PHILADELPHIA BATTLEFIELDS

PHILADELPHIA BATTLEFIELDS

Disruptive Campaigns
and Upset Elections in a Changing City

JOHN KROMER

TEMPLE UNIVERSITY PRESS
Philadelphia • Rome • Tokyo

TEMPLE UNIVERSITY PRESS
Philadelphia, Pennsylvania 19122
tupress.temple.edu

Published 2020

Library of Congress Cataloging-in-Publication Data

Names: Kromer, John, 1948- author.
Title: Philadelphia battlefields : disruptive campaigns and upset elections in a changing city / John Kromer.
Other titles: Disruptive campaigns and upset elections in a changing city
Description: Philadelphia : Temple University Press, [2020] | Includes index. | Summary: "This book examines political campaigns undertaken in Philadelphia during the late 20th and early 21st centuries that were extraordinarily successful despite the opposition of the city's political establishment. It describes the origins, outcomes, and factors that influenced these successful "insurgent" campaigns."—Provided by publisher.
Identifiers: LCCN 2019052208 (print) | LCCN 2019052209 (ebook) | ISBN 9781439919712 (cloth) | ISBN 9781439919729 (paperback) | ISBN 9781439919736 (pdf)
Subjects: LCSH: Philadelphia (Pa.)—Politics and government—20th century. | Elections—Pennsylvania—Philadelphia.
Classification: LCC F158.52 .K76 2020 (print) | LCC F158.52 (ebook) | DDC 974.8/11043—dc23
LC record available at https://lccn.loc.gov/2019052208
LC ebook record available at https://lccn.loc.gov/2019052209

♾ The paper used in this publication meets the requirements of the American National Standard for Information Sciences—Permanence of Paper for Printed Library Materials, ANSI Z39.48-1992

Printed in the United States of America

9 8 7 6 5 4 3 2 1

Contents

★★★★★

PART III: COMMON THREADS

Acknowledgments

Although I have previously written about the relationship between ward-and-division politics and civic engagement,[1] the idea of writing this book did not occur to me until I had read Karen Bojar's *Green Shoots of Democracy in the Philadelphia Democratic Party*.[2] The reporting, personal observations, and interviews that she weaves together make her book a great introduction to a complicated topic. Although my background and some of my personal perspectives differ from Karen's, those who are familiar with her work will understand how much I benefitted from it. Comments and suggestions from Karen and Richard Bojar during various stages of this project were constructive and very helpful.

My wife, Kathleen Nelson, aided me in many ways, large and small, during the challenging time in which this book was planned, organized, and written. Getting this project completed without the benefit of her love, patience, and good advice would have been impossible.

To design and complete the map illustrations that appear in most chapters of this book, Michael Fichman had to endure two years of false starts, unanticipated do-overs, inaccurate directions, and inadequate explanations, all of which I am responsible for. Michael's creative work is an essential component of this book, and I am very grateful to have been the beneficiary of his intelligence, patience, and forbearance. Amy Hillier generously provided shapefiles that she had previously used to design a map illustrating Home Owners' Loan Corporation (HOLC) underwriting criteria.

Tara Powers and Basma Abouelenein of Elevate Healthcare generously contributed graphic services associated with most of the illustrations, other than maps, that appear in these pages, producing high-quality results on very short notice.

Carolyn Adams provided some early encouragement and helped me get acquainted with Temple University Press. Editor-in-chief Aaron Javsicas and his colleagues Ashley Petrucci, Kate Nichols, and Anne-Marie Anderson were consistently encouraging and supportive, and they devoted special attention to getting *Philadelphia Battlefields* published at a time when public interest in related issues was likely to be high. Gary Kramer provided invaluable guidance regarding marketing and promotion. Rebecca Logan and colleagues at Newgen completed copyediting, typesetting, and indexing tasks expertly and on time.

I very much appreciate having had the opportunity to review original documents from the Natalie Saxe Randall Papers at the Historical Society of Pennsylvania, a collection that provided valuable information and insights about the underappreciated accomplishments of this dynamic policy maker and administrator from the Clark/Dilworth era.

At Temple University's Urban Archives, located in the University Library's Special Collections Research Center, I found a wealth of primary-source material about municipal government operations and Philadelphia political campaigns that would not have been available anywhere else. Reviewing interview transcripts from the Walter Massey Phillips Oral Histories, also housed at the Urban Archives, helped deepen my understanding of ways in which mid-twentieth-century government and civic leaders viewed and acted on opportunities to influence social and political change in Philadelphia. Josue Hurtado, librarian and coordinator of public services, and Courtney Smerz were especially helpful in making it possible for me to obtain the photos of Chaka Fattah and Ed Rendell that appear on the cover.

The experience of entering the 2011 Philadelphia Democratic primary election as a candidate for sheriff (described in the Introduction) gave me insights into the political process that could not have been gained in any other way. My underresourced campaign would never have survived the months leading up to election day without the steadfast commitment and good advice provided by my campaign team: chairwoman Happy Fernandez (still greatly missed by many Philadelphians since her untimely passing in 2013), campaign manager David Zega, campaign treasurer Matt Kremer, Chris Kingsley, and Andy Dennison. The following year, Andy created an e-book documenting my campaign strategy, as well as those of Brett Mandel (a candidate for city controller in 2009 and 2013) and Stephanie Singer (a candidate for city commission in 2011), both of whom graciously agreed to participate in filmed interviews. For Andy's publication, Julie Proulx produced digitized maps of election results, similar to those shown in Chapter 1 of this book and elsewhere.

During the first phase of my research, City Commissioner Al Schmidt and Chief Deputy Commissioner Seth Bluestein were extraordinarily helpful in providing me with access to Registration Commission records dating back to the 1940s, as well as offering additional information and advice about past election records. Deputy City Commissioner Nick Custodio helped me gain access to ward and division election results copied from the ledgers in which they had been recorded during the predigital era. Digital media coordinator Michelle Montalvo provided assistance and found archived files on short notice on several occasions while my research was under way.

As described in Chapter 8, Stephanie Singer is the person most responsible for making Philadelphia election-results data available to the public. On her own initiative as a private citizen, Singer obtained these data and posted them online at a time when the city commissioners were unwilling or unable to do so. In 2011, Singer was elected to a seat on the City Commission, and during her single term in office, she and Commissioner Schmidt (also elected in 2011) oversaw the posting of current and archived election results data on the city commissioners' website. The pioneer whose accomplishments predated these initiatives is Ed Goppelt, who created Hallwatch.org in 2001 and maintained it for nearly a decade as a vehicle for posting election results, campaign finance reports, and other detailed information about municipal government operations.

David Lynn, who has completed election data and campaign finance analyses associated with many campaigns, frequently on a pro bono basis, helped me adapt the summary of expenditures by the campaign committees of selected common pleas court candidates that appears in Chapter 7.

I benefitted from having access to past newspaper reporting and commentary about political activity that took place in Philadelphia during the turbulent final decades of the twentieth century. The capable writers whose work I consulted in connection with research for *Philadelphia Battlefields* include Peter Binzen, Paul Critchlow, Dave Davies, Larry Eichel, Tom Ferrick, Patrick Kerkstra, Acel Moore, Linda Wright Moore, S. A. Paolantonio, Walter Roche, and Vanessa Williams. The *Philadelphia Tribune*, a major resource for political news reporting and analysis throughout this period and beyond, was an essential resource for most chapters of the book.

During and after the turn of the century, an especially capable and well-informed generation of reporters and commentators emerged, whose work now appears online and in some print media. In my research for this book,

I have benefitted greatly from the work of Jake Blumgart, Ryan Briggs, Max Marin, Holly Otterbein, Jonathan Tannen, and others, as well as that of print-media veterans John Baer, Chris Brennan, and Chris Satullo.

My affiliation with the University of Pennsylvania, initially as a staff member at the Fels Institute of Government and subsequently as an adjunct instructor in the Department of Urban Studies, provided me with invaluable research experience. Department of Urban Studies cochair Elaine Simon has been a consistent source of encouragement and advice, and Victoria Karkov has been an invaluable information provider and problem solver. Interactions with students in my fall semester "Politics of Housing and Urban Development" class helped me think about the best ways to communicate information about a topic with which many people are not very familiar.

I appreciate the help of the many people who made themselves available for in-person interviews, including Gregory Benjamin, Judge Mark I. Bernstein, Todd Bernstein, Brandy Bones, Richard Chapman, Patrick Christmas, Cara Crosby, Judge Legrome D. Davis, Judge Nelson A. Díaz, George Donnelly, Lucy Erdelac, Congressman Chaka Fattah, Graham Finney, Jon Geeting, Mary Goldman, Maya Gutierrez, Councilperson Curtis Jones Jr., Judge C. Darnell Jones II, House Speaker Robert W. O'Donnell, Councilperson Cherelle Parker, Alison Perelman, Councilperson Maria D. Quiñones-Sánchez, Governor Edward G. Rendell, City Controller Rebecca Rhynhart, Judge Annette M. Rizzo, Nikil Saval, Jennifer Schultz (not yet a judge at the time when this book was being completed), Sarah Clark Stuart, Councilperson Marian Tasco, David Thornburgh (who served as executive director of the Fels Institute of Government during part of my tenure there), Joseph Vignola (who has served the city of Philadelphia in several official capacities), Kellan White (who was especially helpful in providing a detailed briefing on the Rhynhart campaign), Judge Flora Barth Wolf, and Shelly Yanoff.

Reverend Dr. W. Wilson Goode Sr. of the Amachi Program, Katie Day of United Lutheran Seminary, John DiIulio of the Fels Institute of Government, and Sister Mary Scullion of Project HOME provided information and thought-provoking suggestions about how to consider the role of congregations of faith in supporting voter education and political activism. Interviews with Pastor Derick Brennan of Canaan Baptist Church, Reverend Robin Hynicka of Arch Street United Methodist Church, Reverend William B. Moore of Tenth Memorial Baptist Church, Reverend Dr. Alyn E. Waller of Enon Tabernacle Baptist Church, and Rabbi Adam Zeff of Germantown Jewish Centre helped deepen my understanding of these issues. The experience of participating in a Lenten Sunday worship service at Old First Reformed Church and hearing Reverend Michael Caine's observations on the prodigal son parable were especially helpful to me. Nancy Megley of

Arch Street United Methodist Church provided me with an excellent briefing on POWER and a description of its accomplishments to date. David Mosenkis briefed me on his analysis of disparities in state funding for public education and on the outcomes of related advocacy by POWER.

Others who helped me when it really mattered include Clarence Armbrister, Megan Barry, Robert Cheetham, Frank DiCicco, Katherine Dowdell, Noel Eisenstat, Frances Fattah, Shirley Hamilton, Betty Harper, Elizabeth Ireland, Frances Jones, Peggy Kovich, Carol Kuniholm, Brigid McCloskey, Melissa Piccoli, Heather Pierce, Abigail Poses, Eleanor Sharpe, Kyasha Tyson, Jane Whitehouse, and Susan Windle.

I found three books especially useful throughout this project, and I consulted them frequently: *Philadelphia: A 300-Year History*, edited by Russell F. Weigley; *Rizzo: The Last Big Man in Big City America*, by Sal Paolantonio; and *Black Voters Mattered: A Philadelphia Story*, by W. Wilson Goode Sr.[3] For anyone who would like to become better informed about Philadelphia's twentieth-century history, these three books provide the equivalent of an excellent short course.

PHILADELPHIA BATTLEFIELDS

★★★★★★★

Introduction

Philadelphia Battlefields: Disruptive Candidacies and Upset Elections in a Changing City is about political campaigns undertaken in Philadelphia during the late twentieth and early twenty-first centuries that were extraordinarily successful despite the opposition of the city's political establishment. The book describes the origins, outcomes, and factors that influenced successful "insurgent" campaigns, based on an analysis of election data, descriptions of the social and economic environment in which these campaigns were organized and implemented, and interviews with participants.

The book's purpose is to describe and analyze urban political dynamics in a typical postindustrial city by focusing on how strategies for these campaigns were operationalized, as well as to show how they were influenced by local history, economic conditions, and population trends. The research makes use of election data and data-mapping tools that have become much more accessible in recent years, making it possible to describe and analyze voting patterns at the neighborhood, district, and citywide levels in greater depth and to explain how they influenced election outcomes.

This topic is particularly deserving of attention for several reasons:

- Although urban Democratic Party organizations that have traditionally been dominant in most older cities continue to possess significant political power, their influence has weakened substantially during recent decades. A description of the campaign strategies that proved successful in overcoming party opposition and an explanation of how changes in urban demographics, governance, and the economy contributed to the outcomes of insurgent candidacies sheds new light on the factors that have influenced social change, political activism, and municipal governance during the past half-century.

- The period following the 2016 presidential election has been characterized by a resurgence in political activism, and much of this activism has originated and grown in older metropolitan areas. By providing detailed information and insights about the ways in which insurgent candidacies have succeeded, I hope that this book may serve as a frame of reference for individuals and groups seeking to organize or participate in political campaigns or reform initiatives.
- The creators of all of the strategies described in this book were seeking, among other goals, to inspire constructive civic engagement—to encourage citizens to exercise their citizenship by becoming more knowledgeable about candidates and policy issues and participating enthusiastically in campaigns and elections. The chronically low voter turnout in many U.S. elections provides ample evidence of the need to find better ways to get citizens involved—to more closely align civic engagement with individual and group self-interest.

Municipal Politics and the Urban Economy

Most students of urban development would agree that older cities recovering from postindustrial economic disinvestment need responsible municipal leadership and capable governance to achieve future success. However, relatively little attention has been devoted to the process by which municipal leaders have been chosen during the past half-century and the circumstances under which political activism or political reform movements have brought about the election of outstanding leaders. As more older central cities begin to experience downtown revitalization accompanied by gentrification in some neighborhoods and an influx of immigrants in others, a greater understanding of the electoral process can guide the design and implementation of policies to stimulate increased voter turnout, promote broader civic engagement, and support the election of capable, well-qualified leaders.

Philadelphia is a city that has undergone significant economic hardships but has also achieved some noteworthy success in stimulating reinvestment during recent years; it is also a place where, under some circumstances, insurgent candidates for office have won elections despite the opposition of the city's dominant political party. Their successes were based on creative and timely campaign strategies combined with the successful candidates' perceived responsiveness to voter concerns about broader social and economic issues such as jobs, taxes, racial divisions, and neighborhood change. Gaining a better understanding of the relationship between these successful strategies and the context in which they are designed and implemented can provide useful insights into the best ways to achieve higher levels of community participation in the electoral process and help capable individuals gain election to office.

Organization of the Book

Philadelphia Battlefields is organized as a three-part work.

Part I consists of eight chapters, seven of which describe a campaign or a sequence of related campaigns: newcomer Rebecca Rhynhart's landslide victory over a veteran incumbent in a citywide 2017 race for Philadelphia city controller; a Democratic takeover of Philadelphia city government, engineered by business and civic leaders in 1951, following a century of dominance by Republican administrations; Chaka Fattah's successful use of the communication and organizing skills he developed as a neighborhood activist to mobilize participation in successful campaigns for the Pennsylvania legislature and U.S. Congress; strategies undertaken by Thomas Foglietta and his supporters to pursue the opportunity to introduce capable new leadership into South Philadelphia politics in the wake of the 1980 Abscam scandal; the approach adopted by former prosecutor Edward Rendell to defeat an incumbent Philadelphia district attorney at a time when warring factions were battling for control of the Democratic Party; Maria Quiñones-Sánchez's success in winning a city council seat, the first Hispanic woman to do so, despite the active opposition of Hispanic elected officials allied with veteran party leaders; and the differing experiences of individual members of a reform slate of judicial candidates, nominated by Pennsylvania governor Robert Casey and known as the "Casey Five," as they worked to secure Democratic Party support for election to common pleas court over the opposition of key party leaders. Each of these chapters includes a chronology table that shows the relationship between the election that is the primary focus of the chapter and other elections that preceded it and that, in some instances, influenced the campaign strategies of one or more of the candidates in these elections.

This part ends with a description of similarities among the campaigns, as well as a discussion of whether their successful outcomes should be interpreted as representing fundamental changes in local government or simply viewed as one-off victories, based largely on serendipitous circumstances that advanced individual political careers.

Part II consists of four chapters, focusing on the experience of political activism from different perspectives, including those of three women who entered the local political environment at different phases in Philadelphia's late-twentieth-century and early-twenty-first-century history; representatives of three advocacy organizations: Americans for Democratic Action, the Committee of Seventy, and Philadelphia 3.0; participants in three Democratic ward organizations that differ from their predecessors in ways that suggest new opportunities for change; and representatives of congregations of faith who have been active in local politics in different ways.

Part III ends the book with two chapters. The first describes the expectations surrounding Philadelphia's May 2019 Democratic primary elections, which many activists viewed as presenting an opportunity to place reformers in key positions in city government, as well as the factors that influenced the successful and unsuccessful outcomes of these elections. The book concludes with a description of the challenges that need to be addressed to increase the effectiveness of the political process, improve municipal governance, and introduce a new generation of political leadership at the local and state level.

Learning from Experience

Not long after graduating from college, I won an uncontested election and became a Democratic committeeperson in West Philadelphia's 46th Ward, representing a division that included a substantial population of University of Pennsylvania students, faculty, and staff, as well as doctors and lawyers, schoolteachers, health and human service workers, and unemployed, retired, and homebound families and elderly people.

The first ward meeting I attended was held in a cramped storefront a few blocks away from the Penn campus. The ward leader was Lucien Blackwell, a city council member who was also head of the local chapter of the longshoremen's union and who had been a boxer before entering the armed forces. Councilman Blackwell called the meeting to order, and the other committeepeople, about fifty of them, took their seats on folding chairs organized in rows, classroom style.

In previous years, I had participated in many meetings of neighborhood organizations and civic groups; but the composition of this group was more diverse, in terms of age, race, income, educational attainment, employment, and household status than that of any other meeting I had ever attended.

Imagining Councilman Blackwell as a boxer was not difficult. He spoke forcefully and without nuance. Arthur Hicks, a fellow committeeperson who had become acquainted with Blackwell when both were working on the Delaware River docks, would say, "Lucien isn't the period—he's the exclamation mark."

But Councilman Blackwell was not an authoritarian leader. He went out of his way to ensure that every voice was heard and that every individual had a chance to participate. During the weeks preceding the annual Democratic primary elections, candidates for office came to the ward meeting, presented themselves, and responded to questions. Blackwell's stature as a Democratic City Committee leader ensured that candidates would show up and would be responsive to questions from the committeepeople.

West Philadelphia state representative James Williams passed away while in office, and a well-attended funeral service was held at Hickman Temple Memorial Church. Several rows of pews had been reserved for the 46th Ward committeepeople, up front and to the side, and the committeepeople entered as a group and took their seats together. It was as though we were members of a team—a group of people who might not all be well acquainted with one another individually, but who respected one another, took one another seriously, and got together when needed to uphold an important responsibility.

Before each election day, I circulated a letter containing information about the upcoming election, a description of the offices that would appear on the ballot, and information about candidates whom I recommended. In the letter that I circulated before one primary, I recommended that voters vote no on the question of whether to retain Bernard Snyder, an incumbent common pleas court judge who had been endorsed by the Democratic Party but who had been charged with misconduct in office. The "no" votes in my division, along with many other "no" votes cast citywide, resulted in Snyder's removal from the judiciary. After the election, I sent Councilman Blackwell a letter explaining that I was returning my "street money" (the cash that ward leaders routinely distribute to committeepeople before elections, ostensibly to cover "election day expenses," but rarely documented in campaign finance reports) because I had not supported one of the endorsed candidates. I received a letter from him two days later, along with the street money. The letter said, "You are an excellent committeeperson, and this money belongs to you."

At the time, I had also been active in Cedar Park Neighbors (CPN), a community organization whose members had become concerned about a city fire station located at a five-points intersection on the Baltimore Avenue neighborhood commercial corridor. The building had been vacated when the fire company relocated to new quarters a few blocks away. With others who were interested in finding an appropriate reuse for the building before it deteriorated and became a nuisance or hazard, I participated in a series of neighborhood meetings to discuss alternatives. The result was a proposal by CPN to create a joint-venture partnership that would take ownership of the building and develop it as a neighborhood retail center organized as a farmers market hall. The city administration, which had a policy of selling surplus properties at auction, opposed the proposal, but Councilman Blackwell supported it, probably because of my involvement, and the property was transferred to the new partnership. After years of uncertainty, missteps, and controversy, the building became the location of Dock Street Brewery, a valued neighborhood asset. The only other realistic alternative that had been proposed during the dialogue leading to this outcome was the demolition of the building for use as a surface parking lot.[1]

At the time, Baltimore Avenue had been experiencing years of economic disinvestment, and a public auction of the firehouse building would probably not have attracted a lot of interest. If the real estate market had been stronger, Councilman Blackwell might not have supported the CPN proposal, despite my involvement; committeeperson status did not guarantee that every wish would be fulfilled. However, this experience helped me understand how participation in political activism at the grassroots level could help advance neighborhood organization and community reinvestment goals.

In later years, I participated in political campaigns as a campaign treasurer and campaign manager; then I ran as a candidate for Philadelphia sheriff in the 2011 Democratic primary. At the time, the sheriff's office was under federal investigation for mismanaging tax sales, the auctions at which tax-delinquent properties are sold to recover unpaid tax revenue. As a former city housing director (from 1992 to 2001), I had been concerned about the purchase of tax sale properties by speculators and negligent absentee investors, and I had written commentary pieces, subsequently published in the citywide news media, calling for the sheriff's office to be reformed or replaced. Accordingly, my candidacy was based on a pledge that, once elected, I would work to transfer the responsibilities of the sheriff's office to municipal departments that were already managing similar responsibilities (such as the Law Department and the Department of Public Property), after which I would close the office and resign. I did not harbor any unrealistic expectations about the outcome of my candidacy—which, needless to say, was not given serious consideration by Democratic Party leadership—but I felt that it was important to draw more attention to these issues. Campaigning for office gave me an opportunity to share my views with neighborhood audiences in every area of the city, and the experience gave me new insights about how an insurgent candidacy can succeed or fail (with my candidacy as a good example of the latter).

All of these experiences helped me view the political process as, at its best, an engine of democracy and gain a better understanding of the ways in which we, the citizens of this republic, have grown accustomed to the use of a highly inefficient vehicle—the political party system in its current form—to deliver this value. *Philadelphia Battlefields* is intended to pose a related question: In the interest of advancing toward true democracy, can we find new ways of making this vehicle function effectively or replacing it with something much better?

Limitations and Aspirations

Because this book is narrowly focused on campaigns and elections, many of the broader topics that would ordinarily be part of a work of this kind are addressed only briefly or not at all. To devote attention to political dynamics, I have tried to limit coverage of urban history, demographic and economic trends, and public policy issues to include only basic information that I think is needed to place the political campaigns in context. A more comprehensive work would have devoted much more attention to the powerful influence of African American and Latino media on voter choices during the past half-century; to the growing influence of LGBTQ constituencies in municipal politics; to the growth of political activism in Philadelphia's Asian American community; to the role that building trades, municipal employee, and service worker unions have played in Philadelphia politics; to the different ways in which congregations of faith across different denominations support voter education and encourage political activism; and to campaign financing strategies and campaign finance oversight policies. I hope that these important topics will be regarded as attractive prospects for future research by others.

Although it would be relevant to include comparisons between Philadelphia and other cities in a book of this kind, they do not appear in *Philadelphia Battlefields*, in part because I wanted to focus in depth on the political environment in a city that I know well but also because of significant differences between Philadelphia and other cities that pose particular research challenges. In many other cities, for example, elections are managed by county governments; in Philadelphia, county government functions are consolidated within the municipal infrastructure, making apples-to-apples comparisons more complicated. In addition, digitized election records are more accessible in Philadelphia than they are in many other places, for reasons described in the Acknowledgments. As digitized election data, both current and historical, become more readily available in other places, new opportunities to conduct worthwhile comparative research will emerge.

I encourage readers of *Philadelphia Battlefields* to bear in mind that more than a few of the political leaders who currently have the most influence in shaping statewide and national policies—both for better and for worse—began their careers as elected officials representing relatively small legislative districts or as officeholders who were elected to manage relatively discrete municipal and county government responsibilities. With this consideration in mind, I hope that this book will encourage readers to consider participating in politics at the grassroots level, to support the election of candidates who are both principled and pragmatic, and to seek new ways to promote true democracy in an imperfect world.

PART I

The Bold Ones

1

★★★★★★★

Razor Thin

She was a political neophyte. He was a veteran politician.

She had never campaigned for elective office. He had been victorious in state and local elections for a quarter-century.

Only one of Philadelphia's sixty-six ward organizations had endorsed her candidacy; most of the ward leaders had no idea who she was. All of them knew who he was; he had been one of them for years.

On New Year's Day 2017, with five-and-a-half months to go until the primary election, her campaign committee had less than $40,000 in the bank. His campaign committee started the year with nearly three times that amount.

Endorsements of her candidacy came from good-government advocates and other sources that were respected but not guaranteed big-vote generators, including Philadelphia's two citywide newspapers, former Pennsylvania governor Edward G. Rendell, and the Laborers' District Council. Endorsements of his candidacy came from sources that had consistently been successful in bringing crowds of supportive voters to the polls: the Democratic City Committee, the Philadelphia Building and Construction Trades Council, the Philadelphia Council of the AFL-CIO, and the city's two public-employee unions, to name a few.

She had gained the support of the Black Clergy of Philadelphia and Vicinity, the National Organization for Women, and Millennials in Action, a recently formed recruitment and training organization for young activists. But nearly all of the city's elected officials, including the Democratic members of City Council, supported him. So did the local chapter of Americans for Democratic Action, a standard-bearer for Philadelphia's liberal electorate for more than a half-century. So did Philadelphia Neighborhood Networks, a resource for community activism that had been experiencing a resurgence in the wake of the 2016 presidential election.

Philadelphia mayor James Kenney, who had been her boss the previous year, when she had served as the city's chief administrative officer, was no friend of his, but he was not endorsing her candidacy either. Kenney had decided not to get involved in the controller race at all.

So why was Rebecca Rhynhart's victory over incumbent city controller Alan Butkovitz in the May 16, 2017, Democratic primary election such a spectacular success? "We expected the margin to be razor thin," recalled Kellan White, who played a key role in organizing and executing Rhynhart's campaign strategy.[1] But the margin was the opposite of razor thin. Rhynhart won with nearly 80,000 votes, compared with roughly 56,000 votes for Butkovitz. Rhynhart won a majority in forty-nine of Philadelphia's sixty-six wards. As shown in Figure 1.1, she won all of Greater Center City—the wards in and surrounding Philadelphia's central business district. She won all of West Philadelphia. She won most of South Philadelphia and most of Northwest Philadelphia.

Butkovitz was able to gain majorities in Northeast Philadelphia, where his home ward, the 54th, and the district he had previously represented in the state's General Assembly were located. But voter turnout and the resulting Butkovitz majorities in these wards were low, compared with turnout and Rhynhart's margins of victory in other sections of the city.

In an ordinary year, a political challenge to Philadelphia's established party organization would have been unlikely to succeed. However, 2017 was not an ordinary year. Although success could not be guaranteed in any particular election, national and local trends would seem to have favored an insurgent campaign in Philadelphia, particularly one led by a female candidate with no ties to the city's seemingly monolithic Democratic Party. Donald Trump's victory in the November 2016 presidential election, in which he carried Pennsylvania by a margin of about 44,000 votes, stimulated an upsurge in political activism in Philadelphia and the suburbs. A week after the presidential election, a blog post on the website of Philadelphia 3.0 (a political organization supporting "independent-minded candidates" and "efforts to reform and modernize City Hall"[2]) encouraged readers to "get mad, then get elected"; the post described opportunities to participate in upcoming political campaigns and encouraged readers to consider running for committeeperson, a neighborhood-level political office, in the May 2018 primary election.[3] Nearly two hundred people showed up for two subsequent orientation/recruitment meetings, and many of them became

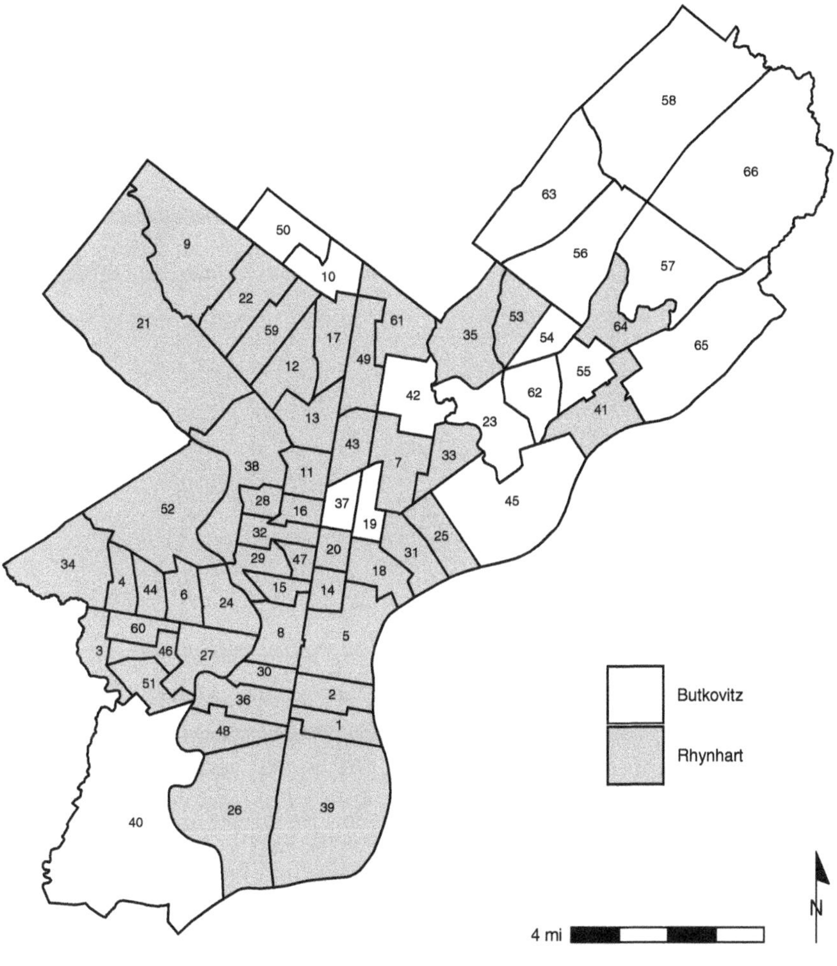

Figure 1.1 May 2017 Democratic primary results for city controller by ward

Source: Data from Philadelphia City Commissioners, "Archived Data Sets: 2017 Primary," https://www.philadelphiavotes.com/en/resources-a-data/ballot-box-app/additional-election-results-data; map by Michael Fichman.

first-time candidates for committeeperson seats. Table 1.1 shows key elections leading up to the 2017 Democratic primary.

On a national level, more women were running for elected office. A report by the Rutgers Center for American Women and Politics found that, in November 2017, 198 women candidates were challenging incumbent members of the opposing party for a seat in the U.S. House of Representatives, almost four times the comparable number in 2015 (in general, the center found that "there *are* more women running for office . . . but that the increases in candidacies vary by level of office").[4]

TABLE 1.1 KEY ELECTIONS LEADING UP TO 2017 DEMOCRATIC PRIMARY

Year elected	Mayor	District attorney	City controller	Democratic City Committee chair
Incumbent in 2006	John F. Street	Lynne Abraham	Alan L. Butkovitz	Robert A. Brady
2007	Michael A. Nutter			
2008				
2009		R. Seth Williams	Alan L. Butkovitz	
2010				
2011	Michael A. Nutter			
2012				
2013		R. Seth Williams	Alan L. Butkovitz	
2014				
2015	James F. Kenney			
2016				
2017		Lawrence S. Krasner	Rebecca Rhynhart	

Source: Philadelphia City Commissioners, *View Election Results* database, https://www.philadelphiavotes.com/en/resources-a-data/ballot-box-app.

The district attorney (DA) election was the top-of-the-ballot race in the May 2017 Philadelphia Democratic primary. Seven candidates were competing to replace former district attorney Seth Williams, who, before being indicted on corruption and bribery-related charges, had announced in February that he would not seek reelection. The highest-profile candidate was Lawrence S. Krasner, a defense attorney with a criminal defense and civil rights practice who had filed dozens of lawsuits against the police and had represented protestors at the Democratic and Republican conventions, as well as members of Black Lives Matter and Occupy Philadelphia. Krasner's candidacy was the beneficiary of media advertisements funded through a political action committee associated with George Soros, the billionaire investor and philanthropist who regularly contributed to liberal causes, but his campaign was not necessarily assured of success. One of Krasner's opponents, Joe Khan, was a respected former city and federal prosecutor. Another opponent, Richard Negrin, had established strong ties with neighborhood and civic organizations during his tenure as the city's managing director in the administration of former mayor Michael Nutter.

The DA race was an open primary; no candidate had been endorsed by the Democratic City Committee, Philadelphia's party leadership organization. DA candidates traveled around the city, courting ward leaders and delivering campaign pitches at candidates-night ward meetings. No single candidate succeeded in capturing a decisive-looking number of ward endorsements. Five of them each obtained between seven and nine ward endorsements; a sixth, Jack O'Neill, got eleven.[5]

In addition, eight building trade unions announced their endorsement of O'Neill, and a union-linked political action committee began funding cable and broadcast advertisements in support of his candidacy. Perhaps in an effort to show solidarity with the unions that backed his own candidacy, Butkovitz endorsed O'Neill as well. According to White of the Rhynhart campaign, "This created an opportunity for us."[6]

White recalled advice that, years earlier, Congressman Chaka Fattah had given another candidate: When your campaign endorses someone running for another office in the same election, 50 percent of that candidate's supporters might support you—but 100 percent of that candidate's opponents will oppose you. Mindful of this advice, the Rhynhart campaign took action after Butkovitz's pledge of support to O'Neill. "After Alan endorsed Jack O'Neill," White explained, "we could call the other DA candidates and say, 'Did you know that Alan Butkovitz endorsed your opponent?' So we were able to get help from the other campaigns."[7]

Former governor Rendell was "very involved" in the campaign, according to Rhynhart, and he provided support in various ways during the campaign period.[8] Rhynhart made some smart proactive moves. She reached out to Ryan Boyer of the Laborers' Union, and the two of them got acquainted at a time when the union was supporting DA candidate Tariq El-Shabazz. The Rhynhart campaign was subsequently able to enlist the help of this union, particularly with respect to bringing out votes for Rhynhart in African American neighborhoods.

At the start of the campaign year, there seemed to be no question that the Democratic City Committee and Philadelphia's most influential ward leaders would be endorsing Butkovitz for city controller. Aware of this political reality, Rhynhart refrained from making any significant contributions of campaign funds to City Committee or the ward organizations.

Instead, the campaign team worked on persuading DA candidates to list Rhynhart as the endorsed candidate for city controller on the sample ballots that their supporters would be handing out to voters as they arrived at the polls. Four sample ballots supporting Rhynhart's candidacy are shown in Figure 1.2. The cost of making this happen was relatively low. Shortly before the primary election, Rhynhart's campaign made contributions to three DA candidates who listed her on their sample ballots: $2,500 to Michael Untermeyer, $5,000 to Joe Khan, and $7,500 to Rich Negrin.

By contrast, the Butkovitz campaign contributed nearly four times as much—$55,000—to the Democratic Campaign Committee of Philadelphia before the election. Notwithstanding Butkovitz's endorsement by the party, the value of this contribution turned out to be negligible, given his subsequent defeat in three-quarters of the city's wards, including the 34th, where Democratic City Committee chair Bob Brady served as ward leader.

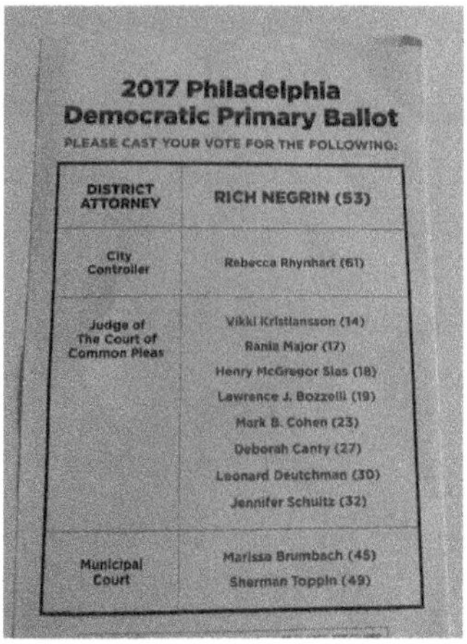

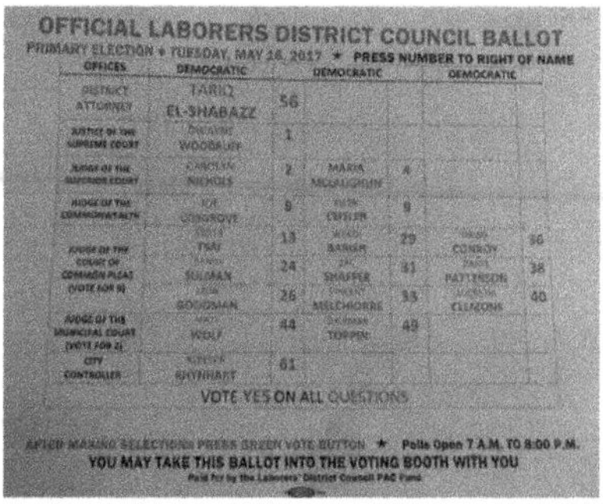

Figure 1.2 Rebecca Rhynhart listed on four district attorney candidates' sample ballots *Source:* Negrin, Untermeyer, and Khan campaigns; Laborers' District Council

In that ward, Rhynhart outpolled Butkovitz by nearly 300 votes, 2,234 to 1,936.

Because the election for district attorney was attracting the most attention in the May 2017 Democratic primary and because the Democratic Party had not endorsed any particular candidate for DA, many voters were likely to pay the most attention to information associated with the candidate they supported for DA. Because campaign workers for multiple DA candidates were distributing sample ballots that also promoted Rhynhart's candidacy for controller, the benefits for Rhynhart were likely to be significant.

"I don't know if sample ballots really work," White said, "but getting Rebecca's name on the sample ballots of DA candidates didn't hurt. In the 22nd Ward [one of a half-dozen consistently high-turnout wards in the

TABLE 1.2 VOTE TOTALS FOR LEADING DA CANDIDATES BY WARD, COMPARED WITH RHYNHART'S VOTE TOTALS

	Top Ten Krasner Wards									
	46	50	5	22	2	8	10	9	21	34
Lawrence S. Krasner	3,102	2,844	2,702	2,700	2,684	2,557	1,876	1,738	1,738	1,690
Rebecca Rhynhart	2,653	1,710	*4,199*	*3,052*	*3,536*	*4,112*	1,264	*2,647*	*3,201*	*2,234*
	Top Ten Khan Wards									
	8	21	5	9	22	30	2	15	34	50
Joe Khan	1,893	1,819	1,805	1,579	1,361	1,336	1,183	1,068	768	716
Rebecca Rhynhart	*4,112*	*3,201*	*4,199*	*2,647*	*3,052*	*2,075*	*3,536*	*2,512*	*2,234*	*1,710*

Source: Philadelphia City Commissioners, *View Election Results* database, https://www.philadelphiavotes.com/en/resources-a-data/ballot-box-app.
Note: Numbers for wards in which Rhynhart's totals exceeded Krasner's or Khan's totals are shown in italics.

city], the ward committee didn't distribute any sample ballots—but we had six ballots on the street with Rebecca's name on them."[9]

Krasner won a plurality in the DA race, receiving 59,368 votes (38 percent) to 31,480 votes for Khan (20 percent) and 22,048 votes for Negrin (14 percent); the other candidates shared the remainder of the vote.

Given the high level of interest in this race, could Rhynhart's victory be attributed, at least in part, to a coattails effect, in which voters who came to the polls to vote for one of the DA candidates cast votes for Rhynhart as well? This contention is not supported by ward-level results for the winning and runner-up DA candidates. As shown in Table 1.2, in seven of the ten wards in which Krasner received his highest vote totals, Rhynhart won more votes than he did. In all ten of the wards in which Khan received his highest vote totals, Rhynhart won more votes than Khan did.[10]

Timing, circumstance, and candidate profile and presentation all influence the outcome of a municipal election to varying degrees; but these factors, in isolation, do not guarantee success. During the campaign period, these and other factors are tested on a playing field that consists of the city's wards and divisions. The use of ward-and-division geography as a context for examining election outcomes helps explain why the Rhynhart campaign was successful in the 2017 primary and how Butkovitz had succeeded in fending off challenges in previous years.

Philadelphia's Political Geography

For election-management purposes, Philadelphia is divided into sixty-six wards, shown in Figure 1.3. Ward boundaries rarely correspond to neighborhood boundaries and, unlike the boundaries of many legislative districts, are

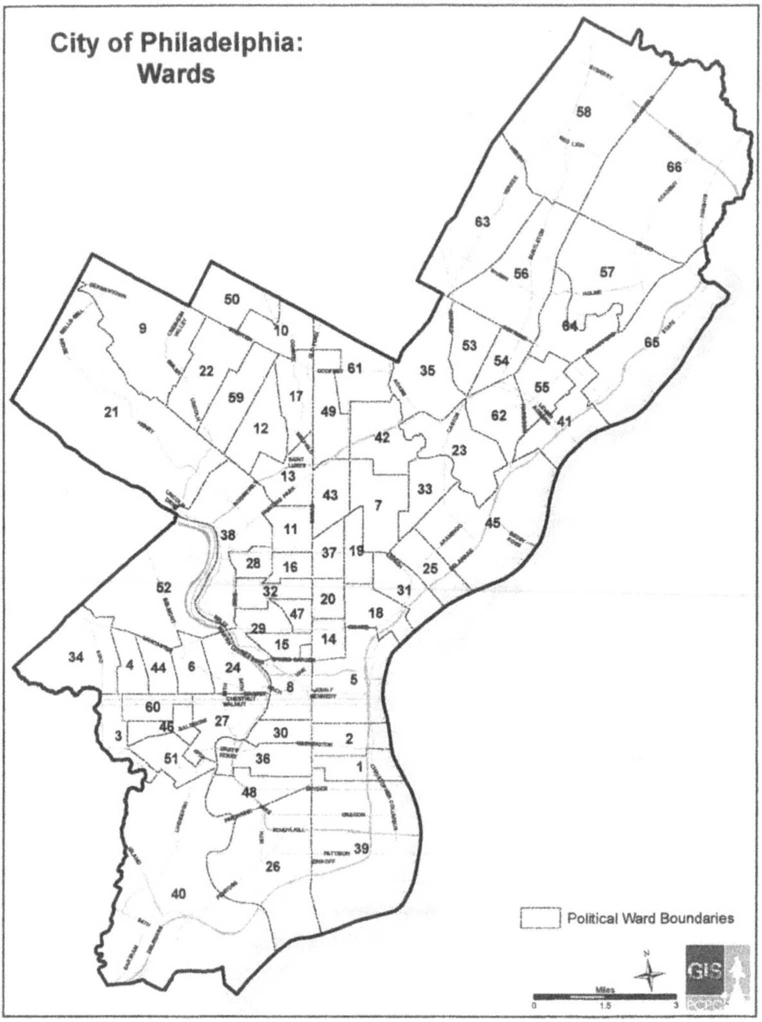

Figure 1.3 Philadelphia ward boundaries (approved in 1965; still in effect in May 2017)

Source: John Daley and Allen Weinberg, *Genealogy of Philadelphia County Subdivisions*, 2nd ed. (Philadelphia: City of Philadelphia Department of Records, 1966), 91.

not required by law to be realigned periodically to ensure that all wards contain approximately equivalent numbers of registered voters. The ward boundaries that were in effect at the time of the 2017 Democratic primary were approved in 1965 and had not been redrawn since then. During the intervening years, large areas of North, West, and South Philadelphia lost thousands of residents, in large part because of the postindustrial depopulation that

Philadelphia, like many older cities, experienced in the decades after World War II. In some neighborhoods, a reversal of this trend began to occur during the years leading up to and after the turn of the twenty-first century, as new housing construction stimulated population growth in outlying areas of the city, while gentrification and immigration led to population increases in several other neighborhoods. By 2017, these changes were reflected in large variations in the number of registered voters from one ward to another.

Voter turnout—the number of voters who come to the polls and cast votes in any particular election—is just as significant as total ward population. Philadelphia's overall voter turnout, like that in other U.S. cities, is notoriously low, and low voter participation can have serious consequences. In the November 2016 presidential election, more than 390,000 registered voters in Philadelphia failed to vote. If fewer than 12 percent of these voters had participated in the election and had cast votes for Hillary Clinton (the choice of 82 percent of the Philadelphia voters who did participate), then Donald Trump's 44,000-vote margin of victory in Pennsylvania would have been erased.

In every election, the same wards almost always generate the highest voter turnout. All of the high-turnout wards have similar characteristics: higher income levels than the citywide median; higher levels of educational attainment, with many college graduates; and high levels of employment, with many residents working in public-sector and professional-service jobs. The resident population of many, but not all, of these wards is predominantly white.

One-third of all votes in the 2017 city controller primary election—44,936 votes, out of a total of 134,807 votes citywide—were cast in just ten of the city's sixty-six wards. As shown in Table 1.3, Rhynhart was victorious in all ten of these wards and won substantial majorities in eight of them.

The 2017 primary election results demonstrate the extent to which vote totals in the highest-turnout wards can exceed vote totals in lower-turnout wards. In the 54th Ward, where Butkovitz served as ward leader, only 647 people voted in the controller election, and Butkovitz outpolled Rhynhart by just 78 votes (362 to 284). By contrast, in Center City's vote-rich 8th Ward, where Rhynhart lived, total turnout in the controller election was 5,769, and Rhynhart won the ward decisively, 4,112 to 1,657.

The minimum number of votes that Rhynhart would have needed to defeat Butkovitz in the May 2017 primary was 55,594—one vote higher than Butkovitz's citywide vote total of 55,593. Rhynhart generated that number of votes in just twenty-eight wards—the ones that produced the biggest voter majorities for her candidacy. She could have won the election without receiving a single vote in the remaining thirty-eight wards, more than half the wards in the city. As shown in Table 1.4, Rhynhart's vote total in the 5th

TABLE 1.3 PERCENTAGE OF VOTES FOR RHYNHART FOR CONTROLLER IN TEN WARDS

Ward	Total votes	Rhynhart votes	Rhynhart percentage of total votes
5	5,518	4,199	76
8	5,769	4,112	71
2	4,512	3,536	78
21	4,935	3,201	65
22	4,977	3,052	61
46	3,978	2,653	67
9	3,877	2,647	68
15	3,442	2,512	73
34	4,170	2,234	54
39	3,758	2,114	56
Total	44,936	30,260	67

Source: Philadelphia City Commissioners, *View Election Results* database, https://www.philadelphiavotes.com/en/resources-a-data/ballot-box-app.

TABLE 1.4 RHYNHART VOTES IN 5TH WARD COMPARED WITH TWELVE LOW-TURNOUT WARDS

Ward	Number of Rhynhart votes
5th Ward	*4,199*
Low-turnout wards	*3,963*
25	446
62	435
45	403
16	397
64	377
47	374
37	360
20	308
54	284
33	244
7	194
19	141

Source: Philadelphia City Commissioners, *View Election Results* database, https://www.philadelphiavotes.com/en/resources-a-data/ballot-box-app.

Ward alone exceeded the combined vote totals she received in the twelve wards that produced the lowest numbers of votes for her.

The Rhynhart campaign was not anticipating this outcome, and she had prepared herself to present her candidacy to any audience. "She was willing to go anywhere," White said. "When you speak with certain community groups, you may only get an audience of five people, but those five people may each get twenty others to vote."[11]

Rhynhart also took advantage of her status as an unendorsed candidate. "Because Rebecca was such an outsider," White said, "she'd be candid about things that she felt were unfair. You can't say that the city's ten-year tax abatement [a generous tax incentive that provided major benefits to downtown developers] is unfair if you're tied to the building trades. You can have conversations that your opponent wouldn't think of having."[12]

At the same time, Rhynhart made substantial commitments of time to scheduling meet-and-greet parties and fundraising events in the higher-turnout downtown wards where she already knew many people socially and could readily get acquainted with other residents whose professional backgrounds were similar to hers.

"She had to raise enough money to get on TV," White said. "She would do three or four house parties a night—it was a slog, but it was well worth it in the end. A lot of people would give $500 and then max out [make additional contributions up to the maximum amount permitted by the city's campaign finance law] later on."[13]

Not all campaign events produced promising results. One supporter came to an event to mobilize volunteers who wanted to circulate petitions for her; she found only three other people in attendance—and one of them was Rhynhart's husband.

But the campaign's fundraising strategy, based largely on direct communication with individual donors, began to pay off. Sarah Stuart, executive director of the Bicycle Coalition of Greater Philadelphia, who had supported candidates for Philadelphia City Council in previous years, cohosted a fundraising party for Rhynhart. As the date of the event approached, Stuart began to worry about whether anyone would come; twenty-five people showed up. The cohosts' goal for the event had been to raise $2,000; they raised $3,000.

Stuart had attended city council budget hearings at which Rhynhart had testified on behalf of the city administration. Based on this experience, she characterized Rhynhart as "young, bright, fearless, and super-confident," and added, "You have to have nerves of steel to work in that environment."[14]

A woman with many years of experience as a consultant to the federal government said, "I'm a process person, and [Rebecca] gets it; she gets how the process needs to be improved—just the basics of fixing the nuts and bolts of government, making it run more effectively. She was just better [than Butkovitz] at talking about how to run government efficiently."[15]

An attorney with many years' experience in the auditing field said, "After the 2016 election, like a lot of women in the country, I thought about what I could do. I felt that Alan Butkovitz was annoying—the way he worked to promote himself rather than to help people. He was all about the press conference."[16]

Not everyone was enthusiastic about Rhynhart's candidacy. One politically active resident of the 22nd Ward, who enthusiastically promoted Krasner's DA candidacy, also supported Butkovitz because she was suspicious about Rhynhart's Wall Street connections and because she felt that Butkovitz "seemed to be someone who'd fight corruption."[17]

Controlled versus Inspired versus Undecided

Any serious candidate for elective office needs to organize a campaign that is based on a realistic response to an obvious question: How many votes will it take to win? In a typical Philadelphia election that takes place during a year in which no candidates for national office are on the ballot, the number of votes needed to win is a number equal to or greater than the *controlled* vote: the number of voters that the city's Democratic Party organization can reasonably expect to be cast in support of party-endorsed candidates on election day.

In the context of municipal elections that take place in cities like Philadelphia, a controlled vote is decisively influenced by an organized political or civic entity; the voter's choice is based primarily on that entity's endorsement of the candidate. A controlled voter may be a person who consistently supports the Democratic Party–endorsed ticket, who votes only for judicial candidates approved by the bar association, or who supports legislators endorsed by organizations concerned with a specific issue, such as the National Rifle Association or Emily's List. For these voters, the entity's endorsement is as important as, or more important than, in-depth knowledge of the candidate's experience and qualifications.

An *inspired* voter is one who has made a firm decision about supporting a particular candidate based primarily on factors other than an endorsement by a political party or advocacy group. Instead, this choice is likely to be associated with the voter's perception of the candidate's personality and temperament; the candidate's identification with a particular constituency (racial/ethnic, urban or rural, industrial or agricultural) or a particular issue (abortion, family planning, immigration, the environment, LGBTQ equality); or the voter's feelings of animosity toward the candidate's opponent.

Charismatic candidates, particularly those who have attracted attention nationally, can draw many inspired voters to the polls. In the period leading up to the 2016 presidential primary elections, many of the most enthusiastic supporters of Bernie Sanders and Donald Trump were not overly concerned about the party affiliation of either of these candidates. In Philadelphia, Frank Rizzo, a candidate who was highly popular with white, working-class constituencies, campaigned as a Democrat in two successful mayoral races (1971 and 1975) but later switched parties and became the Republican nominee for mayor in the 1987 and 1991 elections. His 1991 campaign had been gathering momentum before being cut short by his death in July of the election year.

In most elections there are no charismatic candidates on the ballot, and in many elections, large numbers of voters do not find the offices, the candidates, or the candidates' identification with particular constituencies or issues to be relevant or important enough to attract them to the polls. As a result, overall turnout in most elections is low, and the outcome of many elections is based in large part on the extent to which party organizations or groups representing particular constituencies can be effective in delivering what are often termed "like-minded voters" to the polls.

Although the political power of Philadelphia's Democratic Party has weakened significantly in recent decades, the party still has more capability to consistently influence voter decisions than most other political, civic, or advocacy organizations that are active in the city. A large number of voters can be counted on to support the party-endorsed ballot in every election. Other voters who come to the polls to support a particular candidate for a major office, such as president, U.S. senator, or governor, may decide to vote for party-endorsed candidates running for down-ballot judicial and state offices about which they may not be well informed—or know nothing at all. These inspired voters who default their other choices with respect to candidates for lower-profile offices may also be considered controlled votes to a more limited extent.

Voters in a third category, those truly undecided voters who have no allegiance to the party ballot and no commitment to any particular candidate, appear at polling places in smaller numbers on every election day. An undecided voter may not have any familiarity with the candidates or offices on the ballot, and that voter's decision may be based largely or entirely on information received by chance before entering the polling place. Although genuinely undecided voters may represent a relatively small percentage of total turnout, an effective strategy for influencing those voters who are undecided or not committed to a lesser-known, unendorsed candidate can have a game-changing impact.

How many votes does it take to be elected as the Democratic candidate for controller in an ordinary Philadelphia primary election? In his two previous primary campaigns for controller in 2009 and 2013, Butkovitz's winning vote totals were between 35,000 and 40,000. However, these two elections differed significantly from each other.

In 2009, as in 2017, the incumbent district attorney was not running for reelection, and five candidates were competing for the Democratic Party DA nomination, generating a somewhat higher total voter turnout than in previous years. Butkovitz, the incumbent for the city controller position, faced two challengers: John L. Braxton, a retired African American judge, and Brett Mandel, a tax reform advocate who had previously served as a policy analyst under former controller Jonathan Saidel.

If Braxton and Mandel had joined forces, their consolidated voter support would likely have been sufficient to have defeated Butkovitz. As it turned out, Braxton and Mandel split the opposition votes (receiving 30 percent and 28 percent of the vote, respectively), producing a ten-thousand-vote margin of victory for the incumbent. Butkovitz secured most of his votes in Northeast, Northwest, and South Philadelphia, as shown in Figure 1.4.

Butkovitz and Mandel had a rematch four years later, in 2013. That year, Mandel's campaign returned with a substantially larger campaign budget, and Judge Braxton, his competitor for anti-Butkovitz votes in 2009, was not on the ballot. In that year's district attorney election, Seth Williams, who had been elected in 2009, was running unopposed. As a result, total votes in the DA election dropped by nearly half, from 104,600 in 2009 to 57,998 in 2013.

Butkovitz promoted his candidacy heavily in African American communities that had delivered many votes to Braxton in 2009. He also earned many more votes in the downtown Philadelphia wards that had produced high vote totals for Mandel in the previous election. As a result, although Mandel again won Center City's 5th and 8th wards, as he had in 2009, his 2013 margins of victory were much lower: 961 votes in the 5th, compared with 1,672 votes in 2009, and 1,543 in the 8th, compared with 2,298 in 2009. In large part on the basis of his successful performance in areas of the city where he had been weak in 2009, Butkovitz again prevailed in 2013, this time with a slightly higher vote total, but with a decisive majority (61 percent), as opposed to the 42 percent plurality he had achieved in 2009. The geographic dispersion of Butkovitz's ward majorities is shown in Figure 1.5.

Using the results of the two prior controller elections as a frame of reference, it would appear that the number of votes a party-endorsed candidate for controller needed to win, running in a year in which neither the controller nor the DA race was very competitive—a year similar to 2013—would be about 30,000 votes. The number of votes needed to win in a year in which the controller race, the DA race, or both involved more competition or higher-profile candidates might be more like 50,000 to 60,000 votes (on the basis of the 2009 results, with the Braxton and Mandel votes combined).

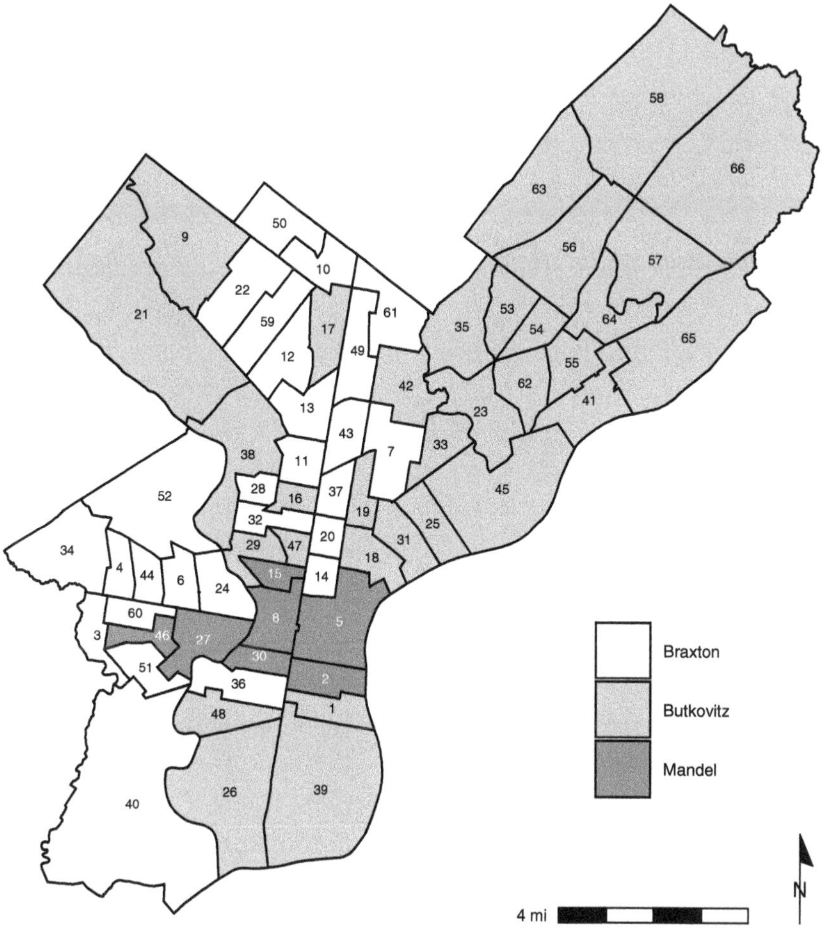

Figure 1.4 2009 Democratic primary election results, Philadelphia city controller

Source: Data from Philadelphia City Commissioners, "Archived Data Sets: 2009 Primary," https://www.philadelphiavotes.com/en/resources-a-data/ballot-box-app/additional-election-results-data; map by Michael Fichman.

In 2017, the Butkovitz campaign pursued an approach similar to the one that had been successful in 2013, focused on winning endorsements from the Democratic City Committee, ward organizations, and unions. His vote total in that year was about 56,000 votes, higher than the amounts needed to win in 2009 and 2013. So why were 56,000 votes, many of them controlled votes, not enough to win in 2017? There are several likely explanations.

The district attorney race was a much higher-profile event in 2017 than it had been in 2009, the most recent previous instance in which multiple candidates had been competing in a DA election with no incumbent. Citizen

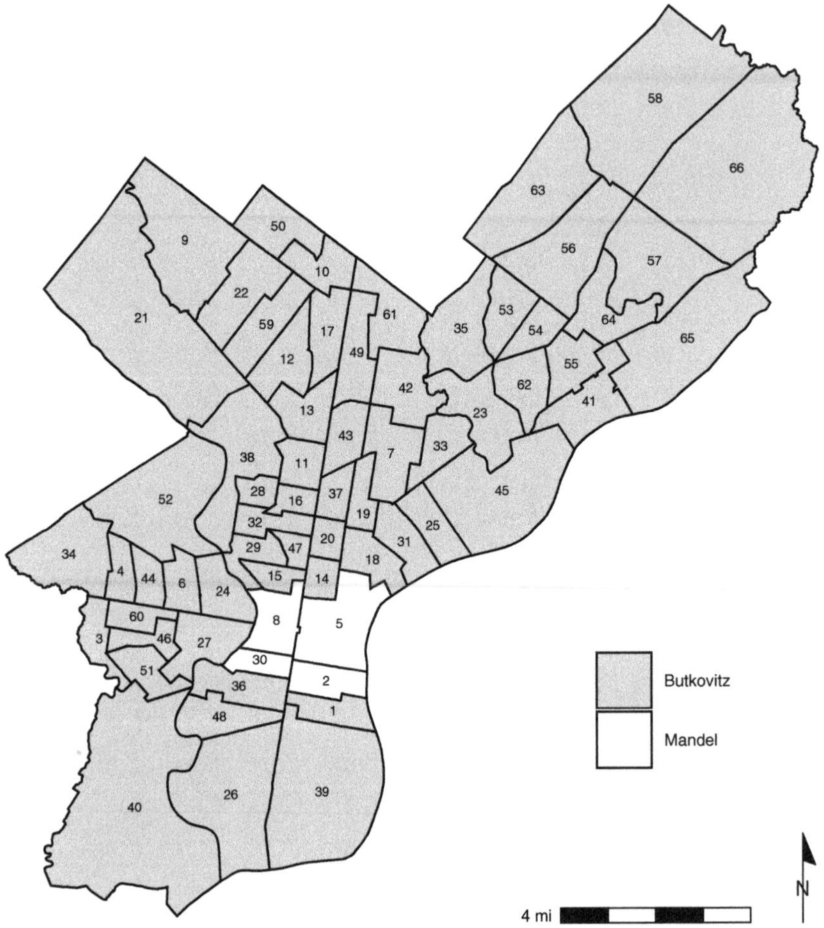

Figure 1.5 2013 Democratic primary election results, Philadelphia city controller

Source: Data from Philadelphia City Commissioners, "Archived Data Sets: 2013 Primary," https://www.philadelphiavotes.com/en/resources-a-data/ballot-box-app/additional-election-results-data; map by Michael Fichman.

outrage over the well-publicized abuses of public office that had led to incumbent Seth Williams's indictment and resignation in February of the election year were likely to have influenced a significant turnout for Joe Khan and Rich Negrin, two DA candidates with commendable past records of public service. Lawrence Krasner's engagement in civil rights litigation against the Philadelphia Police Department, his representation of Black Lives Matter activists, and his endorsement by MoveOn Political Action also were likely to have increased his name recognition and stimulated a higher voter turnout. The vote total for all DA candidates in 2017 was

155,246, a third larger than the 104,600 overall vote total in the multiple-candidate 2009 DA primary.

Although Rebecca Rhynhart was probably less well known at the start of 2017 than Brett Mandel had been in 2009 and 2013, and although Mandel had established his activist credentials and initiated his critique of the controller's office well before running for the office, Rhynhart's use of television advertising in the final weeks of the campaign enabled her to strengthen her name recognition and put Butkovitz on the defensive. According to Kellan White:

> We spent enough money to give Rebecca good TV exposure [during the final weeks preceding election day], and that changed everything. Alan tried to respond, and it backfired. I understood that his strategy had been to do heavy mailings and then change over to TV. A series of four or five mailings would have been effective. Rebecca had some potential negatives—her past employment at Bear Stearns, for example—but they're hard to portray on TV and much easier to portray through mailings.
>
> In the past, [Butkovitz] had pissed some people off, but he eventually gained enough support to win. So in the 2017 primary, he just had to be like a winning football team—make every play, make every tackle, don't give up any interceptions.[18]

The Butkovitz campaign apparently scrambled to get their candidate on TV earlier than planned, but the initiative had been lost. Rhynhart's early TV exposure, combined with her relentless networking, was already having an effect.

In the wake of the Trump election and the postinauguration Women's March, the opportunity to bring a competent woman with no political background into public office was likely to have broad appeal. For voters who were angered and disheartened by the results of the presidential election but who had no opportunity to effect immediate change on a national level, the Krasner and Rhynhart campaigns offered a chance to do so locally. Recognition of this opportunity with reference to a woman's candidacy was likely to have been an especially significant factor, as evidenced by the election results: Rhynhart outpolled Krasner by twenty thousand votes.

The Grassroots Landscape

The political contests that take place on a citywide level are replicated on a smaller scale within Philadelphia's sixty-six wards. Each of these wards is divided into geographic units known as divisions (sometimes called precincts in other cities) that contain at least 100 and no more than 1,200 registered voters.[19] Unlike ward boundaries, division boundaries must be realigned after each decennial census as needed to comply with the 100-to-1,200 registered voter parameter. As a result, wards in which the population grew during the decades after the most recent drafting of ward boundaries in 1965 contain more divisions than wards in which the population declined or remained about the same during this period. For example, the 14th Ward, located in an area of North Philadelphia where crowded public housing towers were demolished and replaced with low-rise, lower-density housing, contains only eleven divisions. The 40th Ward, where the Korman Corporation constructed thousands of suburban-style homes during the last four decades of the twentieth century, contains fifty-one divisions. Each division in the city has a single polling place.

In older neighborhoods that contain row houses and multifamily apartment buildings, divisions can be relatively compact. For example, within the division highlighted in Figure 1.6, the 5th Division, located in Northwest Philadelphia's 22nd Ward, one could walk the length of every street in the division in an hour or two.

The 22nd Ward, which consists of twenty-nine divisions, is part of the 200th Pennsylvania House District, along with two neighboring wards: the 9th, with seventeen divisions, and the 50th, with thirty divisions. Because of this geography, the next person to be elected state representative for the 200th Pennsylvania House District will be chosen by a majority of voters from a total of seventy-six divisions that are located within a relatively small area of the city.

In a primary election held every four years, voters from the Democratic and Republican parties elect two committeepeople from each division to represent the party's interests on a neighborhood level. A committeeperson, who must be a registered party member living within the division boundaries, is an unpaid party representative who is responsible for informing voters about the party's candidates in each election and for responding to voter requests for information and assistance. The committeeperson's role is distinct from that of the election board members who work inside the polling place to sign in voters, supervise the voting process, and resolve any related problems in their capacity as nonpartisan election officials performing a task on behalf of the government entity responsible for administering elections.

All of the committeepeople in the city are elected in the same primary election. A short time after the election, committeepeople in each ward meet and vote on the selection of a ward leader who will represent the ward

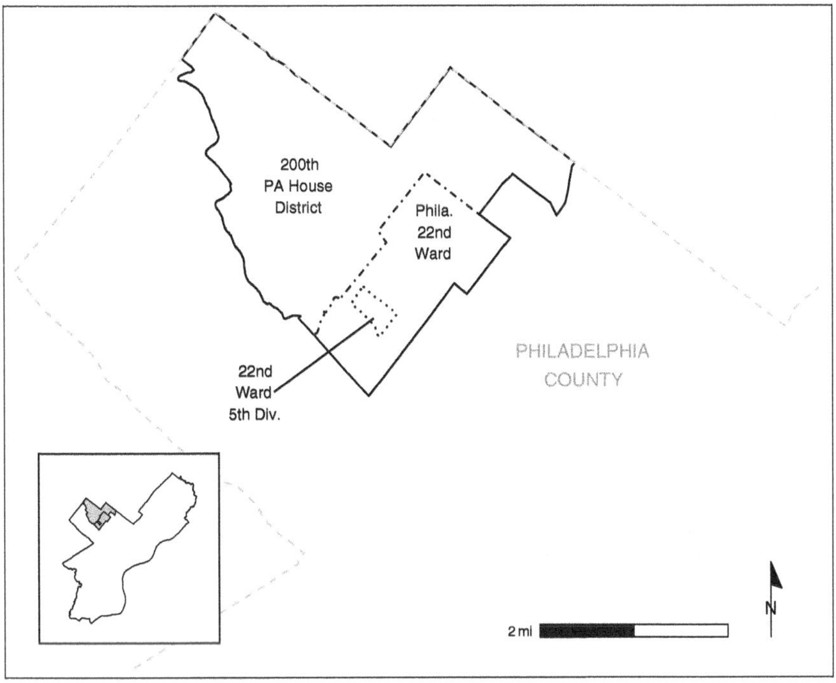

Figure 1.6 Three district boundaries: 5th Division, 22nd Ward, and 200th Pennsylvania House District

Source: Ward boundaries data from John Daley and Allen Weinberg, *Genealogy of Philadelphia County Subdivisions*, 2nd ed. (Philadelphia: City of Philadelphia Department of Records, 1966), 91; Pennsylvania House District boundaries data from Philadelphia City Planning Commission, "City of Philadelphia: Legislative Districts," https://files7.philadelphiavotes.com/maps/state-rep-maps/All_State_Representative_Districts.pdf#_ga=2.202051281.192143267.1585344776-1970273490.1584814299 (accessed April 15, 2020); map by Michael Fichman.

in Philadelphia's citywide party organization, the Democratic City Committee. The elected ward leaders then convene and elect a City Committee chair to serve as the city party leader.

In each ward, the ward leader and committeepeople usually meet several times a year. In some wards, the meetings are held on a regular schedule that is known to all participants in advance; in other wards, the scheduling of meetings can be ad hoc and unpredictable. In a typical year, the most important ward meetings are those held during the weeks leading up to each primary election, when candidates for office may be given an opportunity to make presentations to committeepeople. Some wards offer any candidate the opportunity to deliver a presentation. In other wards, only selected candidates—in some instances, candidates who have already been endorsed by City Committee or who are favored by the ward leader—are admitted to the ward meeting. Each ward makes its own determination about the extent to which it will welcome or prohibit candidates' campaign pitches.

When an incumbent Democratic officeholder runs for reelection, City Committee almost invariably gives its endorsement to the incumbent (although there are some exceptions to this practice). In elections in which no incumbent is on the ballot, City Committee may support one of the contenders or (as in the 2017 DA primary) none of them. City Committee deliberations are conducted behind closed doors and may not be subject to *Robert's Rules of Order* guidelines or other parliamentary procedures. However, because maintaining party unity and demonstrating respect for ward leaders are high priorities, any City Committee endorsement is likely to be consistent with the views of a majority of the ward leaders or the result of horse trading involving mutually agreed-on endorsements of multiple candidates that produces reasonably satisfactory results for participants with different views and preferences.

Although divisions are designed to contain voter populations that are roughly equivalent, actual voter turnout can vary widely from one division to another within the same ward. Some of the same factors that influence turnout at the ward level—income, educational attainment, and employment status—have a similar effect within a division. However, race is a less significant factor at the division level; some of the city's highest-turnout divisions have a substantial or majority African American population. In addition, the level of homeownership within a division is likely to influence turnout. Many more homeowners than renters are likely to be long-term residents who know more of their neighbors, have stronger ties with neighborhood-based entities such as block organizations and local congregations of faith, and have more interest in issues affecting their long-term well-being and their investment in their homes.

The 22nd Ward provides an illustration of the extent to which turnout can vary from one division to another. In the 2017 Democratic primary election for city controller, the high-turnout 1st Division generated a turnout of 391 voters, more than three times the combined turnout of the lower-turnout 25th, 26th, and 28th Divisions, as shown in Table 1.5. As with ward turnout, turnout at the division level is relatively consistent from election to election; many of the same divisions will have the highest- and lowest-turnout status each time.

In an earlier era, when ward organizations were powerful brokers of government jobs, city contracts, and public services, the ward and division structure was much stronger and more cohesive. As the Democratic Party's influence weakened during the late twentieth century, this structure became fragmented. In current primary elections, some ward organizations do not

TABLE 1.5 SELECTED HIGHER- AND LOWER-TURNOUT DIVISIONS IN THE 22ND WARD

	Higher-turnout divisions			Lower-turnout divisions		
Candidate	**1**	**2**	**6**	**25**	**26**	**28**
Rebecca Rhynhart	246	203	159	63	76	67
Alan Butkovitz	145	155	90	57	45	56
Write-in	0	1	0	0	0	0
Total	391	359	249	120	121	123

Source: Philadelphia City Commissioners, *View Election Results* database, https://www.philadelphiavotes.com/en/resources-a-data/ballot-box-app.

always endorse the candidates that City Committee has endorsed; at the division level, some committeepeople do not support candidates that the ward organization endorses.

The most active committeepeople have a highly visible presence on election day. They can often be found outside the polling place, greeting voters and distributing information about favored candidates—most frequently in the form of sample ballots printed by City Committee or the ward organization. Many committeepeople are longtime neighborhood residents who are well known in the community; as voters approach the polling place, they tend to gravitate to the committeepeople rather than to campaign workers or volunteers from outside the community who have shown up for the first time on that day to promote a particular candidate. Some committeepeople compose and distribute a letter that contains information about the offices on the ballot and about recommended candidates. Through these activities, a committeeperson in a higher-turnout division can significantly influence election outcomes within a particular ward.

The outcome of the 2016 Democratic primary election for state representative in the 200th Pennsylvania House District provides a good illustration of the significance of division-level activism. In December 2015, Cherelle Parker resigned her position as state representative for the 200th District after winning election to the Philadelphia City Council. Since Parker had completed only one year of her two-year term, a special election was held in March 2016 to fill this vacancy through the end of the year. The winner of the special election was Tonyelle Cook-Artis, who had previously been Parker's chief of staff.

As a result of the timing of Representative Parker's resignation and the scheduling of the special election, Cook-Artis was in an unusual position. After winning the special election in March 2016 and being sworn into office on April 5, she also needed to win election in the April 26 primary—three weeks later—to remain in office for the new legislative term that would begin in January 2017.

TABLE 1.6 2016 DEMOCRATIC PRIMARY ELECTION RESULTS BY WARD, 200TH LEGISLATIVE DISTRICT

Candidate	9th Ward	22nd Ward	50th Ward	Total
Chris Rabb	4,105	3,672	2,522	10,299
Tonyelle Cook-Artis	706	2,854	5,306	8,866
Bobby Curry	421	1,074	1,145	2,640
Write-in	2	1	0	3
Total	5,234	7,601	8,973	21,808

Source: Philadelphia City Commissioners, *View Election Results* database, https://www.philadelphiavotes.com/en/resources-a-data/ballot-box-app.

In the April Democratic primary election, Cook-Artis was challenged by Chris Rabb, a 9th Ward committeeperson who had not previously held any higher elective office. Consistent with customary practice, Cook-Artis's candidacy was endorsed by the Democratic City Committee and numerous Democratic officeholders, including Mayor James Kenney, Democratic members of City Council, and Democratic legislators representing other Philadelphia districts in the state's General Assembly.

However, Rabb conducted an ambitious door-to-door campaign and mobilized a strong get-out-the-vote initiative on election day. Rabb's energetic campaign, combined with what may have been overconfidence on the part of his opponent and her supporters, produced an unexpected victory for him, as shown in Table 1.6.

Predictably, the 50th Ward produced the highest turnout and the most votes for Cook-Artis, the ward-endorsed candidate. Rabb's combined votes in the 50th and 9th Wards gave him a small lead over Cook-Artis, but his results in the 22nd Ward produced a decisive win for him, notwithstanding the ward leader's endorsement of Cook-Artis.

The three high-turnout 22nd Ward divisions shown in Table 1.5 produced large margins of victory for Rabb. His votes in these three divisions alone represented more than 20 percent of all the votes he received in the 22nd Ward.

Although defeating an incumbent, especially a party-endorsed incumbent, is extremely difficult in any election, Rabb's success in 2016 demonstrates that it can be done. Although upsets such as the one he achieved are rare, another one occurred in the same election: in Northeast Philadelphia's 202nd Legislative District, challenger Jared Solomon defeated incumbent Mark Cohen, who had been the state's longest-serving state representative.

A Rusting Machine

Conceptually, Philadelphia's ward and division structure is consistent with the fundamentals of democracy and representative government. A municipality is divided into compact, walkable, village-sized areas, known as divisions. Voters in each division elect two residents, their committeepeople, to represent the interests of the political party to which they belong. Groups of divisions are aggregated into neighborhood-sized wards. The committeepeople elected from divisions within a ward meet to elect a ward leader. Then all the elected ward leaders meet to elect a leader of their party's city committee, who represents the party at the city level. In concept, this inclusive, grassroots approach is an ideal mechanism for advancing democracy and collective action, one that should ensure high levels of citizen engagement and voter turnout in every election.

Unfortunately, present reality is not consistent with this ideal. On a citywide basis, relatively few people know the names of the committeepeople who represent the division where they live—or even know what a committeeperson is or does. Although many committeepeople are fully engaged in carrying out their responsibilities, many others fail to attend ward meetings and are more absent than present at the polls on election days. Ward meetings are held behind closed doors, and many ward leaders make candidate endorsements unilaterally, rather than by a vote of a majority of the committeepeople. Some ward organizations and ward leaders accept contributions from candidates without explaining why the money is being accepted and how it will be spent. *Philadelphia Inquirer* reporter Tom Ferrick described a conversation with one ward leader: "Asked what he did to earn a $10,000 consulting fee before the Democratic primary, Ronald Couser, leader of Germantown's 22nd Ward, had a succinct answer: 'Give advice.'"[20] Although transactions such as this one are required to be documented in campaign finance reports, many ward organizations consistently fail to file them.

Given the secretive, insular fashion in which ward organizations conduct their affairs, it is not surprising that these organizations may endorse candidates that a majority of voters do not support. Returns from the 22nd Ward in three elections illustrate this disconnect.

- In the April 2016 primary election for state representative, challenger Chris Rabb outpolled ward-endorsed candidate Tonyelle Cook-Artis by more than eight hundred votes in the 22nd Ward.
- In the May 2017 Democratic primary election for city controller, ward-endorsed candidate Alan Butkovitz was defeated by Rebecca Rhynhart by more than one thousand votes.
- In the same primary, Lawrence Krasner received more than three times as many votes as ward-endorsed candidate Tariq El-Shabazz.

Many voters do support ward-endorsed candidates, often with little knowledge of the candidate's qualifications or fitness for office. If more voters had greater awareness of these characteristics, they might avoid electing individuals who subsequently mismanage their responsibilities or break the law. As described previously, Philadelphia's district attorney resigned in disgrace in 2017. A year earlier, U.S. Congressman Chaka Fattah was convicted on charges of fraud, racketeering, and money laundering. In 2014, a Northwest Philadelphia state senator was found guilty of conflict-of-interest charges, and a year earlier, four state representatives pled guilty or no contest to charges of accepting money in exchange for political favors.

Who should be held responsible for Philadelphia's chronic failure to use the ward and division structure as a vehicle for encouraging participation in the democratic process and electing responsible candidates to public office? In 2017, U.S. Congressman Bob Brady was chair of the Democratic City Committee, an office he had held for thirty-one years. Brady's success is due in large part to his consistent support of the city's Democratic ward leaders. As he told a reporter:

> I happen to subscribe to the fact that I love my ward leaders and I love my committee people, and they don't get enough recognition! "Oh, you get them a job?" You're goddamn right I get them a job! Because they work hard! They're community people! They know their neighbors! Why shouldn't a Councilman that they supported hire them? Why shouldn't a Congressman? Everybody in my staff is involved in politics. Why not? Why not?[21]

To help ensure that party-endorsed candidates are elected, Brady maintains party unity by upholding the status quo. He would never take it on himself to propose that ward meetings be open to the public, that all ward endorsements be made on the basis of a majority vote of committeepeople, that ward leaders refrain from accepting money from candidates for "advice," or that ward committees file financial reports to document any such transactions—and if he did, he would not be likely to remain head of City Committee for long.

Since the ward leaders who elect the party chair are elected by committeepeople who, in turn, are elected by voters in each division, the ultimate responsibility for the current dysfunctional state of the party lies with two groups of registered Democrats: those who voted for the committeepeople now in office, with or without having much knowledge of the responsibilities of this position or awareness of the candidates' qualifications, and a much larger group—those who failed to vote at all. Congressman Brady may own a share of the blame for the current condition of the party, but the voters own the problem outright.

Rebecca Rhynhart's victory demonstrated that a citywide election could be won decisively by a candidate who entered the race with almost no support from Philadelphia's Democratic Party establishment and who did not actively seek party endorsements during the campaign. Her success was due in part to her team's perceptive and well-managed campaign strategy and in part to the degree to which her candidacy resonated with deep concerns held by many voters in 2017. At various times in Philadelphia's history, other candidates had achieved comparable successes as a result of a similar combination of campaign management and circumstance. Was Rhynhart's win another one of these infrequent insurgent-candidate successes, or was her victory the first solid evidence that the Democratic Party's dominant role in Philadelphia politics was finally coming to an end?

2

★★★★★★★

Origin Story

The history of the Philadelphia reform movement that resulted in the overthrow of the Republican machine and the subsequent decade of municipal reform that took place during the mayoral administrations of Joseph S. Clark Jr. and Richardson Dilworth (1952–1956 and 1956–1962, respectively) have been well documented.[1] This chapter is about the trends in voting, voter registration, and voter turnout at the citywide and neighborhood level that made these changes possible and subsequently established the Democratic City Committee, for better and for worse, as a leading influence in Philadelphia city politics for the remainder of the century. (See Table 2.1 for a snapshot of key elections before and after the elections of Clark and Dilworth.)

On election night in 1947, incumbent mayor Bernard Samuel's victory margin left Dilworth and Clark very dejected and fearful that the reform movement was dead before it had truly begun. The two men went to the roof of the hotel where they had received the returns. There the mood was electric. "We saw all these volunteers up there and they were jubilant," recalled Dilworth. "The election was lost, but they were seeing the future."[2]

Preoccupied with their disappointment over the unsuccessful outcome of his reform candidacy for mayor, Dilworth and Clark were unaware that they were witnessing the beginning of the end of a nearly century-long Republican stranglehold on Philadelphia politics.

Viewed in the context of Philadelphia's political history up until then, their pessimism about the prospects for future reform is understandable. In 1947, 70 percent of Philadelphia's registered voters were Republicans—

TABLE 2.1 KEY ELECTIONS LEADING UP TO AND FOLLOWING CLARK AND DILWORTH ELECTIONS

Year elected	Governor	Mayor	District attorney	Democratic City Committee chair
Incumbent in 1947	James H. Duff	Bernard Samuel	John H. Maurer	
1948				James A. Finnegan
1949				
1950	John S. Fine			
1951		*Joseph S. Clark Jr.*	*Richardson Dilworth*	
1952				
1953				William J. Green Jr.
1954	George M. Leader			
1955		*Richardson Dilworth*	Victor H. Blanc	
1956				
1957			Victor H. Blanc	
1958	David L. Lawrence			
1959		*Richardson Dilworth*		
1960				
1961			James C. Crumlish Jr.	
1962	William W. Scranton	James H. J. Tate (appointed)		
1963		James H. J. Tate		Francis R. Smith
1964				
1965			Arlen Specter	

Source: Data for governor, mayor, and district attorney from Philadelphia Registration Commission, *Annual Reports* (Philadelphia: City of Philadelphia, 1947, 1950, 1951, 1953, 1954, 1955, 1957, 1958, 1959, 1961, 1962, 1963, 1965); data for Democratic City Committee chair from Russell F. Weigley, ed., *Philadelphia: A 300-Year History* (New York: W. W. Norton, 1982), 653, 659, 662.

693,535 out of 1,003,464 registered voters citywide.[3] Republican state senators and state representatives from Philadelphia held key positions in Pennsylvania's General Assembly, as they had for decades; and because Philadelphia had not yet achieved "home rule" status, the city was, in effect, "merely a legislative agency of the state . . . not an independent sovereignty"[4] and was subject to the power of state elected officials.

The influence of the Republican party bosses and the political machine had been pervasive during the previous half-century, as the following examples illustrate:

- In the first decade of the twentieth century, approximately 94 percent of all city employees illegally paid assessments to the

Republican organization. In addition to paying between 1 and 4 percent of their salary to City Committee, employees were required to contribute half that amount to their local ward committees.[5]
- False voter registration, "helping" voters mark their ballots, and providing premarked ballots, as well as false counting, ballot box stuffing, and vote buying were common election practices.[6]
- A grand jury convened in 1928 to investigate "connections between the police, the bootleggers, and the gambling rings" resulted in the arrest of 63 members of the police force and the dismissal of 174 members of the force over a seven-month period. Ten years later, a similar grand jury investigation exposed a comparable alliance between the police and organized crime.[7]

Decade after decade, key positions in municipal government had been held by Republicans. Reform movements emerged and some reformers were elected to municipal office, but the power of Republican bosses and the political organization they oversaw remained largely intact until the years after World War II.

Predigital Data Resources

Annual reports submitted to the governor of Pennsylvania by the Registration Commission for the City of Philadelphia provide detailed information about Philadelphia voters and major election results during the postwar period. The commission was responsible for registering citizens to vote, purging from voter files the names of voters who were deceased or had moved, and recording changes of address, among other responsibilities. Much of the commission's work was accomplished by traveling registrars and other employees who conducted door-to-door canvassing in what the commission termed "more transient" divisions. In 1947, for example, their activities resulted in the registration of 85,099 new voters and the removal of 31,029 names from the voter rolls.[8]

Computers became part of Philadelphia's election-management system a few years later. The annual report for 1951 describes how information collected by traveling registrars is sorted by ward and then "sent to the I.B.M. room":

> The room is of major importance in the operation. . . . The completed data for each new registration is taken off and key punched on a card, which is later used to address city-wide mail check cards and to compile the official street and jury lists as well as to make the

> official registration count for each election. You may wonder how one little card could do so much but it is done by automatically feeding this key punched card through various counters and printers.[9]

Each annual report provides a breakdown of registered voters by ward and party affiliation.

During this period, the report also identified the number of "Native Born," "White," and "Colored" voters, as well as "Foreign Born" voters, in each ward, as shown in Figure 2.1. At that time, most "Foreign Born" voters are likely to have been Irish, Italian, and Eastern European.[10]

REGISTRATION AND VOTE—FALL, 1948

Table showing by wards the comparative number of native-born, white and colored, and foreign-born registered as of December 31, 1948, and the vote cast for the office of President parties on November 2, 1948, as computed by the County Bo[a]

WARDS	REGISTRATION: Native Born: White	Native Born: Colored	Foreign Born	Rep.	Dem.	N. P.	Misc.	Total	Truman	Dewey
1st	13,675	236	5,280	13,477	4,544	268	2	18,291	7,222	7,001
2d	5,901	2,316	1,082	7,987	2,093	88	1	10,169	2,849	5,420
3d	3,147	1,709	1,225	4,901	1,123	53	4	6,081	1,546	3,486
4th	2,230	2,663	985	4,980	995	52	1	5,988	1,060	3,604
5th	2,280	963	970	3,445	706	56	4	4,212	1,145	2,155
6th	290	160	46	417	86	1	—	504	90	305
7th	5,482	5,769	647	8,957	2,822	292	27	12,098	3,281	5,760
8th	6,066	220	924	5,657	1,815	310	18	7,800	1,489	4,195
9th	1,064	40	139	1,018	197	27	1	1,243	274	709
10th	4,633	406	500	4,985	473	95	5	5,558	759	3,414
11th	1,062	677	370	1,891	194	24	—	2,109	446	1,280
12th	1,769	683	660	2,544	717	48	3	3,312	1,034	1,625
13th	2,680	4,086	829	6,151	1,388	34	2	7,575	1,098	3,903
14th	2,196	4,421	481	5,007	1,890	39	2	7,098	2,155	3,029
15th	14,528	2,421	3,136	13,655	5,134	283	13	19,085	7,349	7,645
16th	2,986	283	971	2,715	1,452	72	1	4,240	1,959	1,434
17th	3,440	106	871	3,284	1,065	66	2	4,417	1,756	1,796
18th	8,479	18	1,008	6,736	2,631	134	4	9,505	4,350	3,677
19th	17,703	565	2,668	14,758	5,769	405	4	20,936	9,571	7,839
20th	7,531	12,938	3,315	17,924	5,618	233	9	23,784	8,706	8,925
21st	20,276	442	2,045	19,412	3,058	286	7	22,763	7,034	12,029
22d	48,621	8,059	6,013	43,801	13,913	1,921	58	59,693	18,937	31,758
23d	22,559	906	3,241	19,947	6,341	503	15	26,706	11,083	12,044
24th	10,826	12,427	3,410	18,209	7,976	437	41	26,663	10,589	9,295
25th	17,088	286	3,003	14,807	5,505	269	5	20,386	9,705	7,803
26th	21,063	3,453	6,663	23,649	7,132	384	3	31,168	13,311	12,009
27th	9,302	1,636	911	8,912	2,499	411	26	11,848	3,396	5,849
28th	15,202	7,471	5,094	17,757	9,561	488	21	27,827	13,008	7,810
29th	9,348	6,048	3,057	11,985	5,184	218	11	17,448	7,496	5,955
30th	1,678	11,251	286	9,219	3,867	104	5	13,215	5,658	4,054
31st	12,402	9	1,127	10,197	3,164	171	6	13,538	5,783	5,814
32d	5,950	14,698	2,687	14,078	8,784	427	81	23,365	11,277	6,845
33d	28,833	58	4,876	21,696	10,946	680	25	33,267	17,236	11,191
34th	18,680	1,341	4,275	17,768	6,061	512	5	24,366	9,906	10,402
35th	52,598	109	9,118	48,502	12,516	1,746	56	62,820	23,273	31,095
36th	12,986	11,189	2,983	17,167	9,786	247	7	27,157	14,867	7,415
37th	7,940	1,638	972	7,306	2,862	268	4	10,440	4,482	4,065
38th	29,252	2,879	5,330	25,180	11,366	885	30	37,461	17,182	14,208
39th	22,072	970	9,357	22,300	10,240	758	11	33,399	16,441	10,703
40th	24,368	2,692	3,499	22,086	7,805	558	11	30,549	14,152	11,365
41st	23,106	216	2,545	19,861	6,547	530	8	26,966	12,821	11,150
42d	25,581	12	6,082	19,665	10,880	1,017	14	31,576	13,049	13,575
43d	22,140	465	4,340	19,379	7,070	486	10	26,945	12,388	10,618
44th	8,831	9,148	1,725	13,695	5,771	226	12	19,704	8,910	6,157
45th	13,645	78	2,409	11,086	5,018	282	6	16,392	8,267	5,716
46th	38,199	931	8,461	30,838	15,317	1,409	27	47,591	19,374	18,636
47th	3,147	12,720	637	11,047	5,292	149	16	16,504	7,089	4,700
48th	12,468	451	3,009	13,445	3,227	252	4	16,928	7,328	7,227
49th	23,276	340	6,770	18,912	10,225	1,126	22	30,286	12,842	12,278
50th	29,949	42	4,980	23,925	9,676	1,349	21	34,971	12,892	17,631
51st	21,209	1,676	2,766	18,263	6,926	451	11	25,651	11,381	9,965
52d	14,599	10,283	4,587	17,293	11,446	707	22	29,468	13,907	8,978
Totals	780,106	161,706	182,805	742,330	285,623	21,909	656	1,050,417	432,699	426,962

Figure 2.1 Registration summary, with racial and ethnic characteristics, 1948

Source: Philadelphia Registration Commission, *Forty-Third Annual Report* (Philadelphia: City of Philadelphia, 1948), 26, 27.

As the population of Northeast Philadelphia grew during the postwar years, new wards were created in this part of the city, and ward boundaries were redrawn in some other areas that had experienced recent population increases. However, in many respects, the 1947 ward map is similar to the 2019 ward map shown in Chapter 1.

Reasons for Optimism

Why were the volunteers on the hotel rooftop feeling so upbeat on election night 1947? Incumbent Republican Mayor Bernard Samuel had just beaten Dilworth, the Democratic challenger, by about 92,000 votes, with support from 56 percent of the voters, winning the majority vote in forty-two of Philadelphia's fifty-two wards. From this perspective, Dilworth's performance had been slightly worse than that of the Democratic candidate for city controller two years earlier, in 1945. In that general election, the successful Republican candidate, former state representative Frank J. Tiemann, also won 56 percent of the vote and received majority votes in all but thirteen wards. So what was all the excitement about?

When examined at the ward level, the 1947 results could be viewed by reform Democrats as evidence of progress. Table 2.2 shows the percentage of votes received by the Republican candidate in fifteen wards in the 1945 general election for city controller and the 1947 general election for mayor. The wards shown produced the most votes for Mayor Samuel in 1947. As shown in this table, the Republican candidate's percentage of the total vote declined between 1945 and 1947 in eight of the fifteen wards. In six of them, the decline was 5 percent or greater.

This comparison of the 1947 election results for Samuel, an incumbent candidate who had held a citywide office for nearly four years, with the 1945 results for Tiemann, a politician who had not even been able to win reelection to his state House seat in 1944, provides evidence of a significant erosion of support for the top-of-the-ballot Republican Party candidates between 1945 and 1947, as shown in Table 2.2.

Foundation for Reform

Two years after the celebration on the hotel roof, Dilworth won the 1949 general election for city treasurer, and Clark was elected city controller. The energetic citywide campaign that Dilworth had conducted in 1947, in close collaboration with Clark, had attracted the interest of a new generation of reform-minded Philadelphians. In addition, as G. Terry Madonna and John Morrison McLarnon III put it, "Between 1947 and 1949, a serendipitous

TABLE 2.2 PERCENTAGE OF VOTES RECEIVED BY REPUBLICAN CANDIDATES IN FIFTEEN WARDS, 1945 AND 1947

	1945 controller election			1947 mayoral election			
Ward	Total votes	Votes for Republican candidate	Republican % of all votes	Total votes	Votes for Republican candidate	Republican % of all votes	Change in Republican % of total, 1945–1947
35	31,692	20,321	64	43,394	25,028	58	−6
22	29,783	18,332	62	39,003	20,922	54	−8
46	29,178	12,717	44	32,481	15,739	48	4
26	18,399	12,266	67	22,353	14,921	67	0
39	21,900	11,389	52	26,175	14,881	57	5
20	14,226	8,935	63	17,512	12,405	71	8
38	22,399	10,801	48	25,591	12,293	48	0
50	19,891	9,838	49	25,281	12,018	48	−1
21	13,120	9,429	72	16,922	11,312	67	−5
33	19,562	9,724	50	24,436	10,982	45	−5
40	16,380	9,142	56	21,188	10,908	51	−5
42	20,676	9,252	45	23,862	10,433	44	−1
24	14,178	7,658	54	16,805	10,402	62	8
28	15,561	6,962	45	19,426	10,345	53	8
23	15,140	9,115	60	18,974	10,323	54	−6
All wards	601,971	335,786	56	734,560	413,091	56	0

Source: Philadelphia Registration Commission, *Fortieth Annual Report* (Philadelphia: City of Philadelphia, 1945); Philadelphia Registration Commission, *Forty-First Annual Report* (Philadelphia: City of Philadelphia, 1947).

Note: Wards shown are wards that produced the most votes for Samuel in the 1947 mayoral election.

confluence of events significantly improved the reformers' prospects,"[11] including the following:

- Dilworth and Clark established a working relationship with Democratic Party Chair James A. Finnegan, based in part on an understanding that the two reform leaders, notwithstanding their membership in the Democratic Party, would be conducting organizing and fundraising activities independently of the party organization.
- A committee appointed by City Council to find ways to increase city revenues and reduce expenses to avoid a tax hike uncovered numerous instances of corruption in municipal government that were well publicized in the city's newspapers. A succession of investigations, arrests, prosecutions, and convictions were to follow.
- Members of the Greater Philadelphia Movement, a group organized by Republican business leaders to advocate for the approval of a home rule charter, became convinced that political change was essential as well. They established the "Independent Republicans for the 1949 Democratic ticket" with a goal of convincing 100,000 registered Republicans to vote for Dilworth and Clark in 1949.[12]
- The Philadelphia chapter of Americans for Democratic Action (ADA), described as a group that included in its membership "Philadelphia Gentlemen, trade union leaders, ex-Socialists, reform-minded politicos, and civic activists," played a vital role in organizing a citywide constituency for reform.[13] During the years leading up to the 1949 election, the ADA trained nearly six hundred volunteers in its "School for Practical Politics," published fact sheets and political analyses, conducted telephone and street-corner outreach, and even produced a series of politically oriented television programs.[14]

In the 1949 election for treasurer, Dilworth received 465,490 votes, compared with 353,168 votes for his Republican opponent, William Seiler. Seiler received the most votes in only two of the eleven large wards that Samuel had won in 1947. The decline in support for the Republican ticket had become even more pronounced. As Table 2.3 shows, the percentage of votes received by the Republican candidates declined in all fifteen wards between these two elections, with declines of 12 percent or more in twelve of them.

The votes contributing to the Democratic victory in 1949 were highly concentrated within a relatively small number of wards located in certain

TABLE 2.3 PERCENTAGE OF VOTES RECEIVED BY REPUBLICAN CANDIDATES IN FIFTEEN WARDS, 1947 AND 1949

	1947 mayoral election			1949 treasurer election			
Ward	Total votes cast	Votes for Republican candidate	Republican % of all votes	Total votes	Votes for Republican candidate	Republican % of all votes	Change in Republican % of total, 1947–1949
35	43,394	25,028	58	54,725	22,976	42	–16
22	39,003	20,922	54	45,535	18,238	40	–14
46	32,481	15,739	48	36,461	12,823	35	–13
26	22,353	14,921	67	24,872	12,324	50	–17
39	26,175	14,881	57	27,588	12,320	45	–12
20	17,512	12,405	71	17,239	10,179	59	–12
38	25,591	12,293	48	29,724	10,391	35	–13
50	25,281	12,018	48	30,054	9,795	33	–15
21	16,922	11,312	67	18,927	10,006	53	–14
33	24,436	10,982	45	27,643	9,446	34	–11
40	21,188	10,908	51	24,449	9,754	40	–11
42	23,862	10,433	44	25,760	8,621	33	–11
24	16,805	10,402	62	18,710	8,644	46	–16
28	19,426	10,345	53	19,585	7,846	40	–13
23	18,974	10,323	54	21,531	9,029	42	–12
All wards	734,560	413,091	56	822,895	353,168	43	

Source: Philadelphia Registration Commission, *Forty-First Annual Report* (Philadelphia: City of Philadelphia, 1947); Philadelphia Registration Commission, *Forty-Third Annual Report* (Philadelphia: City of Philadelphia, 1949).

TABLE 2.4 HIGHEST VOTE TOTALS IN WARDS WITH MAJORITY VOTES FOR DILWORTH CANDIDACIES, 1947 AND 1949

Ward	1947 mayoral election	1949 treasurer election
35	18,366	31,504
22	18,081	27,132
46	16,742	23,344
33	13,454	18,088
42	13,429	17,016
38	13,298	19,235
50	13,263	20,086
49	11,887	16,169
39	11,294	15,129
52	11,004	14,951
40	10,280	14,625
41	9,655	14,759
43	9,652	14,034
51	9,224	13,141
Other*	9,081	12,694
Total votes from top fifteen wards	188,710	271,907
Percentage of candidate's total votes	59	58
Candidate's total votes	321,469	465,490

Source: Philadelphia Registration Commission, *Forty-First Annual Report* (Philadelphia: City of Philadelphia, 1947); Philadelphia Registration Commission, *Forty-Third Annual Report* (Philadelphia: City of Philadelphia, 1949).

* 28th Ward in 1947; 36th Ward in 1949.

areas of the city, as they had been in 1947. In both elections, just fifteen of the city's fifty-two wards produced nearly 60 percent of Dilworth's votes. As shown in Table 2.4, fourteen of these wards produced the highest number of votes for Dilworth in both elections.

As shown on the map in Figure 2.2, all of the wards in which Dilworth received the most votes in these two elections were located outside the city's central core: west of the Schuylkill River, outside the industrial and row house neighborhood zones north and south of the downtown area, and outside the Delaware River wards.

Nine of these wards (plus the 28th Ward in the 1947 election) are the same wards that produced large numbers of votes for Republicans in the 1945, 1947, and 1949 general elections, as shown in Tables 2.2 and 2.3. The fifteen wards shown in Tables 2.2 and 2.3 contributed about half of the total votes that the leading Republican candidates received citywide in these three elections.

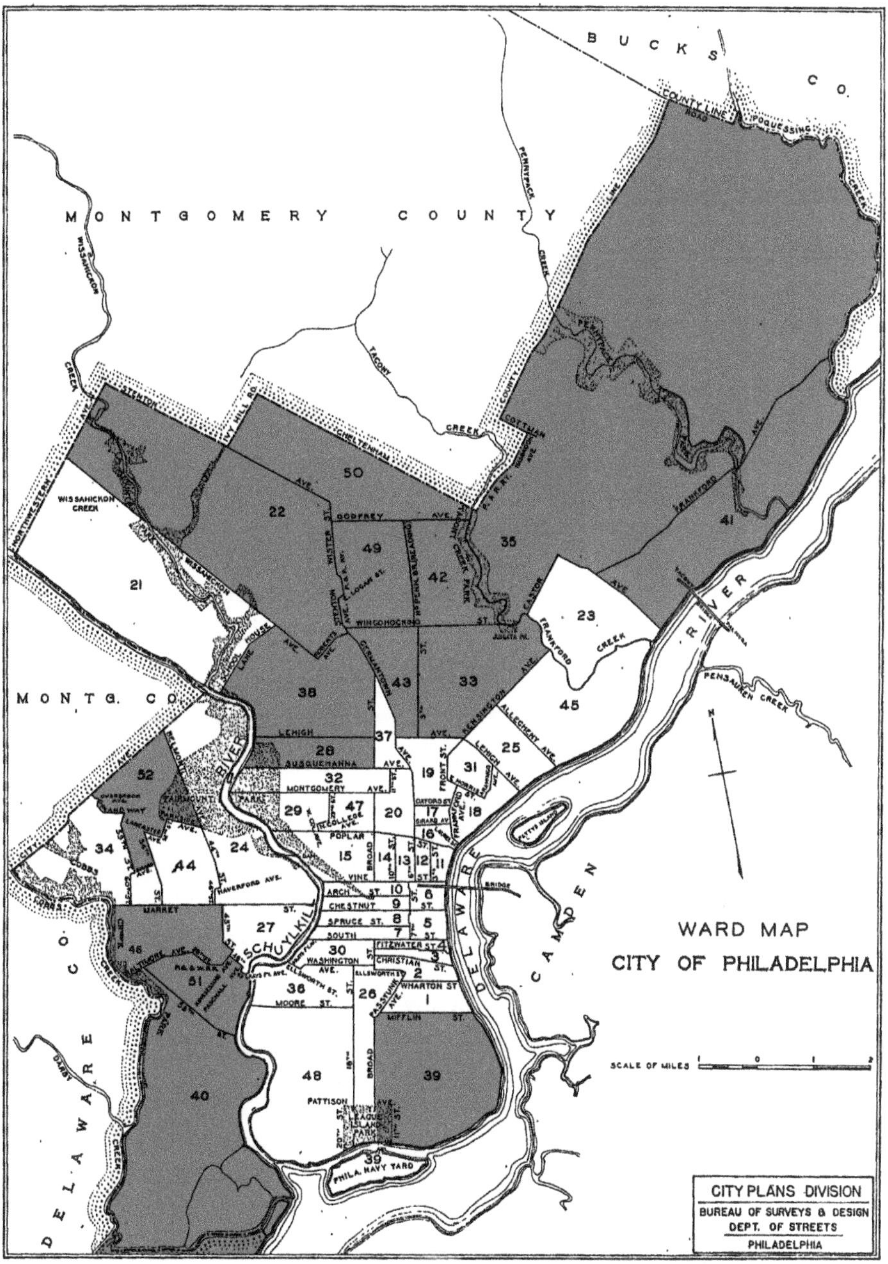

Figure 2.2 Wards with highest vote totals for Dilworth candidacies, 1947 and 1949

Source: Map from John Daley and Allen Weinberg, *Genealogy of Philadelphia County Subdivisions*, 2nd ed. (Philadelphia: City of Philadelphia Department of Records, 1966), 87; data from Philadelphia Registration Commission, *Annual Report, 1947* (Philadelphia: City of Philadelphia, 1947); and Philadelphia Registration Commission, *Annual Report, 1949* (Philadelphia: City of Philadelphia, 1949).

Not Entirely Golden

The election of Clark as mayor and Dilworth as district attorney in 1951 was accompanied by voter approval of a home rule charter for Philadelphia in the same year. During Clark's administration and Dilworth's two subsequent mayoral terms, the second of which ended with his resignation to run for governor in 1962, fundamental changes in the structure of municipal government and major improvements in the quality of the urban environment were conceived and implemented. City departments were reorganized and professionalized. A reenergized Civil Service Commission supervised test-based hiring of city personnel, and talented individuals were recruited from other cities to take on leadership positions.[15]

Dilworth brought integrity to the district attorney's office,

> eliminating political control and establishing for the first time in many years a set of reliable criminal case records. . . . [His staff] cut the period prior to trial in nonbail cases from ninety to thirty days, and the delay in reaching trial in bail cases from nearly two years to seven months . . . Dilworth worked closely with Police Commissioner [Thomas] Gibbons to break up long-standing alliances between ward politicians and the police.[16]

Major improvements in the city's downtown and neighborhoods attracted national attention. Edmund N. Bacon, who had become executive director of the City Planning Commission in 1949, directed or influenced transformative changes that took shape during and after the Clark and Dilworth administrations. Although Bacon supervised or contributed to plans for public investment throughout the city, he was most widely recognized for his leadership role in the design and implementation of downtown redevelopment projects, including Penn Center and Market East, as well as renewal activities in the Independence Hall and Society Hill redevelopment areas.[17]

Mayor Clark worked closely with Democratic City Committee chair Finnegan, who had been elected president of City Council in 1951. Although Democratic Party support was a factor influencing some departmental appointments, key leadership positions were filled by qualified individuals.[18]

At the same time, the relationship between the reform leaders and City Committee was far from problem free. Party leaders were especially frustrated by the institution of civil service standards, which denied them the opportunity to readily place constituents in city jobs, as their Republican counterparts had been able to do for decades before charter approval and the ascendancy of the reformers.

Congressman William J. Green became chair of the Democratic City Committee in 1953, and by the time Dilworth took office as mayor, it was known that, if he chose to do so, Green could deliver a majority vote in City Council supporting a charter amendment that would exempt some employees from merit-hiring provisions. Seeking to reach a compromise that would prevent such an action from taking place, Dilworth announced his support for a less radical charter amendment that would create exemptions for a certain class of municipal employees: those who performed county-government administrative functions such as the recorder of deeds and registrar of wills. However, a referendum question on this amendment was decisively defeated by voters in the 1956 primary election. Dilworth had failed to deliver the outcome that would have improved his working relationship with the party leaders; and he had angered the activists who had supported his and Clark's reform agenda in previous elections.[19]

Other conflicts had emerged during Dilworth's first term as mayor. When Dilworth resigned from his position as district attorney to run for mayor, Victor H. Blanc, not a favorite of Dilworth, was elected to complete his term. Then, in preparation for the 1957 election, Congressman Green used his influence as City Committee chair to obtain party endorsement for Blanc's election to a full four-year term as DA, over Dilworth's objections.[20]

Some of the ADA members who had been most active during the period leading up to the 1949 election were unhappy with the compromises that Clark and Dilworth had subsequently made with party leaders. Most of the women who had taken on key leadership roles (as described in depth by G. Terry Madonna and John Morrison McLarnon) moved on to take part in other government and civic activities, in Philadelphia or elsewhere.[21]

When Dilworth resigned to run for governor in 1962, City Council President James H. J. Tate, a Democratic Party stalwart, became acting mayor. In 1963, a mayoral election year, the Democratic Party endorsed Tate's candidacy for a full four-year term. In opposition to Tate, Walter M. Phillips, who had played a central role in Philadelphia's reform movement for more than a decade, declared his candidacy for the Democratic nomination. Phillips attracted the support of independent Democrats, including ADA members, but their effort to mobilize citywide turnout for their candidate was unsuccessful. Phillips was easily defeated by Tate, and a not entirely golden age of twentieth-century reform in Philadelphia came to an end.

Growth and Decline

Although the total number of votes for the Democratic candidates shown in Table 2.5 increased from 321,469 in 1947 to 438,278 in 1959, most of this increase was associated with relatively few wards, particularly those in

TABLE 2.5 HIGHEST VOTE TOTALS FOR DILWORTH AND CLARK IN SELECTED WARDS, 1947–1959

Ward	Dilworth votes, 1947 (mayor)	Dilworth votes, 1949 (treasurer)	Dilworth votes, 1950 (governor)	Clark votes, 1951 (mayor)	Dilworth votes, 1955 (mayor)	Dilworth votes, 1959 (mayor)
35*	18,366	31,504	30,055	36,821	38,841	53,183
22	18,081	27,132	22,000	26,206	21,193	13,594
46	16,742	23,344	21,309	21,486	17,808	16,892
33	13,454	18,088	17,779	16,621	15,068	15,580
42	13,429	17,016	14,463	15,183	13,201	13,319
38	13,298	19,235	17,468	16,944	13,726	13,807
50	13,263	20,086	17,569	20,560	22,146	24,456
49	11,887	16,169	14,841	15,025	14,434	14,626
39	11,294	15,129	16,004	15,055	13,437	12,967
52	11,004	14,951	14,650	14,693	15,150	14,903
40	10,280	14,625	14,840	14,379	13,194	11,193
41	9,655	14,759	13,367	13,620	11,680	12,808
43	9,652	14,034	13,044	12,541	10,896	10,683
Total votes from selected wards	170,405	246,072	227,389	239,134	220,774	228,011
Percentage of candidate's total votes	53	53	50	53	52	52
Candidate's total votes	321,469	465,490	452,055	448,973	423,017	438,278

Source: Philadelphia Registration Commission, *Annual Reports* (Philadelphia: City of Philadelphia, 1947, 1949, 1950, 1951, 1955, 1959).

* In 1957, the area previously occupied by the 35th Ward was subdivided to add six wards. The votes in the 1959 column are votes from the aggregated area, the boundaries of which are identical to those of the pre-1957 35th Ward.

Northeast and Northwest Philadelphia. To accommodate Northeast Philadelphia population growth during the 1950s, the 35th Ward in Northeast Philadelphia was subdivided in 1957 to add six wards, the 53rd through the 58th, to occupy the same area that had been previously occupied by the 35th alone. In this aggregated area, the 1959 vote totals exceeded the 1947 totals for the same area by 34,817 votes. In Northwest Philadelphia's 50th Ward, the 1959 totals exceeded the 1947 totals by 11,193 votes.

For most of these wards, the 1949 election was a high-water mark, with more votes generated for Richardson Dilworth in this election than for Dilworth or Clark in the four subsequent elections. In 1959, Dilworth received fewer votes than he had in 1949 in eleven of the thirteen wards shown in Table 2.5. In ten of these wards, Dilworth received fewer votes for his 1955 mayoral candidacy than Clark had received for his 1951 candidacy for the same office.

The inconsistencies in Table 2.5—a few wards generating more votes for Democratic candidates after 1949, while many other wards generated fewer votes for these candidates—can be explained in part by two trends that were emerging during this decade. New housing development and associated population growth were producing an increase in the number of registered voters in some wards, especially in Northeast Philadelphia's 35th Ward.

> Generous government benefits, namely the Servicemen's Readjustment Act of 1944 (GI Bill) and FHA home lending policies, assisted returning veterans, the majority of whom were white, in their quest to move from Philadelphia's densely packed industrial neighborhoods to the quasi-suburban atmosphere of Northeast Philadelphia following World War II. Prominent builders, most notably Hyman Korman (1891–1964) and A.P. Orleans (1888–1981), capitalized on these circumstances to expand home construction west of Roosevelt Boulevard in the Near Northeast, especially in Rhawnhurst, Lawndale, and Oxford Circle, in the late 1940s and 1950s.[22]

At the same time, Philadelphia was beginning to experience postindustrial population loss, and citywide population would continue to decline through the remaining decades of the twentieth century. These trends likely contributed to declines in the number of registered voters in some wards, particularly those located in row house neighborhoods in or near the city's central core or along the Delaware River.

Mortgage underwriting standards that had been instituted years earlier favored new construction in areas such as Northeast and Northwest Philadelphia and created disadvantages for older neighborhoods that were experiencing disinvestment. In 1935, the Federal Home Loan Bank Board and the Home Owners' Loan Corporation (HOLC) initiated the City Survey Program, designed in part to identify communities in which federally supported mortgage financing programs should be promoted and to provide real estate investors with insights into the varying degrees of risk associated with lending in different urban neighborhoods. As Amy Hillier explains, the program was influenced in part by an "ecological" theory of neighborhood change, which held that "neighborhoods naturally decline as some residents move to find more suitable habitats. In this view, African-Americans, Jews, and certain immigrant groups were seen as invaders, warning signs that neighborhoods had reached the last phase of their decline."[23] Much of this growth occurred in areas that had been designated as "best" and "desirable" in a 1937 HOLC map, while much of the decline occurred in areas designated as "declining" and "hazardous."

Hillier found that HOLC's coded map for Philadelphia did not influence mortgage lending practices in Philadelphia between 1937 and 1950; in fact, her analysis of a random sample of mortgages made by private lenders during this period showed a disproportionately higher level of lending in areas of the city that had been designated as "hazardous." However, as she and others have pointed out, underwriting guidelines adopted by the Federal Housing Administration (FHA), which facilitated postwar mortgage lending on a large scale in metropolitan areas across the country, "assumed a racial and ecological conception of neighborhood change" consistent with that shown in the HOLC map.[24]

As FHA policies contributed to residential development, population growth, and increases in registered-voter population in areas such as Northeast Philadelphia, these policies also likely influenced disinvestment, depopulation, and decreases in registered voter population in other areas of the city during the two and a half decades after the 1937 map was published.

The New Political Narrative

The year 1952 began with the institution of "home rule" and the inauguration of two municipal leaders whose election had been energetically supported by a highly organized reform movement, as well as by the city's Democratic Party leadership, Republican business leaders, and many Republican and independent voters. The weakening of the city's Republican Party began almost immediately and continued during the remainder of the decade and beyond.

The Home Rule Charter empowered Philadelphia's mayor and City Council with responsibility for the administration of municipal government and, in doing so, removed state elected officials' longstanding control over most local government functions. In addition, charter-mandated stan-

TABLE 2.6 PARTY REGISTRATION TRENDS, 1945–2016

Year	Democrat	Republican	Other	Total	Percentage Democrat
1945	336,320	598,279	21,851	956,450	35
1950	308,338	718,123	21,243	1,047,704	29
1955	408,396	548,910	20,850	978,156	42
1960	587,182	408,762	22,048	1,017,992	58
2016	853,098	125,522	123,944	1,102,564	77

Source: 1945–1960 data from Philadelphia Registration Commission, *Annual Reports* (Philadelphia: City of Philadelphia, 1945, 1950, 1955, 1960); 2016 data from Philadelphia City Commissioners, "Voter Registration by Party, 1940–2019," https://files7.philadelphiavotes.com/department-reports/Historical_Registration_1940-2019G.pdf#_ga=2.52315820.404044973.1584814299-1970273490.1584814299 (accessed April 20, 2020).

dards for employee recruitment and promotion and for the procurement of goods and services significantly reduced opportunities to secure jobs or contracts for politically connected individuals or organizations.

After nearly a century of hegemony, the Republican Party found itself with little capability to compete effectively in the new political environment. In the decades that followed the 1951 election, every mayor and every president of City Council would be a member of the Democratic Party. In the first session of City Council after the adoption of the Home Rule Charter, nine out of the ten elected district council members would be Democrats, and Democrats would continue to hold a majority of council seats from that time on.

In terms of voter registration, Philadelphia remained a Republican-majority city until after the mid-1950s, as shown in Table 2.6. However, in addition to electing Democrat Richardson Dilworth as mayor in 1955 and 1959, Philadelphia voters overwhelmingly supported Democratic candidates for U.S. president (Adlai Stevenson over Dwight Eisenhower, 557,352 to 396,874, in 1952; and Stevenson over Eisenhower, 507,289 to 383,414, in 1956) and for governor of Pennsylvania (George Leader in 1954; David Lawrence in 1958). By 1960, the proportion of city voters who were registered Democrats had reached nearly 60 percent; by 2016, it had risen to nearly 80 percent. After 1960, the Republican Party was rarely competitive in a Philadelphia election. The city had returned to single-party domination, but now with Democrats in power.

Standards for municipal governance that were embedded in the Home Rule Charter helped ensure that Philadelphia would not return to a period of corruption and mismanagement resembling that which had existed during the worst years of Republican hegemony. However, the domination of local politics by a single party over an extended period has had other consequences with significant implications for local governance.

Chronic Corruption and Mismanagement. Quasi-public authorities such as the Philadelphia Redevelopment Authority, Philadelphia Housing Authority, and Philadelphia Parking Authority are created by state legislation and are not subject to the hiring and procurement standards set forth in Philadelphia's Home Rule Charter. As a result, these state-chartered authorities have the benefit of more flexibility and fewer limitations with respect to actions such as hiring professional staff, negotiating contracts, and expediting payments to vendors.

At various times during the past half-century, quasi-public authorities have made use of this capability to organize and implement ambitious real estate development ventures and to participate in public-private partnerships that a municipal department operating under Home Rule Charter-mandated processes would not have been able to manage as efficiently and cost-effectively. However, the fact that these agencies are not constrained by Home Rule Charter requirements provides them with opportunities to reward politically connected individuals with contracts and jobs.

Public authority mismanagement and corruption can drain an agency of the public-benefit value that authorities were created to provide, as illustrated by the findings of two performance audits of the Philadelphia Parking Authority released in 2017. One audit found that the authority's board of directors had failed to address sexual harassment allegations against the executive director and that the board's lack of oversight had enabled the executive director to manipulate his own employee leave records "for his own personal gain."[25] The other audit found that a total of $1.17 million in parking revenues that the authority should have paid to the Philadelphia School District was spent on "incorrect, questionable, and excessive" expense items.[26]

Long-Term Incumbency. In a one-party system, the party organization will, with rare exceptions, consistently support the reelection of incumbent candidates. This practice helps ensure continuity in party leadership and a continuation of the status quo valued by party leaders. To the extent that incumbents continue to receive party endorsements and continue to be reelected, challengers are less likely to emerge, and the party organization becomes increasingly monolithic and ossified.

Mark B. Cohen served in the Pennsylvania House of Representatives from 1974 until 2016, when, as referenced in Chapter 1, he was defeated by challenger Jared Solomon. John Baer of the *Philadelphia Daily News* characterized Cohen as a legislator who

> possessed unparalleled skills for padding his salary with tens of thousands of dollars a year in expenses called per diems, currently $185 per day—money with no accountability, no receipts required.

> . . . He ran up more than $104,000 in expenses in one legislative session. That included $44,000 in per diems; $11,000 in airline tickets to fly between Philly and Harrisburg because, he said, "driving wears me out" (he was 41 at the time); $5,700 in parking fees, mostly at Philadelphia International [Airport].[27]

After losing reelection to his House seat in 2016, Cohen competed for one of nine available seats on the Court of Common Pleas on the ballot in the 2017 Democratic primary election. Despite having received a "Not Recommended" rating from the Philadelphia Bar Association, Cohen came in eighth, with 36,461 votes.

Weakening of Civic Infrastructure. If incumbent officeholders are routinely supported for reelection and if "open" elections (in which the Democratic City Committee does not endorse any particular candidate) become increasingly rare, then many people will conclude, justifiably, that the political deck of cards is stacked and that opportunities to influence positive change are limited or nonexistent. Based on this perspective, many individuals who might be regarded as activists in other respects—in terms of their participation in neighborhood or civic organizations or in congregations of faith—may refrain from getting involved in political activity at the ward and division level. Although these individuals possess knowledge and experience that could contribute substantial added value to the political system, many of them are uninvolved in any political activity other than voting on election day.

One consequence of this opting-out on the part of individuals who might otherwise be characterized as neighborhood activists is the dearth of candidates for committeeperson positions. Despite the post-2016 groundswell of voter activity that produced successes for two unconventional candidates in Philadelphia's 2017 elections—Lawrence Krasner for district attorney and Rebecca Rhynhart for city controller—the number of individuals who chose to run for committeeperson in the 2018 Democratic primary election was approximately the same as the number of candidates who had filed nominating petitions in the previous committeeperson elections in 2014.[28]

Reduced Turnout. As Philadelphia has transitioned from a two-party to a single-party system, voter turnout—the percentage of registered voters who cast a vote in a particular election—has steadily decreased. During the 1950s and 1960s, turnout for presidential elections was never lower than 80 percent, and turnout for mayoral elections was, with one exception, higher than 70 percent (the exception was 1959, in which turnout was

69 percent). By contrast, turnout for presidential elections in the twenty-first century exceeded 65 percent only once (in 2008), and turnout for mayoral elections after 2000 exceeded 30 percent in only one out of five elections (2003).

In one sense, Philadelphia's twenty-first century began in the same way as its twentieth century had, with one party dominating the city's political system. Although, in both instances, the dominant party was not invincible, the candidates it endorsed were, for the most part, odds-on favorites in any given political competition. The party was like "the house" in the gambling games that were facilitated by corrupt police officers in the underground economy of the early twentieth century and that subsequently surfaced with legislative authorization in Philadelphia casinos a hundred years later.

No serious initiative to replace the dominant party with something else—something other than the party not in power at the time—was attempted during the twentieth century. Instead, candidates for office worked to secure the support of key members of the party establishment or to become identified with voter constituencies that, because of the circumstances of a particular time, appeared to have the potential to beat the odds and cause one or more candidates to win election without party support, as Rebecca Rhynhart had done in 2017. Any future attempt to fundamentally change the local political system will benefit from an understanding of how these initiatives succeeded or failed and of how they were influenced by the city's economic condition and social environment.

3

Entrepreneur

The postwar Democratic takeover of city government was facilitated in large part by a network of individuals who were already influential in their own right and who, in many instances, were connected with one another through business and social relationships. The election of 1951 was not a revolution; it was a dramatic transfer of political power from one group of elites to another. The activists who brought about this change were, to a large extent, part of Philadelphia's establishment, members of the city's ruling class. With relatively few exceptions, the city's underlying social structure remained intact afterward. The city's traditional winners and losers remained in their places.

Under both Republican and Democratic municipal rule, some political power was given away to members of disenfranchised communities or disadvantaged constituencies, often in the form of government jobs or public service contracts. The associated value was not insignificant. A traffic court judgeship could go on for decades. A housing inspector job could support a head of household for a lifetime. The value of these accommodations to members of constituencies that possessed relatively little power was recognized and respected. Many of the beneficiaries of these accommodations were recognized and respected as well; some of them became civic and political leaders in their communities.

For an increasing number of African Americans who grew up during the early postwar decades, participating in a system of political accommodation was no longer acceptable; but seeking to take over the city's top elective offices, as the reformers had done in 1951, would not be feasible—at least not in the short term. Chaka Fattah's experience as a successful candidate for state representative, and later for Congress, illustrates the ways in which black political activists developed a creative and effective approach to gaining political power as Philadelphia changed.

A generation after Richardson Dilworth and Joseph Clark were successfully implementing their reform campaigns, Chaka Fattah and Curtis Jones were brainstorming their strategy for the May 15, 1979, Democratic primary. The two of them had met and become acquainted through the House of Umoja, an urban Boys Town founded by Fattah's mother, Sister Falaka Fattah, as a safe community for current and would-be street gang members. On the basis of their mutual interest in political activism, Fattah and Jones organized a grassroots group called the Youth Movement to Clean Up Politics, and they became high-profile participants in political and social-change campaigns organized by African American leadership groups in West Philadelphia and elsewhere.

Fattah and Jones were ambitious, energetic political entrepreneurs, and both of them were interested in the possibility of becoming candidates in the 1979 primary. Many offices would be on the ballot: mayor, all seventeen city council seats, and a handful of lesser-known municipal government offices such as registrar of wills and recorder of deeds. Fattah and Jones both wanted to be candidates, but they wanted to run as partners, not as competitors for the same position.

Their solution was to file as candidates for two seats on the three-member Philadelphia City Commission, the agency responsible for supervising elections, recording election results, maintaining voting machines, and handling other components of the election-management infrastructure. Taking two seats on the City Commission would be a logical next step for the leaders of the Youth Movement to Clean Up Politics, which had conducted voter registration drives and sponsored its own candidate forums as ways of encouraging more citizens to become active and informed voters.[1]

They picked up nominating petitions, collected signatures from more than the required number of registered Democrats, and submitted the necessary paperwork. Their nomination filings were approved, and they were both listed on the Democratic primary ballot. No one involved apparently took note of the fact that the threshold age for candidacy for City Commission was twenty-five; or, if anyone did take note of it, no one did anything about it. On May 15, 1979, Fattah would be twenty-two years old, and Jones would be twenty-one.

They found creative ways to promote their joint campaign in a down-ballot race that ordinarily would not have attracted much attention. Each day they would phone the campaign headquarters of Charles Bowser, a former deputy mayor and the only African American mayoral candidate in the

1979 primary, and after introducing themselves as reporters for Temple University's student newspaper, they would request Bowser's itinerary for the day. "We would show up first and make our pitch," Jones said. "And then we would leapfrog him and arrive before him at his next stop. Young people who saw us were inspired to join us. We kept it entertaining."[2]

They talked up their candidacy with state representative David Richardson, who had made a priority of getting young African American men engaged in community activism and neighborhood politics. "Dave Richardson listened to what we had to say, and he didn't laugh us out of the room," Jones later recalled. "He took us by the hand and led us up to Georgie Woods's show on WDAS."[3]

Georgie Woods was a highly popular Philadelphia radio host who had been active in the 1960s civil rights movement and who frequently devoted generous amounts of airtime to commentary on social and political issues. Jones recalled:

> Georgie Woods introduced us to the world as two young activists who should be listened to. He said, "Introduce yourself. Why are you running?" Then he got up and left the studio. Panic set in, but we kept talking for half an hour, while he went out and got breakfast. Then he came back, started eating, and chimed right in—he never missed a beat. He was able to grasp what we were doing and to get right into the conversation. After that, we were born. We were part of Philly's political family.[4]

They campaigned on college campuses, at youth gatherings, at high schools. They opened a campaign headquarters in a building at 51st and Arch Streets, the same building that housed Bowser's mayoral campaign, as well as state representative Hardy Williams's reelection campaign. They received advice and support from Bowser and Williams, as well as from W. Wilson Goode, who would be elected Philadelphia's first African American mayor in 1983.

The campaign gained momentum. Fattah and Jones received the endorsement of the 400-delegate Black Political Convention on March 11.[5] With other African American candidates on March 24, they participated in a motorcade, led by Representative Richardson as grand marshal, that passed through more than half of the city's neighborhoods.[6] On May 10, the *Philadelphia Inquirer* endorsed Fattah's candidacy, calling him "perhaps the most knowledgeable and most enthusiastic candidate."[7]

On May 15, Fattah received 43,788 votes, placing fourth in a field of twenty-four candidates, and Jones placed eighth. Both of them remained members of Philadelphia's "political family" for decades to come. Table 3.1 shows key elections leading up to Fattah's elections.

TABLE 3.1 KEY ELECTIONS LEADING UP TO CHAKA FATTAH'S ELECTIONS

Year elected/ appointed	Mayor	PA House member, 192nd District	PA senator, 7th District	U.S. Congress member, 2nd District
Incumbent in 1973	Frank L. Rizzo	Anita Palermo Kelly	Freeman Hankins	Robert N. C. Nix Sr.
1974		Anita Palermo Kelly		Robert N. C. Nix Sr.
1975	Frank L. Rizzo			
1976		Anita Palermo Kelly	Freeman Hankins	Robert N. C. Nix Sr.
1977				
1978		Nicholas A. Pucciarelli		William H. Gray III
1979	William J. Green III			
1980		Nicholas A. Pucciarelli	Freeman Hankins	William H. Gray III
1981				
1982		*Chaka Fattah*		William H. Gray III
1983	W. Wilson Goode			
1984		*Chaka Fattah*	Freeman Hankins	William H. Gray III
1985				
1986		*Chaka Fattah*		William H. Gray III
1987	W. Wilson Goode			
1988		Louise Williams Bishop	*Chaka Fattah*	William H. Gray III
1989				
1990		Louise Williams Bishop		William H. Gray III
1991	Edward G. Rendell			Lucien E. Blackwell
1992		Louise Williams Bishop	*Chaka Fattah*	Lucien E. Blackwell
1993				
1994		Louise Williams Bishop	Vincent J. Hughes	*Chaka Fattah*

Source: Access to election data provided to the author by Philadelphia City Commissioners.

A Changed Landscape

Philadelphia's African American population grew substantially at different times during the first half of the twentieth century. Between 1900 and 1920, the number of black Philadelphians doubled, from 63,000 to 134,000, with the highest concentrations of black residency near the city's center, between Spruce Street and Washington Avenue.[8]

Another surge in African American population took place during and after World War II, with a 5 percent increase in black population during the 1940s and 1950s, and a 10 percent increase in the 1960s.[9]

Black population remained relatively stable during the last half of the twentieth century, a period when Philadelphia, like many older cities, was experiencing a protracted trend of population decline, primarily a result of deindustrialization, white flight, and suburban expansion financed in large part by federal funding for highways and homeowner housing. The loss of white population was the biggest contributor to this trend. In 1960, the number of white residents of Philadelphia exceeded the number of black residents by nearly a million. By 1990, this margin had dropped to slightly over 200,000.[10]

For most of this period, Philadelphia's African American population remained highly concentrated within certain areas of the city. In an analysis of residential patterns in U.S. metropolitan areas, Douglas S. Massey and Nancy A. Denton ranked Philadelphia as the nation's fifth most segregated central city in 1980.[11] In a doctoral dissertation completed in 1985, Ira Goldstein found that "only 12 of the city's 365 Census tracts are truly integrated, with blacks and whites living side-by-side in a high percentage of the blocks. . . . Other tracts that may appear integrated overall were actually segregated by blocks."[12]

In many neighborhoods experiencing depopulation, African Americans who might have moved in to replace outgoing whites were met with community opposition and violence or threats of violence. A demonstration by four hundred white residents at the home of a black family that had moved into a Southwest Philadelphia neighborhood received national news coverage. In that year, the city's Commission on Human Relations responded to incidents "in which racial or ethnic tension rose when someone moved to an inhospitable neighborhood" in traditional blue-collar Kensington and Southwest Philadelphia communities, as well as in Northeast and Northwest Philadelphia.[13]

Even in some of the city's more diverse neighborhoods, residents shared an understanding of the blocks where African Americans would be allowed to live without being bothered or threatened. Referring to this period in a 2011 publication by Cedar Park Neighbors, a community organization representing a neighborhood not far from the University of Pennsylvania, Sarah A. Mack commented, "This area with its Victorian houses was viewed as an oasis of discrimination by most blacks living just six blocks south. . . . Beaumont and Windsor Avenue homes were closed to us as a people as far as sales were concerned."[14]

During the 1950s and 1960s, African American candidates were elected to represent some areas of Philadelphia where large numbers of black voters lived. However, most of these candidates would not have been successful without the endorsement of the Democratic City Committee. Mayor Goode described this political dependency in his book, *Black Voters Mattered: A Philadelphia Story*:

> Prior to 1968, Black elected officials in Philadelphia had been handpicked by the Democratic Party leaders of the time. Notable Black elected officials, like Raymond Pace Alexander and Edgar Campbell, served well but were chosen as candidates by the Party leadership. African Americans who ran against the wishes of the Democratic Party political machine lost, and lost badly.[15]

Characterizing the party leadership of that time and subsequent years, Curtis Jones said, "They wanted to keep the status quo. You fought to be a committeeperson, and if you got elected and were loyal to the party's slate, then you went up in the ranks. If you were lucky, you became ward chair or ward leader, and your loyalty was rewarded."[16]

The career of Ulysses Shelton, state representative in North Philadelphia's 181st District, illustrates this progression. After serving in the air force, Shelton worked as a clerk in the city's Department of Records and then served as an aide to Congressman Michael Bradley before running successfully for the Pennsylvania House in 1960. He was reelected eight times.

On the basis of the demographic trends and political realities of this period, most legislators who represented Philadelphia's African American communities in 1970 could be grouped into two categories: black officeholders who had won the favor of the Democratic Party and white officeholders whose districts had experienced a significant change in racial makeup during their terms of office.

The map in Figure 3.1 shows House boundaries overlaid onto areas with majority-black population, according to the 1970 and 1980 censuses. Several white officeholders served multiple terms while the demographic changes shown in this map were taking place. Francis J. Lynch represented a House district that included a section of North Philadelphia (the 195th) from 1969 until 1974. In West Philadelphia, Anita Palermo Kelly (192nd District) represented the Wynnefield and Overbrook neighborhoods from 1969 until 1978. One area of the city with substantial majority-black population, Northwest Philadelphia, had no African Americans in the state House of Representatives in 1970. In that year, Rose Toll represented the 200th District, Francis J. Rush represented the 201st District, and Peter E. Perry represented the 203rd District. All of these elected officials except Toll had

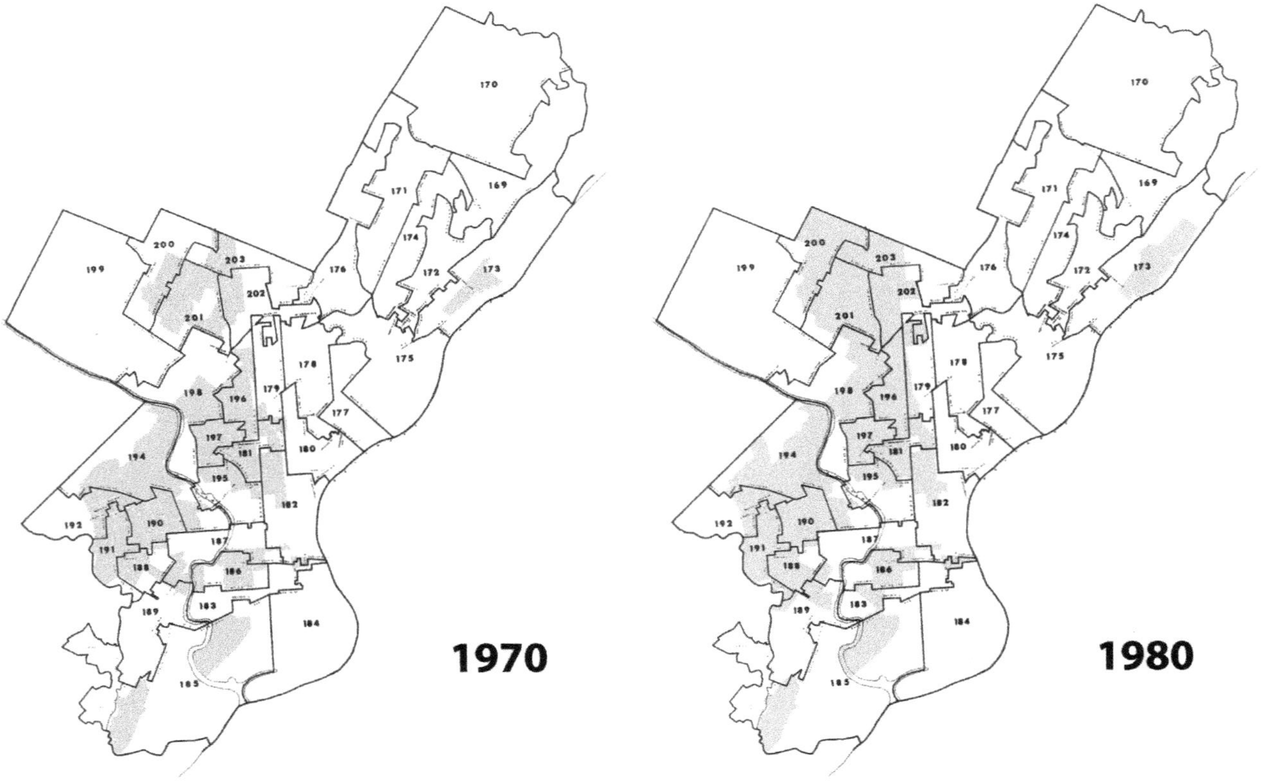

Figure 3.1 Pennsylvania House districts and majority-black areas of Philadelphia, 1970 and 1980

Source: Map from Pennsylvania Department of General Services, *The Pennsylvania Manual*, vol. 102 (Harrisburg: Commonwealth of Pennsylvania, 1976), 206; graphic overlay by Michael Fichman.

Note: Gray shading shows majority-black areas.

served in the House before 1969, during a time in which all Philadelphia House members were elected on an at-large basis, representing the city as a whole. Starting with the 1969 term, the city was subdivided into legislative districts, with voters in each district electing one candidate as their state representative, with no at-large members.

The New Generation

This political pattern began to fundamentally change after Hardy Williams was elected to represent West Philadelphia's 191st District in 1970. Williams was the first member of a new generation of black candidates who were successful in winning office without having sought the endorsement of the Democratic Party establishment.

After completing military service and law school, Williams worked in the Philadelphia City Solicitor's Office and in one of Philadelphia's African American law firms. He ran for City Council in 1965 and was defeated by the party-supported incumbent, Charles Durham. Three years later, however, he became leader of the 3rd Ward, defeating Mary Brennan—a rare instance of a challenger overcoming an incumbent ward leader.

The 1970 Democratic primary, in which Williams defeated veteran officeholder Paul Lawson to represent state House District 191, was the only race for a Philadelphia House seat in which a challenger succeeded in displacing an incumbent. High voter turnout for Williams, the result of an energetic campaign that reached every block in the district, made the difference. The campaign enlisted the participation of hundreds of supporters in a massive field operation that included many young people who knew about the candidate's past advocacy for ending youth gang warfare and improving the city's public education system. "Children respond to reality," Williams told the *Philadelphia Tribune*. "They want to participate toward a goal. When they realized how politics affects them, a political identity was created among them."[17]

Williams's 1970 victory, in which he received 3,408 votes compared with 2,333 for Lawson, was a milestone in the history of the Black Political Forum (BPF), an organization that had been founded two years earlier under the leadership of Hardy Williams, Wilson Goode, and John White Sr. The BPF's primary goal was to elect a new generation of black officeholders who would effectively represent the interests of the city's African American communities independently of the Democratic Party. At that time, although Philadelphia had experienced more than a century of African American political activism, the black community had yet to be represented in any top leadership positions in municipal or state government.[18]

As Wilson Goode described it:

> The BPF was comprised of committed men and women who were actively striving to bring political education to the Black community and to encourage Blacks to develop independent voting habits. To pursue its mission the BPF planned retreats, formed political education institutes, including an hour-long radio program on WHAT with Mary Mason; arranged poll watcher training; organized strategy sessions; and provided support for candidates who were running independently of the major parties.[19]

During his campaign for reelection two years later, Hardy Williams told the *Philadelphia Tribune*:

> My election . . . was the beginning of a new kind of Black politics, a kind in which the people actually choose their own candidate. . . .
>
> The issue we're placing before the people in this campaign is this: Shall we allow the forces of gang warfare, unemployment, a controlled educational system, a fire department that is seven percent Black, and a policy that divides the Black man with crumbs and no bread, to govern our lives?
>
> I say that for the future and development of our young people, both Black and white, we will master the use of the ballot and create our own Reconstruction in this part of history.[20]

The BPF's approach represented a welcome alternative to the only route to political success that had traditionally been available to prospective African American candidates: devoting years of service to the Democratic Party in hopes of eventually being, as Goode put it, "hand-picked" for a political reward. Instead, the BPF's goal was to mobilize citizens to take control of the existing political infrastructure by voting to replace ineffective political leaders at the ward and division level, then participating in neighborhood and citywide coalitions to elect qualified African American candidates to state and local government office.

During a twelve-year period that followed the 1970 election, four other African Americans who had been active participants in the BPF and the Williams campaign were elected to the state House of Representatives, replacing white officeholders who were older than they were—in some instances, much older. As shown in Table 3.2, three of the departing officeholders were replaced by newcomers half their age. One of these newcomers was Chaka Fattah.

Opportunities for African American candidates to achieve political success in citywide elections, as well as legislative-district elections, were becoming more apparent. In the 1979 Democratic primary in which Chaka

TABLE 3.2 SELECTED PENNSYLVANIA HOUSE OF REPRESENTATIVE MEMBERS, BY AGE

District	Candidate	Year inaugurated	Age at start of inaugural year	Predecessor	Age of predecessor at end of final year in office
191	Hardy Williams	1971	39	Paul M. Lawson	56
201	David P. Richardson Jr.	1973	24	Francis J. Rush	51
200	John F. White Jr.	1977	27	Rose Toll	65
203	Dwight Evans	1981	26	James F. Jones Jr.	46
192	Chaka Fattah	1983	26	Nicholas A. Pucciarelli	59

Source: Pennsylvania House of Representatives, "House Historical Biographies," https://www.legis.state.pa.us/cfdocs/legis/BiosHistory/serRes.cfm?search&body=H&cnty=57 (accessed April 20, 2020).

Fattah and Curtis Jones had campaigned for City Commissioner seats, mayoral candidate Charles Bowser came within 37,000 votes of defeating party-endorsed candidate William Green. "It really woke people up that Philadelphia could elect a black mayor, that it was possible," Bowser was to recall.[21] Bowser chose not to run for office again, but the encouraging results of his 1979 campaign provided evidence that an African American mayoral candidacy could be successful. At the time when Fattah was launching his campaign for state representative in the 1982 primary, a possible mayoral candidacy by Wilson Goode in the following year was already under discussion in political circles.[22]

Borders and Shading

"I went to sleep in Hardy Williams's district, and I woke up the next morning in Nicholas Pucciarelli's district," Chaka Fattah recalled in a 2018 interview, describing the results of the 1982 legislative reapportionment—the redrawing of certain legislative district boundaries that follows each decennial census.[23] Although the realignment of Pennsylvania House of Representatives boundaries resulting from reapportionment did not ensure that Fattah, or any other challenger to incumbent state representative Nicholas A. Pucciarelli, would be successful in the 1982 Democratic primary election, the remapping was advantageous in two respects: it enabled Fattah to run as a candidate for the Pennsylvania House against Pucciarelli, rather than against Williams, an ally and supporter; and it added a significant number of African American residents to the redrawn district that Pucciarelli would have to defend.[24] As the *Philadelphia Inquirer* reported a week before the May 18 primary election day, "When [Pucciarelli] won election to the state House of Representatives for the second time two years ago, his district . . . was 59.9 percent white. Now he is up for a third term, but his old district has been reapportioned and has wound up 59.9 percent black."[25]

The Pennsylvania House of Representatives consists of 203 members who are elected to two-year terms. The House reapportionment process that occurs after every decennial census mandates the redrawing of House district boundaries when needed to ensure that each of the 203 districts across the state contains an approximately equivalent number of residents.

In a city that has experienced significant population loss from one census to another, as Philadelphia did during the late twentieth century, some House districts need to be enlarged to increase district population to the extent needed to achieve equivalency with that of other districts where population remained stable or increased. In some instances, the only way to achieve this result is to eliminate one or more districts altogether so the remaining districts can expand their boundaries and gain additional residents. For example, the state House redistricting that followed the 1980 census (after a decade in which Philadelphia lost more than a quarter of a million residents) resulted in the city's loss of five state House districts, as shown in Figure 3.2.

The redistricting process had serious political consequences for the five state representatives whose districts were eliminated as a result of the redistricting that followed the 1980 census: they had to decide whether to run for election in the expanded districts that now included many residents who had never voted for them or retire. In West Philadelphia, the 189th House District, which state representative Martin P. Mullen had represented since 1955, disappeared from the map as a result of the post-1980 realignment, as shown in Figure 3.2. Mullen subsequently ran for election in the 1982 Democratic primary as a candidate for the House seat in the newly expanded 191st District, which now included his home address, and he lost. He never held elective office again.

The Pennsylvania Constitution calls for the state legislative redistricting process to be undertaken by a five-member commission consisting of the majority and minority leaders of the House and Senate, as well as a fifth member, appointed by the other four, who serves as chair. If the four legislative leaders are unable to reach agreement on the commission chair appointment, the state supreme court makes the decision.

A redistricting plan is not subject to approval by the governor or by a vote of the legislature. Although the commission holds public hearings before approving a redistricting plan, the only opportunity available to a citizen who opposes a plan produced by the commission is to file an appeal with the Pennsylvania Supreme Court. The Fair Districts PA website

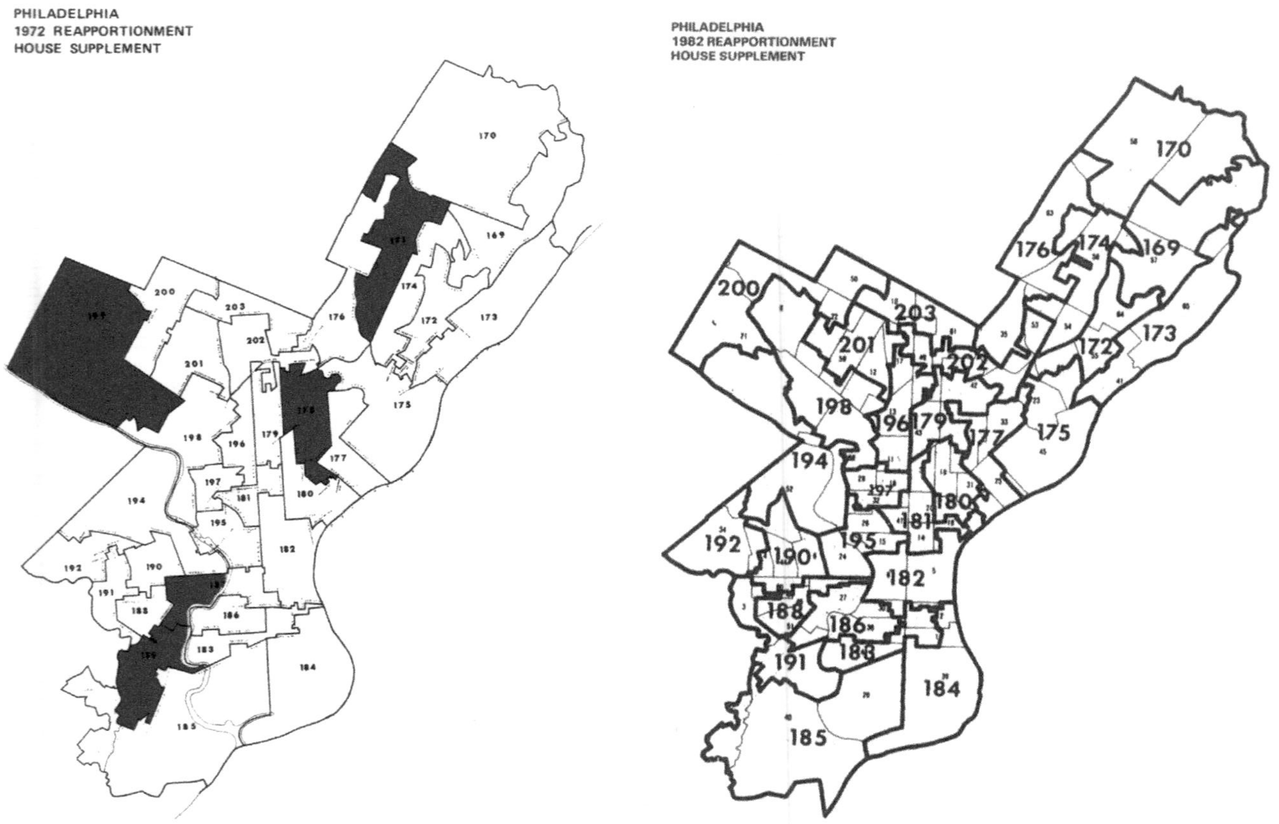

Figure 3.2 Pennsylvania House districts eliminated in 1982 reapportionment and post-reapportionment House district map

Source: Maps from Pennsylvania Department of General Services, *The Pennsylvania Manual*, vol. 102 (Harrisburg: Commonwealth of Pennsylvania, 1976), 206; and Pennsylvania Department of General Services, *The Pennsylvania Manual*, vol. 107 (Harrisburg: Commonwealth of Pennsylvania, 1986), 206; graphic overlays by Michael Fichman.

characterizes this process as one that "gives party leaders enormous power over the mapping process" and "lets incumbents draw their own districts—a clear conflict of interest from the start."[26]

However, the redistricting process for state House and Senate districts is much fairer than the one associated with the realignment of federal congressional districts. The commission-led approach requires that the leaders of the two political parties achieve a compromise; if they are unable to do so, the supreme court makes the decision. In contrast, congressional redistricting is authorized by a majority vote of the state legislature. In those states where one party holds a majority in both houses during a reapportionment year, that party, in effect, owns the redistricting process. The resulting map may include bizarrely configured districts that are designed to create electoral majorities for the party in as many districts as possible.

Elements of a Campaign

In Chaka Fattah's view, the prospects for winning an election depend on three factors: the strength of a campaign organization, the effectiveness of personal communication with voters at the neighborhood level, and the "glue" that makes voters enthusiastic about the candidate and committed to showing up on election day.[27]

Hardy Williams and the new generation of African American candidates that followed him, including Fattah, did not seek to organize a new political party. Instead, they competed in primary elections, often running against Democratic Party–endorsed candidates, to win the Democratic nomination for the offices they sought. If successful, they would be placed on the November ballot as the Democratic nominees—and, increasingly, they were successful. At the division level, these candidates worked closely with Democratic committeepeople who supported them.

But they did not stop there. In those divisions where committeepeople were not supportive, they recruited residents to run against them, and they trained these challengers to do everything that a committeeperson would do—distribute campaign information, conduct door-to-door canvassing during the weeks leading up to the election, and work to get out the vote and create a campaign presence outside the polling place on election day.

Describing these organizing strategies and their relationship to voter engagement, Fattah recalled that

> Hardy Williams created campaign offices in people's homes everywhere [in the districts where Williams campaigned for office]. Wilson Goode had ten regional offices across the city [to support his 1983 campaign for mayor].

> We used current block captains or created new block captains, just asking people to cover their own block as a contribution to the campaign.[28]

African American church congregations were a critical factor in many campaigns. Speaking of the successful 1978 congressional campaign of Reverend William H. Gray III (following a narrow defeat two years earlier), Fattah commented that "the key was Bright Hope Baptist Church [where Gray served as pastor]. That congregation could deliver hundreds of votes."[29] An important supporter in Fattah's 1982 campaign was Philadelphia City Councilman John C. Anderson. Members of Fattah's and Anderson's families were longstanding parishioners at the African Episcopal Church of St. Thomas, the first black church in Philadelphia, where Anderson's father had served as rector from 1944 to 1975.

To mobilize the campaign against Pucciarelli, Fattah said, "We undertook a massive registration drive. We knocked on every door. We registered thousands of new voters."[30] Outreach efforts undertaken by Fattah and other African American candidates is likely to have contributed significantly to the growth in black voter registration in the three West Philadelphia wards shown in Table 3.3. These wards encompass the 192nd District where Fattah and Pucciarelli were competing for the state House seat.

Chaka Fattah started implementing his voter outreach strategy a full year before the 1982 election. Through past experience, he had gained an understanding of what it took to engage directly with prospective voters on an areawide basis: recruit volunteers, organize registration drives, ring doorbells on every block, stage events, get out the vote on election day.

TABLE 3.3 BLACK AND WHITE REGISTERED VOTERS IN 4TH, 34TH, AND 52ND WARDS, 1975–1982

Year	Black	White
1975	252,129	560,786
1976	313,816	606,224
1977	301,467	583,770
1978	391,461	603,991
1979	369,257	567,557
1980	371,295	585,203
1981	362,455	570,372
1982	345,986	576,105
Change from 1975 to 1982	93,857	15,319
	37%	3%

Source: Philadelphia Registration Commission, *Annual Reports* (Philadelphia: City of Philadelphia, 1975–1982).

Fattah also understood the critical importance of the "glue" that would bind people to the campaign and make them enthusiastic about voting for the candidate. Speaking of the 1982 campaign and others in a 2018 interview, Fattah said, "You need to promise tangible things—to open a district office, to hold neighborhood meetings, to bring services to the people. We created an Unemployment Club [to help job seekers], and we invited everyone in the division to participate. We just started acting as though we were already in office."[31]

Fattah had been engaged in one issue that was critically important to voters: ending youth gang violence in West Philadelphia.

> The [Wynnefield] neighborhood was a substantial, integrated, middle-class area that felt exempt from youth gang violence. Then one weekend, there were two killings, one in retaliation for the other. My father and I set up meetings between the two groups. There was a picture of me in the *Philadelphia Inquirer.* I was a teenager—sixteen or seventeen. We facilitated a dialogue.[32]

Fattah also focused on neighborhood resident employment and the need to prepare young people for good jobs in a changing economy. In a February 1982 interview with the *Philadelphia Tribune*, Fattah described unemployment and increased crime as being interrelated and stated, "We need . . . to look at where we're going. The manufacturing town is gone, and for all intents and purposes, it's not coming back. It is a service center, a tourist center, and we need to understand it . . . and start training kids for those jobs."[33] The *Tribune* also noted that Fattah has "addressed the issue of housing abandonment . . . that is beginning to attack the Overbrook community."[34] During the two years preceding the campaign, Fattah had held two housing-related positions in the mayoral administration of William J. Green III, where Wilson Goode served as managing director.

Democratic Party leaders took sides in the Pucciarelli-Fattah battle. Pucciarelli was a protégé of George X. Schwartz, leader of the 34th Ward and former city council president (at the time of the 1982 primary, Schwartz was appealing his indictment in the Abscam scandal; the Pennsylvania Supreme Court upheld the indictment later that year). Edgar Campbell, leader of the 4th Ward, who held the elective office of clerk of quarter sessions in the county judicial system, enlisted a protégé of his own, Barbara Scott, to enter the race, a move that was said to have been intended "to hurt Fattah by taking some votes in the predominantly black wards that were added to the district by reapportionment."[35]

However, other political leaders brought new resources and new energy to the Fattah campaign. Fattah noted:

> [Congressman] Bill Gray endorsed me a week before the election and loaned the campaign $1,800. It might not seem like a lot, but the total budget for the campaign was $13,000. Charles Bowser wrote a letter that went out to all the households. [State representatives] Dwight Evans, John White Jr., and David Richardson all helped. They trained people and campaigned with me.[36]

After candidate nominating petitions had been filed, Pucciarelli challenged Fattah's candidacy with a claim that Fattah did not reside in the district. The challenge proved unsuccessful, and Fattah's name was placed on the ballot.

A day after the primary, the *Philadelphia Inquirer* deemed the 192nd District election too close to call; with 96 percent of the vote counted, Fattah led by twenty-six votes.[37] A few weeks later, the primary election results were certified, and Fattah was declared the winner. His official margin of victory was fifty-eight votes. The Pucciarelli campaign demanded a recount. Gregory M. Harvey, a renowned election lawyer and former head of the Southeastern Chapter of Americans for Democratic Action, monitored the process on behalf of the Fattah campaign. The results confirmed Fattah's victory.

Eight months later, Chaka Fattah entered the state capitol in Harrisburg to begin his term of office. At age twenty-six, he was the youngest person to hold the office of state representative.

Transactional versus Transformational

The mayor called it "simplistic and impractical." The acting president of the Mantua Hall Apartments Tenant Council said, "I think in all honesty it is kind of a far-fetched idea." "Stop turning people on with these wishes," scolded another tenant council leader.[38]

The year was 1990, seven years after Chaka Fattah took his seat in the Pennsylvania House. The idea—moving eighteen thousand residents of deteriorated public housing sites into formerly vacant properties rehabilitated by private and nonprofit developers—was his. "The design and density of public housing does not work well for families," Fattah said. "Yet [the Philadelphia Housing Authority] is now requesting more than $900 million from the federal government to rehabilitate high-rises." Announcing his proposal in March 1990, Fattah convened a task force, the Citizens' Collaborative to Reform Public Housing, consisting of representatives of municipal government, the judiciary, public housing tenant organizations, and the building industry to conduct related fact-finding. He charged the group with completing its work and producing a report within ninety days.[39]

Over the years, many people had criticized big-city public housing as a failed system, but no one of Fattah's stature had launched a reform plan with a financing component that, arguably, seemed feasible: a state government bond issue with interest payments funded in part through savings achieved by eliminating maintenance expenses associated with the housing authority's dilapidated inventory.[40]

In some important respects, Fattah's proposal anticipated a program that would be introduced two years later by the U.S. Department of Housing and Urban Development (HUD). HOPE VI, a high-profile Clinton administration initiative, would call for the replacement of public housing projects standing in disrepair on isolated campuses with mixed-income housing designed to blend with the surrounding neighborhood environment. Judge Nelson Díaz, a member of Fattah's Citizens' Collaborative to Reform Public Housing, would be hired as HUD general counsel by Secretary Henry G. Cisneros and would play an important role in overseeing HOPE VI implementation.

In 1990, when Fattah announced his proposal, he had served three terms as state representative, then had been elected to the Pennsylvania Senate. During his tenure in both houses of the General Assembly, Fattah had advanced proposals to support and increase the effectiveness of education and workforce development policies and programs. So why was he devoting so much energy to promoting a major new initiative associated with the public housing system, which, unlike state-sponsored schools and jobs programs, was administered and funded almost exclusively by the federal government?

Fattah was adhering to two principles that had been integral to the success of his political career so far: start the campaign for your next office well ahead of the election year; and, in choosing new policies and legislative initiatives to promote, act as though you have already been elected to that office. Fattah had won a seat in the Pennsylvania Senate in 1987, after nudging a long-incumbent state senator, Freeman Hankins, into retirement. Setting the stage for a campaign for federal office would be a logical next step.

Reverend William H. Gray III, the incumbent officeholder in the 2nd Congressional District, was the highest-ranking African American lawmaker in the country,[41] as well as one of Philadelphia's most influential political leaders, and he had been a supporter of Fattah's campaign against Pucciarelli. If Fattah decided to run against Gray, mobilizing the resources needed to mount a credible campaign would have been a significant challenge. As it turned out, Fattah had no need to make a choice; Gray unexpectedly resigned from office in June 1991.

Fattah competed in a special election that was held that November to fill the vacant 2nd District seat for the remainder of Gray's term, which would extend through the end of 1992. The Democratic Party endorsed Lucien E. Blackwell, a former Philadelphia city councilperson who had been an unsuccessful candidate for mayor the year before. In the special election, Blackwell received only 39 percent of the total vote; but the two other Democratic Party members in the race,[42] Fattah and John F. White Jr., split most of the remainder (about 53 percent of the vote), enabling Blackwell to win.[43]

To retain his office for the 1993–1994 congressional term, Blackwell had to defend his seat just a few months later in the April 1992 Democratic primary election. Because Fattah had expressed the view that the winner of the special election should be given the opportunity to remain in office for a full two-year term, he refrained from participating in the April primary (although he later expressed regret for having done so).[44] John White chose not to run either, and as a result, Blackwell's only opponent in April was C. DeLores Tucker, former Pennsylvania secretary of state. Although Fattah might have been a more formidable candidate, Tucker's name recognition and strong get-out-the-vote presence on election day brought her within eight percentage points of defeating Blackwell—not a bad outcome for a first-time candidate. However, Blackwell had now succeeded in overcoming challengers in two elections, and he appeared to be well positioned for reelection in 1994.

Like many other prominent Philadelphia politicians, both African American and white, Blackwell had worked his way up through the Democratic Party ranks to become a leader in the party organization. He had been a two-term state representative and a five-term city councilperson, and he had achieved success as the head of a strong ward organization.

Blackwell had also established strong political credentials independently of the party hierarchy. He had served as head of the local chapter of the International Longshoremen's Association from 1973 to 1991. He had effectively managed relationships with the diverse political constituencies that could be found within his ward and his council district. The latter included some of the city's highest-poverty neighborhoods, as well as the University of Pennsylvania and adjacent neighborhoods populated with large numbers of students and faculty.

Blackwell and Chaka Fattah were well acquainted. Blackwell had enlisted Fattah and Curtis Jones to supervise his mayoral campaign organization in the 1991 Democratic Primary, with Jones serving as campaign manager. However, their past acquaintance did not stop Fattah from challenging Blackwell in the special election held in the fall of that year to fill Gray's congressional seat or from doing so again in the May 1994 Democratic primary. He announced his candidacy in November 1993.

Fattah had anticipated that some of Philadelphia's highest-profile political leaders—including Mayor Edward Rendell, council president John Street, state representative Dwight Evans, and city councilperson Marian Tasco—would come out in support of Blackwell's reelection, and he was undeterred. During his tenure in the state legislature, he had built a broad base of political support within his state House and Senate districts, both of which fell within the boundaries of the 2nd Congressional District. He had also attracted the interest of prospective financial supporters from outside Philadelphia as a result of his innovative approach to public policy issues of statewide and national significance. One example of the latter is the annual Graduate Opportunities Conference, which he founded in 1987 as a vehicle for increasing minority student enrollment in graduate programs in the STEM fields, and which continued for years afterward. Another example is the two-day American Cities Conference, convened in February 1992 to advance his plan for simultaneously remaking the public housing system and rehabilitating thousands of vacant houses.

Although Blackwell and Fattah were both recognized as "solid liberals whose campaign platforms are built on promises of more jobs, safer streets and better schools,"[45] they were viewed by many as representing two generations of African American political leadership:

> Blackwell, 62, epitomizes the traditional big-city politician—the activist-turned-insider. He scrapped his way from a $1.88-an-hour job on the Philadelphia docks to the presidency of Local 1332 of the International Longshoremen's Association. . . .
>
> Fattah embodies the new generation of African American political leadership—the policy wonk. He holds a master's degree in public administration from the University of Pennsylvania. He churns out proposals and holds round tables on federal urban policy, education, and drug treatment.[46]

Years later, Fattah characterized Blackwell as a "transactional" politician, himself as "transformational":

> Our message was that I knew how to use clout to benefit our community. I was not just another candidate. The difference between my candidacy and Lucien's was substance. I could say, "We'll vote about the same, but there will only be two or three bills that are about jobs and hiring, and I'm going to write them."[47]

At the same time, he recognized that being identified with a transformative approach to public policy would not be sufficient to win an election against an incumbent who was well known to many residents of the congressional district. As he had in the campaign against Pucciarelli, Fattah pursued opportunities to win over current ward leaders and committeepeople or to replace them. "Our goal was to get half of the ward leaders to support us or to create an opponent for ward leaders that did not support us," he recalled. "I called Carol Campbell [leader of the 4th Ward and secretary of the Democratic City Committee, known as 'one of Philadelphia's most influential power brokers'[48]] every day."[49]

He also needed to find the best way for his campaign to reach out individually to as many of the "likely voters" in the district as possible. He commissioned a poll at the start of the campaign, and as he recalled in 2018, the outcome was instructive:

> The polling results said that I would win if people got my message and that I should focus on delivering my message to African American women. They were the likely voters who could make a difference, just like they made the difference in the Virginia governor's race [years later, in the November 2017 election, in which Democrat Ralph Northam defeated Republican Ed Gillespie, who ran a Trump-style campaign[50]]. They have a higher propensity to vote. Men in a barbershop will talk, but many of them will not vote. It's the same with churches: the majority of the congregation consists of women and kids.
>
> So 98 percent of the campaign was devoted to that bloc. Ruth Hayre [Ruth Wright Hayre, a highly regarded African American public school educator and administrator] did a radio message for us. She started by saying, "I've never supported a candidate for office publicly until now." We got Susan Taylor, the editor of *Essence* magazine, to produce a letter of support that we included in a mailer to African American women. It said, "I've never endorsed a candidate for political office before, but focusing on families and children is critical in this election." To provide some balance, we had a similar message from a woman who lived in the 34th Ward [a racially diverse section of the congressional district]. These were messages from people who are not known for their political views.
>
> Then I spent all my time in hair salons introducing myself to women and handing out information—giving them something to read while they were sitting there under the dryers.[51]

The presence that Fattah had already established in his state Senate district provided a big advantage. As a matter of routine, he had visited and spoken with students in a different public school classroom in the district every week. Every graduating high school senior had received a congratulatory certificate from him. He had showed up at the well-attended opening days for the area's Little League teams, which had broad community support in many of the district's neighborhoods. In many instances, Fattah was returning to places where he was already well known, rather than introducing himself for the first time. Blackwell was not as well known or as well regarded in many of these places.

Northwest Philadelphia, where John White had won three high-turnout wards (the 9th, the 22nd, and the 50th) in the 1991 special election, represented a particular challenge and a potentially big reward. The two people with the greatest capability to influence an election in this area—Marian Tasco and Dwight Evans—were supporting Lucien Blackwell. As a response, in Fattah's words, "We created a whole organization around Cindy Bass."[52] Before joining Fattah's state Senate staff, Bass had managed housing counseling services at Mount Airy USA, a well-regarded community development corporation based in the 22nd Ward, which encompasses most of the liberal, mixed-race East and West Mount Airy neighborhoods (Bass would be elected to Philadelphia City Council in 2011 and would become Democratic ward leader for the 22nd Ward in 2018).

How effective was Cindy Bass's organization in working to generate support in this part of the congressional district? *Philadelphia Inquirer* reporter Vanessa Williams describes the Mount Airy Day Festival that took place the weekend before the primary:

> Both candidates had listed the event on their schedules. When the festival got under way that morning, Fattah's organization was in place. There were tables filled with campaign brochures, newspaper clippings, and blue and white "Fattah for Congress" buttons. People wearing Fattah's portrait on their T-shirts and baseball caps worked the crowd. A little before noon a yellow school bus showed up, and a children's drill team emerged: When it stepped off, Fattah was out front, waving to people who yelled his name as he strode up Germantown Avenue.
>
> Women at nearby beauty parlors ran outside, their tresses dripping, to wave and squeal as he passed. Motorists honked and teenagers hopped alongside the mini-parade. By the time Fattah was escorted into the main festival area, dozens in the racially mixed, middle-class crowd were wearing his buttons and clutching his literature. . . .
>
> Blackwell never showed up.[53]

Realigned for Success

Although Fattah had not participated in the 1992 primary election, that year proved to be pivotal in terms of his congressional ambitions. As a state senator, Fattah was in a position to influence the redrawing of the congressional district boundaries in the redistricting process that took place that year. As described earlier, the boundary-designation process for congressional districts is unlike the approach for realigning state House and Senate districts, which requires both parties to compromise or to risk defaulting boundary-designation decisions to the state supreme court. Instead, congressional redistricting is subject to the legislative process: the introduction of a bill that is subject to state House and Senate approval and the governor's signature. For this reason, the outcome of congressional redistricting is strongly influenced by the leaders of the political party or parties in control of the House, Senate, and governor's office during a redistricting year.

The 1992 congressional redistricting was a particularly contentious process that could not be resolved until October of that year, when the U.S. Supreme Court rejected Republican challenges to redistricting proposals that had been previously approved for both state legislative and congressional districts.[54] Fattah later termed the congressional redistricting plan that the federal court had allowed to remain in place "the least illegal" version of the alternative plans that had been the subject of prolonged debate during the preceding months.[55]

The 1992 redistricting was significant in that it created a second majority black congressional district in Philadelphia. As a result of the new boundary designations, the African American population in the 1st Congressional District (covering much of South Philadelphia, North Philadelphia, and Center City) rose from 34 percent to 52 percent. The 2nd District, in which Lucien Blackwell was the incumbent officeholder, remained majority black; however, the 1992 redistricting reduced African American voter population in this district from 82 percent to 62 percent, eliminating several wards that had previously produced large vote totals for Blackwell and including more of Fattah's state Senate district.[56]

Table 3.4 shows results in the 1991 special election in seven wards that were removed from the 2nd Congressional District in the 1992 redistricting. Four of these wards had generated large vote totals for Blackwell in 1991.

Despite the disadvantages that the 1992 remapping created for Lucien Blackwell, the boundary changes did not necessarily guarantee success for Fattah. For example, Fattah's candidacy was opposed by key political leaders in the three Northwest Philadelphia wards that John White had won in 1991. However, through his aggressive campaigning in this area, as illustrated by the Mount Airy Day anecdote, Fattah carried all three of these wards in 1994, as shown in Table 3.5.

The 1994 primary was a landslide victory for Fattah. As Figure 3.3 shows, Fattah carried all the wards that he had won in 1991, many of the wards that Blackwell had won that year, and all three of the wards that

TABLE 3.4 1991 SPECIAL ELECTION RESULTS IN WARDS DELETED AS A RESULT OF 1992 REDISTRICTING

Ward	Fattah	Blackwell	White
11	803	2,211	1,014
12	1,868	2,275	1,339
16	710	2,352	884
17	1,559	3,381	2,363
30	800	500	475
32	890	3,254	1,387
40	52	182	12
Total	6,682	14,155	7,474

Source: Access to election data provided to the author by Philadelphia City Commissioners.

TABLE 3.5 2ND CONGRESSIONAL DISTRICT ELECTION RESULTS IN THREE NORTHWEST PHILADELPHIA WARDS: 1991 SPECIAL ELECTION AND 1994 DEMOCRATIC PRIMARY

1991 special election				
Ward	Fattah	Blackwell	White	Fattah (%)
9	738	190	741	44
22	3,053	1,957	3,398	36
50	1,834	2,054	6,044	18
Total	5,625	4,201	10,183	28
1994 Democratic primary				
Ward	Fattah	Blackwell		Fattah (%)
9	2,594	609		81
22	4,079	2,162		65
50	4,374	3,019		59
Total	11,047	5,790		66

Source: Access to election data provided to the author by Philadelphia City Commissioners.

White had won. Fattah captured nearly 60 percent of the vote, defeating Blackwell 53,416 to 38,831.

On election night, Fattah and his team met at the home of his finance chair, James Wade, in the East Falls neighborhood, as campaign operatives called in voting results, division by division. When they learned that Fattah would win decisively, they got in their cars and drove downtown, where Henry Nicholas, head of the Hospital and Health Care Employees Union, was hosting the campaign's election night party at the union headquarters. As Fattah's car pulled into a parking space, announcers on the local news

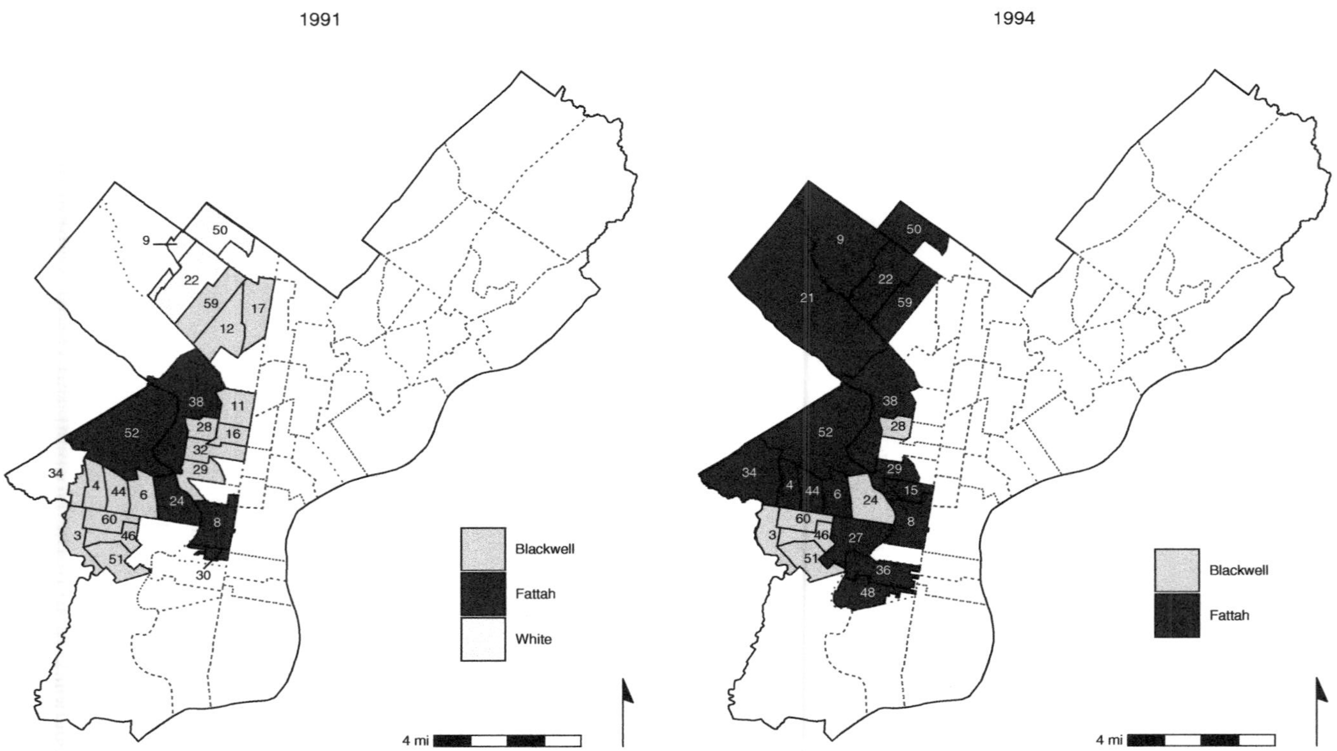

Figure 3.3 Results of 1991 special election and 1994 Democratic primary, 2nd Congressional District

Source: Access to election data provided to the author by Philadelphia City Commissioners; maps by Michael Fichman.

radio station were discussing what they still believed would be an assured win for Blackwell. They, like others, had apparently concluded that Blackwell, characterized as a political veteran closely tied to Philadelphia neighborhoods, would be unbeatable. "That expectation was the white liberal view as opposed to the black row house reality," Fattah commented later. Because "Lucien was connected with the traditional party structure," the news commentators had assumed that the party-endorsed candidate would prevail. "The white talking heads were misinformed," Fattah said.[57]

The Fairest Map of All

The redrawing of the 2nd Congressional District boundaries played an important but not decisive role in Fattah's 1994 victory. The new configuration of the district, as illustrated in Figure 3.3, did not differ significantly from that of the old one, and the new map was, in some important respects, an accurate reflection of the diversity of Philadelphia's population and neighborhoods. Fattah's campaign in the 1994 primary had proven to be so effective that he might well have carried most or all of the wards that had been deleted from the old district map, as well as the new wards that were being included in the district for the first time. Factors other than redistricting were greater contributors to Fattah's success. However, the redistricting decisions made before this election and before the 1982 primary (in which Fattah challenged Pucciarelli) illustrate how incumbent state legislators may be able to influence the redrawing of district boundaries in ways that could be advantageous for them in the future.

A much more dramatic illustration is Philadelphia's experience in the congressional redistricting that followed the 2010 census, during a period in which Republicans held both houses of the state legislature and the governor's office. Uncharacteristically, Philadelphia Democratic City Chairman Bob Brady (who was then the incumbent congressman in the 1st Congressional District) worked closely with state elected officials to produce thirty-six Democratic votes, primarily from Philadelphia-area legislators, in favor of a GOP-supported redistricting plan.

Brady's involvement and the level of Democratic support for the Republican plan was particularly noteworthy because the plan called for the creation of thirteen districts that contained a majority of Republican voters and only three districts with a majority of Democratic voters, in a state where vote totals for Democratic congressional candidates had substantially exceeded vote totals for Republican candidates—2,701,820, to 2,626,995—in the most recent congressional election.[58] Karen Bojar cites data produced by Azavea (a geospatial software design and data analytics firm) for the Redistricting the Nation project as evidence that Brady's underlying goal may have been to alter the racial composition of his congressional district to increase the district's white voter population and to make it less likely that an African American candidate would be able to beat him in the next election.[59] Brady's efforts were successful, and he was reelected several times without a serious challenger before retiring in 2018.

Also in 2018, coincidentally, litigation initiated by the League of Women Voters, with widespread support from fair-election advocates, resulted in the Pennsylvania Supreme Court redrawing the state's congressional districts.

As the *Washington Post* reported:

> The original Republican-drawn map had become the butt of national jokes due to its reliance on strange, sprawling shapes to create a balance of electoral power heavily tilted toward the GOP. . . .
>
> The court-drawn map splits just 13 counties between multiple districts, fewer than half as many as the Republicans' 2011 map. And the court-drawn districts are twice as compact as the 2011 districts, based on one common measure of geographic compactness.[60]

The supreme court remapping produced favorable results for Democrats; the party gained three seats in the congressional elections that were held later that year.

As Bojar points out, "Bob Brady could get away with undermining the Democratic Party's future prospects because redistricting is not the kind of subject to which the average voter pays attention."[61]

Given the likelihood that the average voter will continue to be relatively uninformed about redistricting, are there ways in which the congressional redistricting process could be changed to reduce the potential for political interference? Fair Districts PA frames the challenge in this way:

> Redistricting is a complex issue combining people, geography, political affiliations, history, and more, making a simple definition of "fairness" difficult. But without clear standards, the Supreme Court has been reluctant to address partisan gerrymandering. That's why we believe that fair standards must apply a nuanced set of criteria in a way that can be verified through objective tests.[62]

Among the criteria being considered by Fair Districts PA (and the associated question that each criterion is intended to address) are *population equality* (Does each district have the same number of people in it?), *geographic compactness* (Is the shape of each district as regular and simple as possible?), *community integrity* (Are counties, cities, and towns kept in a single district, whenever possible?), and *partisan fairness* (Do districts fairly represent voters from all political parties?).

As spatial analytics technology has become both increasingly sophisticated and increasingly accessible, more attention has been devoted to the design of algorithms that could be used to evaluate the outcomes associated with the application of criteria such as those identified by Fair Districts PA.[63] These efforts will continue, and they should be supported and encouraged, although with an awareness of two facts: because people will define "fairness" in different ways, no algorithm will be capable of generating maps that are indisputably fair; and because people in general are unlikely to be as knowledgeable about congressional redistricting as, in an ideal society, they should be, the most effective defense against future gerrymandering—an informed electorate—will never be as powerful as fair-elections advocates would wish it to be.

4

★★★★★★★

Navigator

The machines that served as vehicles for Philadelphia's industrial-era economy had several characteristics in common. Under normal circumstances, they performed iterative routines reliably and efficiently. When they broke, they were repaired. Accidents were followed by cleanups and the resumption of routine activity. For some industries, existential challenges did not emerge for decades. Changes in shipbuilding practices would require new capital investment and workforce reorganization at certain times; but during much of this period—the years between the mid-1800s and the mid-1900s, for example—there was relatively little awareness that shipbuilding, like other industries of that era, would undergo fundamental structural changes (such as the changes associated with the emergence of container vessels and supertankers) that would make it almost unrecognizable to individuals who had grown up and thrived in the old economy.

The political machines that operated in Philadelphia's working-class neighborhoods during this period had similar characteristics. They had a hierarchical, highly regimented structure not unlike that of a factory. Performance goals, quantified in terms of voter registration and controlled-vote turnout, were established, and ward leaders closely supervised committeepeople to ensure that these goals were met or exceeded. Certain ward leaders had control over the hiring and continued employment of many public-sector workers and their managers. The power of the ward organization needed to be respected and taken seriously.

During the late twentieth century, the South Philadelphia affiliates of Philadelphia's political machine—the Democratic ward committees representing wards in neighborhoods south of South Street—were, as a whole, the most effective in the city. But even these high-performing organizations were far less reliable than the machines that operated on South Philadelphia factory floors. Political leaders, on the whole, were no more intelligent or emotionally stable than other citizens, and some of their decisions were strongly influenced by their desires, fears, and anxieties rather than based on rational choice. Certain elected officials and political operatives were corrupt or corruptible. Promises could be broken, commitments could go unfulfilled, and rules could be circumvented. Political alliances could be unmade and reconstituted, creating new opportunities for some and shutting out others.

The successful congressional campaigns of Thomas Foglietta during the 1980s illustrate both the weaknesses and strengths of a traditional political machine—its vulnerability to disruptions as well as its capability to recover from crises (see Table 4.1). Foglietta's successes were based on his supporters'

TABLE 4.1 KEY ELECTIONS LEADING UP TO THOMAS FOGLIETTA'S ELECTIONS

Year elected/ appointed	Mayor	U.S. Congress member, 1st District	U.S. Congress member, 3rd District	Democratic City Committee chair
Incumbent in 1976	Frank L. Rizzo	Michael J. "Ozzie" Myers	Raymond F. Lederer	Martin Weinberg
1977				
1978		Michael J. "Ozzie" Myers	Raymond F. Lederer	
1979	William J. Green III			
1980		*Thomas M. Foglietta**	Raymond F. Lederer	David Glancey
1981			Joseph F. Smith	
1982		*Thomas M. Foglietta*†		
1983	W. Wilson Goode			Joseph F. Smith
1984		*Thomas M. Foglietta*‡		
1985				
1986		*Thomas M. Foglietta*‡		Robert A. Brady

Source: Access to data for mayor and Congress members provided to the author by Philadelphia City Commissioners; data for Democratic City Committee chair from S. A. Paolantonio, *Frank Rizzo: The Last Big Man in Big City America* (Philadelphia: Camino Books, 1993), 206, 258; Mark Wagenfeld and Rusty Pray, "Obituary: Joseph F. Smith, 80, Longtime Politician," *Philadelphia Inquirer*, May 18, 1999, p. B4; and Roll Call, "Robert A. Brady," http://media.cq.com/members/408 (accessed April 20, 2020).

* Defeated Michael J. "Ozzie" Myers

† Defeated Joseph F. Smith

‡ Defeated James J. Tayoun

understanding of how both these qualities could be advantageous to their candidate at a time when South Philadelphia's political environment was particularly unstable.

On February 2, 1980, Nicholas Pucciarelli was halfway through his second term as state representative. Chaka Fattah, newly employed as an aide to Philadelphia's housing director, was yet to emerge as a career-ending threat. Joseph Vignola was sitting in his home on Fitzwater Street in South Philadelphia when the phone rang.

"Is your TV on?" It was Freddy Del Rossi, the Democratic ward chairman for the 2nd Ward, where Vignola was Democratic ward leader. Vignola switched on the television and tuned to Channel 6. That was how, in an oh-my-God moment, he found out about Abscam.[1]

Vignola was more than an interested TV viewer of the sting operation in which several prominent local politicians were caught on tape agreeing to accept bribes offered by an FBI informant posing as an Arab sheik. One of them was congressman Michael "Ozzie" Myers, who from then on would be remembered for the videotaped sound bite, "Money talks, and bullshit walks." Congressman Myers was Vignola's boss.

The Big Peninsula

South Philadelphia is laid out in a grid of square blocks flanked by two rivers—a chessboard overlaid onto a two-and-a-half-mile wide peninsula. Broad Street is the north-south axis, with numbered streets running parallel on either side: 2nd, 3rd, 4th, all the way out to 34th, 35th, and 36th Streets, and named streets—Bainbridge, Fitzwater, Catharine—extending east and west, with some blocks bisected by narrow streets or wider avenues. Port facilities, industrial zones, and retail commercial corridors that emerged during the eighteenth and nineteenth centuries became centers of commerce, and they were surrounded by row house blocks that, in pre-gentrification 1980, were still populated by participants in the industrial-age workforce. As shown in Figure 4.1, the area included seven wards.

For many decades, South Philadelphia's political realm had a king: 1st District Congressman William Barrett, known to many as simply "the Congressman." Like the king on a chessboard, Barrett moved in a predictable pattern from one spot to the next, turn by turn. On a day when Congress was in session, the Congressman traveled to Washington; then, at the end of the day, he returned to ward headquarters in Grays Ferry to meet with constituents, ward leaders, and committeepeople during the evening hours. DC, Grays Ferry; DC, Grays Ferry, week after week, year after year.

Barrett had started his career as a liquor distributor and bootlegger. After winning election as a Democrat and being sworn into Congress in

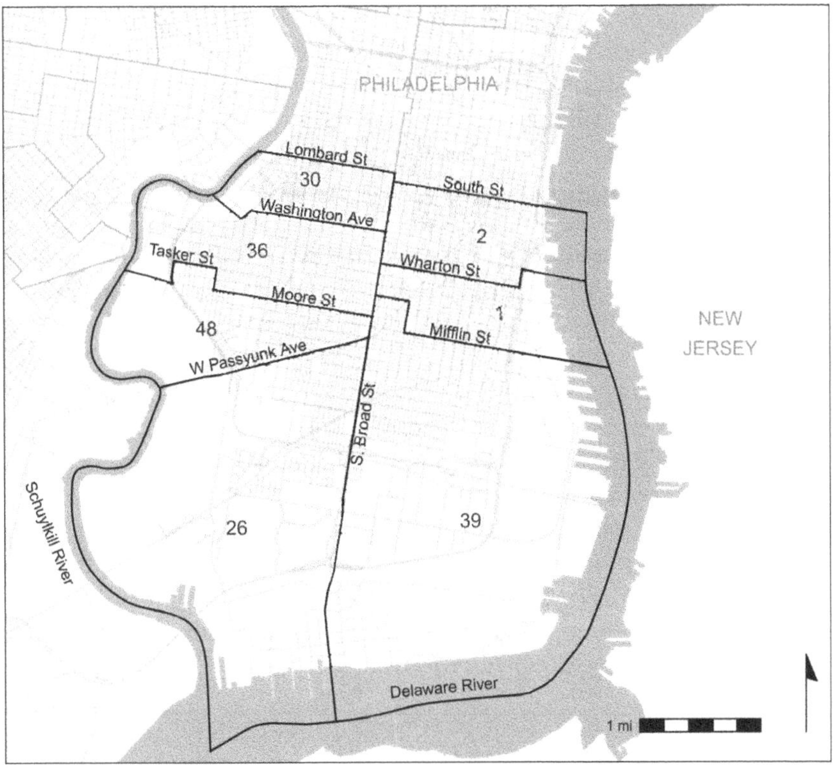

Figure 4.1 South Philadelphia wards and Philadelphia ward map

Source: Data from John Daley and Allen Weinberg, *Genealogy of Philadelphia County Subdivisions*, 2nd ed. (Philadelphia: City of Philadelphia Department of Records, 1966), 91; map by Michael Fichman.

1945, he left off trading in bottles and began trading in jobs and services. He understood what Chaka Fattah would learn years later in West Philadelphia: patronage and services are the glue that holds a political network together. In Barrett's working-class district, his office became a neighborhood employment agency and a neighborhood health and human services center.

At the time when Barrett joined Congress, political patronage had been an integral part of Philadelphia's municipal government for a century. Although the approval of the Home Rule Charter in 1951 brought about fundamental structural changes that reduced opportunities for political intervention in city hiring, contracting, and procurement, political patronage did not end altogether—far from it. A person of influence could still get you a public-sector job. Someone once told Curtis Jones that, in those days, Barrett could hand a card to a constituent in need of employment, and when the card was shown to the appropriate person downtown, the jobseeker would be placed on the payroll of a city agency, a public authority, or a public utility as a clerk, an inspector, a property maintenance worker, or an administrative assistant.[2] What Jones heard may or may not have been an exaggeration, but it was not an inaccurate characterization of Barrett's ability to deliver value for his constituents.

Barrett brokered jobs-and-services transactions through the network of ward leaders and committeepeople who were the political representatives of neighborhoods in his district. By making these transactions his top priority over the years, the Congressman became the most powerful politician in South Philadelphia. Commenting on Barrett's approach in a 2019 interview, Joseph Vignola remarked:

> It was constituent service—but there was a price to pay for that. At the time when Bill Barrett was the third most senior member of Congress [in 1975], the Marine Corps closed the supply depot at Broad and Washington—in his own neighborhood! At the same time, they were opening up a naval hospital in Louisiana. The only water anywhere nearby was the edge of the Mississippi River. By coming home [every day when Congress was in session], he gave up a lot of power that he could have wielded.

Bob Brady, who became head of the Democratic City Committee in 1986 and held the 1st Congressional District seat from 1998 to 2019, would never have allowed the Marine supply depot to be moved out of town. He was constantly looking for opportunities to bring economic value to his district—in many instances, to the city as a whole—and keep it there. But Brady's view of his role was similar to Barrett's. Like Barrett, he had no ambition to be a statesman or policy maker. Maintaining and strengthening working relationships with key participants in the neighborhood-level political infrastructure was a top priority for both of them.

Barrett and Brady had another characteristic in common: neither one devoted a lot of time to recruiting and nurturing the next generation of political leaders. Joseph Vignola observed:

> Bill did not want any rivals for power. He was very fearful of my Uncle Henry [Cianfrani], my Uncle Henry's younger brother, Victor, and my cousin Buddy.[3]
>
> He also did not foster growth in the party. For example, if [Mayor Frank] Rizzo called him up and said, "Bill, give me the name of someone you want to be revenue commissioner," he'd go, "Frank, can I have three clerk jobs?" He never tried to promote anybody.

Brady had a similar aversion to party building and the recruitment of the next generation of leaders. Writing in 2017, Holly Otterbein commented that

> Brady [has not] done enough to address the thin bench for Democrats in this town, which leaves both the party and Philadelphia without a coming generation of leaders. . . . Brady didn't get where he is to kick the bums out of City Hall or enact a grand vision for the Democratic Party. He's there to do what he always does: get shit done.[4]

Brady chose not to run for reelection to Congress in 2018. That election took place in the wake of the Pennsylvania Supreme Court–mandated redistricting described in Chapter 3. The district map that had favored Brady's reelection prospects over a prospective African American candidate was replaced. In 2019, Brady's home ward, the 34th, would be represented in Congress by an African American, Dwight Evans.

Divisions

South Philadelphia experienced a level of population loss comparable to that which occurred in many of the city's other older neighborhoods after World War II. Total population declined by 39 percent, with a loss of nearly half the white population. Because the decline in black population was substantially lower, this demographic group came to represent a much larger proportion of area residents, growing from less than a quarter of the total population in 1950 to nearly one-third in 1980. The foreign-born population declined substantially during this period, with a total decline of 70 percent over the four decades.

In 1980, South Philadelphia was as racially segregated as other parts of Philadelphia, with high concentrations of either white or African American populations in most census tracts, as shown in Figure 4.2.

In 1980, according to the U.S. Census, 61,038 South Philadelphians identified themselves as Italian (with reference to their birthplace or the birthplace of their parents or ancestors), 11,758 as Irish, and about 3,300 each as Polish, English, and German.[5] During the mid- to late twentieth century, many of Philadelphia's leading political figures were people of Irish and Italian descent. James A. Finnegan became president of City Council in 1951, and he was succeeded by James H. J. Tate in 1955. Tate became mayor in 1962, and his council presidency was taken over by Paul D'Ortona, an Italian-born South Philadelphian, who remained as head of council until 1972.

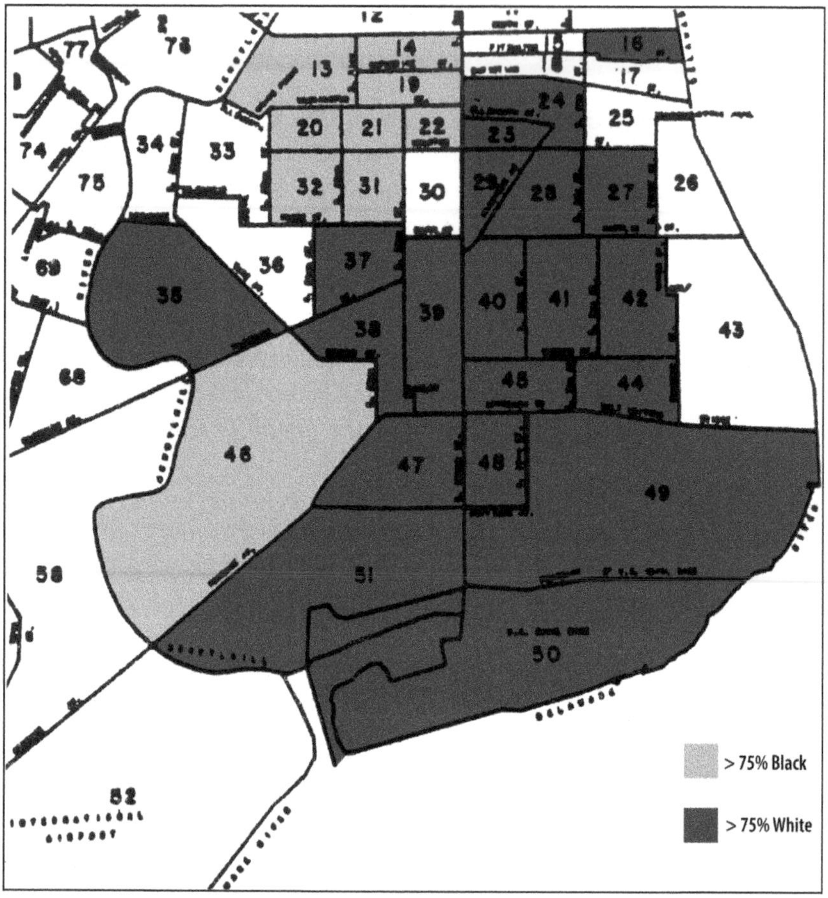

Figure 4.2 Concentrations of white and African American population in South Philadelphia census tracts, 1980

Source: John Maneval, *An Ethnic History of South Philadelphia, 1870–1980* (Philadelphia: Balch Institute for Ethnic Studies, 1991), II-106, II-107.

Political alliances frequently transcended ethnic divisions. Although Congressman Barrett helped many people enter the political infrastructure, few could be regarded as his protégés. Two individuals whose careers Barrett helped advance, however, were of Italian descent: William Cibotti, who represented City Council's 2nd District from 1968 to 1975 (he died in office and was succeeded by his daughter, Anna Cibotti Verna); and G. Fred DiBona, who became a common pleas court judge.

And it was not impossible for an ambitious person who did not belong to one of the area's dominant ethnic groups to achieve success in South Philadelphia politics. James Tayoun, the son of a Lebanese immigrant, won election to the Pennsylvania House in 1968, then to Philadelphia City Council in 1975, where he represented the east-of-Broad 1st Council District. Frank DiCicco, who became 1st District councilperson years later, called Tayoun "the hardest working campaigner" he had ever seen.[6]

> He had a base around the corner from where I lived at 10th and Ellsworth, and he was running against Buddy Cianfrani's candidate. Tayoun was in everyone's face, day and night. If you called him at four in the morning [with a constituent service request], he'd be there at your house at five after four. Whether anybody liked him or not, the guy was an amazing campaigner. He was just tireless—and that made a difference.[7]

Ward Math

"My maternal grandfather was a businessperson," Joseph Vignola said. "He was in the scrap business—metals and rags, paper products, and stuff like that. So you needed political protection." Vignola's grandfather worked during a period in which the Republican Party was in everybody's business. The Republican political machine's dominance over municipal government, characterized as "one-party political rule," was strongest from the mid-1890s to the early 1930s.[8]

The influence of the Republican Party began to wane during the presidency of Franklin Roosevelt and (as described in Chapter 2) after World War II, when Bill Barrett's political career was just beginning. As the Democrats gained power, they continued to use the ward and division system as a vehicle for delivering jobs and services in exchange for controlled votes. Martin Weinberg, who grew up in South Philadelphia and later became a valued member of Frank Rizzo's inner circle, described the system as it had existed during the years when his father, Emanuel Weinberg, was Democratic leader of the 39th Ward:

> In those days, if you had any kinds of needs with the city, . . . the committeeman was the guy who took care of you. . . .
>
> In an area like South Philadelphia, there were so many immigrants. That's why it became the hotbed of machine politics. Those immigrants really needed the help of their committeepeople to exist. . . .
>
> You didn't knock on the door two weeks before the election and discuss abortion or issues. . . . Nobody really gave a shit about people's positions. It was a very, very service-oriented job. You voted for your committeeman.[9]

Weinberg described an election-day system that was highly organized:

> You have your workers at the division [polling place] who would check off people as they came to vote. And then around 3 p.m. when I came home from school, I would . . . go to the houses that hadn't voted yet and knock on doors. Then I'd go out again at six.
>
> And then the big boss, my mother, would come out about 7 o'clock and make sure they came out to vote. Each street had somebody like myself to make sure that everybody who could came out to vote on election day. That's one of the reasons why the percentage of voters [was] so much higher in those days. . . .
>
> [After the polls closed] all the committeemen would come in . . . they'd have to stand in front of everybody and announce the results of their division and hand in the official return to my father, so they couldn't phony it up. . . . After you were done, you would sit there and wait because everybody who came in had to announce in front of everybody, and nobody could leave until everybody was through.[10]

In a row house community populated by many families who are related to one another by birth and marriage, where everyone on the block knows everyone else on the block, and where the local polling place is a short walk away, a vote-delivery system of this kind is highly effective.

Emanuel Weinberg had begun his first term as a Democratic ward leader during the 1930s, when Republicans still retained power in South Philadelphia. In the 1939 election, Republican candidates captured all three City Council seats in South Philadelphia's 1st District (at that time, the city charter provided for council districts to be represented by multiple members).[11] The district remained under Republican control for the next twelve years.

The Republican Party's power had been so all-encompassing that even the Democrats were Republicans: Democratic City Committee chair John O'Donnell was on the Republican payroll.[12] At the neighborhood level, Republican Party operatives, known as "O'Donnell Democrats," registered as Democrats so they could be elected as Democratic ward leaders and take control of other offices available to the minority party. Joseph Vignola's Uncle Henry (Cianfrani) had been one of them, and he remained with the party after it broke free of Republican control. Cianfrani was elected as a Democratic member of the state House of Representatives in 1952, the year after Joseph Clark was elected mayor, and he served six terms.

South Philadelphia had not contributed to the electoral successes of Clark and Richardson Dilworth in a big way, and some other areas of the city received far more benefits than South Philadelphia during the administrations of these two mayors. Northeast Philadelphia got thousands of new houses, populated with white homeowners, while South Philadelphia experienced years of depopulation. Society Hill in Center City and Yorktown in North Philadelphia got major investments of federal funding to support the development of new homeowner housing, while South Philadelphia inherited steadily deteriorating public housing sites—Southwark Plaza, Martin Luther King Plaza, Tasker Homes, Wilson Park—which would become eyesores and crime magnets and would remain that way for decades. No public housing could be found in Mayor Clark's Chestnut Hill neighborhood or anywhere near the Society Hill townhouse where Mayor Dilworth lived.

In 1961, a year before he resigned the mayoralty to run for governor, Dilworth angered South Philadelphians by proposing the issuance of parking permits as a way of addressing the area's street-parking congestion. At a public meeting, "Dilworth was pelted with lemons and tomatoes. Afterward, he referred to South Philadelphians as 'greasers,' the first time his ethnic [prejudice] had slipped out."[13]

The reformers had not been extremely popular in South Philadelphia from the start. In the pivotal 1951 election, Joseph Clark's margin of victory over a lackluster opponent, Daniel A. Poling, was six percentage points lower in South Philadelphia than in the remainder of the city.

During the years after William Meehan inherited the leadership of the Republican City Committee from his father, Austin Meehan, in 1961, many South Philadelphia voters continued to support Republican candidates, despite the ongoing decline in party membership. When a good opportunity presented itself, Meehan was able to capture votes from many Democrats and independent voters to add muscle to the weakened Republican base. In the 1967 mayoral election, for example, four of South Philadelphia's six wards produced a majority of votes for the Republican candidate, former district attorney Arlen Specter, who ran against incumbent Democrat Mayor James H. J. Tate. On a citywide basis, at a time when the Democratic Party had nearly 200,000 more registered voters than the Republicans, Specter came within 11,000 votes of defeating Tate. A key factor in the election was Tate's appointment of Frank Rizzo, a South Philadelphia native, as police commissioner. Rizzo had been a lifelong Republican until that year, when he changed his party affiliation after the announcement of his appointment.[14]

South Philadelphia voters were more conservative than voters elsewhere in the city. In the 1968 presidential election, 44 percent of South Philadelphia voters supported Richard Nixon or George Wallace, compared with 37 percent in the rest of the city, as shown in Table 4.2. In 1972, when George McGovern won Philadelphia, 56 percent to 44 percent, Nixon won South Philadelphia, 52 percent to 48 percent.

TABLE 4.2 VOTE TOTALS FOR 1968 AND 1972 PRESIDENTIAL ELECTIONS

		Citywide		South Philadelphia		Remainder of city	
Year	Candidate	Number	%	Number	%	Number	%
1968	Hubert Humphrey	525,768	62	58,462	56	467,306	63
	Richard Nixon	254,153	30	35,373	34	218,780	30
	George Wallace	63,506	8	10,133	10	53,373	7
	Total	843,427		103,968		739,459	
1972	George McGovern	430,901	56	46,371	48	384,530	57
	Richard Nixon	343,553	44	49,739	52	293,814	43
	Total	774,454		96,110		678,344	

Source: Philadelphia Registration Commission, *Sixty-Second Annual Report* (Philadelphia: City of Philadelphia, 1968); Philadelphia Registration Commission, *Sixty-Sixth Annual Report* (Philadelphia: City of Philadelphia, 1972).

However, when Frank Rizzo became a candidate for mayor in 1971, the gap between Democratic and Republican voters widened, and it never came near closing again. In 1969, Democrats had outnumbered Republicans in South Philadelphia, 67,524 to 51,049. In 1971, the numbers were 78,396 to 45,685; and in 1975, when Rizzo ran for reelection, Democrats led Republicans 82,510 to 27,608 in South Philadelphia and 620,652 to 225,182 citywide.[15]

"Rizzo took traditional Republicans, especially those who left South Philly and moved to the Northeast, and made them Democrats," Joseph Vignola said. "That was Marty Weinberg's smart card—Billy Meehan didn't see it happening [Martin Weinberg had worked closely with Bill Barrett to strengthen Rizzo's political base for several years before the 1971 election[16]]. And the South Philadelphia Italians, because of Rizzo, they all became Democrats too."

Meehan had a longstanding friendship with Rizzo, and he was not particularly enthusiastic about the Republican candidates who emerged to oppose Rizzo in the 1971 and 1975 elections. Former city councilperson Thatcher Longstreth, Rizzo's opponent in 1971, had delivered reliable votes for Meehan while on council, "but he was not this dynamic person," Vignola commented. "Rizzo was this person he knew he could do business with. He could keep General Asphalt [the family-owned contracting business] paving streets. He could get bond work for some of his investment banking friends." Meehan was also unenthusiastic about the Republican candidate in the 1975 mayoral election. The only person who appeared to be interested in running against Frank Rizzo was Thomas Foglietta, also a former city councilperson, who was probably not viewed by Meehan as a strong competitor. "Whenever Billy Meehan thought he had a serious

TABLE 4.3 VOTE TOTALS FOR 1971, 1975, AND 1979 MAYORAL ELECTIONS

		Citywide		South Philadelphia		Remainder of city	
		Number	%	Number	%	Number	%
1971	Frank Rizzo (D)	394,067	53	67,255	72	326,812	51
	Thacher Longstreth (R)	345,912	47	26,661	28	319,251	49
	Total	739,979		93,916		646,063	
1975	Frank Rizzo (D)	321,513	57	58,694	75	262,819	54
	Thomas Foglietta (R)	103,565	18	11,008	14	92,557	19
	Charles Bowser (Philadelphia)	138,783	25	8,161	10	130,622	27
	Total	563,861		77,863		485,998	
1979	William Green (D)	317,919	53	39,857	56	278,062	53
	David Marston (R)	174,569	29	22,580	32	151,989	29
	Lucien Blackwell (Consumer)	103,620	17	8,841	12	94,779	18
	Total	596,108		71,278		524,830	

Source: Philadelphia Registration Commission, *Sixty-Fifth Annual Report* (Philadelphia: City of Philadelphia, 1971); Philadelphia Registration Commission, *Sixty-Ninth Annual Report* (Philadelphia: City of Philadelphia, 1975); Philadelphia Registration Commission, *Seventy-Third Annual Report* (Philadelphia: City of Philadelphia, 1979).

chance of winning a mayor's race—going back to Specter versus Tate—he took the shot," Vignola said. "But [1975] was not one of those times."

As shown in Table 4.3, Rizzo's percentages of South Philadelphia votes increased from 72 percent in the 1971 mayoral election to 75 percent in 1975. In the latter election, Foglietta finished third in a three-candidate race. When it came time to choose Rizzo's successor in the 1979 election, South Philadelphia voters delivered 56 percent of their votes to the Democratic candidate, Congressman William J. Green III, a liberal congressperson from a family with strong party connections (his father had been head of the Democratic City Committee from 1953 until his death in 1963 and had served consecutive terms in Congress from 1949 until 1963). Notwithstanding Green's credentials, the percentage of South Philadelphia voters who supported Green in that election was nearly twenty points below the vote percentage that Rizzo had received from South Philadelphia four years previously.

Switching Partners

Congressman Barrett died in office on April 12, 1976. At the time, he had been a candidate for reelection to the House seat that he had held almost continuously since 1945 (he was not reelected for the 1947–1948 term, but he regained his seat in 1949). Barrett's name could not be removed from the ballot in time for the primary election; so the Congressman was elected as the party's candidate a final time postmortem. That fall, the voters chose

Michael "Ozzie" Myers to fill the vacant 1st Congressional District seat. Myers subsequently won a full two-year term in 1978, and he was preparing to run for reelection when the Abscam news broke on February 2, 1980.

The Abscam indictments were the biggest political challenge of Mayor Bill Green's tenure as mayor, which had begun just a few weeks previously on January 7. Two Philadelphia congresspersons—Myers and Raymond Lederer—and three city council members had been recorded accepting bribes from an FBI informant. All five were members of the Democratic Party, the party that Green controlled through his friend, City Committee chair David Glancey.

Because the April primary election was just two months away, Democratic Party operatives had to regroup quickly. Mayor Green called a meeting of the ward leaders whose jurisdictions lay within the 1st Congressional District. He told the group that he had already lined up a candidate to succeed Myers: Alex Bonavitacola, a respected common pleas court judge. Green went around the room and asked each ward leader to pledge support for the judge as the endorsed candidate for Myers's congressional seat.

Before the meeting, Vignola had spoken with Mayor Green. They both understood that, given the disruption caused by the Abscam indictments, Myers's congressional district office in Philadelphia was in particular need of administrative support; so Vignola was going to stay on the job. "Ozzie told me he'd do the right thing by the district," Vignola said to the mayor. The presumption of innocence, which Vignola also mentioned to the mayor, would have been easier to acknowledge if Myers's outrageous performance had not been captured on videotape and broadcast on television. In any event, according to Vignola, when Green came to Vignola as he went around the room at the ward leaders meeting, the mayor said, "I know I can't ask you to do this," and moved on. Every other ward leader pledged support for Bonavitacola.

Myers had known about the meeting, and he heard about the outcome right away. Vignola recalled:

> Ozzie immediately started mobilizing his forces. He was on the Merchant Marine and Fisheries Committee. The Seafarers Union was powerful. He got some labor guys involved.
>
> Then the ward leaders started to renege on their promise [to support Bonavitacola].
>
> At the same time, anyone who had twenty-five bucks and a hundred signatures [that a candidate needed to file a nominating petition to become a candidate in the upcoming election] was on the ballot, from [ward leader] Bernie Avellino all the way down to [criminal defense attorney] Chuck Peruto Jr. It was a zoo.

> Ozzie said, "I'm going to fight this. I did nothing wrong. I'm going to run." I said, "If you're going to run, I'm going to be for you. I'll run the office—you just go out there and campaign and raise money."

Because Myers's office in D.C. was not being adequately managed, Vignola's assistance would be needed there as well as in Philadelphia. So Vignola would remain a member of Myers's staff, but he would stay out of the congressional campaign, except in the 2nd Ward, where he was ward leader. He would continue to shuttle between Philadelphia and Washington for the remainder of that year.

After learning about the erosion of party support for his candidacy, Judge Bonavitacola reevaluated his position. A common pleas court judgeship is, among other things, a guarantee of permanent employment. Although common pleas judges are periodically subject to yes-or-no "retention" votes, it is extremely rare for a judge to be voted out of office by a majority of citywide voters voting no in a retention election. In contrast, resigning from the judiciary to become a candidate in a contested election is a guarantee of nothing, even under circumstances in which the candidate is supported by the mayor and the Democratic City Committee chair. When it became clear that ward leaders were abandoning their pledges, Judge Bonavitacola withdrew his name from consideration for the 1st District congressional seat.

The *Philadelphia Inquirer* reported that "supporters and opponents alike generally agreed . . . that Green had bungled his political response to the Abscam affair" and quoted one "sympathetic South Philadelphia ward leader" as saying:

> He should have called us all into his office one by one . . . and said, "Look, you S.O.B., I want you to support so-and-so, or else I'm coming after you with all I've got." That's the only thing we understand in South Philadelphia—you reward friends and punish enemies.[17]

Myers and fourteen other candidates ended up on the ballot for the April Democratic primary. Vignola reached out to his committeepeople and constituents in the 2nd Ward on Myers's behalf. He wrote a letter to voters in the Queen Village neighborhood east of 6th Street, a "hotbed of progressivism," as Vignola characterized it, where many liberal Democrats lived. Vignola recounted that the letter said, in effect, "Ozzie told me that he's going to do the right thing for the district. With so many people in the race, we don't know what might happen if we go with another candidate. If someone else gets elected who isn't the best person for Congress, then we may be stuck with that person for years. If Ozzie wins and has to leave, then we'll be in a better position to pick a replacement who is qualified."

Myers won the April primary, with about 24,000 votes. The candidate who came closest to defeating him was Hardy Williams, who was about 2,000 votes behind him. Only one of the other twelve candidates, Bernard J. Avellino, received more than 5,000 votes. Vignola's outreach to his constituents had worked. "Ozzie won every division in my ward," he said.

Meanwhile, the prosecution of the Abscam defendants moved along quickly. Myers was convicted in August. However, contrary to the wishes of Mayor Green and Party Chair Glancey, he did not resign from office, and he refused to end his candidacy for reelection. Ozzie Myers was going to appear on the ballot in the November election as the Democratic candidate for the congressional seat.

Vignola told Myers that he should step down, and they had a big falling out. "Ozzie was pissed at me—so pissed he wouldn't talk to me. I told him that I couldn't support him—I would look for somebody else," Vignola explained.

That was when Vignola and, as he put it, "a group of guys I hung out with—Young Turks, all in our twenties"—got into a serious discussion about Tom Foglietta's candidacy. They thought that Democratic Party leaders could be persuaded to support Foglietta as an independent candidate in the November election and that lifelong Democrats in congressional district neighborhoods could be persuaded to vote for him.

So who was Tom Foglietta?

The Friends of Tom Foglietta

Thomas Foglietta might be considered as noteworthy for what he was not as for who he was. Foglietta was not involved in the Abscam scandal. He was not aligned with any of the Democratic Party factions that routinely contended with each other for political power in South Philadelphia; Foglietta was a lifelong Republican. He had not been a candidate in the April 1980 primary. The winning Republican candidate for Congress in that contest was Robert R. Burke, a West Philadelphia lawyer who was unknown to most voters. Foglietta had been an elected official—a five-term Republican member of Philadelphia City Council—but he was not identified with any significant legislative achievements. No one who knew him would characterize him as a policy wonk. S. A. Paolantonio, Frank Rizzo's biographer, wrote, "Tom Foglietta's tenure on City Council was somnambulant. In City Hall he was known as 'the Fog.'"[18]

Notwithstanding these drawbacks, Tom Foglietta possessed characteristics that made him an attractive candidate for office. He was a well-known political figure in South Philadelphia. He was relatively young (fifty-one years old in 1980), sociable, and, to many, likable. He was a man of Italian extraction who had achieved success in America. He had a college degree and a law school diploma. He was courteous and gentlemanly—not like Ozzie Myers, who had received six months' probation after pleading no contest to charges of hitting a cocktail waitress. He was a South Philadelphian who was comfortable socializing with Philadelphia's elites. He and John B. "Jack" Kelly Jr., a fellow city council member and the brother of Princess Grace of Monaco, frequented downtown nightspots together, often in the company of glamorous women.

Foglietta was not an accidental candidate who lacked integrity and personal convictions. He was a moderate Republican—the kind of politician who in later years would have been branded as "Republican in name only" (RINO). As a candidate and elected official in 1980 and afterward, he formed his own opinions about public policy, and his views were not always consistent with those of the South Philadelphia mainstream. He supported a woman's right to choose. He supported affirmative action programs and gay rights. He saw nothing wrong with allowing students who wished to do so to pray in school before classes began. He supported cuts in military spending. He opposed funding the B-1 bomber and the MX missile. Acknowledging that defense spending could bring new jobs to Philadelphia, he said, "I want to provide jobs too . . . but I don't want to do it by building weapons designed to destroy other people."[19]

People who were active in South Philadelphia politics knew him, and many of them were convinced that he was someone they could work with, especially under circumstances in which the Democratic candidate on the November ballot was a convicted felon. Some Democrats who might have been potential competitors against Myers in November had already run in the April primary and lost. Mayor Green and David Glancey liked Foglietta, who had headed a Republicans-for-Green faction during Green's 1979 mayoral campaign. Foglietta was well known in South Philadelphia. It was unlikely that he would try to usurp anyone else's power as a ward leader or candidate for some other office in a future election. No one else who might have had credibility as a candidate was in a position to plunge into a demanding campaign with only a few months remaining until election day.

Most important, Foglietta knew how to navigate the often treacherous waters of South Philadelphia politics. The Fogliettas and the Cianfranis—Vignola's family—came from the same village in Italy—Monteroduni—and when the two families emigrated to Philadelphia, they lived near each other on Fitzwater Street. Members of both families got deeply involved in politics and engaged in alliances and rivalries over the years. Tom's father, Michael, was a dyed-in-the-wool Republican who served on City Council from 1948 to 1952, then helped his twenty-seven-year-old son get elected to a council at-large seat in 1955. The Cianfranis were all Democrats.

To help ensure his son's success at the polls, Michael Foglietta would ask Democratic Party committeepeople with whom he was acquainted to include Tom's name on the sample ballots that they would be distributing to voters on election day. In Philadelphia's council at-large election, seven candidates are selected on a citywide basis by all voters participating in the election. Each voter can vote for five at-large candidates, and the candidates with the highest vote totals win the seven available seats, subject to one qualification: not more than five at-large councilpersons can be members of the same political party; two of them must be members of the minority party. To help his son, Mike Foglietta asked his Democratic Party acquaintances to delete the name of one of the five party-endorsed Democratic candidates from their sample ballots and replace it with Tom's name. Doing so would not reduce any Democratic at-large candidate's prospects for success; given the overwhelming Democratic majority in Philadelphia, all the Democratic at-large candidates were going to win, even if some would-be Democratic votes were flipped to a Republican candidate.

To illustrate the kind of ballot cutting that Michael Foglietta was seeking on behalf of his son, Table 4.4 shows the results of the 1971 election of council at-large candidates, in which Tom Foglietta won his fifth consecutive council term. In that year, the winning Democratic candidates received between 362,746 and 401,550 votes. The vote totals for all five of the Democratic candidates were far greater than the vote totals for any of the winning Republican candidates. As the table shows, the most popular Republican

TABLE 4.4 ELECTION RESULTS FOR COUNCIL AT LARGE, 1971

Candidate	Party	Number of votes
John Kelly	D	401,550
Edgar Campbell	D	390,001
William Boyle	D	371,057
Francis O'Donnell	D	366,768
Edward Cantor	D	362,746
Thomas Foglietta	R	285,994
Beatrice Chernock	R	265,305
Alvin Echols	R	256,618
Thomas Magrann	R	244,303
Anthony Novasitis	R	238,925

Source: Access to election data provided to the author by Philadelphia City Commissioners.
Note: Winners are in italics.

(Foglietta) received nearly 80,000 votes fewer than the least popular Democrat (Edward Cantor).

As indicated above, if ballot cutting in a particular election reduced Democratic vote totals by, for example, 10,000 votes, the overall election results would not change; all the Democratic candidates would still win. However, 10,000 votes shifted from one of the Democratic candidates to one of the Republicans could tip the balance with respect to the election of minority-party members. For example, with respect to the results shown in Table 4.4, the injection of an additional 10,000 votes for Alvin Echols would have enabled Echols to defeat Beatrice Chernock and win one of the minority party seats in 1971.

In a neighborhood with a level of political organization comparable to that which existed when Emanuel Weinberg was leader of the 39th Ward, ballot cutting of this kind could be done with a high degree of precision to deliver a reliable number of votes to a targeted candidate.

The experience of council at-large member Happy Fernandez provides a good illustration of how a well-managed citywide ballot-cutting strategy can deliver many votes. Fernandez, a former college professor and former head of the Philadelphia chapter of the liberal Americans for Democratic Action, ran for council at large in 1987 and finished poorly. After that defeat, her advisers recommended that she engage the services of then-former state senator Henry J. "Buddy" Cianfrani, Vignola's cousin. Fernandez paid Cianfrani $5,500 for his services in the 1991 Democratic primary election, and he delivered; she received 56,956 votes, winning one of the five council at-large positions and outpolling three other Democratic candidates who won at-large seats.

In preparation for her 1995 reelection campaign, she again enlisted Cianfrani's help, paying him $6,000. That year, she came in first with 76,202 votes.

> [Cianfrani] demonstrated that ward leaders would listen to him. The evidence? They put Happy on their sample ballots—and she is a candidate they don't particularly like. . . .
>
> She even got the most votes in Bob Brady's Overbrook-Wynnefield ward, and he is not only the chairman of the city Democratic committee but he was favoring another candidate in the at-large race. . . .
>
> Fernandez came in first in parts of Northeast Philadelphia that have no love for her but an old fondness for Buddy.[20]

Cianfrani helped Fernandez, a Democrat, accumulate votes in a Democratic primary. But why would a Democratic committeeperson agree to consider

Republican Mike Foglietta's request to divert votes to his son in the 1971 general election for council at large? Probably because Foglietta was a fellow South Philadelphian, possibly a relative, possibly a fellow member of a church or social club, possibly because they were paid to do so. And why would an average registered voter who had been accustomed to voting exclusively for Democratic candidates be willing to vote for a Republican candidate listed on a sample ballot distributed by the local committeeperson? Because the committeeperson had been helpful to that voter as a source of information and assistance over the years, and because voting the sample ballot on election day was all that the committeeperson was asking in return.

Now, in 1980, Foglietta was ready to run as an independent candidate, and Vignola and his friends were ready to help him. Vignola spoke at a caucus of South Philadelphia ward leaders. He said, "If Tom is running, this is what we have to do." Shortly afterward, Vignola was interviewed on national television as the first prominent Philadelphia Democrat to break ranks with the party in the upcoming congressional election. Foglietta announced his candidacy, and Bob Barnett, a seasoned campaign operative, ran the campaign. Neil Oxman, a media consultant who would later produce electoral successes for many candidates at every level of government, handled communications.

The upcoming election would be a major ballot-cutting and ticket-splitting challenge, but the Foglietta team was well prepared.

> Robert Barnett, campaign manager for Foglietta, says that his candidate's 20 years as a city councilman, coupled with surveys showing that 70 per cent of the electorate identifies Myers with Abscam, should overcome voter tendency to pick the straight Democratic ticket. "We're counting on them to exhibit one more level of sophistication," he says, citing polls that give Foglietta 47 per cent of the vote and Myers 19 per cent.
>
> But Barnett and Foglietta are taking no chances. Campaign commercials open with a newspaper clipping of Myers' expulsion, then switch to a picture of a ballot. The camera moves down the Democratic ticket, then pans to the right and Foglietta's spot on the independent column—"just to make sure people know," Barnett says.[21]

On Wednesday nights, Vignola would meet with 2nd Ward committee people in groups. He explained:

> I would tell them, this is what we're doing. I explained how to cut the ticket, how to do it right. It's a presidential year; it's a short ballot. You vote for Foglietta and then you go down and vote for the other

> candidates—make it look like a primary. You don't have to pull the big lever. Vote for Foglietta, then vote for whoever you want.

The plan worked. Foglietta beat Myers by about five thousand votes. At his victory party, Foglietta said, "The people of the First District will not accept corruption."[22] At the time, Foglietta was still a Republican. He changed his registration shortly afterward, and when he arrived in Washington, he joined the Democratic caucus.

Despite their misstep a few months earlier with respect to Judge Bonavitacola's candidacy, Mayor Green and David Glancey remained in control of the party apparatus, and that made a difference, according to Vignola. Myers agreed. Commenting on the election results, he told a *Philadelphia Inquirer* reporter, "The biggest problem I had was that the Democratic mayor endorsed the Republican candidate. If the Green administration had not taken a position, I would have won this going away."[23]

The timing of Myers's conviction may also have made a difference. Another Abscam defendant, Congressman Raymond Lederer, whose district, the 3rd, bordered the 1st District on the north, east of Broad Street to the Delaware River, easily won reelection. He had been indicted but had not gone to trial before election day.

Sequels

Lederer's day of reckoning came two months later. He was convicted in January, a week after being sworn into office, and he resigned from Congress in April.

A special election was scheduled for that July to select a new 3rd District congressperson, who would occupy the seat for the remainder of Lederer's term. The election became a test of political power between two candidates: Democratic Party chair David Glancey, who was backed by Mayor Green and the mayor's allies and who was endorsed by the Democratic City Committee; and state senator Joseph Smith, whose supporters included ward leaders and union members who had enjoyed political favor during Mayor Rizzo's tenure and who felt snubbed by the reform-minded Green administration.

Because his opponent had already received the Democratic Party endorsement, Senator Smith's name could not appear on the ballot as a Democrat, so he ran as a Republican, but he also filed as an Independent. As a result, his name appeared twice on the ballot posted in the voting machines, as shown in Figure 4.3.

Registered Democrats in the district outnumbered Republicans by about four to one. With help of Mayor Green and his political allies,

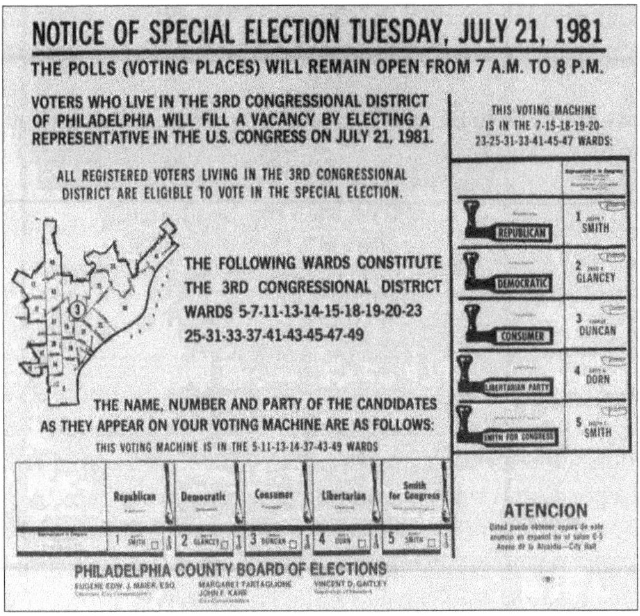

NOTICE OF SPECIAL ELECTION TUESDAY, JULY 21, 1981

THE POLLS (VOTING PLACES) WILL REMAIN OPEN FROM 7 A.M. TO 8 P.M.

VOTERS WHO LIVE IN THE 3RD CONGRESSIONAL DISTRICT OF PHILADELPHIA WILL FILL A VACANCY BY ELECTING A REPRESENTATIVE IN THE U.S. CONGRESS ON JULY 21, 1981.

ALL REGISTERED VOTERS LIVING IN THE 3RD CONGRESSIONAL DISTRICT ARE ELIGIBLE TO VOTE IN THE SPECIAL ELECTION.

THE FOLLOWING WARDS CONSTITUTE THE 3RD CONGRESSIONAL DISTRICT WARDS 5-7-11-13-14-15-18-19-20-23 25-31-33-37-41-43-45-47-49

THE NAME, NUMBER AND PARTY OF THE CANDIDATES AS THEY APPEAR ON YOUR VOTING MACHINE ARE AS FOLLOWS:

THIS VOTING MACHINE IS IN THE 5-11-13-14-37-43-49 WARDS

Republican	Democratic	Consumer	Libertarian	Smith for Congress
1 SMITH	2 GLANCEY	3 DUNCAN	4 DORN	5 SMITH

THIS VOTING MACHINE IS IN THE 7-15-18-19-20-23-25-31-33-41-45-47 WARDS:

REPUBLICAN	1 SMITH
DEMOCRATIC	2 GLANCEY
CONSUMER	3 DUNCAN
LIBERTARIAN PARTY	4 DORN
SMITH FOR CONGRESS	5 SMITH

ATENCION

PHILADELPHIA COUNTY BOARD OF ELECTIONS

Figure 4.3 Ballot in July 1981 special election, 3rd Congressional District

Source: Philadelphia City Commissioners, "Notice of Special Election Tuesday, July 21, 1981," *Philadelphia Inquirer*, July 20, 1981, p. 6A.

Glancey's campaign raised about $200,000, roughly three times as much as Smith's campaign and enough to buy television ad time for Glancey during the weeks preceding the election.[24]

Notwithstanding these advantages, Smith won the election easily, beating Glancey by about seven thousand votes. Smith's winning total consisted of the combined votes for Joseph F. Smith, the Republican candidate (lever 1 in Figure 4.3), and Joseph F. Smith, the Smith for Congress candidate (lever 5). Many voters who pulled lever 5 because they wanted to express preference for an independent candidate who had not been endorsed by either the Democratic or Republican Party may not have been aware that the Smith for Congress candidate and the Republican nominee were the same person.

The outcome of the July special election was a major defeat to Green, who had supported Glancey's candidacy as a high political priority, as well as a reaffirmation of the political influence of Frank Rizzo, who had made phone calls on Smith's behalf.[25]

Months before, it had been clear that the results of this election might jeopardize Tom Foglietta's future in public office because of the possibility that he would have to compete against the winner to remain in Congress.

Reapportionment, the realignment of congressional district boundaries based on the results of the 1980 decennial census, was scheduled to be completed before the 1982 congressional elections. In light of the population decline that Philadelphia had experienced during the 1970s, it was likely that the city would lose one congressional district. It was also likely that this change might be achieved by merging the 1st and 3rd Districts in some way. In the reapportionment process, the district boundaries could be redrawn to favor either Smith or Foglietta, depending on the extent to which the reconstituted district included the river wards, to Smith's benefit, or the downtown area and South Philadelphia, favoring Foglietta.

The state legislature approved the redistricting plan on March 2, 1982, and Foglietta was pleased with the results, shown in Figure 4.4. "I'm very happy with it, and it makes me very confident I will win this election," he said.[26] He claimed to have strong support in nineteen of the twenty-four wards that made up the new district, including high-turnout wards in South Philadelphia and Center City.[27] Smith claimed to be equally pleased with the results, noting that 60 percent of his old district was included in the new one. "I couldn't have drawn it better if they'd given me the pencil," he told the *Inquirer.*[28]

Foglietta's prospects for victory in this election were far from certain. The Democratic City Committee, still under David Glancey's leadership, was going to refrain from making an endorsement, ostensibly because both candidates were incumbents. However, if an endorsement vote were to have been held, it was clear who would have won. As a ward leader and state senator, Smith had built up strong ties with many ward leaders over the years, and most of them were in his camp. Although Mayor Green would work hard for Foglietta, the results of the Smith-Glancey race made it clear that Green's support would not have a decisive influence on the election's outcome; on the contrary, many voters in the river-ward heartland disliked Green. Rizzo, who at the time was considering the possibility of running for mayor in 1983, was a Smith supporter. And South Philadelphia was not necessarily going to deliver the election to him. On the contrary, several influential South Philadelphia political leaders, such as state senator Vincent Fumo, were on Smith's side.

During 1981, already anticipating a tough reelection fight, Bob Barnett had asked Vignola if he would help the Foglietta campaign again, and Vignola indicated his willingness to do so. A few months later, however—much earlier than he expected—Vignola was appointed to fill a vacant seat on the three-member City Commission, the bipartisan board that oversees voter registration and elections. Although he was not required to give up his post as ward leader and was allowed to participate in political activity (except in an election in which city commissioners were on the ballot), Vignola would need to devote most of his available time to overhauling the practices

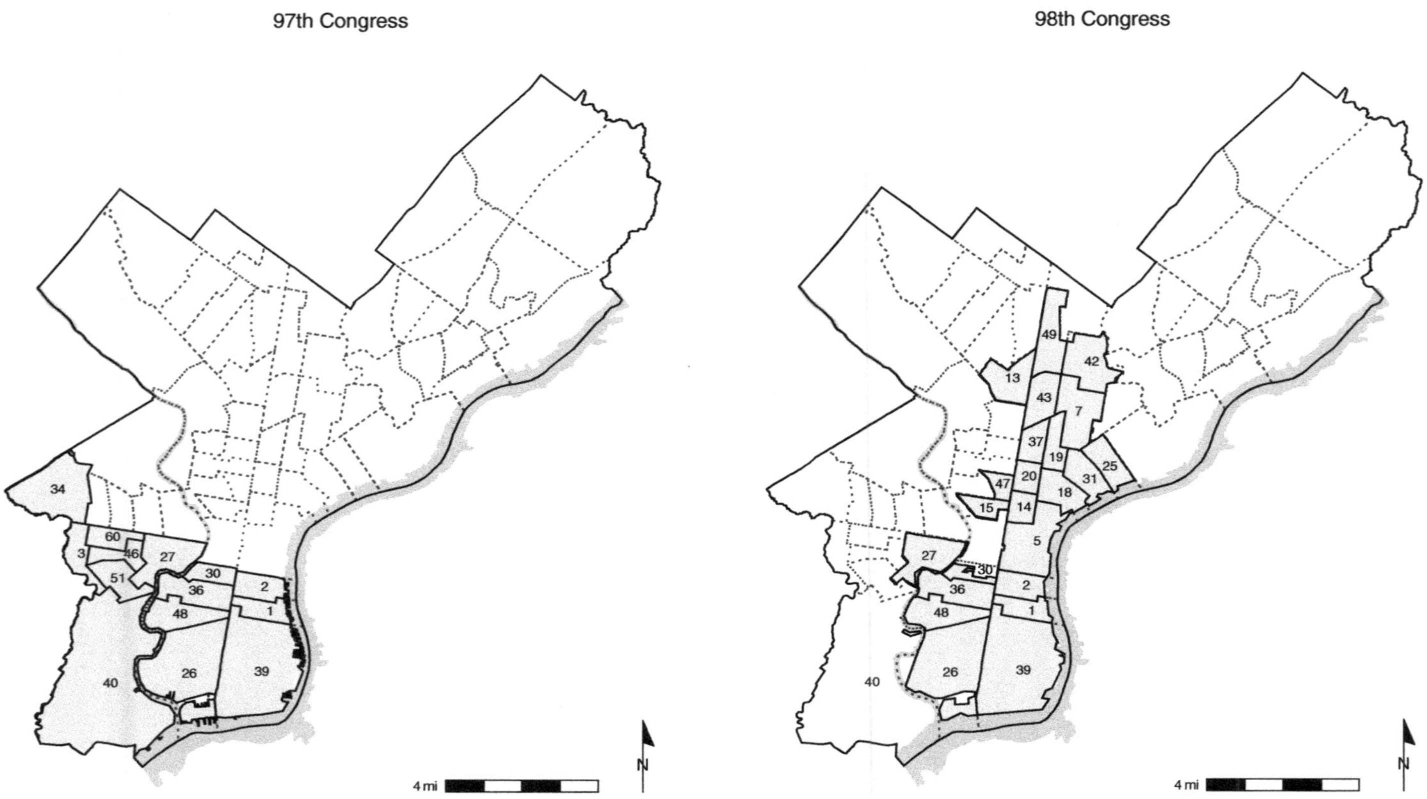

Figure 4.4 The 1st Congressional District, before and after the 1982 reapportionment

Source: Data from Pennsylvania Department of General Services, *The Pennsylvania Manual*, vol. 105 (Harrisburg: Commonwealth of Pennsylvania, 1980), 188; and Pennsylvania Department of General Services, *The Pennsylvania Manual*, vol. 106 (Harrisburg: Commonwealth of Pennsylvania, 1982), 187; maps by Michael Fichman.

of the commission, which had drawn charges of mismanagement and allegations of fraud. A 1979 report had documented:

> money needlessly spent: nearly $1 million to recount the ballots in the May [1979] primary after a tally sheet error cast doubt on the validity of the election. . . .
>
> A suspiciously high number of absentee ballots was cast in the May 1978 primary . . . and massive machine breakdowns occurred in the November 1978 general election.[29]

In addition, "large numbers of voters, mostly in black wards, were disenfranchised by voting machine breakdowns" in the 1979 mayoral election.[30]

Many of these problems, which had not been fully addressed by 1982 when Vignola became chair of the City Commissioners, were associated with Margaret M. Tartaglione, a Democratic ward leader who had chaired the commission before Vignola and was still a commissioner. In 1978, Tartaglione had been charged by District Attorney Edward G. Rendell with election tampering after she ordered several voting machines to be moved from one polling place to another. She was acquitted of the charge after election workers testified that "voting machines were frequently moved about [from one polling place to a newly designated polling place] up to the time the polls opened, despite a state law to the contrary."[31] Tartaglione was a Smith supporter.

A particularly unwelcome barrier to Foglietta's reelection emerged closer to home. Vignola's cousin Buddy was actively working on Smith's behalf in the 2nd Ward. He explained:

> So I'm still the ward leader, and my cousin Buddy comes out of college,[32] and he's for Joe Smith. So Joe Smith is talking with Buddy about the 2nd Ward and not talking to me. From the time of nominations until three or four days after the primary, I never talk to Joe Smith; he never calls me.
>
> And I'm not only doing my job to make sure it's a fair election, but I'm also going to different wards, especially in areas where there are Italians. I'm talking about, "I know the pride you felt about Frank Rizzo being the first Italian American mayor of Philadelphia, and how you felt when he was running for reelection and people started taking shots at him. We should feel the same pride now—this is the first Italian American congressman we've ever had."

Although each candidate touched on policy issues when they felt it necessary to do so, differing policy perspectives were not going to decisively influence the election's outcome. As examples of accomplishments during his brief time in office, Foglietta mentioned securing $34 million for capital improvements to the Philadelphia Navy Yard, saving the Philadelphia district office of the Army Corps of Engineers, and helping to lead the opposition to a Reagan administration proposal to charge shippers "user fees" to help finance the dredging of the Delaware River. Smith said he had spent two months studying foreign policy and had found that every administration's policies were different from one another, with support for Israel and anti-communism being the only consistent ones. Foglietta was rated 90 (out of 100) by Americans for Democratic Action; Smith was rated 50. Smith was rated 100 out of 100 by the AFL-CIO's Committee on Public Education; Foglietta was rated 57.[33]

The 1982 election was an off-year election, one in which the highest-profile races—the U.S. presidency or the Philadelphia mayoralty—were not on the ballot. In such a year, voter turnout will be low; many voters will not be that interested in determining who the next U.S. senator, congressperson, governor, or district attorney will be. The outcome of such an election depends on how effective a particular candidate is in enlisting the support of committeepeople and on how effective these committeepeople will be in encouraging residents to vote for that candidate.

Because most ward leaders were not supporting his candidacy, Foglietta knew he needed to reach out to individual committeepeople—hundreds of them across the district—and market his credentials to them directly. Foglietta had the relevant experience; he was an energetic, accomplished doorbell-ringer who, over the years, had learned how to present himself in a way that would appeal to row house residents. Smith was sixty-two years old. He had been an incumbent state senator since 1971, and he had not needed to mount an energetic campaign on his own behalf for years. Smith could lock in the support of many ward leaders in the district; but Foglietta had the ability to sell has candidacy convincingly to committeepeople, division by division.

As Barnett had anticipated, the election was challenging, but Foglietta's approach proved successful; he won, 31,937 to 30,024.

At the City Commissioners office, Vignola had suspected that Marge Tartaglione would use her position, as she had been suspected of doing in past elections, to increase the odds that a candidate she favored would win. In previous years, the third commissioner, Republican John Kane, had sided with Tartaglione, enabling some of the actions that had brought notoriety to the Commissioners office. Now that Vignola was chair, Kane sided with Vignola. He recounted:

> Marge thinks that John Kane is going to be with her in all the votes, and she's trying to do all this stuff. And I'm just going, "No"—and I've got the votes.

Tom ends up winning, but not by a substantial margin. Then they want to talk about recounts, and I'm saying "No, it's over; it's done with." That's when I get the phone call from Joe Smith. He's pushing to have all the voting machines opened. And I'm saying, "No, we've got the count, we're not going to have the voting machines opened. There's a procedure to go through."

Joe Smith gets angry. He says, "Why are you being so obstinate? I thought you were for me!" And I said, "Did you ever speak with me? You spoke with my cousin Buddy. He's not the ward leader. I am. He doesn't control the ward anymore. I do." And Smith says, "So tell them I'm withdrawing my petitions [for a court action ordering a recount]." So I walk out and say, "I just got off the phone with Congressman Smith, and he's withdrawing his petitions. This is over."

Buddy Cianfrani's best days as a political consultant—when he would produce successes for candidates such as Happy Fernandez—were yet to arrive. In the 1982 election, he had encouraged and worked on behalf of two candidates for state Senate and for another congressional candidate, in addition to helping Smith. He was unsuccessful in all four races—and in the Foglietta-Smith battle, he even lost the 2nd Ward.[34]

Tayoun Times Two

In 1984, Joseph Vignola was city controller (he had been elected in 1983), and he remained leader of the 2nd Ward. Wilson Goode was mayor, and Joseph Smith had replaced David Glancey as chair of the Democratic City Committee. There was no animosity between Vignola and Smith over the 1982 election; they had both moved on.

In anticipation of the April 1984 Democratic primary, ward leaders met to consider candidate endorsements. Under ordinary circumstances, the Democratic Party automatically endorses incumbent officeholders who are running for reelection, and all the ward leaders agreed that Foglietta should receive the endorsement. The issue appeared to have been resolved until, not long after the endorsement decision had been made, ward leaders began hearing from James Tayoun that he was considering becoming a candidate.

Well before his election to City Council in 1975, Tayoun had established himself as a formidable political presence in South Philadelphia. Shortly after he joined the council, a *Philadelphia Magazine* writer reported:

> He is without a doubt the shrewdest, most intelligent newcomer on City Council. . . .

> When a new supermarket was scheduled to open recently in Tayoun's district the owners asked him to intercede on their behalf with city departments and agencies that were holding them up. Tayoun agreed—but for a price. He explained that he would clear up their paperwork overnight if he could place his constituents in their first 40 job openings. They went along with the plan and Tayoun was able to add 40 more foot soldiers to his patronage army. . . .
>
> The other councilmen are scared to death [of Tayoun] because they realize that he can singlehandedly outflank them all. . . . he will mark time as the most feared councilman.[35]

A coworker at the *Philadelphia Public Record*, a newspaper that Tayoun founded later in his career, recalled:

> Like his legendary predecessor Congressman Bill Barrett (D-Phila.), he held office in the district five nights a week, when any constituent who needed help could consult with him. Seasoned hands say they have never seen a councilman who was more hands-on with his constituents.[36]

As word of Tayoun's interest in becoming a candidate began to spread, the ward leaders' support for Foglietta began to erode. According to Vignola, various justifications for reconsidering the Foglietta endorsement were offered: "I've worked with Jimmy for years." "If I had known Jimmy was interested, I would have voted differently."

Unlike Foglietta, Tayoun had been a Democratic Party stalwart for years. Foglietta was a relatively recent addition to the party; he had been a Republican candidate and officeholder for most of his career. Tayoun was leader of South Philadelphia's 1st Ward. Foglietta was not a ward leader.

It soon became clear that Tayoun would become a candidate for the congressional seat. He told an *Inquirer* reporter that he would enter the primary if he obtained the endorsement of the ward leaders—who had already expressed their support for an endorsement of Foglietta a short time earlier. "It has come to my attention there is a great deal of dissatisfaction with the performance of Mr. Foglietta generally," Tayoun commented.[37]

A caucus of the ward leaders who represented wards located within the congressional district was scheduled, and a majority of the ward leaders reversed themselves. They endorsed Tayoun by a fourteen-to-six vote with three absentees.[38]

Tayoun promoted his candidacy as the cornerstone of a "peace ticket" that would resolve a conflict between two powerful Democrats: state senator Vincent Fumo and former state representative Leland Beloff, who had made known his intention to capture Fumo's seat in the 1984 primary. To prevent this conflict, Tayoun proposed that Beloff receive the party's endorsement for the City Council seat that Tayoun would vacate by running against Foglietta for Congress, removing the threat to Fumo while increasing Beloff's political power. The only person who would be left out of this equation would be Foglietta.[39]

The ward leaders subsequently voted to support Fumo's reelection. Tayoun resigned from City Council and filed as a candidate in the congressional primary against Foglietta. Beloff agreed to run for the City Council seat that Tayoun had vacated. The swiftly executed political maneuvers associated with the peace ticket were a testimonial to Tayoun's networking and lobbying skills; or, alternatively, perhaps they were the outcome of a behind-the-scenes agreement by Beloff and Fumo to persuade Tayoun to resign, using their pledge of support for Tayoun's congressional candidacy as bait.

In any case, the ward leaders' buy-in was not a guarantee of success for Tayoun's candidacy against Foglietta. Mayor Goode, who was much more politically engaged and much more effective in the political realm than Mayor Green had been, supported Foglietta. The Democratic City Committee endorsed Foglietta as well, consistent with its policy of supporting incumbent candidates in every primary election, although some ward leaders complained that party chair Smith had not been working hard enough to strengthen Foglietta's political standing.[40]

Tayoun and Foglietta debated each other and attacked each other in the press. They charged each other with failing to assist their constituents with access to public services, with lacking a basic understanding of important public policy issues, with having ties to mobsters.[41] The skirmishes and insult trading may not have made any difference. Foglietta won the April primary decisively, receiving approximately 60 percent of the turnout. Joseph Vignola described the reasons why:

> Tom raised a ton of money. He still had Neil Oxman and Bob Barnett running the campaign. And although Tayoun is a door-knocker, Foglietta worked his tail off, knocked doors, showed up at committeepeople's houses, talked to them, did the whole thing.
>
> While Tayoun was popular, none of the professional politicians trusted him—so it was easy for Tom, who was trustworthy, to go sell that. And it was a hard fought battle.

In a special election held in May, Beloff won Tayoun's council seat, and Fumo retained his Senate office without a serious political threat. Tayoun had not benefitted from the peace ticket as anticipated. However, as a ward leader and as a likely future contender for public office, Tayoun continued to be regarded with both respect and apprehension. Despite Foglietta's substantial margin of victory in the 1984 election, the congressperson and his supporters had to be prepared for another challenge two years later. And they were prepared.

As of early 1986, Tayoun had not announced his candidacy for the 3rd District seat—just as he had not been an announced candidate two years previously when the ward leaders had endorsed Foglietta and then reversed themselves shortly afterward. This time when the ward leaders got together to decide on an endorsement, Vignola was ready. He recounted:

> Bob Barnett and I sat down at the ward leaders' meeting with Duke Little [a fellow ward leader], and I tell Duke, "Whatever I do, second it." Duke says, "What—," and I say, "Duke, whatever I'm doing, just second it."
>
> So we have a caucus of ward leaders. Joe Smith's the chairman. "Nominations are now open."
>
> I raise my hand. "I nominate Tom Foglietta."
>
> Duke Little: "I second it!"
>
> "There being no other nominations. . ."
>
> I go, "Mr. Chairman, I nominate Jim Tayoun."
>
> Joe says, "You just nominated Tom Foglietta."
>
> I say, "I can nominate as many people as I want."
>
> Duke Little goes, "I second it!"
>
> I say, "I move nominations be closed."
>
> I'm asked, "Why'd you do that?"
>
> "Because last time, you all said you didn't know Tayoun was running; if you knew Tayoun was running, you wouldn't have endorsed Foglietta. Now, whether Tayoun runs or not, you have a chance to endorse him. He's a private citizen. Now you can encourage him to run by giving him your endorsement."
>
> Nominations are closed. Now, the vote. Tayoun gets two votes, Tom Foglietta gets thirteen.

Vignola had succeeded in forcing the ward leaders to show their cards. No one could claim afterward that they had not been aware of the opportunity to consider endorsing Tayoun.

Tayoun was furious, and Vignola received an angry phone call from him not long after the meeting. Joe Smith was amused. Tayoun did enter the race soon after the ward leaders' meeting, and in the May primary, he was defeated by a much higher margin than he had been in April 1984. As shown in Figure 4.5, Foglietta won nineteen of twenty-three wards, with large ma-

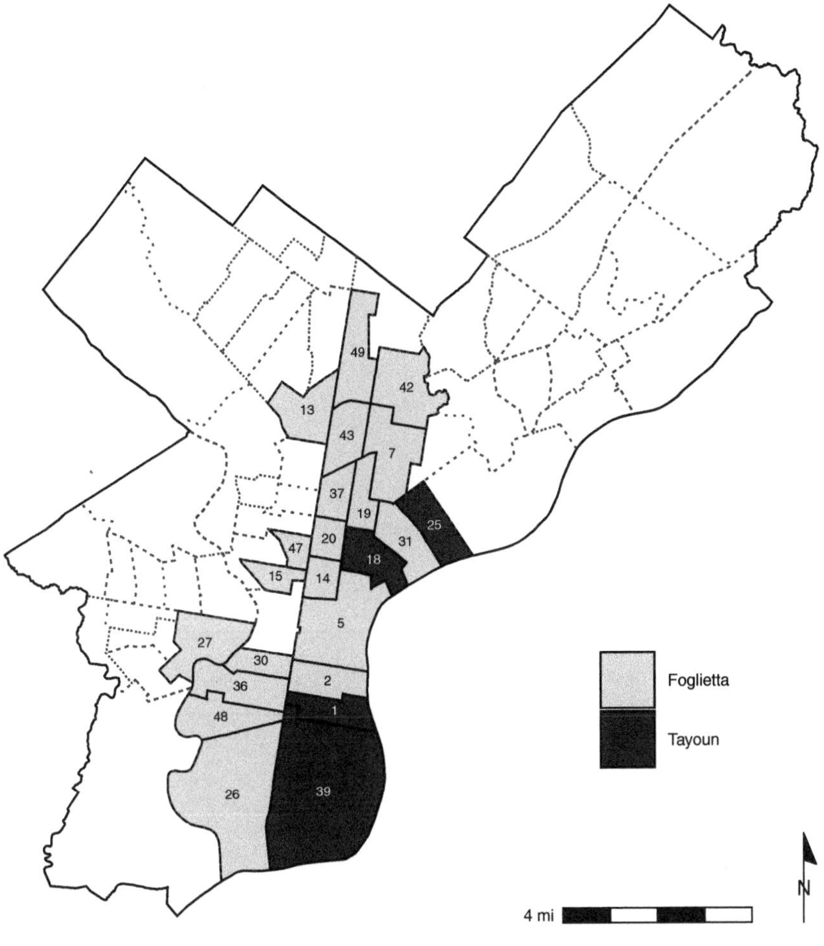

Figure 4.5 Wards won by Foglietta and Tayoun in 1986 primary election

Source: Access to election data provided to the author by Philadelphia City Commissioners; map by Michael Fichman.

jorities in many of them: 2,217 to 1,665 in the 2nd Ward, where Vignola was Democratic ward leader; 2,679 to 635 in the liberal downtown 5th Ward; as well as in the lower North Philadelphia wards with significant numbers of African American voters: 1,234 to 64 in the 47th; 1,030 to 215 in the 20th; 1,618 to 407 in the 37th; and 1,006 to 501 in the 19th.

"We got over 60 percent of the vote," Foglietta commented after the final returns had been reported. "If that doesn't convince him [Tayoun], nothing will."[42]

From a political perspective, Tom Foglietta was Chaka Fattah's opposite. Foglietta was born into a political family; notwithstanding the support he received from Hardy Williams and Williams's allies, Fattah had to grow his own political family. Fattah was an entrepreneur who created new political opportunities by reinvigorating an anemic political infrastructure. Foglietta did not create new political opportunities, but he possessed a quality that produced multiple successes in 1980s South Philadelphia: the ability to recognize opportunities when they emerged and to navigate his way through a changing, high-risk political environment.

5

★★★★★★★

Spoilers

Ed Rendell walked home before the polls closed on May 17, 1977. He took a shower and drafted a concession message in Western Union–style prose: "Dear Emmett, Congratulations. Ed Rendell."[1]

During most of the previous six months, Rendell had devoted all of his waking hours to his campaign against District Attorney F. Emmett Fitzpatrick, the incumbent candidate in the Democratic primary election. He had campaigned every day from dawn until late at night, greeting commuters at subway stations and rail platforms in the early morning and shaking hands with patrons of neighborhood bars as midnight neared.

In a conversation one evening as election day was approaching, James Tayoun offered Rendell some advice.

> Tayoun took me out for a drink one night with about six or seven weeks to go [Rendell recalled years later], and he said, "Look, you've run a great race. You've impressed people. You've got a great future. Withdraw now, and I guarantee you, we'll run you for something."
>
> I said, "I can't do that. I've put so much time into this." And he said, "You can't win because we're going to beat you down here [in South Philadelphia] five to one, and there's nowhere else in the city where you'll make that up."[2]

Owing in large part to the Democratic City Committee's endorsement of his candidacy, Fitzpatrick's campaign was on its way to amassing a budget of about $450,000. Rendell had raised only about $57,000. "I didn't have resources to give the public much information," he said. "I only did, literally, three days of ten-second TV commercials. I didn't have any radio or any direct mail." And the lower the flow of information from the campaign to the voter, Rendell observed, the more likely it is that the party, through its network of ward leaders and committeepeople, will control the election's outcome.[3]

The City Committee's strategy for combatting Rendell had been to ignore him; the alternative, attacking the challenger, might generate publicity that could draw attention to Rendell's campaign. So at the annual Jefferson-Jackson Day Dinner, the party's big campaign season event, Rendell's name was not mentioned by the main speaker, Mayor Frank L. Rizzo. Rizzo encouraged attendees to vote for Fitzpatrick and then moved on to other topics.

Rendell asked to speak at ward meetings, but only one ward committee gave him the opportunity to make a presentation: the one in his home ward, the 8th. The 8th Ward Democratic Committee subsequently endorsed his candidacy. No other ward committee allowed him to speak at a meeting. No other ward committee endorsed his candidacy.

When the polls closed and the vote tally was completed, Tayoun's prediction about the seven South Philadelphia wards was proven correct, to some extent; Rendell lost six of them, although by a much smaller margin than Tayoun had predicted. But Rendell won almost everything else: all of West, Northwest, and Northeast Philadelphia and Center City, as well as most of the Delaware River and North Philadelphia wards, as shown in Figure 5.1.

The outcome of the election was described as a "stunning setback" for Mayor Frank L. Rizzo's political organization, which had taken control of the city's Democratic Party leadership a year earlier.[4]

> [Democratic City Committee chair Martin] Weinberg had ordered the organization's . . . ward leaders to strive for a strictly controlled vote, one in which only the most loyal party members were encouraged to go to the polls.
>
> However, the turnout was higher than expected—about 30 percent—and it was apparent that the voters had defied the organization's wishes. The results also suggested that many of the ward leaders and committeemen may have covertly supported the reform candidates.[5]

The "Dear Emmett" message was never sent. Table 5.1 shows elections that led up to Rendell's victory.

This chapter is only partly about Ed Rendell. Although Rendell's strategy succeeded because it was well organized and relentlessly implemented,

Figure 5.1 1977 Democratic primary election for district attorney election results by ward

Source: Access to election data provided to the author by Philadelphia City Commissioners; map by Michael Fichman.

dissension within Philadelphia's Democratic Party, combined with errors and miscalculations made by influential politicians and the incumbent candidate, unexpectedly provided significant benefit to his campaign.

Specter's Fortunes

If Arlen Specter had not been a particularly ambitious person, he might have remained in office as Philadelphia district attorney for years, and Ed

TABLE 5.1 KEY ELECTIONS AND APPOINTMENT LEADING UP TO EDWARD G. RENDELL'S ELECTION

Year elected/ appointed	Governor	Mayor	District attorney	Democratic City Committee chair
Incumbent in 1960	David L. Lawrence	Richardson Dilworth		William J. Green Jr.
1961			James C. Crumlish Jr.	
1962	William W. Scranton	James H. J. Tate (appointed)		
1963		James H. J. Tate		Francis R. Smith
1964				
1965			Arlen Specter	
1966	Raymond P. Shafer			
1967		James H. J. Tate		William J. Green III
1968				
1969			Arlen Specter	Peter J. Camiel
1970	Milton J. Shapp			
1971		Frank L. Rizzo		
1972				
1973			F. Emmett Fitzpatrick	
1974	Milton J. Shapp			
1975		Frank L. Rizzo		
1976				Martin Weinberg
1977			*Edward G. Rendell*	

Source: Data for governor from National Governors Association, "Former Pennsylvania Governors," https://www.nga.org/former-governors/pennsylvania/ (accessed April 20, 2020); data for mayor and district attorney from Philadelphia Registration Commission, *Annual Reports* (Philadelphia: City of Philadelphia, 1962, 1963, 1965, 1967, 1979, 1971, 1973, 1975, 1977); data for Democratic City Committee chairs from Russell F. Weigley, ed., *Philadelphia: A 300-Year History* (New York: W. W. Norton, 1982), 659, 662, 663; and S. A. Paolantonio, *Frank Rizzo: The Last Big Man in Big City America* (Philadelphia: Camino Books, 1993), 162, 206.

Rendell might have spent much of his career reporting to him as a senior aide. Rendell respected and admired Specter, and he found the work energizing.[6] After years of successful performance in the DA's office, Rendell might subsequently have become a judge and retired after years on the bench.[7] If Specter had not been particularly ambitious about advancing his political fortunes and elevating his stature in the public sector, then Rendell might never have become Philadelphia DA, Philadelphia mayor, and governor of Pennsylvania.

However, Arlen Specter was extremely ambitious. Early in his career, he had served as assistant counsel to the Warren Commission investigating President John F. Kennedy's assassination, and his presentation of the "single-bullet theory"—the basis for the argument that Kennedy's killer acted alone—had attracted national attention. Later, as special assistant attorney general serving under Pennsylvania governor William W. Scranton, Specter had prosecuted cases against corrupt Philadelphia magistrates. He brought in twelve indictments.

In 1965, Specter decided to run for Philadelphia district attorney. Although a registered Democrat, he was unable to secure the party's support for his candidacy, so he made himself available to the Republican Party and obtained the GOP endorsement.

Specter succeeded in dominating the campaign season narrative. He called attention to the city's rising crime rate, charged that incumbent DA James C. Crumlish Jr. had not prosecuted criminal cases aggressively enough, and criticized Mayor James H. J. Tate for planning to increase real estate and wage taxes to fund salary raises for municipal employees.[8] A scary commercial produced by Specter's team drew widespread attention to the campaign and his candidacy by fueling fears of urban crime.[9]

Through the skillful use of these tactics, Specter was able to present himself as a champion of law and order as well as an advocate for good government, appealing to the interests of two constituencies that were not always aligned with each other. Specter's approach was successful. He defeated Crumlish 327,787 to 289,522, a win that the *Philadelphia Inquirer* characterized as a "smashing triumph" and "a severe blow to the Democratic organization, which held a 247,000 registration lead over the Republicans."[10]

The Philadelphia district attorney is an independently elected office that receives funding through the city's operating budget but does not report to the mayor. The mission of the office, as described on its website, is "to protect the community and provide a voice for victims of crime," prosecuting cases "ranging from minor offenses to felonies, including sexual assaults and murders."[11] Much of the staff (about six hundred employees in 2019) consists of assistant district attorneys who prosecute thousands of cases each year.

In Philadelphia, the district attorney's term of office is four years, and the DA is elected in what is known as an "off-year" election, meaning one in which the best-known offices—U.S. president, Pennsylvania governor, or Philadelphia mayor—are not on the ballot. The city controller also holds a four-year term of office and is elected in the same year as the DA. Although the two are elected individually, in some instances a DA candidate and a controller candidate will campaign together or work in coordination with one another as a team when it is felt to be mutually beneficial. In 2017, Rebecca Rhynhart shrewdly adopted a hybrid approach: she did not team up with a particular DA candidate, but, in a sense, she did not run individually either. As described in Chapter 1, she took advantage of the opportunity to have her name listed on the sample ballots of multiple candidates in the hotly contested DA race without endorsing any one of them individually.

The person holding the office of district attorney possesses more political power than many other elected officials. Without needing to consult anyone else, the district attorney can issue press releases and reports, hold news conferences, make speeches, and participate in civic and community events to gain public support for herself or to draw attention to an issue that she feels is important. Lynne Abraham, who held the office from 1991 to 2010, gained national recognition for seeking the death penalty in homicide cases "virtually as often as the law will allow."[12] Early in his first year in office, Lawrence Krasner announced that, as one way of reducing the city's population of unnecessarily incarcerated individuals, his office would stop seeking cash bail for people accused of some misdemeanors and nonviolent felonies.[13]

Arlen Specter used the resources of his office to elevate his already high profile. Among the actions announced during his first weeks in office: instituting a policy of padlocking taprooms that had accumulated multiple liquor code violations;[14] making a commitment to reduce the time required to bring criminal cases to trial, with particular emphasis on eliminating a backlog of more than three hundred rape cases;[15] and calling for a reform of the magistrates' system, announcing that his staff would be inspecting the books and records of these lower-court judges on a quarterly basis.[16]

Republican leaders sensed an opportunity to capitalize on Specter's success, and they began courting him to be the party's candidate for mayor in the November 1967 general election. A poll commissioned by the party indicated that Specter could easily beat either of the two leading contenders for the Democratic nomination: incumbent Mayor Tate and challenger Alexander Hemphill, a former city controller.[17] The poll results were published in February of the election year, and in early March, the Republican Party's candidate selection committee and the party's sixty-six ward leaders announced their unanimous support for Specter as their candidate for mayor.[18] At the time, the Democrats were still engaged in a protracted battle over their party's endorsement. Party chair Francis R. Smith and a group of ward leaders were working to persuade Tate to withdraw from the race, an effort that ultimately proved unsuccessful.[19]

Tate soundly defeated Hemphill in the May primary election, 152,949 to 81,238. Then, in contradiction to the February poll results, Tate beat Specter in the November election. However, Tate's margin of victory was the smallest in more than thirty years; the incumbent mayor won by about 11,000 votes out of a total of roughly 700,000 votes cast.

Tate was successful for several reasons. The city's first Catholic mayor, he had advocated for legislation providing state funding for parochial and private schools (Specter did not take a position on this legislation). The city's labor unions, longstanding supporters, brought Tate funding and campaign workers. Many of the thirty thousand municipal employees "who were given generous pay raises and promised a pension system so liberal that critics suspect it may be actuarily unsound"[20] cast their votes for Tate. Former Mayor Joseph Clark, at that time a U.S. senator, made campaign appearances with Tate, undermining Specter's efforts to portray himself as a candidate who embodied the principles of the 1951–1962 Clark-Dilworth reform era.[21] The factor that may have been most important, however, was Tate's appointment of Rizzo as police commissioner six months earlier, a move that had been encouraged by Congressman William Barrett.[22]

Specter had retained his position as DA during the mayoral campaign, and he easily won reelection in the 1969 fall election, outpolling his Democratic opponent, attorney David Berger, by more than 100,000 votes.

The next DA election, in 1973, was a critical one for both Specter and the Republican Party. City GOP chair William Meehan wanted to keep the DA's office under Republican control, but there was another reason why the 1973 election was important to him. On that date, voters would also elect thirty-nine judges to Common Pleas Court, along with a handful of other judges. According to the *Philadelphia Inquirer*, these judgeships represented more than two thousand patronage jobs in the court system.[23]

In a general election, many voters will be inclined to "pull the big lever" to automatically record votes for all of the candidates nominated by the party to which they belong (an option available on mechanical voting machines in use during the twentieth century). If a popular or well-known candidate is at the top of the ticket—the top of the ticket being, in this instance, the DA election—the greater the likelihood that more committed voters will come to the polls and vote for the party to which that candidate belongs. In this election, Meehan's best bet would be to keep Arlen Specter at the top of the ticket.

However, the party's goals appeared to be in conflict with Specter's ambitions. Specter had previously made known his interest in the prospect of running for governor in the 1974 election; but if he were to run for DA in 1973 and win, he would have to leave office only a few months later to enter the governor's race.

Choosing not to run for reelection would also be problematic. In that event, Meehan would lose Specter as a strong top-of-the-ticket candidate on the November 1973 ballot. Meehan might then show his displeasure with Specter by giving the GOP endorsement to some other candidate for governor in 1974.[24]

So Specter could choose to run for reelection to avoid alienating Meehan. However, because he had publicly expressed his interest on more than one occasion in considering a candidacy for governor, many voters who had supported Specter previously might not feel enthusiastic about reelecting a candidate who might decide to quit the job after a few months in office.

Specter probably concluded that there was no reasonable option other than to run for reelection, and he did; but it was not surprising that voter response to his candidacy in 1973 was far weaker than it had been in 1969.

And he was not successful. Emmett Fitzpatrick's victory was characterized as "a stunning upset" by Ed Rendell, who had been chief of Specter's homicide unit at the time. Specter had been overconfident, Rendell observed. "He really wasn't interested in the job anymore and was preparing to run for governor."[25]

As shown in Figure 5.2, Fitzpatrick outpolled Specter in several Northwest, West, and North Philadelphia wards that Specter had won in 1969. Citywide, 236,907 votes were cast for Fitzpatrick, and 208,731 were cast for Specter.

In the six wards where Specter had received more than 10,000 votes in the 1969 general election, Specter's vote totals in 1973 were much lower, as shown in Table 5.2. In the aggregate, Specter received about 20,000 fewer votes in these wards than in 1969, and he lost one of them (the 40th) altogether.

National politics likely influenced Specter's loss as well. The Watergate scandal dominated the news during 1973, and Philadelphia's November 6 election took place about two weeks after the "Saturday Night Massacre," in which Attorney General Elliott Richardson and his deputy, William G. Ruckelshaus, resigned rather than carry out President Richard Nixon's order to fire special prosecutor Archibald Cox. Celebrating Fitzpatrick's success at the polls on election night, city labor leader Wendell Young credited a "Watergate Whammy" factor, observing, "Watergate has made a lot of people suspicious of the other party." Pennsylvania Governor Milton Shapp had a different view. "More like Rizzogate," he said.[26]

Troubled Alliances

The DA election had major implications for the political future of Mayor Rizzo. During the 1973 election year, Rizzo had been engaged in an all-out battle with Peter J. Camiel, who had become chairman of the Democratic City Committee during the final years of the Tate administration. After the party's Policy Committee endorsed Fitzpatrick for DA and William Klenk for city controller in early March, Rizzo charged that Camiel had not given city managing director Hillel Levinson and two other prospective DA candidates the opportunity to make presentations to the Policy Committee and to be considered for endorsement. He accused Camiel of "bossism" and characterized the endorsement of Fitzpatrick as a "step backward for good government."[27]

Ten ward leaders joined Rizzo in refusing to support the committee's endorsements. One of them, James Tayoun, called Camiel a "dictator" and

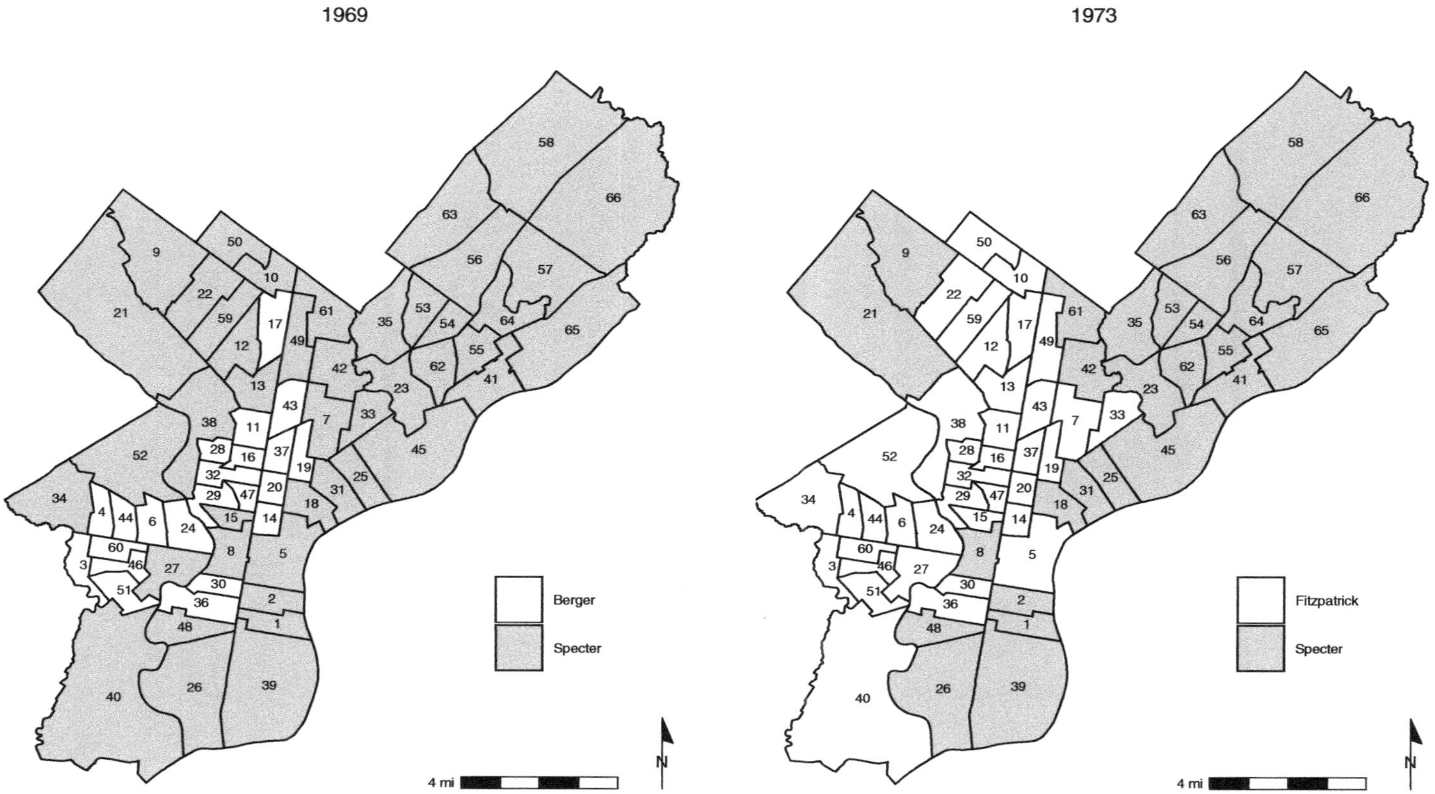

Figure 5.2 Results of November 1969 and November 1973 district attorney elections by ward

Source: Access to election data provided to the author by Philadelphia City Commissioners; map by Michael Fichman.

TABLE 5.2 ARLEN SPECTER'S ELECTION RESULTS IN SIX WARDS IN 1969 AND 1973 GENERAL ELECTIONS FOR DISTRICT ATTORNEY

Ward	1969	1973
21	13,083	8,318
66	12,369	9,400
58	11,556	9,210
39	11,516	8,374
56	10,424	7,595
40	10,002	5,701
Total	68,950	48,598

Source: Access to election data provided to the author by Philadelphia City Commissioners.

charged him with "hand-picking" Fitzpatrick and Klenk.[28] Rizzo announced that he planned to "restructure" the Democratic City Committee and replace Camiel.[29] Responding with charges of his own, Camiel alleged that Rizzo had tried to bribe him several weeks earlier by suggesting that he could give Camiel the ability to select architects who would be awarded city contracts if Camiel would agree to endorse political candidates supported by Rizzo.

Rizzo was as ambitious a politician as Specter, and at the time, he was in a position to consider two options that could lead to future political success: run for a second mayoral term in 1975, or run for governor in 1974. Rizzo had performed well at the polls in 1971, and if he chose to remain in city government, he could run for a second term with a good chance of winning; or he could run for governor against incumbent Milton Shapp—as a Republican. If Rizzo were to switch parties in preparation for a gubernatorial campaign, President Nixon, with whom Rizzo had already begun cultivating a relationship, would be a major supporter. Rizzo had advocated for Nixon's reelection in 1972, and Nixon could return the favor by helping Rizzo win the 1974 governor's race. For Rizzo, both scenarios would necessitate "restructuring" Philadelphia's Democratic Party and getting rid of Camiel.

Arlen Specter's ambition represented a significant problem for Rizzo with respect to both of these options. He and Specter had established a good working relationship during the years in which Rizzo had been police commissioner and Specter had served as DA. If Specter remained DA while Rizzo became governor, this positive relationship could continue, but a Specter candidacy for governor would end it. Although Rizzo would be likely to win a Specter versus Rizzo race for governor, the position of Philadelphia district attorney that Specter would vacate to enter the race would probably be filled by a Democrat who owed his job to Camiel. Then the investigations of police misconduct and municipal corruption (which had already begun, but which Specter had not pursued aggressively as a political priority) would be likely to multiply.

In light of this situation, Rizzo was especially displeased that Camiel had not given him the opportunity to pick a DA candidate for the party to endorse. With that opportunity, Rizzo could have secured the endorsement for a weak candidate—someone like Hillel Levinson—to increase the chances that Specter would win. Instead, Camiel chose the DA candidate that the Policy Committee subsequently endorsed: Emmett Fitzpatrick—exactly the kind of person who, as Camiel's protégé, could make trouble for Rizzo as a Republican governor.

Rizzo did not retract his comments about Fitzpatrick being a "step backward," but he did not endorse Specter either. "I tell you Arlen Specter is an excellent district attorney and does an excellent job," he told an *Inquirer* reporter. "Arlen is a great, fine guy."[30]

The 1973 campaign was dull. The *Philadelphia Inquirer* reported that "[Fitzpatrick's] major campaign theme was that Specter was a politician who planned to resign and run for governor next. . . . He also hammered away at what he said was Specter's failure to make the streets safe after eight years as district attorney." Fitzpatrick completed the campaign season "without having proposed a single major program." Specter, for his part, "ran a decidedly low-key campaign, making as few public appearances as possible, and brushing aside Fitzpatrick's charges as political and untrue."[31]

During the years leading up to his candidacy for district attorney, Emmett Fitzpatrick had earned a reputation as one of Philadelphia's top criminal lawyers. Before then, he had served as an assistant district attorney under James Crumlish, the DA who had preceded Specter and was defeated by him in 1965. As a defense lawyer, Fitzpatrick had represented some unsavory characters, including Major Benjamin Coxson, a drug kingpin.[32] In exchanges with voters during the course of the campaign, Fitzpatrick could display "the criminal lawyer's penchant for stinging debate."[33] His campaign was disorganized and underfunded.[34] He initially stated that he would not give up his private law practice after being elected DA and then changed his mind in the face of strong opposition.[35]

Fitzpatrick's comments on Frank Rizzo had an evenhanded tone early in the campaign but turned negative as election day approached. In a September 9, 1973, interview, Fitzpatrick said, "I would have expected his ringing endorsement," based on Fitzpatrick's recollection that "[Rizzo] took what I regarded as a liking to me" years earlier when Rizzo was a police captain and Fitzpatrick was an assistant DA.[36] A month later, however, Fitzpatrick was calling for the DA's office to investigate the use of private funds to refurbish Rizzo's City Hall office and the financing of a home that had been built for Rizzo by a contractor friend.[37]

Fitzpatrick's positive characteristics could not be considered extraordinary: He would not resign a few months after taking office to run for another office, as Specter might do. He had been endorsed by the Democratic Party. He campaigned hard. He had not done anything that would detract from his candidacy in a serious way, and he had not done anything that would embarrass his supporters. In 1973, that was, apparently, about all it took to surprise Arlen Specter with an upset win.

Fitzpatrick versus Fitzpatrick

Three years passed, 1974 through 1976. Recalling Fitzpatrick's performance in office, Ed Rendell characterized his record as "fair." "He did some good things, and he did some bad things—he was just fair."[38]

By the end of 1976, however, the public's perception of Fitzpatrick as a person—apart from his record as DA—had changed. Fitzpatrick had been beset by problems that, in the aggregate, redefined him in such negative terms that his performance in carrying out the responsibilities of district attorney was, in a way, beside the point.

What did Fitzpatrick do wrong? Upon taking office, he refused to staff the grand jury that Arlen Specter had convened to investigate political corruption. He was suspected of being complicit in the filing of a false report of a crime—a scheme allegedly concocted by a former law firm client to conceal the payment of a debt to the mob. He had refused to testify before a federal grand jury about that incident, invoking the Fifth Amendment.[39] He told participants in a candidates forum convened by several women's groups that he did not see the need to create a special unit in the DA's office to handle rape cases and domestic violence cases.[40] He charged taxpayers for excessive out-of-town travel.

> The crowning blow came when he attended a National District Attorneys Association Conference in Montreal. Upon his return, he put in a voucher for $184 for dinner, which he said he paid for several other cities' DAs at a seafood restaurant called Aquascutom. *The Philadelphia Inquirer* . . . discovered that Aquascutom was not a restaurant but a clothing store and the $184 was for a safari suit purchased by Fitzpatrick. The voucher was an attempt to get the public to pay for it!
>
> The safari suit was the last straw.[41]

Given the accumulation of negative reports about Fitzpatrick, Rendell anticipated that someone would challenge Fitzpatrick in the 1977 Democratic primary, probably some high-profile lawyer or judge. But no one came forward, "primarily because [prospective challengers] were afraid of the mayor and the Democratic machine. The mayor could be and often was vengeful, and the machine was still incredibly strong."[42]

So Rendell decided that he would be the challenger. He had always been interested in the possibility of running for office, and the Democratic primary was his opportunity. Without the luxury of funding to introduce himself through mailings or commercials, he would campaign night and day—literally—in meetings and public places. He and his wife would live off her salary and their savings for five months, mid-December to mid-May.

A lot of voters had heard enough about Fitzpatrick to conclude that they did not want to reelect him, so Rendell did not need to devote a lot of time to telling people about Fitzpatrick's shortcomings. He just had to tell people—a lot of people—that there was an alternative.

> I had the great good fortune of Fitzpatrick being universally unpopular, of being pounded by the papers, being pounded by some TV and radio commentators. People knew that they didn't want to elect Fitzpatrick. So the one thing I did was to let people know that there was someone running against him. My task was to let them know that there was opposition.[43]

Rendell had the advantage of being personable and outgoing. He could strike up a conversation with anyone, and he was rarely at a loss for words. He was a hard-core fan of both college and professional sports, and he would be comfortable talking sports with patrons of any neighborhood bar or diner. Those people would be more interested in joking about the Phillies than in discussing the fine points of prosecutorial policy. And all he wanted was to meet them and have them experience him as a likable person who was an alternative to Fitzpatrick. He wanted to stimulate next-day conversations—"This guy who's running against Fitzpatrick was at the bar last night"—and promote word-of-mouth communication about his candidacy.

In the early months of the campaign, Rendell had to decide how to spend $10,000 that he had available for promotion. He got some advice from former City Committee chair Peter Camiel (who had been deposed as head of City Committee in 1976 after Rizzo's takeover of the party following his reelection as mayor in 1975). Rendell had previously done some volunteer lawyering for City Committee, and he and Camiel were on good terms.

> The question was, should we buy radio? With $10,000 in those days, you could buy a good week of radio, maybe ten days. Or do we buy billboards?

> Camiel suggested billboards. He said, "For $10,000, you could get one hundred billboards that will be up there for two months. Not the big highway billboards but neighborhood billboards. They sit up there, and people pass them time after time on their way to work; it's on their route. Before the election, they'll look at it again and again."
>
> So we did billboards, and they worked. They let people know that there was someone running against Fitzpatrick. [Featuring a vest-attired, stern-looking photo of Rendell], they said, "It's a matter of integrity," which was a big knock against Fitzpatrick.[44]

Rendell also found a way to use the ward and division structure to his campaign's advantage, as a result of information that his team obtained about the outcomes of the most recent ward leader elections. As described in Chapter 1, ward leaders are elected by a majority vote of committeepeople in each ward. Rendell found it beneficial to analyze the results of these elections on a ward-by-ward basis.

> Even though the ward structure was very strong, in almost every ward there are dissidents. We did good research and found that John Jones tried to unseat the ward leader in some ward—he ran against the ward leader and he lost, thirty-six to twenty-eight; but that means that Jones had about half the ward on his side. So we found the twenty-eight dissident committeemen, and a lot of them stood up for us for no money and handed out stuff that said "Rendell." So on election day, you had one guy who was handing out stuff that said "Fitzpatrick" and "the Official Democratic Ballot," and you had another guy handing out stuff that said "Rendell" and "the New Democratic Ballot."[45]

Rendell had not initially planned on coordinating his campaign with that of incumbent city controller William Klenk, who had been endorsed for reelection by a unanimous vote of the Democratic Party's Policy Committee in February, at the same meeting at which Fitzpatrick was endorsed. However, when Klenk publicly took exception to the city finance director's budget projections (charging that Philadelphia's operating deficit would be more than twice as large as the finance director had projected—as much as $70 million, as opposed to $30 million), Rizzo demanded that Klenk be replaced as the party-endorsed candidate. City Committee subsequently recruited Andrew G. Freeman, executive director of the Philadelphia Urban League, to become the endorsed nominee for controller (Freeman had been a registered Republican up until that time). The withdrawal of the party's planned endorsement left Klenk free to coordinate his campaign activities with Rendell, making it possible for the two of them to present themselves as the reform alternative to Rizzo's candidates.[46]

Although Rendell consistently refrained from criticizing Rizzo directly, many people who volunteered for his campaign had been active in the Citizens Committee to Recall Rizzo, a movement that had been organized in 1976 with the goal of removing Rizzo from office. Richard Chapman, executive director of the regional chapter of Americans for Democratic Action, which had played a central role in the recall movement, took charge of field operations for the Rendell campaign.

The recall movement had attracted a wide range of people who were opposed to Rizzo for one or more of three reasons. Rizzo had presented a misleading, no-new-taxes version of the city budget during the 1975 election year; then, a month after being reelected, he called for a massive tax increase. As a cost-saving measure, Rizzo abruptly ordered the closing of Philadelphia General Hospital, the city's only public hospital. And Rizzo had encouraged a blockade of the *Philadelphia Inquirer* building by trade union members after the publication of a satirical column that portrayed the mayor as vulgar and uneducated (city police stood by without intervening, and it was not until federal authorities got involved that the paper was able to resume operations).[47]

Although the Citizens Committee filed petitions containing more than 211,000 signatures, with enough valid signatures to place a recall referendum question on the November 1976 ballot, the recall drive was stopped by a Pennsylvania Supreme Court ruling that the Philadelphia Home Rule Charter provision for recall was unlawful.[48] For frustrated recall-movement participants, the May 1977 election was the next opportunity to take action in support of city government reform.

Years later, Richard Chapman described the value that the recall movement represented to the Rendell campaign. Just after announcing his candidacy, Rendell came to Chapman's office, and Chapman said something that surprised him.

> I said, "Look, you're going to win this hands down."
>
> "Why are you saying that?" Rendell asked.
>
> "It's because I have, sitting here, thousands of names and addresses of people who hate the mayor—who signed their names!" So he would know who they are [and how to reach them].
>
> "We have hundreds of people who went and collected the signatures. And they're all furious at the supreme court for throwing out the recall. They're looking for revenge. And you're it—you're the revenge. I guarantee it."

> Long afterward, Ed told me, "You were the only person that year who said to me, 'You're definitely going to win this election.'"[49]

Although anti-Rizzo sentiment remained high, Rendell knew it would be much more advantageous for him to focus exclusively on anti-Fitzpatrick sentiment. And, Rendell recalled, "Rizzo didn't get engaged because nobody thought I was going to win."[50]

Unexpected help came from other sources. Anthony Ianarelli, who had been fired from his position as executive director of the Philadelphia Parking Authority by Rizzo, apparently in connection with the issue of hiring patronage workers,[51] "clued us in to all [intraparty] dissension in Northeast Philadelphia," according to Rendell.[52]

Six weeks before the election, Rendell and Klenk received the endorsement of the Philadelphia Party, which had been created by Charles W. Bowser as the vehicle for his 1975 candidacy for mayor (and which Bowser intended to serve the same purpose in connection with a 1979 campaign for mayor that he was considering). Bowser promised to campaign for the two candidates and pledged the support of as many as 1,200 poll watchers and election day workers. "The [party-]endorsed candidates are the hand-picked candidates of Frank Rizzo," Bowser said, "and if we don't stop Rizzo in 1977, it's going to be almost impossible to stop him in 1979."[53] Bowser's commitment was a welcome development. At the start of Rendell's campaign, the extent to which African American political activists would engage in the 1977 election had been unclear.

The news media, while not unaware of the progress of Rendell's campaign, underestimated its potential strength. In March, *Inquirer* reporter Paul Critchlow observed:

> Fitzpatrick remains personally popular with many ward leaders. And those leaders in the most tightly controlled wards, where massive margins are routinely rolled up, show no signs of wavering. These include State Sen. Henry J. (Buddy) Cianfrani (2nd Ward). House Speaker Herbert Fineman (52nd) and City Council President George X. Schwartz (34th)—all of whom exert enormous influence on other ward leaders.[54]

As it turned out, Fitzpatrick won the 2nd Ward but lost the "tightly controlled" 52nd and 34th to Rendell.

In May, a week before the election, Critchlow reported:

> Despite his image problems, Fitzpatrick is considered the favorite to win the Democratic nomination. . . .

> Fitzpatrick has solid labor backing, and he remains popular with all but a handful of the Democratic Committee's 69 ward leaders.
>
> Additionally, Mayor Rizzo has begun to campaign strenuously on Fitzpatrick's behalf. . . . The mayor said he had made one of the "most serious mistakes in his life" opposing Fitzpatrick's election four years ago. Rizzo explained that his opposition to Fitzpatrick had resulted from his feud with the now-deposed party chairman, Peter J. Camiel.[55]

None of these factors made an appreciable difference on election day. In addition to winning most of the city's wards, Rendell outpolled city controller William Klenk, the other top-of-the-ticket candidate, by more than twenty thousand votes, notwithstanding the fact that Klenk, as an incumbent candidate, had started the year with greater name recognition than Rendell, the newcomer.

Andrew Freeman, Klenk's opponent for city controller, was not a strong campaigner, according to Rendell, and he had no significant campaign experience. Although Klenk lost six more wards than Rendell, he received almost twice as many votes as Freeman, with strong support in a substantial number of wards with a predominantly African American population.

Years later, Rendell explained that the Democratic City Committee could have avoided an embarrassing defeat by adopting a relatively simple strategy.

> If I had been [City Committee chair] Marty Weinberg, I would have seen that Fitzpatrick was unpopular enough to be in danger of losing. And despite Fitzpatrick's manifest unpopularity, I could have won the primary for him. I would have called three or four lawyers that I knew wanted to get the party's endorsement for judge. I would have said, "It's not your time to be judge yet. We're going to slate you for judge two years from now. But now you've got to get a thousand signatures to file a petition to run for district attorney. You don't have to do anything else—just get your name on the ballot."
>
> So then, when the voters come into the voting booth and look at the ballot, they see Rendell, they see Fitzpatrick, but they also see [three or four other candidates' names]. [Rendell and the three or four other candidates] split the negative vote, and Fitzpatrick wins. If that had happened, I might have won anyway—or I might have come in second, I might have lost. But the organization was overconfident. They didn't bother to do that. They could have done that, and that would have been the end of it.[56]

As it turned out, the May election ended Emmett Fitzpatrick's political career.

After taking office, Rendell did not go out of his way to become Rizzo's political adversary. Reconstituting the DA's office and positioning himself for future reelection were more important priorities. However, Rizzo would have preferred Fitzpatrick, particularly in light of the fact that Rendell owed much of his electoral success to thousands of revenge-seeking Rizzo-recall supporters. Just as, four years earlier, Specter had been overconfident about his prospects for beating Fitzpatrick, Rizzo and his supporters had been overconfident about Fitzpatrick's prospects against Rendell. Just as Fitzpatrick had been the spoiler of Specter's gubernatorial ambitions in 1973, Rendell had become a spoiler (although not the only spoiler) of Rizzo's ambition to increase his control over both the Democratic Party and city government in 1977.

Troubled Town

The author of *Race, Poverty, and Unemployment Task Force: Interim Report* put it bluntly:

> The Task Force was not optimistic about the city's future. This view was generated in part by past trends and in part by the growing conservatism in the country. Needless to say, these two factors, coupled with a nagging uncertainty about the country's future (let alone the city's) made for an understandable reticence when it came to predicting the city's prospects.[57]

The *Interim Report*, part of a wide-ranging research project known as Philadelphia: Past, Present, and Future, was published in the early 1980s, not long after the start of Ronald Reagan's presidential administration. In the preceding decade, Philadelphia had lost more residents than at any time in the city's history; total population had declined from 1,948,609 in 1970 to 1,688,210 in 1980. The unemployment rate had grown from 4.6 percent in 1970 to 11.2 percent in 1980, and the percentage of Philadelphians receiving public assistance had grown from 14.2 percent to 19.8 percent during that time. Between 1979 and 1980 alone, the city had lost nearly 10,000 manufacturing jobs.[58]

The *Interim Report* was published during what would have been Mayor Rizzo's third consecutive term of office, which would have extended from 1980 to 1983. To serve a third term, Rizzo would have had to win reelection in 1979; but for him to run for reelection in 1979, a majority of voters would have had to approve an amendment of Philadelphia's Home Rule Charter to remove the two-term limit to which the position of mayor was subject. Rizzo wanted to run again, and in 1978, he launched a movement to change the charter. The referendum question was placed on the November ballot.

The results of the referendum were dramatically different from the results of the two mayoral primary elections that Rizzo had won earlier that decade; the proposed amendment was rejected by a two-to-one ratio, with "no" votes winning forty-nine of the city's sixty-six wards, exceeding "yes" votes in several wards that Rizzo had won in the past two mayoral primaries. As a comparison of Figures 5.3 and 5.4 shows, Rizzo failed to win "yes" votes in many north and northeast Philadelphia wards that had produced a majority of votes for him in 1971 and 1975. "No" votes won in West Philadelphia's 34th Ward, where City Council president George X. Schwartz was ward leader. "No" votes won in Kensington's blue-collar 18th Ward. Even the late Congressman Barrett's ward, the 36th, delivered a "no" majority.

Although the charter-change election was, in effect, a referendum on Frank Rizzo, it was unlike the two elections in which he had been a candidate. There was no opportunity for Rizzo to take advantage of an opponent's weaknesses or to split the opposition vote between two other contenders.

Many citizens hated Rizzo; they would have voted against him in any election. But why did so many of his supporters, the voters who had turned out in large numbers for him in 1975, fail to get behind the charter-change movement? There was no question that the mayor wanted to seek a third term; so why not give him the opportunity to try?

For some voters, the decision to choose No may have been influenced by the city's distressed condition, combined with a feeling that Rizzo was not improving Philadelphia's economic status and may have been worsening it. Back in the 1950s, it had been in the self-interest of political and business leaders to look the other way when Rizzo, as police inspector, beat up drunken sailors and harassed coffeehouse patrons. But it was not in their self-interest, or in the general public's self-interest, for Rizzo, as mayor, to lie about the city's financial condition and then raise taxes a few weeks after his reelection; to shut down the city's only public hospital without proposing an alternative way of addressing local needs for affordable health care; or to have the police force stand by while union members illegally attempted to stop publication of the city's major newspaper.

In their history of postwar Philadelphia, Joseph and Dennis Clark observed, "The reform movement of the 1940s and 1950s really died when Dilworth resigned as mayor [in 1962 to run for governor],"[59] and the political climate steadily worsened during the years that followed. In 1967, Democratic City Committee chair Francis Smith worked to prevent Tate from being reelected, mobilizing ward leaders to support the candidacy of Alexander Hemphill. Then Tate got rid of Smith after defeating Hemphill.

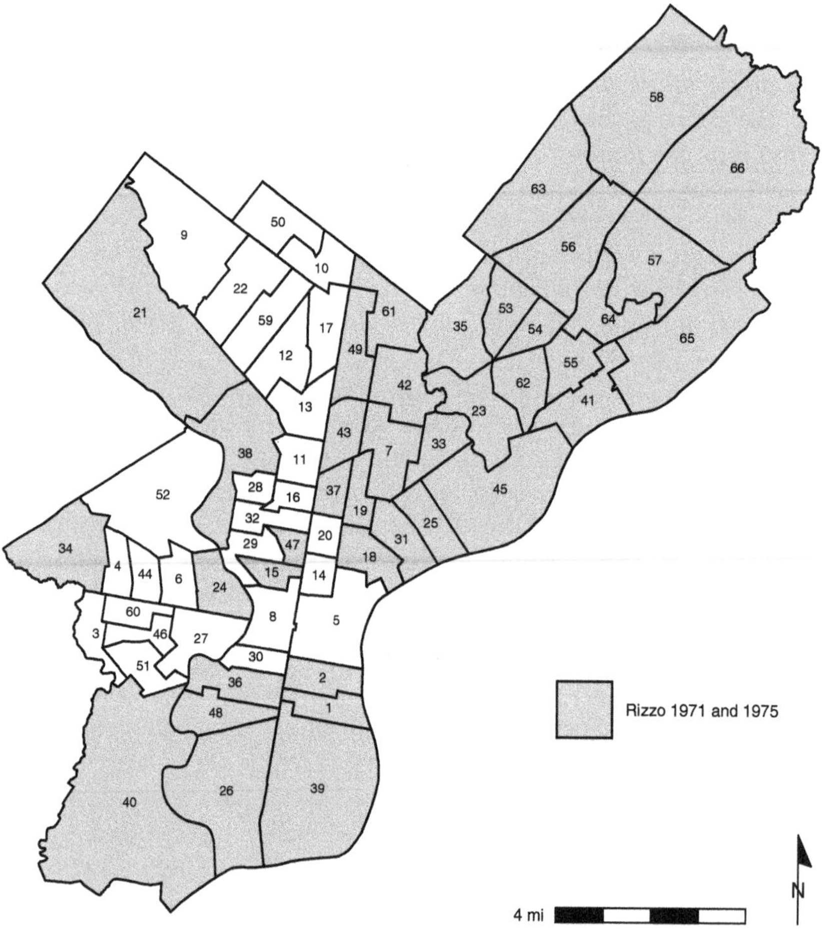

Figure 5.3 Wards won by Rizzo in the 1971 and 1975 general elections

Source: Access to election data provided to the author by Philadelphia City Commissioners; map by Michael Fichman.

Two years later, Congressman William J. Green III, who succeeded Smith, blamed Tate for the party's failure in the 1969 election, in which Arlen Specter defeated the party's candidate, David Berger. "The Mayor had an iron grip on the party machinery," Green said. "The responsibility for defeat should be placed squarely where it belongs."[60]

The relationship became even more adversarial during Rizzo's mayoral tenure, and public awareness of the ongoing city-party conflicts during these years likely dampened many citizens' confidence in the quality and reliability of municipal governance. Rizzo and Peter Camiel, Green's successor as City Committee chair, quickly squared off against each other after

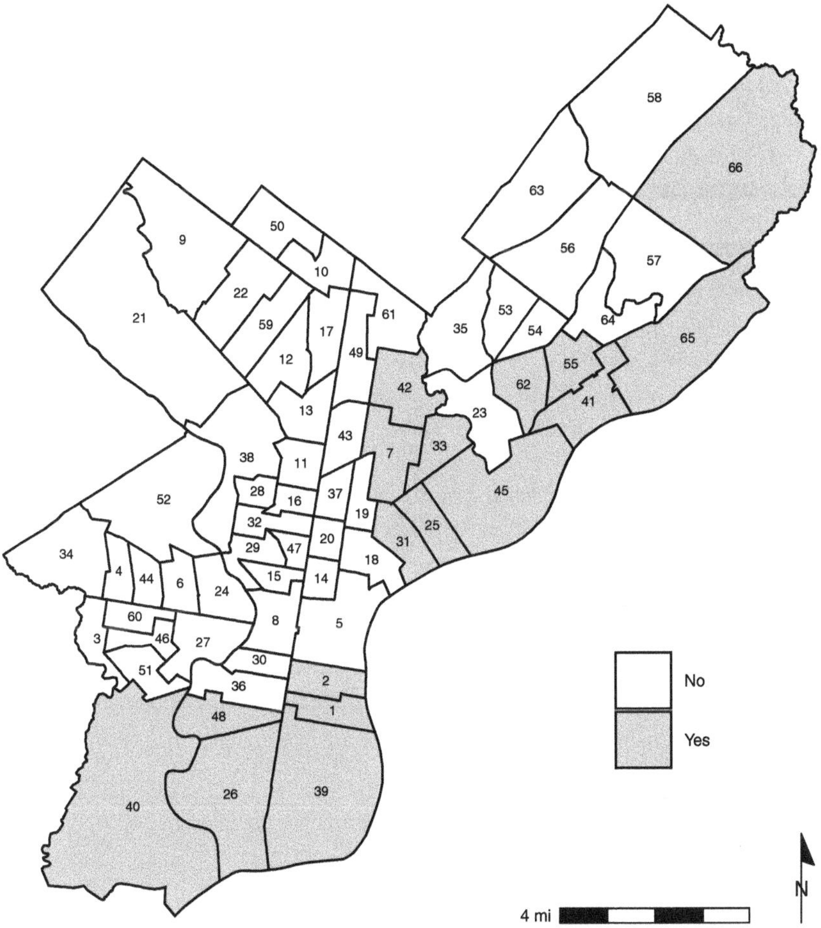

Figure 5.4 Yes and no votes in 1978 Charter Change Referendum by ward

Source: Access to election data provided to the author by Philadelphia City Commissioners; map by Michael Fichman.

Rizzo became mayor. In 1973, when Camiel accused Rizzo of offering him a bribe in connection with the DA candidate-endorsement process, the mayor's denial of the accusation and related charges and countercharges were widely publicized. In response to an invitation from the *Philadelphia Daily News*, Rizzo agreed to take a lie-detector test to resolve the matter, as did Camiel. Rizzo failed the test, and Camiel passed. Likely no one felt that these political conflicts contributed anything to the health of Philadelphia's economy or the well-being of its citizens.

Philadelphians' views about the relationship between the state of the city, Rizzo's leadership, and municipal governance were also reflected in the results of an exit poll that was conducted on May 17, 1983, the primary election day on which Rizzo was defeated by W. Wilson Goode, who had served as managing director in Bill Green's mayoral administration.

> Everyone is concerned about jobs. . . . The concern . . . gripped every section of the city, every income bracket, every political background. . . .
>
> Fully 61 percent of the voters chose negative responses to describe Rizzo. The largest bloc, 30 percent, saw him as "phony." The next most frequent choices were "mismanaged the city" and "can't deal with today's problems." The positive responses—"tough," a "leader" and "gets things done"—were seen as Rizzo's main attributes by only 38 percent of all those polled.[61]

Commenting on Rebecca Rhynhart's spectacular success in the 2017 city controller election, Kellan White said Rhynhart's campaign took advantage of the "chaos in the DA's race,"[62] which had been the central focus of that particular election. In a similar manner, Specter in 1965 and Rendell in 1977 achieved their respective victories by taking advantage of the chaos in the Democratic Party and the widespread anxiety about the city's current condition and future prospects that was characteristic of those years.

6

★★★★★★★

Fearless

How do you become the leading political figure associated with a key Philadelphia demographic? Joseph Clark and Richardson Dilworth, endorsed by city business leaders, drew heavily on support from people like themselves: residents of white, middle- and upper-income neighborhoods who were inspired by the idea that political reform, the revitalization of the city's economy, and a substantial improvement in the well-being of Philadelphia's citizens were achievable in the postwar years. Frank Rizzo's Italian heritage, charisma, and tough-cop persona, as well as his links to Congressman William Barrett and South Philadelphia's political infrastructure, made him an inevitable candidate for mayor during a time when many longtime residents feared that the depopulation and economic disinvestment they were witnessing during the 1970s would lead to social disorder. Wilson Goode organized African American political empowerment campaigns, became a movement leader who was also skilled at collaboration and power sharing, and earned the trust of business leaders through his performance as chair of the state's Public Utility Commission and as the city's managing director during the administration of Mayor William J. Green III.

Given these characteristics, considered in isolation, the person most likely to become the predominant political figure associated with the aspirations of Philadelphia's Hispanic community before and after the turn of the twenty-first century would be Nelson A. Díaz. Díaz thought so; he became a candidate for mayor in the 2015 Democratic primary election. Díaz was well known and respected for his years of service to Philadelphia's Latino community. He had been the first Latino to become a common pleas court judge. He had served as general counsel at the U.S. Department of Housing and Urban Development under Secretary Henry Cisneros and as Philadelphia's city solicitor in the administration of Mayor John F. Street. He served on corporate boards, and he was a partner in Dilworth Paxson, the firm that Richardson Dilworth had joined in 1938. He had developed and maintained strong working relationships with Philadelphia civic, business, and political leaders, and he was ready for a new career challenge.

Díaz was aware that an outstanding record of civic leadership and public service does not necessarily guarantee success in a mayoral campaign. He announced his candidacy in early January 2015 and hired campaign support. He received the endorsement of Latinos United for Political Empowerment (LUPE), a group of Latino political leaders, and he had been actively pursuing an endorsement from a group of Northwest Philadelphia ward leaders who had been consistently successful in generating high turnouts for candidates they supported.

However, Díaz's campaign lost its potential for success well before the May primary. In April, LUPE withdrew its endorsement after Díaz rejected the group's request that he provide more than $100,000 in campaign contributions to politicians associated with LUPE and that he campaign with Manny Morales, who was running for City Council against incumbent Maria Quiñones-Sánchez. Díaz had previously announced that he and Morales were running mates, but he withdrew his support after it was reported that racist and homophobic content had appeared on Morales's Facebook account. In place of Díaz, LUPE endorsed mayoral candidate James Kenney without conditioning its endorsement on a commitment to back Morales (whom Kenney did not support).[1] The electricians union, IBEW Local 98, which was actively and energetically backing Kenney's campaign, made substantial contributions to three LUPE ward leaders who were now supporting Kenney for mayor.[2] According to Díaz, Local 98 leader John Dougherty also "had the money to offer support to all three of my main sources in the Northwest," who subsequently endorsed Kenney as well.[3] Kenney won the primary election in a landslide and was elected mayor in November 2015.

Rising Star

By that time, Maria Quiñones-Sánchez had become well known in Philadelphia, both within and outside the city's Latino community. She had served as a legislative aide to two City Council members, Angel Ortiz and

Marian Tasco. She had become the first female and youngest executive director of ASPIRA Inc. of Pennsylvania, the largest nonprofit organization devoted to education and services for Latino children and families in the state. While at ASPIRA, she oversaw the creation of the first bilingual charter school in Pennsylvania. Subsequently, as regional director for the Puerto Rico Federal Affairs Administration, she supervised voter registration and get-out-the-vote campaigns that produced thirty-two thousand new voters in Pennsylvania and Delaware. First elected to council in 2007, Quiñones-Sánchez was a leading supporter of legislation authorizing the creation of the Philadelphia Land Bank, as well as assistance programs for homeowners threatened by foreclosure, and a variety of education, workforce development, and small business support measures. In 2009, *Philadelphia Magazine* named her one of the "50 Most Influential" in the city of Philadelphia.[4]

Quiñones-Sánchez was elected district councilwoman for the 7th District in 2007, defeating incumbent Daniel J. Savage and another candidate in the Democratic primary. In that election, Quiñones-Sánchez won majorities in most of the district's eleven wards, as shown in Figure 6.1, and defeated Savage by nearly 1,700 votes.

In 2011, Quiñones-Sánchez and Savage competed again. This time Savage won one ward that Quiñones-Sánchez had won four years previously (the 63rd). However, Quiñones-Sánchez's margin of victory was much higher; she won by nearly 2,500 votes. Table 6.1 shows significant elections that led up to and, in some instances, influenced Maria Quiñones-Sánchez's successful campaigns.

The redistricting process that was instituted after the 2011 elections gave the 7th Council District a population that was predominantly Hispanic. Previous iterations of the district map had split the Hispanic population between two or more districts, reducing Hispanic voters' capability to elect one of their own. The newly configured district map included a high concentration of Hispanic residents.

The redistricting and the associated voting power of the Latino population provided a new opportunity for this community to enhance its political standing. Political activists could work to consistently deliver Latino votes to Democratic Party–endorsed candidates in exchange for priority access to certain jobs and services, as South Philadelphia political operatives had done during the late twentieth century; or they could create a parallel ad hoc political infrastructure, in which block captains and civic association leaders took over voter registration, voter education, and get-out-the-vote responsibilities to outflank the committeepeople and ward leaders who populated the existing anemic ward and division system, as Chaka Fattah and others had done in West Philadelphia decades earlier.

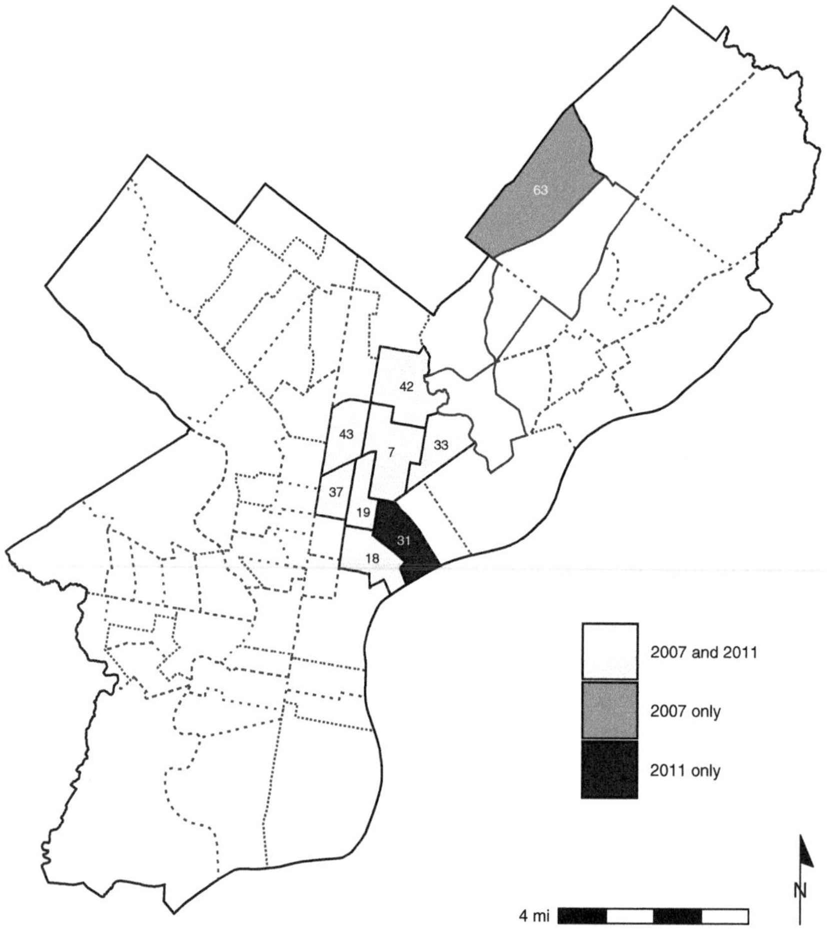

Figure 6.1 Wards won by Maria Quiñones-Sánchez in 2007 and 2011 Democratic primary elections

Source: Data from Philadelphia City Commissioners, "Archived Data Sets: 2007 Primary" and "Archived Data Sets: 2011 Primary," https://www.philadelphiavotes.com/en/resources-a-data/ballot-box-app/additional-election-results-data; map by Michael Fichman.

Obstacles to Empowerment

However, the Latino community possessed significant disadvantages—some inherited from past history, others newly emerging—that would make any political empowerment strategy difficult to achieve in the short term. Some of the highest concentrations of poverty in the city could be found in neighborhoods across the district.[5] A market value analysis completed by the Reinvestment Fund categorized many of the district's neighborhood housing markets as "stressed," with relatively high levels of housing vacancy

TABLE 6.1 KEY ELECTIONS LEADING UP TO AND FOLLOWING MARIA D. QUIÑONES-SÁNCHEZ'S ELECTIONS

Year elected	Mayor	District councilperson, 7th District	PA House member, 180th District	Democratic City Committee chair
Incumbent in 2004	John F. Street	Richard T. Mariano	Angel Cruz	Robert A. Brady
2005				
2006		Daniel J. Savage	Angel Cruz	
2007	Michael A. Nutter	*Maria D. Quiñones-Sánchez**		
2008			Angel Cruz	
2009				
2010			Angel Cruz	
2011	Michael A. Nutter	*Maria D. Quiñones-Sánchez†*		
2012			Angel Cruz	
2013				
2014			Angel Cruz	
2015	James F. Kenney	*Maria D. Quiñones-Sánchez‡*		

Source: Access to 2004 and 2006 data for mayor, district councilperson, and PA House member provided to the author by Philadelphia City Commissioners; 2007, 2011, and 2015 data for mayor, district councilperson, and PA House member from Philadelphia City Commissioners, "Archived Data Sets," https://www.philadelphiavotes.com/en/resources-a-data/ballot-box-app/additional-election-results-data; data for Democratic City Committee chair from Roll Call, "Robert A. Brady," http://media.cq.com/members/408 (accessed April 20, 2020).

* Defeated Daniel J. Savage and Marnie Aument-Loughrey

† Defeated Daniel J. Savage

‡ Defeated Manny Morales

and foreclosure.[6] The district includes industrial zones where vacant multistory factory buildings, former centers of the industrial age manufacturing economy, can be found. Some of them have been successfully repurposed for housing or business uses, but many others have been demolished, or will need to be, because adaptive reuse is too costly. Drug gangs fought each other in the lower part of the district during the 1980s' crack cocaine epidemic, when the area became known as "the Badlands,"[7] and this portion of the district continued to be a center of the drug trade during the opioid epidemic. A major challenge for Mayor Kenney during his first term in office was the need to organize a strategy for clearing encampments of homeless people that had emerged in this area, members of a population that was characterized by "near ubiquitous substance abuse," and to create appropriate housing and service options for them.[8]

High-quality affordable housing, successful neighborhood-based businesses, and capable service agencies such as ASPIRA could also be found in the 7th District; but the area was not like South Philadelphia or West

Philadelphia. No other council district was comparable in terms of the scale and severity of its problems.

Despite Quiñones-Sánchez's success in 2007 and 2011, the area was far from unified politically. In these two elections and in the two elections that followed, a majority of ward leaders in the district endorsed candidates who opposed her. Following their lead, the Democratic City Committee, which can ordinarily be counted on to endorse all incumbent candidates, did not endorse Quiñones-Sánchez in the three elections in which she was an incumbent. In 2014, Quiñones-Sánchez mounted a response: she persuaded her husband and three of her staff members to run against incumbent elected state officials who had opposed her in the past.[9] Although all of these insurgents were unsuccessful in 2014, one of them, Danilo Burgos, won election in 2018 as state representative for the 197th District.

The civic integrity of the area had been undermined by decades of public-sector corruption. Harry P. Jannotti, who served as district councilperson from 1970 to 1984, was convicted and jailed for taking a $10,000 bribe in the Abscam scandal. Upon his release from prison, he resumed his position as leader of the 19th Ward, conducting ward business from his bar at 4th and York Streets. Carlos Matos, a political ally of Jannotti's, who became leader of the 19th Ward some years later, served a three-year sentence in federal prison in connection with a bribery case involving three Atlantic City council members. Richard Mariano, who won election to the 7th District Council seat in 1995, resigned in 2006 after he was arrested for accepting money from businessmen to pay personal expenses. Leslie Acosta, who had defeated Danilo Burgos in the 2014 state representative election, pleaded guilty to a money-laundering scheme in 2016. And in 2017, Carlos Matos's wife, Renee Tartaglione, was convicted "on more than 50 charges, including theft, fraud, and conspiracy for running a bogus treatment program aimed at low-income people struggling with substance abuse near Kensington, which is the epicenter of Philadelphia's opioid crisis."[10]

Corruption and political infighting are likely to have been significant factors discouraging voter participation in the 7th District, where voter turnout is consistently low. The two competitors in the 2011 Democratic primary election for district council (Quiñones-Sánchez and Savage) received a total of about 12,000 votes. In contrast, vote totals ranged from about 15,000 to nearly 23,000 in five of the six other council district elections in which two or more candidates were competing that year. In 2015, the vote total for the two candidates in the 7th District primary (Quiñones-Sánchez and Savage) was again about 12,000. By comparison, in that year's primary for the district council seat in the 2nd District (which includes west of Broad Street areas of South Philadelphia, Center City, and North Philadelphia), about twice as many residents voted.

A pattern of consistently low voter turnout within a certain area of the city has two big implications in terms of campaign strategy. First, a chronically low turnout means that a candidate for a district office (such as district councilperson, state representative, and state senator) will be able to win with a relatively small number of votes, particularly in an election in which more than two candidates are competing. For example, in the 197th District state representative race in which Danilo Burgos was elected in 2018, Burgos won with only 1,317 votes. The remaining 2,254 votes were split between the other two candidates, Frederick Ramirez (with 1,237 votes) and Emilio Vazquez (1,013 votes), with 4 write-in votes. The other implication is that in an election in which all voters in the city participate (such as an election for council at large, mayor, governor, U.S. senator, or president), campaign strategists will be likely to assign lower priority to the interests and concerns of voters residing in such an area—or to ignore them altogether. If, on the basis of past voting behavior, two votes can be generated in the 2nd Council District for each vote in the 7th, then a candidate would be best advised to devote priority attention to the 2nd District and possibly to refrain entirely from campaigning in the 7th.

Another complicating factor is the influence of Local 98, the electricians union, which had been active in 7th District political campaigns for nearly two decades. Since 1993, when John Dougherty became head of the union, Local 98 had raised and spent increasingly large amounts of money, generated primarily through member payroll deductions, to influence campaigns and elections at every level of government. At the end of 2018, COPE, the union's primary political action committee, reported a balance of more than $7 million in funding.[11] The union contributed $269,300 to Richard Mariano's City Council campaigns;[12] then, after Mariano resigned, Local 98 supported the candidacy of 23rd Ward leader Danny Savage, who won a special election to serve the remainder of the council term that Mariano had begun. Local 98's contributions to LUPE in 2015 helped finance the campaign of Manny Morales, Quiñones-Sánchez's opponent in the primary that year. And before the May 2019 primary election, *Al Día* reported that Quiñones-Sánchez had received a total of $7,500 from Local 98, while Angel Cruz, who would become her opponent in that primary, had received $120,000.[13]

New Discord

As described above, the 2015 Democratic primary was the first district council election in which the 7th District had a Latino majority, as a result of the realignment of boundaries that followed the 2010 census. After being defeated by Quiñones-Sánchez in the 2007 and 2011 district council elections, Danny Savage endorsed her candidacy in 2015. "We might not have always agreed in the past on how to get things done," he told a reporter, "but we both have the same goal: to help the people and the communities of the 7th . . . District."[14]

Why did Danny Savage not make an alliance with the other ward leaders to ensure that his former opponent would be defeated in 2015? Quiñones-Sánchez explained:

> Danny comes from a family of public service, and because he had served on this council seat, he knows the complex, hard work that needs to happen in the district. And so while Cruz and the others spent all this time in between the election cycles trying to kiss up to Danny, there's some values that he and I do share around public service. And so, for him, when they put up a candidate like Manny Morales, it just confirmed for him that these guys weren't serious about servicing this complicated district.[15]

The state elected officials who had been challenged by Quiñones-Sánchez-backed candidates in 2014 were not in a similarly conciliatory frame of mind.

"They want to take control of everything," Carlos Matos said of Quiñones-Sánchez and her team. "It's only about her and her alone."[16] "She has failed to be inclusive with others," Angel Cruz observed in 2019. "She doesn't know how to play in the sandbox and share the tools."[17]

Quiñones-Sánchez was unapologetic. Reflecting on the political challenges she faced in 2015, which were to recur in 2019, she said:

> I picked my friends, and I definitely picked my enemies. . . . People who are hostile to my community, who want to take advantage of my community, are not my friends. I'm going to stand up for the constituents I represent, [even] if that means unifying [my enemies] against me, which is what you saw last time [in the 2015 primary, against challenger Manny Morales] and what you'll see this time again [in the 2019 primary].[18]

Quiñones-Sánchez won reelection in 2015, but by fewer than one thousand votes, as shown in Table 6.2. She was most successful in the 23rd Ward where, as a result of Danny Savage's support and the addition of several voting divisions after redistricting, she earned three times as many votes in that ward as she had in 2011. These votes accounted for nearly a quarter of her vote totals. However, the opposition of Cruz and Matos in the 7th and 19th Wards offset these gains. In the 7th Ward, Quiñones-Sánchez received about

TABLE 6.2 ELECTION RESULTS FOR 2011 AND 2015 DEMOCRATIC PRIMARIES, 7TH COUNCIL DISTRICT, BY WARD

	2015 Democratic primary			2011 Democratic primary		
	Maria Quiñones-Sánchez		Manny Morales	Maria Quiñones-Sánchez		Daniel J. Savage
Ward (ward leader)	No. of votes	Percentage of total	No. of votes	No. of votes	Percentage of total	No. of votes
7 (Angel Cruz)	807	12	848	1,377	19	333
18	312	5	299	437	6	110
19 (Carlos Matos)	627	10	1,056	1,512	21	236
23 (Danny Savage)	1,489	23	619	488	7	896
25	78	1	55			
31	62	1	36	48	1	24
33	826	13	629	836	12	398
37				404	6	119
42	744	11	433	599	8	253
43	735	11	389	711	10	309
49	84	1	33			
53				275	4	458
54	206	3	105			
56				487	6	1,514
62 (Margaret Tartaglione)	587	9	1,187			
63				24	0	57
Total	6,557	100	5,689	7,198	100	4,707

Source: Philadelphia City Commissioners, "Archived Data Sets: 2011 Primary" and "Archived Data Sets: 2015 Primary," https://www.philadelphiavotes.com/en/resources-a-data/ballot-box-app/additional-election-results-data.

five hundred fewer votes in 2015 than she had in 2011; and after winning the 19th by more than one thousand votes in 2011, she lost the ward in 2015 by more than four hundred votes. In addition, redistricting added twenty divisions from the 62nd Ward to the geography of the 7th District. The ward leader in the 62nd was Margaret Tartaglione, mother of Renee Tartaglione and Carlos Matos's mother in-law. Together, these three wards generated more than half of Manny Morales's total vote. Although Quiñones-Sánchez won majorities in all but three of the district's wards, as shown in Figure 6.2, the losses she incurred in the remainder almost cost her the election.

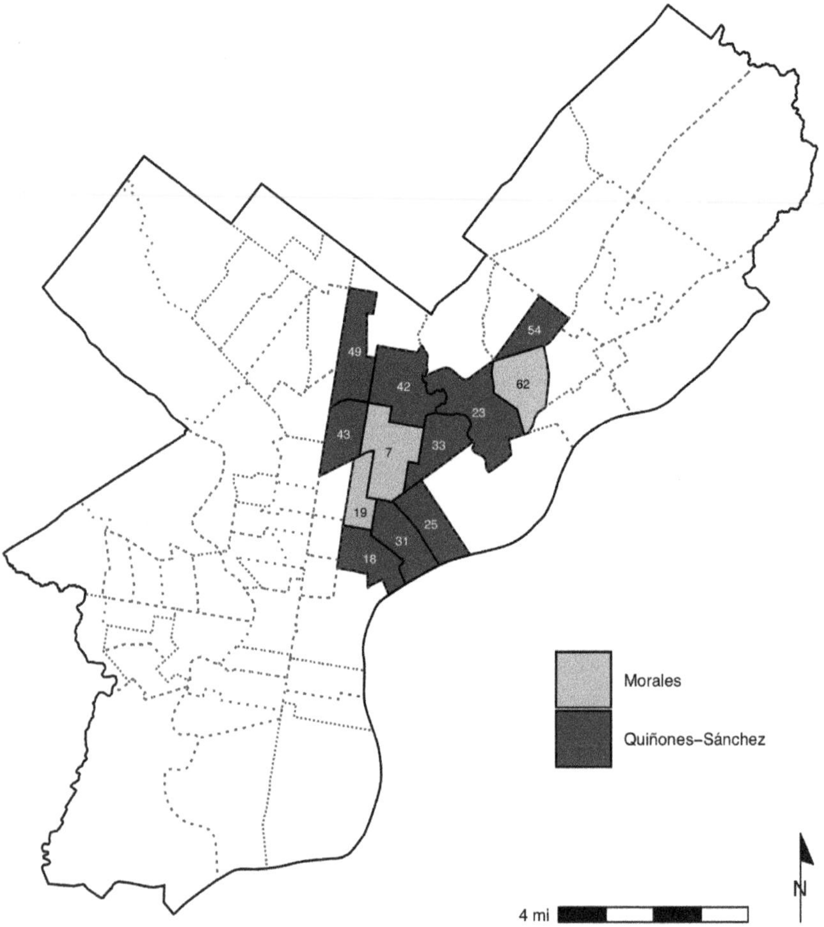

Figure 6.2 Results of 2015 Democratic primary, 7th Council District by ward

Source: Data from Philadelphia City Commissioners, "Archived Data Sets: 2015 Primary," https://www.philadelphiavotes.com/en/resources-a-data/ballot-box-app/additional-election-results-data; map by Michael Fichman.

Morales's strong showing in the 7th, 19th, and 62nd Wards provides a good illustration of how low turnout and controlled voting can make a difference in an election. Despite Morales's shallow experience and qualifications and the appalling content that was discovered on his Facebook page, the influence of Quiñones-Sánchez's political adversaries, along with the funding that Local 98 provided, nearly delivered the election to him.

How could this happen? Nelson Díaz commented on the "colonial mentality" that he viewed as pervasive among Puerto Ricans in Philadelphia and elsewhere.[19] Díaz elaborated on this perspective in his autobiography:

> We are a people who feel grateful just for being allowed to be here. . . . We don't really participate; we just watch from the doorway and think how much worse it would be out in the street. We don't consider ourselves worthy of constitutional rights, and we don't know how to demand them. We fear losing what little we have, because it was granted to us. We didn't earn it. We didn't take it. Ironically, if we did demand those constitutional rights, we'd get a lot more.
>
> But for the foreseeable future, we are a people who are neither here nor there. That's the unofficial motto of the Puerto Rican: *No soy de aquí ni de allá*, which translates in English to, "I am accepted neither here nor there."[20]

In a conversation with me, Díaz observed:

> Maria had a real vision of being able to work within that area, but she had enemies—all those Latino ward leaders who really don't represent our community. There's always been a group in the Puerto Rican community that is controlled by the Democratic Party, and all of them played with [Margaret] Tartaglione. So essentially, they had political control of that whole section of Philadelphia. . . .
>
> They control the vote by either bringing in their voters to vote for the candidate they're working for or suppressing the vote. Maria had to have her own representatives in each one of these polling places because they'll threaten voters who oppose their candidates and try to discourage them from coming in at all. Here we are with an opportunity to vote, and they discourage it.[21]

There is nothing wrong with making sure that voters who will support your candidate get to the polls on election day. And while threatening voters is wrong, taking certain actions that might discourage voters who will not support your candidate may be morally wrong but is technically lawful. However, at a neighborhood polling place and in the surrounding community—especially in a high-poverty community—the boundary that separates a lawful get-out-the-vote plan from a voter-suppression strategy can be crossed.

What is alarming about the election process in Philadelphia is the fact that, in past years, this boundary has been crossed repeatedly by the public officials responsible for election management and oversight. During the many years in which Margaret Tartaglione served as City Commission chair, the commission was cited for numerous instances of mismanagement or dereliction of responsibility (also described in Chapter 4): moving voting machines to new locations without providing proper public notice, paying excessive amounts for voting machine maintenance expenses, failing to maintain employee financial disclosure forms, and "failing to provide sufficient election-related materials and assistance to Spanish-speaking voters."[22]

During Tartaglione's tenure as commission chair, Judge Clarence Newcomer invalidated the results of a 1994 Pennsylvania Senate election, on the basis of a finding that the election outcome was a the result of "an elaborate fraud in which hundreds of residents were encouraged to vote by absentee ballot even though they had no legal reason—like a physical disability or a scheduled trip outside the city—to do so."[23] The Senate district boundaries involved contained many of the neighborhoods included in the 7th Council District.

Documentation supporting Newcomer's decision described the approach adopted by the campaign of candidate William Stinson:

> During the canvassing [completed in "predominately Caucasian areas of the district" months before election day], the canvassers solicited absentee-ballot applications from individuals, including persons registering to vote for the first time, pursuant to a plan to obtain 20 absentee ballots from each division.
>
> Many persons who were hesitant to register because they simply did not want to go to the polls were told that they could fill out an absentee-ballot application and obtain an absentee ballot out of convenience. Many applications were received based on this misrepresentation.[24]

A few weeks before the election, a Stinson campaign worker disclosed that a similar approach would be used in Latino neighborhoods: "The Stinson campaign was going to saturate the Hispanic areas with applications and . . . use the same scheme that was employed earlier. The 'joke' at the campaign was that the Hispanics would sign anything."[25]

Voter assistance provisions in the election regulations have been cited as creating potential opportunities for fraud. According to the "Guide for

Election Board Officials," published by the Philadelphia City Commission, a voter may request and receive assistance at the polling place from an individual who may enter the voting booth with the voter and remain there while votes are cast. A voter may indicate a need for assistance when she registers to vote, in which case, an "Assistance Permitted" notation will appear in the ledger that is used by officials at the polling place to verify voter eligibility. Alternatively, a voter may complete an assistance declaration at the polling place and be allowed to receive assistance. The person providing the assistance may be anyone other than a person belonging to one of three categories: the judge of elections, who supervises polling place activities; the voter's employer or a representative of the voter's employer; or an officer or agent of the voter's union.[26]

In an ethnically and culturally diverse city that includes many elderly residents and residents with disabilities, a voter assistance provision is a necessity. But is it possible that a group of unscrupulous individuals could exploit this provision to ensure that voters—who may have been coerced or offered money—select a particular candidate they support? No evidence of widespread abuse of voter assistance has emerged; but, in a close election, the use of a tactic of this kind in several voting divisions might make a difference.

Preparing for May 2019

During the weeks preceding the May 2019 Democratic primary election for mayor, incumbent James Kenney appeared to be heading for another landslide victory. Polling showed his two opponents—state Senator Anthony Hardy Williams and former city controller Alan Butkovitz—to be far behind.

All City Council seats would be on the May primary ballot as well. Incumbent Maria Quiñones-Sánchez and challenger Angel Cruz were preparing to face off against each other for the 7th District seat. Quiñones-Sánchez's Facebook posts celebrated her role in neighborhood-improvement projects. They exclaimed, "Beautiful day at Feltonville Recreation Playground and Courts for our Ribbon Cutting Ceremony!!"[27] and "We've heard you and we're excited to announce our groundbreaking tomorrow at DENI PLAYGROUND!! This has been a project that we have been working on months for and we're excited to share the plans with the community!"[28] She also chided Cruz's no-show at a media-sponsored debate:

> I'd like to thank Al DÍA News Media and WURD Radio for providing the Community an opportunity to hear me and Angel Cruz discuss the issues that confront our neighborhoods on an everyday

basis. It's a shame that Rep. Cruz didn't show up and that he's unwilling to explain to voters why they should vote for him over me, but I'm not scared! I'm proud of my record and accomplishments on behalf of the residents of the 7th Council District. So my offer to debate Angel Cruz stands: any time, any place, any corner in the district. I'll keep standing on my record and you can keep running from yours![29]

Cruz had a minimal online presence. He told viewers of the 2019 Philly-CAM Video Voter Guide, "I want to clean, secure, and rebuild our neighborhoods."[30]

Across the city, the soda tax was a hot-button election issue. Early in his administration, Mayor Kenney had won council approval for a new tax on sweetened beverages that he proposed to use as a source of funding for citywide prekindergarten programs, the upgrading of city recreation centers, and other public investment in neighborhoods. Quiñones-Sánchez had opposed the tax, charging that it disproportionately affected residents of her district. Two months before the May primary, she joined other City Council members in a resolution calling for a study of the economic impact of the tax. Cruz stated that, while he "is not entirely in favor of the tax . . . he has yet to identify any better options to support early childhood care, community schools, and neighborhood restoration in the district."[31]

A more local hot-button issue was a proposal by a nonprofit organization to open a safe injection site—a place where drug use would be allowed under medical supervision and where drug users would be provided with information about treatment, counseling, housing, and service options. The Kenney administration supported the proposal over the opposition of the U.S. attorney, and, with the May primary approaching, city and federal authorities were engaged in litigation over the matter.[32]

Cruz was not in favor of the proposal; Quiñones-Sánchez took less of a hard line. Cruz said:

> "Well, first of all, I'm not for the safe injection site. That doesn't help. . . . That's part of the problem. And putting it in Kensington, where the most addiction is, the problem will never be solved and it will always stay there in Kensington. . . ."
>
> Quiñones-Sánchez has not been entirely opposed to the idea of such a site. . . . The councilwoman has said that it must be one aspect of a more comprehensive reform approach by the city.[33]

Although voters in the 7th District likely felt strongly about these two issues, neither one appeared to have a decisive impact on the campaigns of either Cruz or Quiñones-Sánchez. Neither issue belonged exclusively to either of them. Both Cruz and Quiñones-Sánchez supported the improvement of neighborhood facilities, but neither of them was wholeheartedly in favor of the soda tax, which had been Mayor Kenney's idea. Cruz opposed the safe injection site; Quiñones-Sánchez was "not entirely opposed" but was not an unequivocal supporter. It might not be entirely out of the question that, at some point, both of them would agree to the opening of such a site if it were part of a broader, more comprehensive approach that had earned some community support.

Approaching the May primary, Quiñones-Sánchez's performance in office compared favorably with the performance of others who had previously represented her constituency in city or state government—Jannotti, Mariano, Acosta, and Tartaglione, for example. She had gained the respect of fellow council members. Her professionalism and effectiveness in office had been praised by community, business, and government leaders, including four former Philadelphia mayors who endorsed her 2015 campaign.[34] And she had been mentioned as a possible candidate for mayor in 2023. So it was ironic that, in 2019, Quiñones-Sánchez was being confronted with a particularly hard challenge within the confines of her home district.

7

★★★★★★★

The Price of a Judge

The relationship between Philadelphia's Democratic Party and local candidates for the judiciary can be characterized as an awkward, uneasy synergy. A candidate for judge needs votes to win citywide elections, and the Democratic Party, under certain circumstances, can be a highly efficient vote-generating machine. The party, in turn, needs money to sustain a citywide political infrastructure, and a judicial campaign committee that receives generous contributions from wealthy attorneys and political action committees can address that need by making substantial payments to the Democratic City Committee and other entities as part of a candidate-endorsement process.

A candidate for judge is not allowed to lead a political campaign—the campaign must be led and managed by a campaign committee that may consist of a handful of inexperienced friends and relatives. The party's City Committee, in contrast, is a seasoned political army boasting dozens of generals and thousands of foot soldiers that operates citywide.

A candidate for judge is prohibited from saying, "Please contribute to my campaign," but party endorsement gives the candidate's campaign committee the prospect of access to a citywide network of contributors, including constituency-group leaders and political action committees.

In turn, after the election is over, many members of the party's army can find or keep jobs in the court system—a system that is governed by judges, many of whom owe their success at the polls to party support.

An endorsement by the Democratic City Committee is not necessarily a guarantee of success on election day. Some unendorsed judicial candidates win elections, and some endorsed candidates lose. The Democratic Party's endorsement is viewed as a plus by some of the frequent voters who routinely vote in every election, while other frequent voters may view it as a negative.

For a judicial candidate, the question of whether to seek a Democratic Party endorsement is complicated. Although the party's power to influence election outcomes remains significant, the party is a lot weaker than it used to be. One candidate for Common Pleas Court who came close to winning without party endorsement expressed the view that "the party is no longer a centralized machine. It has the remnants of something that looks like it, but it isn't one. . . . The party in Philadelphia has to either adapt or risk losing the influence that it has."[1]

With no clear path to success in an uncertain environment, candidates for the judiciary pursue different strategies, some by choice, others by necessity.

Judge Bernstein

Mark Bernstein explained why he wanted to become a judge:

> I was at this political event—it may have been for Mary Rose Cunningham—and across the room, I saw a politician who was under indictment, a guy I had once represented on a small legal matter as a favor to the party. I started across the room to say hello. After all, he's a human being; you're not going to shun him. But before I could get there, this political hanger-on comes up to me and gives me this big hug. "Mark, my buddy! How you doing? He really wants to see you!" It was weird, and I'm thinking, "What was that all about?" Years later, it finally dawned on me: he wanted to find out if I was wearing a bug.
>
> As a lawyer, I found myself practicing before judges that were just as bad as those that had been implicated in the roofers' scandal. They were venal, just unconcerned about justice. They couldn't care less about the law or about doing their job—the important thing was their salary and when they could leave. So I decided to become a judge rather than having to practice before them for the rest of my career.[2]

On February 3, 1987, ten judges in Philadelphia's Common Pleas Court, along with five municipal court judges, were suspended for accepting cash gifts from representatives of the Roofers Union. Later that month, Pennsylvania governor Robert Casey requested that the state Senate approve ten individuals to fill the vacated common pleas seats, on the basis of recommendations from a special commission that Casey had appointed for this purpose. Five of the Casey candidates were endorsed by the Democratic and Republican parties and then approved by the Senate. They were sworn in as interim appointees shortly afterward. The appointments would expire at the end of the year. To remain on the bench, each of them would have to run for election in the 1987 primary and general elections, after which, if successful, they could begin ten-year terms in January 1988.

The other five Casey nominees were not endorsed by the Democratic and Republican parties, and their nominations were not approved by the Senate. If these five individuals entered the 1987 primary and general elections and were elected, then they, like the Casey nominees who had been approved by the Senate, would begin ten-year judicial terms starting in January 1988. (Table 7.1 shows elections that led up to and, in some respects, influenced the successful campaigns of the candidates who would come to be known as the Casey Five.) In the meantime, however, the five vacant court seats for which Casey had recommended the five unendorsed nominees would remain vacant for the remainder of 1987, contributing to a further increase in the Philadelphia court system's ten-thousand-case backlog.

TABLE 7.1 KEY ELECTIONS LEADING UP TO THE CASEY FIVE ELECTIONS

Year elected/ appointed	Governor	Mayor	District attorney	City controller	Casey Five common pleas court candidates
Incumbent in 1982	Richard L. Thornburgh	William J. Green III	Edward G. Rendell	Thomas A. Leonard III	
1983		W. Wilson Goode		Joseph C. Vignola Sr.	
1984					
1985			Ronald D. Castille	Joseph C. Vignola Sr.	
1986	Robert P. Casey Sr.				
1987		W. Wilson Goode			Mark I. Bernstein Legrome D. Davis John W. Herron C. Darnell Jones II Edward R. Summers

Source: Data for governor from National Governors Association, "Former Pennsylvania Governors," https://www.nga.org/former-governors/pennsylvania/ (accessed April 20, 2020); data for mayor and district attorney from Philadelphia Registration Commission, *Annual Reports* (Philadelphia: City of Philadelphia, 1982, 1983, 1985, 1986, 1987); access to data for judicial candidates provided to the author by Philadelphia City Commissioners.

"Once again, when faced with a choice between political expediency and the public welfare, our political leaders unhesitatingly chose the former," commented Benjamin Lerner, head of the Defender Association of Philadelphia.[3]

Mark Bernstein was one of the five nominees who had received Senate approval, and like the other four party-supported nominees, he was a successful candidate in the 1987 elections. Bernstein had arrived in Philadelphia in 1971 to attend law school at the University of Pennsylvania, residing in West Philadelphia's 27th Ward, where a large proportion of the voting population consisted of Penn students, faculty members, and employees. The preceding years had been a time of unprecedented student activism at Penn, with numerous demonstrations and sit-ins on campus, including a 1969 sit-in at College Hall, the university's administration building, that lasted six days.[4] A major focus of this activism was the University City Science Center (UCSC), a research-and-development complex in which Penn was a shareholder. UCSC-related construction that caused substantial residential displacement in neighborhoods adjacent to the campus and UCSC's involvement in military contracts were two flashpoints.

Penn students became politically active off campus as well. "Students were taking over the 27th Ward," Bernstein recalled. Many of them ran for election as Democratic committeepeople and were elected. A Penn student was even elected ward leader, an occurrence that would have been unheard of in any other Philadelphia ward.

Bernstein worked full time for George McGovern's 1972 presidential campaign, and he got involved in ward politics at the neighborhood level as well. In a short time, he became counsel to the 27th Ward Democratic Committee; when the ward leader graduated from Penn and moved out of the area, Bernstein was chosen to take his place. He characterized the ward as "very liberal, very independent, doing its own thing, supporting all the lefty liberal candidates."

After receiving his law degree in 1973, Bernstein remained in Philadelphia and, at the time of his appointment to the judiciary, was a partner in a Center City law firm, Berson, Fineman and Bernstein. During his years in private practice, he had worked hard to establish Democratic Party bona fides, describing the political relationships he formed as "deep and long." He provided legal services and did campaign volunteer tasks to support Democratic candidates running for election or reelection to City Council, the state Senate, the state House of Representatives, and the U.S. Congress. He headed W. Wilson Goode's legal committee in Goode's successful 1983 campaign for mayor, and he served as a deputy to city commissioner Marian Tasco, who subsequently became a leading voice on Philadelphia City Council.

By the time Governor Casey nominated him in 1987 to a judgeship, Bernstein was known and respected by some of Philadelphia's most influential political leaders. His political values were, in some respects, diametrically opposed to those of Democratic City Committee chair Bob Brady; given the opportunity, Brady would never have supported Bernstein's candidacy for a judgeship. But some key party leaders, including Mayor Goode, were among Bernstein's strongest supporters, and they would have regarded the party's failure to endorse his candidacy as an insult. "I can guarantee that, when [Bernstein's supporters] called Brady in 1987, Brady said, 'I'll take care of it,'" Bernstein said.

Bernstein characterized the commission-managed vetting process that produced the Casey nominees as only the "front door," the process that was visible to the public. What mattered more was the "back door" process managed by key party leaders who would confer privately to decide on endorsements. "The question is, who is going to be in the room and who in the room is going to mention your name," Bernstein said. "Because if no one in the room is going to mention your name, you can be the absolute second choice of everyone who's there, but you won't get an endorsement."

Bernstein was not in the room (which may have existed only in a figurative sense), but he did not have to be; apparently, his endorsement was a given. "I'm not sure I was even discussed," he said. The questions that are addressed in the room are: Whose turn is it (within the group of party leaders) to choose a candidate to endorse this time around? And for that person whose turn it is, who is your candidate? No one is allowed to propose endorsing two candidates; doing so means that neither candidate gets endorsed. One year West Philadelphia ward leader Isadore Shrager brought in two names for endorsement, knowing he would come away with none; it was his way of showing responsiveness to two influential supporters, each of whom had been pressuring him for an endorsement. With this outcome guaranteed, he could say to each of them, "Sorry, I really tried."

After endorsements were made, party leaders used various strategies to thin the ranks of unendorsed candidates. "It's not your turn," Republican Party boss William Meehan told one prospective candidate in the 1987 judicial elections. The candidate withdrew from the race as a result. His turn apparently came up two years later; he was elected to the judiciary in 1989.

A candidate with a favorable ballot position—one of the names listed at or near the top of the ballot—might be told, "If you stay in the race, we'll make sure you lose. But if you withdraw, we'll help you win next time." This option is pitched to multiple candidates, each of whom might conclude that he or she will be the party's top priority in the next election cycle. But ballot positions are established by lottery; in the next election cycle, that individual's position on the ballot might be less favorable—so much less favorable that the candidate might decide to withdraw again, regardless of whether a party endorsement seemed to be forthcoming.

A candidate whose endorsement was not ensured, as Bernstein's had been, would have to answer some questions. "They'd want to know, 'If you're not endorsed, will you still run?'" Bernstein said. "If you say you will, that's disrespecting the party." They would also try to find an appropriate way to phrase the question, "Will you hire the people we ask you to hire?" possibly with a question such as, "When there's a job opening, will you accept recommendations from the party?"

> I had a feeling that [this process] was a script—the same one that had previously worked for the Republicans in the 1930s. It was like the party had no ability to change the script. It was what had always worked; it's what we do.
>
> Now, in electing judges, I don't even know if a Democratic City Committee endorsement is worth the money you have to spend. When I was running, there were fifteen to seventeen wards that mattered [in terms of generating enough votes to ensure success for a judicial candidate]; now it's five, six, or seven of them.

Judge Jones

C. Darnell Jones II explained, "I got an appointment with Lucien Blackwell and introduced myself." In 1987, Lucien E. Blackwell was a member of the Philadelphia City Council and a Democratic City Committee leader. Jones continued, "His first question was, 'What have you done for the party lately?' And I said, 'I'm not allowed to do anything for the party. I took an oath as a public defender. We're not allowed to engage in political activity.' And he said, 'That's good. Have a nice day.'"[5]

C. Darnell Jones II came to Philadelphia from Claremore, Oklahoma, by way of Southwestern College in Winfield, Kansas, and American University in Washington, D.C., from which he received his law degree in 1975. During his final year in law school, Jones was offered a job in the Philadelphia District Attorney's Office. However, his best friend, who had moved to the city a year earlier and was working at the Defender Association of Philadelphia, persuaded him to make an appointment for an interview there. Jones did so and was offered a job on the spot. He accepted the offer and remained at the Defender Association for twelve years. Jones's tenure at the Defender Association coincided with the years in which Mark Bernstein entered private practice and became increasingly involved in Democratic Party politics.

Late one night in late February 1987, Jones learned that Governor Casey had recommended him to fill one of the recently vacated common pleas court seats. Frederic Tulsky, a *Philadelphia Inquirer* reporter who was a friend and a frequent golfing partner, was on the phone. "Congratulations!" he exclaimed, "You're going to be one of the governor's picks!"

Not long afterward, Jones ran into Kevin Vaughan, an aide to City Councilman at Large Angel Ortiz, outside City Hall. "He said, 'This is going to be great!' Then he said, 'Listen, who's your ward leader?' and I said, 'What's a ward leader?' He looked at me and said, 'You'd better come inside.'"

Vaughan and Councilman Ortiz briefed Jones about the need to form a campaign committee and start communicating with Democratic Party leaders. Vaughan happened to be leader of the 27th Ward, the same ward in which Mark Bernstein had served as ward leader in the previous decade. Vaughan introduced Jones to a woman who was active in the ward organization, and she agreed to help organize a campaign committee. The committee would serve as a vehicle for raising money and obtaining endorsements in support of Jones's candidacy in the 1987 primary and general elections. As explained above, a Senate vote in favor of Governor Casey's nomination of Jones would authorize an interim appointment only through the end of 1987. Jones would need to be a successful candidate in the 1987 elections to keep his position on the bench and start a ten-year term in January 1988.

Benjamin Lerner, head of the Defender Association, offered his congratulations. "We're so proud that you'll be the first public defender to be appointed to the bench directly from the Defender Association," he said. Then they discussed a related issue: because Defender Association attorneys were not allowed to engage in political activity, Jones should resign. For similar reasons, two of Jones's fellow nominees, Legrome Davis and John Herron, would have to resign from their positions in the district attorney's office.

Meanwhile, leaders of the city's Democratic Party organization, angered that the governor had announced nominations without consulting them first, endorsed only five of the ten common pleas nominees. Mark Bernstein was one of them. He and the other four endorsed nominees were approved by the Senate in April, and Bernstein was seated that month. Darnell Jones was one of the five Casey nominees who were not endorsed and not approved by the Senate. The five common pleas seats that the governor had intended these nominees to fill remained vacant.

Although Jones, Davis, and Herron lacked political credentials, all of them were well qualified for the judiciary. Jones had been a public defender, John W. Herron had been an assistant district attorney, and Legrome D. Davis had been chief of the district attorney's rape-prosecution unit. All of them had resigned from their positions upon being nominated. The party leaders either did not take this important background information into account, or else they viewed it as a negative.

"I went from being on the highest peak imaginable to being in the lowest valley I could ever imagine," Jones said. "We realized that not only were we going to lose our jobs, but the party wasn't going to support us. We quickly became aware of the fact that we were essentially persona non grata in a large number of the ward meetings across the city. They were anti-Casey and anti-reform."

Jones recalled that all the judicial candidates would routinely get notifications about ward meetings that were being held each night. However, the understanding was, as he put it, "Everyone come—except the Casey folks."

The unendorsed nominees persisted in seeking opportunities to introduce themselves to the party rank and file. On the way to a ward meeting one night, Jones saw Russell Nigro, a judicial candidate who was not a Casey nominee, parking his Porsche across the street. They were acquainted but did not know each other very well. As Nigro exited his car, Jones joked, "Is that what you get when you become a judge?" Nigro laughed, and they walked to the building together. Nigro said, "Come with me." He told the men at the door, "He's coming in," and they walked into the meeting.

That was how Jones got an opportunity to speak. "And from that point on," he said, "I think people realized, 'He's not so bad.' I was a commoner; I wasn't this elitist pick. I worked hard to get where I am."

Jones did not have strong relationships with partners in the city's biggest law firms or other wealthy individuals. His friends in the legal profession were more likely to be other modestly paid public defenders. But Jones had numerous friends and acquaintances at Zion Baptist Church, one of the largest congregations of faith in the United States at that time. Pastor Leon Sullivan was internationally known for his leading role in advancing numerous social justice and self-help initiatives, including (while a member of General Motors' Board of Directors) his successful advocacy for GM and other large corporations to withdraw from doing business in South Africa while the system of apartheid remained in effect. "No one was more powerful than Reverend Sullivan," Jones said.

Jones met with Reverend Sullivan, and they discussed his candidacy. Jones was the only one of the Casey Five who belonged to Zion's congregation, and Sullivan said to him, "You're a member of our church; I'll support you."

> So that following Sunday, Reverend Sullivan got up in the pulpit and announced that I was one of the Casey Five, I was a candidate, and

> he wanted me to stand up so everyone in the church could see who I was. And then he just started yelling out my name, yelling my name, and people just kept applauding and applauding and applauding. It was an incredible, incredible moment.

Understandably, Jones had found Councilman Blackwell's dismissive remark deeply discouraging. "When he said that, I'm thinking, I don't have a chance in the world." But before long, the prospects improved for him and the other four unendorsed candidates. "You'd see editorials in the papers: 'Support the Casey Five.' At 6:00 in the evening, when the local news came on, they'd have these editorials: 'Support the Casey Five.' So things started picking up. People would say, 'Wow, you're one of the Casey Five!' We were becoming known."

Governor Casey and Henry Reath, a prominent Philadelphia lawyer with a long history of engagement in social activism, went to work raising funds to support the campaigns of the three unendorsed candidates, providing the capital they desperately needed. "We were relying on Casey and Reath," Jones said. "I remember seeing a figure in the paper about the other contributions to my campaign committee. It was people in my church and public defenders." He laughed. "They only raised about six thousand dollars. So thank goodness for the governor and Henry Reath."

During the course of the campaign, the three unendorsed members of the Casey Five were shocked by what they learned about the Democratic Party–Philadelphia court system synergy and by the insights they gained about the—to use Mark Bernstein's term—venal characters who benefitted from it.

> Worse [than the burden of having to solicit friends and co-workers for campaign funds], according to all three, is the expectation that they would give money to political figures in return for support on election day. All three describe having been told, either directly or indirectly, of the cost to have their names appear on the sample ballot of a ward.
>
> [Legrome] Davis said that two months ago, he would not have believed federal-court testimony last week that City Councilman Leland M. Beloff had bragged of having "15 to 20 judges" under his "control." Now, Davis said, he can understand how political leaders believe that they have such control.
>
> [John] Herron said one ward leader told him flat-out that any money for election-day support in that area would be paid directly to him.

> "The implication is understood that political leaders expect to be paid for their support and expect me also to be available later on," Herron said.[6]

A common pleas judge who is successful at the polls is rewarded with a guaranteed ten-year job with excellent salary and benefits, as well as a small staff. That judge can show appreciation for the party's support of his candidacy by providing party insiders with access to jobs in the court system.

> [In 1987] the court system employs more than 2,000 people in positions not controlled by civil service. The judges, sitting together, also make additional appointments to various city agencies.
>
> "I don't think there is all that much calling of judges by committeemen on active cases," said Gregory Harvey, a Center City lawyer and Democratic committeeman who actively supports Casey's candidates. "What is most at stake is not any broad issue, but jobs."[7]

Although the Democratic Party slated candidates to run against them, all of the Casey Five candidates were elected. Afterward, some party representatives were not hesitant about seeking favors from Jones.

> Party leaders would ask for this, that, and the other thing. I'd say, "I have a house in Oklahoma that my mom and dad had, and I've got friends at home. I don't need this, and I will never tarnish my reputation to give anyone anything. I'm not going to do anything that's going to shame my family name. If people want to see me on a case, they come in the front door. I teach evidence; I know what the rules are." That caught some people by surprise, but other people said, "By all means. That's the kind of person we want."

"A lot of judges had to get their secretaries from the party [through referrals from party insiders]," Judge Jones said, but his secretary—who, in 2018, was in her thirtieth year of service in his office—was a fellow parishioner at Zion Baptist Church, and he had recruited another staff person from the Defender Association Social Services Division.

Judge Davis

Years after the Casey Five drama had come to an end, Governor Casey's son, U.S. senator Robert Casey Jr., told Legrome Davis that his father had regarded the outcome of this initiative as the accomplishment of which he was proudest.

"Casey was one of the most ideologically pure people that I've ever had the pleasure of meeting," Davis said. "When you have fifteen judges out of a ninety-six-person bench being removed for receiving money, you have a public issue. If you can't get excited about that as a politician, then there's something wrong with you. Casey saw it, felt it, believed it, and acted upon it."[8]

During nearly a decade as a prosecutor at the district attorney's office, Davis had become well aware of the need to improve the judicial system. With respect to many of the cases assigned to him, he would intuit in advance how a particular judge would rule, even before the trial had begun. Because the uneven quality of the judiciary frustrated and disappointed him, he was inspired and encouraged by Casey's appointment of a commission to recommend candidates to fill the vacant seats. "The commission believed the same thing I did—that the city needed a judiciary that didn't shame them," he said. "That's where I got my energy" during the months of uncertainty that followed the governor's announcement.

Another one of the Casey Five, John W. Herron, had worked in the DA's office along with Davis, and the two of them decided to share information and strategize during the months leading up to the election. "Early on, we realized that we couldn't win on our own," Davis recalled. "We would have to build some kind of a coalition, and we were working on that."

Davis was already aware that his candidacy would be opposed by some influential political leaders. He recounted that before the governor's nomination, state senator Vincent Fumo, a South Philadelphia political kingpin, had told him, "You're the last person on the face of the earth that I'd want to see as a judge."

Then Henry Reath called, introducing himself as a fellow Princetonian (class of 1942; Davis was a 1973 graduate). Reath had the same idea as Davis and Herron: put together a committee. He recruited some high-profile individuals to join a Committee to Support the Governor's Nominees: Wilson Goode and Ed Rendell, who were competing against each other in the 1987 Democratic mayoral primary; Joseph Vignola, who had been elected city controller in 1983; Philadelphia Bar Association chancellor Seymour Kurland; and several well-known religious and civic leaders. "All of a sudden, you're not standing alone," Davis said.

Davis explained that before Governor Casey's nomination of Davis and the other judicial candidates, Jerome Mondesire, influential aide to Congressman William H. Gray III, had observed that, as a prospective candidate, Davis "has everything it takes, except a sponsor." Congressman Gray subsequently became a key member of the Reath committee.

Davis and Herron pursued opportunities to speak at ward meetings, and they succeeded in getting invited to introduce themselves to ward organizations in Center City, Northwest, and West Philadelphia. The months leading up to the election were a time of constant activity and unrelenting pressure. Davis's wife, pregnant with their daughter, left to live with her mother in England until the election was over (their marriage remains intact). Reath and others worked to persuade Governor Casey to do more to make the challenge facing the five candidates a kind of *cause célèbre*, and Casey did so. The governor contacted people on the committee's behalf and made public appearances in Philadelphia to support the candidates.

The ballot for common pleas judges that would appear in the voting booths on the primary election day would consist of twenty-four slots—three rows of eight names each. In the lottery that was held to determine the order in which candidates' names would be displayed, Davis drew the next-to-last slot, in the far right-hand column known popularly as "death row." After the election, Davis was told that no candidate whose name occupied that position had ever won before; Davis won by about 2,500 votes.

Davis served in Common Pleas Court from 1987 to 2002 and was appointed to a federal judgeship in 2002 after three successive nominations—two by President Bill Clinton in 1998 and 1999 and a third by President George W. Bush in 2002—before receiving Senate approval. In 2017, he became senior judge of the U.S. District Court for the Eastern District of Pennsylvania. His experience in the judiciary over the years had not made him feel more sanguine about the prospects for judicial reform:

> The day after the [1987] election, an editorial was published in the *Inquirer* that said, in effect, this isn't going to change things. It just takes too much energy. At the time, I was young, and I believed that the system would change. I had believed our experiences might change the process—that people might see what could be done. But as the years passed while I was on the bench, with each successive group of judicial nominations, I saw the governor getting farther and farther away from his original idea—he paid increased attention to the politicians. I concluded that the cost of fighting the battle that he had just won was probably very high.
>
> Most of the people that I dealt with in the Philadelphia political system were honest, and certainly good people come through the political process—Bernstein, for example, was a wonderful judge. But given the nature of elective judicial politics in Philadelphia, you have to make political compromises. It does not matter how talented you might be; you cannot win a judicial election in Philadelphia these days without deep involvement in politics.

True Democracy

"Having to go out and see people and answer questions is good," observed Flora Barth Wolf, who was elected to Common Pleas Court in 1991. "It's the last time you're going to do it."[9] Wolf was referring to the fact that, after winning election and then completing an initial ten-year term of office, a common pleas judge does not have to face challengers at the polls again. To remain in office, the judge's name has to be placed on the ballot only for a yes-or-no retention vote, similar to the vote on a bond issue referendum question. A majority yes vote is almost guaranteed; it is extremely rare for a judge to be voted out of office with a no retention vote.

Under these circumstances, the only time a common pleas court candidate is likely to have to encounter voters face-to-face is during a primary-election campaign season that lasts just a few months (because the Democratic Party has dominated Philadelphia politics for decades, a judge who wins nomination in the Democratic primary is assured of success in the fall general election). During this brief period, direct engagement with the voters is essential.

The popular election of judges at the municipal level has one distinct advantage over the appointment of judges by a merit selection committee: campaigning for election requires candidates to get acquainted with community members face-to-face in the neighborhoods where they live. To the extent that judicial candidates are able to gain admission to ward meetings and are allowed to present themselves to those in attendance, the knowledge and insights gained will be beneficial to all concerned.

"I had to run all over the city," Judge Bernstein said.

> I had to go to places where I had never been—to neighborhoods where there were no street signs and where the streets were paved with cobblestones. I visited one Latino ward, and I gave my usual speech. Everyone was very friendly—they offered me cake. Later I realized no one understood a word you were saying—no one speaks English! Afterwards, when you're a judge and someone's on the witness stand who doesn't speak English, you understand. You've gained a better understanding of the city. As a result of that experience [of visiting neighborhoods], the Mark Bernstein on the day I was sworn in was a different person from the one who had filed nominating petitions a few months earlier.[10]

Judge Darnell Jones said of his experience as a candidate:

> There was no greater benefit than going to wards and meeting people and kind of walking in their shoes—going to the neighborhoods

> where they lived. To me, that's just humanity; it's recognizing that people are people. I'm no better than anyone else. I just got some breaks. It's good that people have to go out there and be seen. There are a lot of folks around here [in the courthouse] that would never be in Lower Kensington—they need to see that. If you limit exposure and access, then you end up with someone who's going to sit there—holier than thou, if you will—incredibly judgmental and never ever having set foot in a particular area.
>
> There are certain sections of Philadelphia where you'd be afraid to go—but people live there. Then, later on, if you've got to sentence a person from that place, the child of someone who worked their butt off—single-parent home or whatever—then maybe you'd look at that child a little differently and be a little more tolerant of his or her conduct.[11]

Flora Wolf's husband, Edwin D. Wolf, a highly respected civil rights and legal aid attorney, passed away in 1976 at age thirty-seven. After having spent years at home raising their children, Wolf enrolled at Penn Law and, after becoming a member of the bar, was hired by the Philadelphia City Solicitor's Office. She remained employed there for a decade as an attorney handling legal matters for the city's Department of Licenses and Inspections. In considering her career options during this time, Wolf decided that her first preference would be to become a judge, someone who would "look at cases . . . in a way that would impact other people's lives."[12]

Based on her engagement in civic and social activities over the years, she felt that she could draw on a broad network of prospective supporters rather than having to be as dependent on the Democratic Party, as some other candidates would be.

> I got enough confidence to wing it. I didn't go after endorsements; I just did it. At the time I decided to run, I didn't even know who my ward leader was.
>
> I went to the 59th Ward [in Northwest Philadelphia] and gave some sort of speech. [State representative] Dave Richardson looked at me sympathetically. He told the committeepeople in the room, "She was married to Ned Wolf; she's good people." Afterward he took me into a back room and said, "You need to learn how to give a speech."
>
> I learned a set speech—ninety seconds—and I went all over the city to deliver it. It ended with, "Just this once, let the woman in the door and put her on the bench." My fellow candidates gagged.[13]

Wolf's campaign was a success. She was elected to Common Pleas Court in 1991 and served until 2011.

Like Judge Wolf, Judge Annette Rizzo, who was elected to Common Pleas Court in 1999 (after being appointed by then-governor Tom Ridge to fill a vacancy on the court in 1998), also began her career in the city solicitor's office. However, Rizzo soon moved into private practice, remaining there for the better part of a decade, and then was employed as corporate counsel for CIGNA "until I got the call in 1998."[14]

Rizzo had nurtured a longstanding desire to run for public office, had worked on local and statewide political campaigns, and "had tentacles in lots of places."[15] Because her responsibilities with CIGNA had required her to spend a lot of time outside Philadelphia, she knew she had to catch up with competing candidates who had been more deeply engaged in the political system.

> A lot of people in Philadelphia who have an interest in running for judge start by having a connection with a ward leader or the ward system. They start out by being kind of a lawyer for the party. They make themselves available to do volunteer work or help someone's constituent with a legal matter. This is a normal path. I was not in that cohort because, as corporate counsel, I wasn't permitted to step out of that role and do any individual representation. I couldn't ride that wave.
>
> So I really made the most of the opportunity to campaign. If there was an endorsement to be sought, I'm there. Unions, legal advocacy groups, the Fraternal Order of Police, the Black Clergy, an organization in Chinatown—I went everywhere to make sure I had the breadth of the city, and I felt that was necessary. The most important component of taking the bench is understanding your connection to the community, and the election process assures that in a way that merit selection never would.[16]

Having the same surname as a Philadelphia icon was a mixed blessing. Judge Rizzo was not related to Frank L. Rizzo, the former Philadelphia police commissioner who served as mayor during the tumultuous 1970s. She made a point of emphasizing this distinction to audiences, regardless of whether she felt it would matter. Her caveat was frequently overlooked or not absorbed; the name had a powerful effect. She received chilly receptions when visiting the liberal wards where Mayor Rizzo's fiercest opponents lived. She was greeted with enthusiastic applause from an audience of Fraternal Order of Police members. On several occasions, after making her presentation in one of the city's distressed neighborhoods, she would be approached by an older African American resident who would tell her, "We loved your father. He was the only one who came up to us and kept us safe."[17]

Like Bernstein, Jones, and Wolf, Rizzo recognized the importance of direct communication with voters across the city, some of whom might have previously come into contact with the court system or who might find themselves in a courtroom at some time in the future.

> I made a point to hit every ward. My whole line was, "I'm a South Philly girl, and I know how important neighborhoods are, and I wanted to make sure that I came to this one." I had never been to parts of the Great Northeast and North Philadelphia, and it made a great difference to me as a judge to understand these neighborhoods. When I started to see addresses from these areas in a lot of cases that came before me, I realized how important it was.[18]

Judicial selection by the electorate does not work effectively on a statewide level, at least not in Pennsylvania, where county party chairpersons can decide whether to allow a candidate to speak to an audience of party members. The practice of denying candidates the opportunity to speak has occurred in metropolitan suburbs as well as in remote rural areas. Judge Jones, who campaigned for a seat on the Pennsylvania Supreme Court in 2007, encountered this situation in suburban Montgomery County, only a dozen or so miles away from the chambers where he served as president judge of Philadelphia Common Pleas Court.

> Some of the party faithful wanted to hear what [Jones] had to say about his candidacy for the state's highest court. Jones waited in the back of the room, his raincoat folded over a chair.
>
> But [Democratic Chairman Marcel] Groen refused—and Jones left, disappointed.
>
> "When you're a judge for 20 years and you consistently uphold the rights of others—one of the most important being freedom of speech—to come here and be told an executive decision has been made not to allow me to speak is shocking," Jones said after he was barred from addressing the crowd.
>
> The scene at the Montgomery County Democratic convention underscores how hard it is to run for statewide judicial office in Pennsylvania, as well as how tough it can be for a candidate without state party backing. . . .
>
> Jones said he had been buoyed by the endorsements he got at conventions in counties where he was permitted to speak—Bucks, Chester, Cumberland, Dauphin and Lancaster.

> "You see the judicial character in him when he speaks to people," said Janet Spleen, the Lancaster city clerk who nominated Jones from the floor. She said she thought it important to have an African American on the high court.[19]

"If [the election] is local," Judge Jones observed, "there's a greater chance for minorities to get on the bench. But between here and Pittsburgh, and even in Pittsburgh, there are not many African Americans and Asians and Latinos on the bench. So I think that [for statewide judgeships] the appointment system is best. The courts have celebrated more than two hundred years of existence, and how many black persons have you seen on the [state] courts?"[20]

Naming Rights

Like other candidates for citywide office, a candidate seeking the Democratic nomination for Common Pleas Court has to make choices about investing (through the campaign committee) in a pay-as-you-go project that is likely to last about 120 days, starting in early January of the campaign year.

Every campaign committee has to pay filing fees and spend some money on administrative expenses, on the production and distribution of printed material, and on campaign event space rentals and supplies. These expenses need to be funded at an early stage with contributions of dollars or in-kind goods and services.

A campaign committee may also choose to pay a consultant—an individual or a firm—to circulate nominating petitions; to design, launch, and manage a campaign website; to oversee a door-to-door distribution of campaign material in targeted neighborhoods; or to recruit and supervise a cadre of workers to promote the candidate on the streets or outside polling places on election day. These services cost thousands of dollars, and there is no guarantee that they will produce the desired results. The impact they have, if any, depends on the reliability of the service provider, on the circumstances of that year's election, and on the strength of competing candidates. In many instances, a candidate with no prior campaign experience cannot determine in advance whether the money paid for these services by the campaign committee will have been well spent or wasted.

With few exceptions, a candidate seeking the Democratic City Committee endorsement will be asked to contribute money to the party that is identified in campaign finance reports in generic terms—as "contribution," for example, rather than "payment for party endorsement." The amount that an endorsed candidate is asked to pay the party is often the same for each endorsed candidate. However, that amount may change significantly from one election year to another.

A candidate also has the opportunity to spend money on a higher-priced "consultant"—a person or organization reputed to have connections to political networks that will help the candidate gain more support and receive more votes from certain constituencies (e.g., African American voters), from certain areas of the city (e.g., Northeast Philadelphia), or from the electorate as a whole. These consultants are unlike the lower-tier consultants, described above, that provide specific campaign organization or management services. Instead, they market themselves primarily as sources of insider advice and as facilitators of access to politically influential leaders or organizations.

Table 7.2, adapted from a summary produced by campaign data analyst David A. Lynn for the *Public Record*, identifies payments to the Democratic

TABLE 7.2 PAYMENTS TO THE DEMOCRATIC CITY COMMITTEE AND SELECTED POLITICAL CONSULTANTS FROM SELECTED CANDIDATES IN THE MAY 2017 DEMOCRATIC COMMON PLEAS COURT PRIMARY ELECTION

Candidate	Democratic City Committee	Liberty Square PAC	Genesis IV	Square Group	Total payments	Total votes	Cost per vote
Winning candidates							
Stella M. Tsai*	$35,000	$20,000	$25,000	$10,000	$90,000	63,980	$1.41
Vikki Kristiansson		$20,000			$20,000	62,656	$0.32
Lucretia C. Clemons*	$35,000		$2,500	$30,000	$67,500	47,015	$1.44
Deborah Cianfrani	$35,000	$20,000	$25,000	$15,000	$95,000	43,838	$2.17
Zac Shaffer	$35,000	$20,000	$25,000		$80,000	39,633	$2.02
Deborah Canty					$0	39,239	—
Shanese Johnson	$35,000		$25,000		$60,000	36,792	$1.63
Mark Cohen					$0	36,461	—
Vincent Furlong†					$0	35,904	—
Unsuccessful candidates							
Jennifer Schultz					$0	34,224	—
Daniel R. Sulman	$35,000	$20,000	$25,000	$10,000	$90,000	33,984	$2.65
Leon Goodman					$0	33,338	—
Wendy Barish					$0	31,831	—
Henry McGregor Sias					$0	31,526	—
Rania Major					$0	30,393	—
John Macoretta					$0	29,829	—
David Conroy	$35,000	$20,000	$25,000	$15,000	$95,000	28,453	$3.34
Brian McLaughlin					$0	26,214	—
Crystal B. Powell	$35,000				$35,000	24,756	$1.41
Vincent Melchiorre	$15,000	$20,000	$25,000	$15,000	$75,000	24,360	$3.08

Source: David A. Lynn, based on campaign finance reports filed with the Pennsylvania Department of State.
* Incumbent
† Incumbent, registered Republican

City Committee and to certain political consultants by selected candidates for Philadelphia Common Pleas Court in the May 2017 Democratic primary election.

Each candidate in this primary election was competing to win one of nine open Common Pleas seats. Three candidates, Lucretia C. Clemons, Stella M. Tsai, and Vincent Furlong, were incumbents; like Mark Bernstein in 1987, they had been appointed to fill vacancies on the court, and their appointments had been approved by the state Senate. Also like Judge Bernstein, they needed to run for election to be seated for ten-year terms after their interim appointments ended.

Vincent Furlong is the only registered Republican who won one of the seats in this election (in primary elections, candidates for judge are permitted to run on both the Democratic and Republican ballots). Given this status, a contribution from him to the Democratic City Committee would not have been expected. Mark Cohen, another winner who did not pay the Democratic City Committee, was a Northeast Philadelphia ward leader and had served as a state representative for more than forty years until (as described in Chapter 1) he was defeated in the 2016 Democratic primary election.

As Table 7.2 indicates, some candidates who did pay the Democratic City Committee and the political consultants shown on the table were successful, and others who paid were not. With the exception of Furlong and Cohen, Deborah Canty was the only successful candidate who did not pay the Democratic City Committee or the consultants shown on Table 7.2. The other candidates who did not pay either City Committee or one or more of the political consultants were not successful.

Table 7.2 does not include candidate payments to political consultants other than those shown, to ward organizations, or to political and civic groups, all of which may have decisively influenced the victories of the successful candidates. However, the table does show how important payments to the party and to some of the best-known consultants are regarded by some candidates. It also shows the difficulty of relating these payments to vote totals. The "Cost per vote" column shows the result of dividing the figure in each candidate's "Total votes" column by the corresponding number in the "Total payments" column.

As indicated, one candidate with a high cost per vote (Vincent Melchiorre) received the fewest votes of the candidates listed on the table. The two highest vote-getters, Stella M. Tsai and Vikki Kristiansson, were the only candidates to receive more than 60,000 votes. However, Kristiansson only needed to spend \$20,000 to come within about 1,300 votes of beating Tsai, who spent \$90,000.

In the 2017 primary, four candidates who paid the Democratic City Committee and who were endorsed by the party—Daniel R. Sulman, David

Conroy, Crystal B. Powell, and Melchiorre—were defeated, and only one of them (Sulman) came very close to winning. Factors other than party support clearly made a difference for these candidates, just as other factors influenced the election outcomes for the party-endorsed candidates.

Jennifer Schultz

The experience of Jennifer Schultz as a candidate in 2015 and 2017 illustrates how one unendorsed candidate outpolled several endorsed candidates and came very close to winning.

After receiving her law degree from Cornell and clerking for a federal judge, Schultz took a job as a staff attorney at Community Legal Services (CLS). Her office in CLS's Law Center North Central branch was located in one of Philadelphia's highest-poverty areas. Schultz played a key role in representing indigent families, many of them Spanish-speaking, who had been victimized by real estate investor Robert N. Coyle Sr. in a rent-to-own housing scam. After years of litigation, Coyle was convicted of bank fraud in 2013.

Schultz spent a decade at CLS before considering her first run for the judiciary as a Common Pleas candidate in 2015. "The 2015 election cycle was kind of a historic moment," Schultz observed. "There were twelve open seats for judges—that was about ten percent of the bench in Philadelphia."[21]

Schultz was one of several attorneys working for nonprofit organizations who were invited to a brunch hosted by the Independence Foundation, a local philanthropic organization that had been a longtime funder of legal services programs. The purpose of the event was to encourage nonprofit service organization attorneys to consider running for the judiciary. Candidates for judgeships often come from the district attorney's office or from private practice, and brunch organizers felt that judges with experience in the public-interest sector would come to the bench with a different perspective and a different frame of reference, and that would help make the system of justice in Philadelphia healthier.

The brunch was not a political event; it was an informal briefing and conversation about how the judicial election system worked. Schultz became interested right away.

"I heard people speak about the process, and I'm like, 'I could do that!' So I threw my hat in the ring. . . . I was a complete, absolute outsider. I had never been involved in organized politics at all. I had to start at square one."

Schultz formed a campaign committee. She circulated nominating petitions, collected signatures in support of her candidacy, and filed the completed petitions on time. As mandated by state law, a drawing was held to determine the order in which the candidates' names would appear on the ballot. Schultz landed a favorable position: eleventh in an election with twelve available seats. She contributed her own funds to her campaign and raised modest amounts of funding from relatives and other supporters. She maxed out her use of the leave days she had earned at CLS to campaign full time from March until election day in May.

At the top of the 2015 ballot was the election of a mayor to succeed Michael A. Nutter, who was completing his second term in office that year (Philadelphia mayors are limited to two four-year terms). The Democratic City Committee had declared the mayoral election an "open primary" in which the party would not endorse a candidate. In Schultz's view, 2015 was the election year in which cracks began to appear in the party machinery. "There had always been a history of certain alliances among ward leaders, of certain groups working together and voting together"; but she felt that in 2015, more ward leaders seemed to be making decisions on their own.

With respect to the endorsement of a judicial candidate, "There's deference to the ward leader," Schultz observed. "So if your ward leader doesn't recommend you, it's basically a gentleman's veto."

In some wards, party-endorsed candidates were the only ones allowed to speak at ward meetings, and in those places Schultz was not given an opportunity to make a presentation. In other wards, a candidate would have to pay $100 just to get admitted to the ward meeting, then wait to be called on to give a short presentation. The ward leader controlled the room and decided on the order in which candidates would be called. "You might have to stand there for three hours, smiling the whole time, until they let you speak—and then half the room has already left."

"The system had lots of ways to keep people from engaging in this process," Schultz said. But she soon developed an effective approach.

> I had a platform, as opposed to everyone else who just talked about themselves. When you're a candidate for the judiciary, you're allowed to speak about the administration of justice. So I would say, "Access to justice is what a judge is all about—it's what my career is all about. I want to be a judge so that all voices can be heard."
>
> And an amazing thing happened. After a few weeks, everyone was talking about access to justice. I had changed the conversation. I heard lines from my speech coming from other candidates' mouths.
>
> I'd get a line of people asking me legal service questions, and I started carrying referral sheets. I didn't just hand them out and walk away—I told people what to do in order to get help. To me this was nothing special, but people came to me and said, "You're for real, you really care." Maybe unintentionally, I was showing people what I was all about.

TABLE 7.3 HIGHEST VOTES RECEIVED IN THE DEMOCRATIC COMMON PLEAS COURT PRIMARY ELECTIONS, 2015 AND 2017

2015		2017	
Candidate	Number of votes	Candidate	Number of votes
Ken Powell	54,320	Stella Tsai	63,980
Kai Scott	52,646	Vikki Kristiansson	62,656
Tracy B. Roman	51,643	Lucretia C. Clemons	47,015
Abbe Fletman	47,298	Deborah Cianfrani	43,838
Mia Roberts Perez	43,388	Zac Shaffer	39,633
Lyris Younge	41,242	Deborah Canty	39,239
Rainy Papademetriou	40,324	Shanese Johnson	36,792
Scott DiClaudio	40,163	Mark B. Cohen	36,461
Daine Grey Jr.	38,690	Vincent Furlong	35,904
Chris Mallios	35,005	Jennifer Schultz	34,224
Michael Fanning	33,726		
Stephanie M. Sawyer	33,690		
Jennifer Schultz	33,402		

Source: Philadelphia City Commissioners, "Archived Data Sets: 2015 Primary" and "Archived Data Sets: 2017 Primary," https://www.philadelphiavotes.com/en/resources-a-data/ballot-box-app/additional-election-results-data.

Note: In both elections all listed candidates won, except Jennifer Schultz. In the 2015 election, there were thirty other candidates with lower vote totals. In the 2017 election, there were seventeen other candidates with lower vote totals.

Although Schultz was unsuccessful in both the 2015 and 2017 elections, the results she achieved are noteworthy. As shown in Table 7.3, she was first runner-up in both elections. In the 2015 contest for twelve seats in the judiciary, Schultz came in thirteenth in a field of forty-three candidates, earning 33,402 votes and trailing Stephanie M. Sawyer, the twelfth-place winner, by fewer than 300 votes. In 2017, among twenty-seven competitors for nine open seats, Schultz came in tenth with 34,224 votes, about 1,700 votes behind the ninth-place winner, despite having a much less favorable ballot position.

In an election involving a significant number of candidates competing for the same position, candidate names are arranged in multiple columns in an order determined by the outcome of a government-administered lottery. To what extent, if any, does the location of a candidate's name on the ballot make a difference with respect to election outcomes, particularly in an election involving many candidates competing for a down-ballot office? To address this question, Jonathan Tannen analyzed the results of four Democratic primary elections for Common Pleas Court, describing the results in a December 2016 blog post for Econsult Solutions Inc., a Philadelphia-based consulting firm.

> So, how much does ballot position effect votes? *A lot*. . . . [In each of four elections analyzed] the very first candidate [i.e., the candidate whose name appeared at the top of the left-hand column] received 6.5% of the vote, and won in every election. Everyone listed in the first column did well, as did many in the second column. By contrast, no single ballot position in columns 3–7 received as many votes on average as any position in the first column.[22]

Tannen also evaluated the impact of candidate endorsements by the Democratic City Committee, the Philadelphia Bar Association, and the *Philadelphia Inquirer* and found that ballot position was a more significant factor in determining election outcome than any and all of these endorsements, leading to the conclusion that

> the largest factor in deciding who is chosen to be Philadelphia's judges is an *entirely random lottery*. We have a system in which the luck of being randomly picked is worth as much as the endorsements of the city's dominant political party and the city's most influential newspaper *combined*.[23]

To reinforce his point, Tannen cites the example of one of the 2015 winners, Scott DiClaudio, whose name was listed at the top of the ballot in that election, as shown in Figure 7.1. DiClaudio won a seat on the judiciary, receiving the eighth-highest number of votes "despite having been repeatedly and publicly censured for his poor performance as an attorney."[24]

Schultz was competitive, and nearly successful, in the 2015 and 2017 elections without obtaining Democratic Party endorsement and without spending as much money as some of the other candidates, including some who spent much more but came in behind her.

JUDGE OF THE COURT OF COMMON PLEAS (Vote for not more than 12) / Juez de la Corte de Primeras Instancias (Vota por no mas de 12)							
	SCOTT DICLAUDIO 11	BRIAN T ORTELERE 18	WAYNE M D BENNETT 25	RANIA MAJOR 31	FRANKLIN A BENNETT III 37	MICHAEL FANNING 43	TANGIE M BOSTON 49
	KEN POWELL 12	JAMES F SERARDINELLI 19	SHERRIAN TOPPIN 26	JOSHUA HILL 32	IRA ROBERTS PEREZ 38	BETSY WAHL 44	
	TRACY B ROMAN 13	DANIE GREY JR 20	VINCE GIUSINI 27	SANDRA WEAVER 33	SHANESE JOHNSON 39	VINCENT N MELCHIORRE 45	CHRIS MCCABE 51
	JON MARSHALL 14	JENNIFER SCHULTZ 21	LEON A KING II 28	LYNNE M SUMMERS 34	LUCRETIA CLEMONS 40	CHRIS MALLIOS 46	STEPHANIE B SAWYER 52
	EDWARD WILLIAM LOUDEN JR 15	HARRY PAPADEMETRIOU 22	THOMAS MARTIN 29	STELLA TSAI 35	FRANCES FATTAH 41	MARISSA BRUMBACH 47	STANN MARSHALL CASH 53
	LEON GOODMAN 16	ABBE FLETMAN 23	ANTHONY KYRIAKAKIS 30	KAI SCOTT 36	JOSH LOBEL 42	WILLIAM J CIANCAGLINI 48	DEBORAH WATSON STOKES 54
	LYRIS YOUNGE 17	VINCENT FURLONG 24					Write In / Por Escrito

Figure 7.1 Ballot in 2015 Democratic common pleas court primary election, with Scott DiClaudio in favored position

Source: Philadelphia City Commissioners, "Election Notice," *Philadelphia Inquirer*, May 15, 2015, p. A19.

How to Choose

The decision that a judge makes could cost a person her income, her savings, her job, or her liberty. A bad decision by a judge could ruin the life of an innocent person and cause lifelong hardship for that person's family. A wrong ruling by a judge could cause citizens to question the validity of the entire justice system.

Although many voters in cities similar to Philadelphia are influenced by candidate endorsements promoted by the Democratic Party, it is unlikely that most voters will vote for a judicial candidate, even a party-endorsed candidate, who is known to be manifestly unqualified for the office. So what's the best way to help voters distinguish the Jennifer Schultzes from the Scott DiClaudios? In Philadelphia, many of the city's best-educated voters would not be able to explain the difference between Municipal Court, Common Pleas Court, Superior Court, and Commonwealth Court. So how could we expect the general public to comprehend the differences between, for example, the forty-three candidates on the 2015 common pleas ballot and the twenty-seven candidates on the 2017 common pleas ballot?

The Philadelphia Bar Association has established a process that is designed to help address this concern.[25] Before every election involving candidates for the judiciary, a bar association Commission on Judicial Selection and Retention evaluates each candidate, resulting, in most cases, in a candidate rating (highly recommended, recommended, or not recommended) that is made public before election day. The evaluation process is conducted by an Investigative Division consisting of "not more than one hundred and twenty members, one-third of whom shall be lay persons."[26] To receive an evaluation, a candidate must complete a questionnaire and authorize the commission to obtain access to information about the candidate from the court system and from oversight bodies such as the Philadelphia Board of Ethics and the Pennsylvania Judicial Conduct Board.

Members of the Investigative Division are grouped into review teams that are assigned to assess the experience and qualifications of individual candidates. Each review team is charged with evaluating the candidate in terms of ten standards, ranging from "legal ability sufficient to have earned the respect of lawyers and members of the bench" to a "record of community involvement."[27]

Although the bar association guidelines state that "it is desirable for a candidate to have had substantial trial experience and a knowledge of the litigation process," candidates without trial experience are not necessarily excluded from consideration.

> Other types of legal experience should also be carefully considered, such as negotiation and mediation skills. A private practitioner, a law teacher or corporate, government or public interest attorney may have experience which will contribute to successful judicial performance. Outstanding persons with such experience should not be deemed unqualified solely because of lack of trial experience. The depth and breadth of that professional experience and the competence with which it has been performed, rather than the candidate's particular type of professional experience should be considered.[28]

The review team submits its evaluation to the full commission, and the candidate is required to appear before the commission on two occasions. The process is comprehensive, fair, and transparent.

The bar association ratings are published in major newspapers and elsewhere, but most voters probably come to their polling places on election day without being aware that these ratings exist or are any different from political endorsements. As a way of testing the possibility that broader dissemination of the ratings might influence more voters to select highly recommended and recommended candidates, Econsult Solutions and the bar association's Young Lawyers Division assembled teams of volunteers who distributed fliers containing bar association recommendations for Court of Common Pleas candidates at randomly selected polling places on primary election day in 2017, in which nine individuals were selected for common pleas seats. The test proved successful.

> [The] results were large enough to significantly change the candidates that won in the polling places assigned volunteers. . . . In the election as a whole . . . three out of nine winning candidates were Not Recommended. In the treatment group [the polling places where volunteers distributed fliers], only one was. . . . The Treatment Group results can be read as predictions of what would happen if the entire city had volunteers assigned.
>
> The effect differed by the income and demographics of the neighborhood: moderate income White and Hispanic polling places experienced the largest effect.[29]

On the basis of these findings, if it had been possible to mobilize volunteers citywide at that election, then it seems likely that Jennifer Schultz would have won a nomination to Common Pleas Court, instead of falling short of success by about 1,700 votes. However, the bar association has no capability to mobilize a real citywide initiative of this kind. So are there other ways of making information about judicial candidates available to voters?

"I wish the [government] voting system rather than the political system could do a better job of providing information," Schultz said. "The law prevents government websites to have links to candidate websites. But wouldn't it be great if you could click on a candidate's name and get connected to their website? For the modern voter, that's what people expect."[30]

The question of whether and how merit selection of judges, at both the local and state level, could improve the quality of the judiciary remains unresolved in Pennsylvania. If the approach used in a merit selection process is judicial appointment by a commission with a diverse and distinguished membership, then the question of "who picks the pickers"—the members of the commission—becomes critical. Judge Bernstein and others commented that even ostensibly nonpartisan members of such a commission could be subject to political influence. For example, selecting law school deans to serve on such a commission would seem to be appropriate; but universities count on the state as a funding source, and a law school dean's vote might be affected by a concern that the university's budget might be jeopardized if her vote were to anger powerful members of the state's General Assembly.

Any merit selection methodology proposed for the state judiciary is bound to be imperfect; but a less-than-perfect approach may be a substantial improvement over an existing system that consistently fails to produce judges who are representative of the state's diversity.[31]

With reference to local elections, such as the common pleas elections, a citywide volunteer force already exists; it consists of the committeepeople who, with varying levels of commitment and capability, work at the neighborhood level to get out the vote and inform voters about the candidates. When committeepeople are actively engaged—and many are—they can be very effective in guiding voters to make intelligent choices. Because Schultz did not seek a Democratic Party endorsement, her candidacy would not be supported by committeepeople who advocated exclusively for party-backed candidates. But some committeepeople who heard her speak at ward meetings in 2015 asked for copies of her campaign materials so they could distribute them to constituents, and more commiteepeople did so during her 2017 campaign. Schultz respected the value that committeepeople can provide at the grassroots level:

> We all rely upon trusted sources. Some people print out the bar association list [of highly recommended and recommended candidates], but other people don't trust the bar association. They're more

> likely to trust a neighbor. For them, why would my opinion about a candidate be more valuable than a neighbor's opinion?[32]

Commenting on the failure of various merit selection proposals over the years, Judge Bernstein said, "The solution is to change politics—for kids to care about the public purpose and become committeepeople and ward leaders."[33]

Would it be possible to increase the number of committeepeople, and the ward leaders they elect, who make it their business to inform voters about the best choices for the judiciary? To the extent that it would be possible to do so, an infrastructure that has supported a self-interested hierarchy for decades, under both Democratic and Republican leadership, can start to become an effective resource for serving the public interest.

8

★★★★★★★

Commonalities

For a prospective candidate seeking Democratic Party endorsement, the route to success is often well-defined, regardless of the office. Most often, the candidate needs to establish a position within the party infrastructure by getting elected as a committeeperson, becoming an aide to an influential political figure, or providing services to the party. Then the individual must wait for the next opportunity to become an endorsed candidate, often following the resignation, retirement, or death of an incumbent.

In contrast, many campaigns in which an unendorsed challenger is opposing a party-backed incumbent are different from one another in terms of organization, the candidate's relationship to the existing party hierarchy, and the characteristics of the area where the voters live. The successful strategy that Joseph Vignola and a handful of younger-generation South Philadelphia Democrats devised to advance Tom Foglietta's candidacy involved persuading committeepeople and consistent supporters of party-endorsed candidates to make an exception to past practice by backing a Republican in the November 1980 congressional election. Chaka Fattah's strategies for winning seats in the Pennsylvania House and U.S. Congress were radically different. On the basis of his awareness that many committeepeople would not support him, he recruited and trained block leaders and civic association members to perform the voter education and get-out-the-vote tasks that would ordinarily have been undertaken by supportive committeepeople and party loyalists. Vignola and his allies were successful in persuading voters to support Foglietta because they occupied positions within the party infrastructure. Fattah and his allies were successful in gaining support for Fattah's campaigns because of their influence within the neighborhood environment.

These two campaign approaches—traditional and unconventional—are not mutually exclusive. Some party-endorsed candidates have employed strategies similar to Fattah's, particularly in those instances in which their endorsement is not universally supported by ward leaders and committeepeople. By the same token, some challengers may find opportunities to tap into the existing party infrastructure and use it to their own ends, as Ed Rendell did when he identified dissident committeepeople—the losers in the most recent ward-leader elections—and succeeded in recruiting some of them to back his candidacy.

Examining issues that are common to all campaigns can provide further insight into how insurgent candidacies such as the ones described in the preceding chapters differ from conventional candidacies and from one another.

Identity

Philadelphia Citizen editor Larry Platt described a telling incident that occurred during a May 9, 2017, debate between incumbent city controller Alan Butkovitz and challenger Rebecca Rhynhart, an event that his publication and the Committee of Seventy had sponsored. "In the back of the room, a public official leaned over and whispered in my ear: 'Alan's a good public servant. But you know what I see on that stage? *New versus old.*'"[1]

Another *Philadelphia Citizen* writer elaborated on the differences between the two candidates, based on what she saw at that debate:

> The most striking aspect of the debate . . . was what [the candidates] presented to voters: a stark choice.
>
> Do you want an old-style in-your-face anti-corruption crusader who boasts of things like the bodyguards he needed to keep himself from being shot when he investigated [Philadelphia Sheriff John] Green? (Disbelieving chuckles from the crowd). Then Butkovitz is your choice.
>
> Do you want someone who thinks collaboration, transparency and modernization are the ways to ensure taxpayer money is well-spent? Then Rhynhart gets your vote.[2]

Rhynhart was readily recognized as "new," but also as "younger" (as opposed to "old-style"), unconstrained by obligations to the existing political hierarchy—and, not least, as the woman candidate. Many winning candidates in Greater Philadelphia and other regions of the country during 2017 and 2018 had similar characteristics. In the May 2018 Democratic primary, Elizabeth Fiedler, a veteran public radio reporter who had never previously campaigned for public office, won the Democratic nomination for state representative in South Philadelphia's 184th District, beating a candidate who had been strongly supported by party leaders and the powerful Electrical Workers Union. Also in May 2018, Mary Gay Scanlon decisively defeated former Philadelphia deputy mayor Richard Lazer and eight other candidates to win the Democratic nomination for the 5th Congressional District, which includes a portion of southwest Philadelphia and many suburban communities. Scanlon had been a staff attorney at the Education Law Center of Pennsylvania and pro bono counsel at one of Philadelphia's leading law firms; she had not previously run for public office either. Lazer, much of whose past work experience had been associated with Philadelphia Mayor James Kenney and the Electrical Workers Union, had started his campaign with the benefit of more than $500,000 in advertising spent by a super PAC in support of his candidacy.[3]

Rhynhart, Fiedler, and Scanlon were part of a rising tide of women candidates who won election in 2017 and 2018. According to the Rutgers University Center for American Women and Politics, the freshman class of women entering the U.S. House of Representatives in 2019 was the largest ever, consisting of thirty-six nonincumbent women, bringing the total number of women serving in the 116th Congress to 102.[4] A record number of women were also elected to state legislatures nationwide, with 503 women serving in upper chambers and 1,609 women in lower houses (beating the previous records of 450 and 1,425, respectively).[5]

Chaka Fattah benefitted from being a candidate during an earlier rising-tide period, in which large numbers of voters supported a new generation of African American challengers against incumbents who were, for the most part, white, older, and closely linked to the party. As Matthew Countryman describes it:

> Perhaps the most important legacy of the Black Power movement in Philadelphia [during the late 1960s and early 1970s] . . . was its impact on the nature of black political leadership in the city. . . . The Black Power movement's commitment to community-based leadership . . . truly democratized black leadership in Philadelphia. . . . The leadership of future black movement organizations and campaigns in Philadelphia would include significant and substantive representation of working-class activists from the city's poor black neighborhoods.[6]

However, as has been proven in many elections, a candidate's identity as a member of a particular constituency—even a constituency that is striving to bring more of its members into elective office—does not necessarily guarantee that large numbers of voters belonging to that constituency will support the candidate. In the 1971 mayoral election, in which Frank Rizzo defeated Hardy Williams and Bill Green, "Green earned more votes in Black wards than Williams did—illustrating that Black voters were voting for the most viable candidate as opposed to just voting based upon race."[7] The failure of Rizzo-supported city controller candidate Andrew Freeman's campaign against incumbent William Klenk in 1977 provides additional evidence that a candidate's identity as a member of a voter group does not guarantee that group's support.

In the many other elections that are not reflective of a rising tide, voter turnout is likely to be lower, and the influence of established ward leaders and committeepeople is likely to be greater. Under these circumstances, insurgent candidates must find ways to establish and promote an identity of their own that is likely to appeal to voters. In the 1977 district attorney election, the identity that Ed Rendell promoted as a candidate could be characterized in terms of three factors: he was an alternative to the highly unpopular Emmett Fitzpatrick; he represented "integrity"; and, for many of those who met him during the thousands of hours he spent campaigning, he was likable and personable. As a candidate in the 1980 congressional election, Tom Foglietta was likable and personable as well—and he was also a politician with a clean record whose family was well known in South Philadelphia. These characteristics gave Foglietta a distinct advantage over the many candidates who scrambled to have their names placed on the ballot after the news of Michael "Ozzie" Myers' indictment.

Education

One of Philadelphia's most effective voter education and training initiatives was created by leaders of the Philadelphia Americans for Democratic Action (ADA) after the 1947 election. As described in Chapter 2, the ADA's School for Practical Politics trained nearly six hundred volunteers in less than two years, producing a generation of activists that was the driving force behind the 1949 election in which Richardson Dilworth was elected city treasurer and Joseph Clark was elected city controller.

> The notion of the school was two-fold. . . . One was training volunteers that we had collected in the 1947 [Dilworth mayoral] campaign . . . they were an extremely naïve bunch in terms of how one conducts an election, what a [poll] watcher is supposed to do to

make sure an election isn't stolen and the like. The second reason [and] biggest part was building an even greater force of volunteers and keeping them active.

[Natalie] Saxe and [Molly] Yard provided "instruction on how to become a committeeman or woman," briefed people on Philadelphia issues, and organized support for Clark and Dilworth's street-corner rallies. Saxe and Yard, as much as anyone in the reform movement, were responsible for forging the army of trained campaign workers who "took to the streets and telephones in the fall of 1949."[8]

Years later, state representative David Richardson gave Chaka Fattah's friend Curtis Jones some advice. "Registering people to vote without educating them about what to vote for," he said, "is like giving people driver's licenses without teaching them how to drive." The events of the 1940s had given the ADA activists and the people they influenced an understanding of the what-to-vote-for factor as it related to the need for municipal reform. Emily Sunstein, an active participant in the ADA during the organization's formative years, found fellow member John Patterson's observations on why people voted for reform particularly relevant.

He said that it was a post-war movement. He said that because people had come back from service, or from several years of public dedication in the military sense, in a sense of national cohesion in an emergency, that they wanted it to count for something. And when they came back home they carried that idealism and desire to see change into their civic life. And a great deal of the momentum of the reform movement, and its dedication came from those people who didn't want things to be the way they were. They . . . wanted to do something better. . . . If you can conjure what the thing would have been like had it gotten its start . . . say, in 1950 or '55 or '60 . . . when everybody'd settled down to a normal life, or what they considered a regular life . . . you can see, I think, that it might have been quite different. *Much* harder to do.[9]

The Black Political Forum (BPF), founded in 1968, was designed in part to educate African American citizens about what to vote for. BPF cofounder W. Wilson Goode wrote:

The organization was founded on three core beliefs: Black people must control the institutions that control their lives; political power is the major force for gaining that control; and the Black community must be liberated from political enslavement as soon as possible.

> This last belief was aimed to remedy the stranglehold that the Democratic Party had on the Black community and Black candidates.[10]

BPF members wanted Philadelphia to follow the example of other cities that had already elected African American mayors, such as Cleveland and Gary, Indiana, where Carl Stokes and Richard Hatcher were serving as these cities' chief executives. Mayor Hatcher was the keynote speaker at the BPF's first banquet, held in 1970. Members of the BPF and Hardy Williams's state legislative campaign team traveled to Cleveland and Gary to learn about campaign strategies and operational practices that had proven successful in those cities, and they worked to replicate those practices in Philadelphia.[11]

> From a West Philadelphia storefront, BPF activists trained potential candidates, street campaigners, poll watchers, and voter registration canvassers from black neighborhoods across the city. In addition, the BPF held seminars after each election to analyze the returns and the effectiveness of its candidates' campaign strategies. . . . Those attending BPF training sessions in the early 1970s included a number of future elected officials, including . . . Chaka Fattah.[12]

Through these and other activities, the BPF played an important catalytic role in a decade-long political realignment. The organization made a critical difference in the successful campaigns of numerous African American challengers, starting with Hardy Williams's election as a ward leader in 1968 and his election as a state representative in 1970.

Three years after the founding of the BPF and in the aftermath of Frank Rizzo's election as mayor, the Philadelphia Women's Political Caucus (PWPC) launched a political education initiative designed to encourage more women to engage in political activity at the ward and division level and to recruit women to run for office.

> The organizational genius behind the political education effort was Florence Cohen. . . . According to Cohen, "We have to get a new type of woman—an independent woman—involved in politics." . . . someone motivated by issues rather than by political allegiances and loyalties. . . .
>
> [She] noted that in 1971 only 7 out of 66 Democratic ward leaders were women, but according to Cohen "none whom you'd call independent women."[13]

The initiative achieved an early success. In the 1972 Democratic primary, three PWPC members were elected to the Democratic National Convention and nineteen PWPC members won election as Democratic committeepeople.[14]

Elizabeth Fiedler's campaign for state representative in the May 2018 Democratic primary election included a voter education component that resembled the ADA, BPF, and PWPC initiatives in terms of its large scale and its emphasis on engaging voters in dialogue rather than simply asking them to vote for the candidate.

> Fiedler's campaign manager, Amanda McIllmurray, was a Bernie Sanders staffer responsible for organizing South Philly, and a delegate to the 2016 Democratic National Convention. McIllmurray cofounded Reclaim Philadelphia with fellow staffers after Sanders' loss in the 2016 Pennsylvania Democratic Presidential primary. . . .
>
> The group, following McIllmurray, mobilized behind Fiedler. In all, the team says that their patchwork foot-soldier canvassing effort—comprised of Reclaim members, returning citizens, volunteers, individual residents, and others—knocked on 50,000 doors in the district and increased turnout in a number of wards.
>
> The team trained to make their outreach more than spiel. They trained volunteers to discuss their own reasons for supporting the candidate and to listen to the feedback from their neighbors so they could consider incorporating their concerns into the broader platform.[15]

This approach was similar to one that Jennifer Schultz adopted in her 2015 campaign for Common Pleas Court, in terms of its responsiveness to individual voters. Rather than spending a lot of time talking about herself, as candidates for the judiciary frequently do in campaign-season presentations, Schultz spoke about how the judicial system could help individuals address serious problems that they had or might encounter; when people asked her specific questions related to their individual legal needs, she explained how they could get assistance. This form of voter engagement, like that practiced by the Fiedler supporters, was an indirect but effective way of educating people about what to vote for—with the goal of educating the candidate as well as the voter.

Two Philadelphia labor unions have been particularly active in conducting voter education linked to advocacy in support of certain candidates and legislative measures, both before and after the turn of the twenty-first century.

The International Brotherhood of Electrical Workers Local Union 98, chartered in 1900, has made substantial contributions to candidates' campaigns, particularly incumbent candidates, at every level of government.

Members of Local 98 are a high-profile presence on election days, both downtown and at neighborhood polling places. Under the leadership of John J. Dougherty, who became business manager in 1993, Local 98 has strongly or decisively influenced many elections. However, the defeat of the union-backed candidate in the 2017 city controller election and in the state and federal legislative races won by Elizabeth Fielder and Mary Gay Scanlon provides evidence that Local 98 support does not guarantee success. Because many members live outside the city, Local 98's direct impact as a source of votes—as opposed to an influencer of votes by others—cannot be precisely determined.

The union also has the ability to influence government decisions directly. District Councilperson Bobby Henon, who had been Local 98's political director before being elected to City Council in 2011, continued to be employed by the union after entering office. This practice is not prohibited by Philadelphia's Home Rule Charter; other council members have also been paid for work in the private sector. For example, council member James Kenney earned nearly $70,000 for services to a local architecture firm during 2015, the year in which he was elected mayor.[16] To date, calls for ending this practice have not gained political traction, and an attorney representing Henon has argued that state law allows it.[17]

In January 2019, Dougherty, Henon, and six others were charged in a federal indictment that cited 116 counts of public corruption, misuse of funds, and false statements. In a related news conference, a representative of the U.S. Attorney's Office said, "[Bobby Henon] made decisions on behalf of John Dougherty rather than the people who elected him to City Council."[18] Although more information about the latter was not available at the time the indictment was announced, Henon may have had numerous opportunities to use the powers of his office to support Dougherty and other political allies without having violated the law, given the absence of an outside-employment prohibition in the city charter.

District 1199C, an affiliate of the National Union of Hospital and Health Care Employees, AFSCME, AFL-CIO, has been led by Henry Nicholas since the 1970s, when Nicholas started organizing nursing home and hospital workers and the union began establishing a presence in Philadelphia. District 1199C quickly became a resource for voter education and outreach activities, particularly—although not exclusively—in support of African American candidates for office. The 1199C membership is much more reflective of Philadelphia's racial and ethnic characteristics than Local 98, and a review of membership data would likely reveal that most 1199C members are city residents, while a large number of Local 98 members live in the suburbs.

The value that these outreach and education initiatives deliver is significant but limited. The people who implement them may succeed in reaching lots of registered voters, but because of limitations of resources and capacity, they will not reach most of them. With respect to many offices on the ballot, the voter education they provide occurs on election day as (some) voters look over material that is handed to them as they approach their polling places.

For the most part, the sample ballots and leaflets that are distributed outside polling places on election days are not designed to educate in any substantive way. Any material that does happen to have educational content, such as the fliers containing Philadelphia Bar Association recommendations for common pleas court judges that were offered at selected polling places in the 2017 primary and again in the 2019 primary, competes for attention with other handouts that have a purely promotional purpose.

In some areas of Philadelphia, particularly in high-poverty neighborhoods, an individual working outside the polls will hand a voter a list of numbers handwritten on a scrap of paper. The numbers are the ballot numbers of recommended candidates. The voter enters the polling place and, after voting, sometimes hands the scrap of paper back so it can be used again.

Why would a voter show up at the polls and vote for a series of numbers without considering any information about the candidates and the offices? For some people who want to vote and have little or no access to information, relying on a neighbor's recommendations may be the best way to ensure that their vote reflects their self-interest and that of their community. The numbers on the list may not necessarily be the ballot positions of Democratic Party–endorsed candidates, and it would be a mistake to assume that lower-income people are party-controlled voters—or that they will automatically vote for the candidates whose numbers are handed to them. Regarding the latter, Ed Rendell recalled his experience at the Southwark Plaza public housing site on election day.

> I went in around 3:00. Welfare moms come in to vote. The [Democratic] committeeman hands them a card; it just has numbers on it—no names. In that division I won eighty-four to twenty-seven or something like that—meaning that those welfare moms took the card, nodded to the committeeman, then went in and voted against Fitzpatrick. That's how powerful the anti-Fitzpatrick message had been. And it wasn't just a message that was delivered during the campaign; it was a message that had been delivered over two or three years.[19]

As a South Philadelphia ward leader, Joseph Vignola had a similar experience in the 1978 general election, in which the governor's race was at the top of the ticket. Many African American voters disliked Democratic nominee Pete Flaherty, who, as mayor of Pittsburgh, had opposed busing in support of school integration. In the divisions where public housing developments were located, "the ticket-splitting was unbelievable," Vignola recalled;[20] many residents made a point of voting for Flaherty's Republican opponent, Dick Thornburgh—or not voting for a gubernatorial candidate at all—and then voting for Democratic candidates for all the other offices on the ballot.

Voters have the opportunity to educate themselves about local candidates and campaigns by consulting news media and political commentary associated with trusted news sources; however, the nature of this opportunity is different from what it used to be. Foglietta, Rendell, and the Casey Five candidates were fortunate to be running for election during the 1970s and 1980s, two decades in which local newspapers and television stations were still covering local politics in depth and in which editorial boards were influential. The Philadelphia media "hammered" Fitzpatrick, in Rendell's words, setting the stage for his reform candidacy.[21] Darnell Jones witnessed the power of the media in helping the Casey Five gain widespread recognition.

To some extent, the shrinking or disappearance of conventional print media before and after the turn of the twenty-first century has been offset by online coverage of candidates and campaigns, although multiple sources need to be consulted to get the full benefit of the latter.

Voter self-education in Philadelphia is facilitated by the city's open-data policies. Philadelphia's relatively early adoption of these policies as they relate to campaign and election data was made possible by the activism of a private citizen, Stephanie Singer. Singer successfully advocated for the release of digitized election results, which she subsequently made accessible to the public through a website that she managed. After being elected as one of Philadelphia's three city commissioners in 2011, Singer, in collaboration with fellow commissioner Al Schmidt (also elected that year), instituted the posting of election result data on the commissioners' website as an ongoing policy.

Before the digital data era, ward and division election results, after being certified by the City Commissioners, were entered on ledger pages in massive books that were stored in a city vault. One year the storage area experienced water damage during a flood. As a result, many of these records were destroyed and are no longer available.[22]

Party

The Democratic Party is a machine. The party is a monolith, massive and intractable. The party is a dinosaur; it used to be powerful, but it is now headed toward extinction.

How accurate are these characterizations? For example, how powerful was the party back in the years of its late-twentieth-century golden age? In the 1965 district attorney primary, Arlen Specter, running as a Republican, beat the party's candidate, James Crumlish, by nearly forty thousand votes. The *Philadelphia Inquirer* characterized his victory as "a severe blow to the Democratic organization, which held a 247,000 registration lead over the Republicans."[23] But other severe blows were to follow. Two years later, in the 1967 mayoral primary, incumbent Mayor James H. J. Tate defeated Alexander Hemphill, the endorsed candidate of the Democratic City Committee chair, by what was characterized as evidence of "the disintegration of the Philadelphia Democratic machine."[24] Then, in the 1977 DA primary, Ed Rendell defeated the party-endorsed candidate by about seventy thousand votes in an outcome that the *Philadelphia Inquirer* described once again as "a severe blow to the Democratic organization."[25]

These defeats occurred during a period in which the Democratic Party was considered to be stronger than it is now—but given these illustrations of failure, how powerful could the Democratic Party actually have been? And how powerful is it now? The outcome of the 2017 city controller primary election provides a more recent illustration of unsatisfactory Democratic Party performance. As described in Chapter 1, Rebecca Rhynhart, an inexperienced newcomer, defeated veteran politician Alan Butkovitz in almost every area of the city.

It could be argued that top-of-the-ballot races are sometimes influenced by factors beyond a political party's control; Rhynhart's victory was very likely to have been influenced by the outpouring of support for women candidates after the 2016 presidential election. But the party was not that effective with respect to some down-ballot races either. As also described in Chapter 1, challenger Chris Rabb won the 2018 Democratic primary election for state representative in Northwest Philadelphia, despite the fact that his opponent had been endorsed by the Democratic City Committee and nearly every Democratic elected official, from Mayor James Kenney down. In the 2018 primary election, the party was not even able to find candidates to run for all of the party's foot-soldier positions, the committeeperson seats. More than 250 of these positions were filled by write-in candidates, many of whom won by a single vote—presumably their own.

Party endorsement clearly makes a difference with respect to the election of judges, as described in Chapter 7. However, as revealed by Jonathan Tannen's analysis of the 2017 election (described in that chapter), a candidate's ballot position, determined at random through a drawing of ballot numbers, is a significantly more influential factor than party endorsement.

Money paid to the party, to ward leaders, or to political consultants who may claim to have special connections to Democratic City Committee leaders or ward organizations is no guarantee of success. As revealed by David Lynn's analysis, summarized in Table 7.2, some candidates in the 2017 common pleas court primary made payments of this kind and won, while others who did so lost, some by substantial margins.

Notwithstanding these examples of Democratic Party failure and underachievement, the party's influence in Philadelphia politics is not inconsequential. The party's endorsement still makes the difference between success and failure for many candidates. So what is the real nature of "the party"?

Robert W. O'Donnell, who represented a Northwest Philadelphia district in the Pennsylvania House from 1974 to 1993 and who served as majority leader and house speaker during his final years in office, commented:

> To think about the party as an entity is not the most useful thing. And to think of candidates who oppose incumbents as independents—which may suggest that they're the reformers—doesn't really represent what actually occurs.
>
> In 1971 [the 1971 mayoral election, in which Frank Rizzo defeated Hardy Williams and Bill Green], was there really a party candidate—a candidate who was closely associated with the Democratic Party? Frank Rizzo was hardly a party guy. Bill Green? Sort of a party guy, but sort of independent and liberal. Hardy Williams had a West Philadelphia organization, but he wasn't really a party guy. David Cohen [the liberal city council member who had declared his candidacy for mayor but subsequently withdrew and threw his support to Green] was a successful ward leader—but was he a party guy?
>
> The party is neither a monolith nor an organization that's falling apart. The truth is that the party is just like a place where people come together. The party doesn't pick somebody—never did. A group of people get together at a place called the party.[26]

In describing the party's endorsement of him as a judicial candidate (related in Chapter 7), Mark Bernstein indirectly made reference to a "place" as well, speaking of a relatively open "front door" vetting process, in which all candidates appear to be given the benefit of consideration, contrasted with the "backdoor" decision-making process through which party leaders may take turns deciding which candidates will actually be endorsed for vacant judicial seats.

Some political decisions may still be made in smoke-filled rooms, but most are probably not. In the 1971 election cited by O'Donnell, the three competing candidates were all Democratic Party members, and all of them mobilized large numbers of supporters who were Democratic Party members; but it is unlikely that any major decisions about their campaigns were made at the Democratic City Committee headquarters, then located at Broad and Walnut Streets—or that they spent much time there at all.

References to "the place called the party" and the "front door" and "back door" are used metaphorically to characterize environments in which political transactions take place.[27] These references are not unlike the use of the term "real estate market" to characterize the environment in which real property transactions occur. The political marketplace is where votes and money are transacted—in a room, over the phone, or on the Internet.

As is the case with real estate data, voting data can be analyzed and used as the basis for forecasting; but both the real estate and political marketplaces are subject to unpredictable disruptions and shocks that can have profound long-term effects. The party has the ability, through its promotion of endorsed candidates, to control a large number of votes; but that does not mean that the party can guarantee outcomes. In preparing for the 1977 DA primary election, Democratic City Committee chair Martin Weinberg anticipated a low voter turnout and instructed ward leaders to focus on bringing out controlled votes to produce a win for incumbent Emmett Fitzpatrick, as described in Chapter 5. However, turnout was much higher than expected, and Ed Rendell's supporters (who must have included many committeepeople, as well as some ward leaders) was much greater than Weinberg had foreseen.

As with another marketplace, the stock market, a decision to spend a lot of money to support a particular investment does not necessarily guarantee successful outcomes and, in some instances, does not even improve the odds. A super PAC supported by three suburban hedge fund financiers provided the 2015 mayoral campaign of state senator Anthony Hardy Williams (the son of Hardy Williams, the 1971 mayoral candidate) with $7 million, an amount nearly equal to the funding of all five other candidates in the race. However, Williams finished in second place, behind Jim Kenney, who received more than twice as many votes.[28]

As Jim Tayoun's comments to DA candidate Ed Rendell indicated, South Philadelphia wards traditionally had a greater capacity to deliver controlled votes and to buck trends—as most of the seven wards in that section of the city were able to do in the 1977 DA primary, delivering majorities to Emmett Fitzpatrick on a day when Rendell won almost every other ward in the city. In the late twentieth century, before South Philadelphia demographics were radically altered by gentrification, a knowledgeable person could invest in controlled votes for a particular candidate and be reasonably assured of getting the desired results. Joseph Vignola described his experience in the 1987 Casey Five election.

> I sat down with [media consultant] Saul Shorr, and we went through and said, "How many votes do we need to win?" and "Where can we buy the votes? Where can we influence the Democratic organization to have these people on their ballot, to print their ballot, whatever we've got to do."
>
> So I said [to political operatives], "I have $1,000 for you—I want one thousand votes. I don't care how you get them; I want one thousand votes. You can put them on the noon ballot, the brunch ballot, the afternoon ballot, I don't care." That's the way we did it. And every one of the Casey judges won.[29]

Rebecca Rhynhart's victory in the 2017 city controller primary provides evidence that the controlled-vote characteristics of South Philadelphia did not persist into the twenty-first century; Rhynhart defeated the party-endorsed candidate in all of the South Philadelphia wards without (apparently) buying any votes. In the 2018 state representative primary, unendorsed candidate Elizabeth Fiedler was nearly as successful; she won the election with majority votes in two of the three South Philadelphia wards included in that legislative district.

In the early twentieth century, the Republican Party owned Philadelphia's political marketplace and controlled Philadelphia's city government. In the early twenty-first century, the Democratic Party does not own the marketplace, and its influence on municipal government is limited and shared with other influencers, including business leaders with no party ties, labor unions, nonprofit service organizations, community and civic organizations, and advocacy groups. Although the Democratic Party remains the most visible presence in Philadelphia's political marketplace, visible presence is not the same as ownership, a fact that is becoming increasingly clear to the newest generation of voters.

The party reduces its exposure to challenges by discouraging participation. Nominating petitions filed by aspiring committeeperson candidates may be challenged by incumbents, the latter of whom may be represented by lawyers who have offered to provide pro bono legal services to the Democratic City Committee in the hope of being endorsed for judgeships at some later time. The challenges may be based on claims that the petitions do not contain the required number of valid signatures or that names and other information have been entered incorrectly.

Being elected committeeperson does not guarantee an opportunity for full participation. As a young man, years before he became a City Council staffer, then a council member, and then council president, Darrell Clarke was elected committeeperson in the North Philadelphia division where he lived. He showed up at the first ward meeting that had been scheduled after election day. Heads turned when he entered the room. "Who are you?" someone asked. He introduced himself as an elected committeeperson. Then two men got up from their chairs. They escorted him out the door and left him on the sidewalk.[30]

Although elected committeepeople may not be ejected from ward meetings anymore, most of them are, in some important respects, witnesses to, rather than active participants in, Democratic Party decision-making. As described in Chapter 1, most ward organizations are not open wards, in which decisions about the endorsement of candidates in every election are made on the basis of a majority vote by the ward's committeepeople. Instead, in most wards, the committeepeople are told which candidates the ward organization will be supporting. In a conversation during the 2011 campaign cycle, then–22nd Ward leader Ron Cousar told me, "I'm the ward leader, not the ward follower." Although Cousar retired in 2018, many current ward leaders share his point of view.

The stories related in the preceding chapters illustrate three challenges that a candidate for office in Philadelphia's current political environment must address to be successful.

- Answer the question that Georgie Woods asked Chaka Fattah and Curtis Jones in the WDAS studios before he left to pick up breakfast: "Why are you running?" The opening sentence of your answer needs to be compelling, or voters' attention will start drifting almost immediately and may be lost for good.
- Decide how to address the question that is implicit in David Richardson's observation regarding the need to educate citizens about what to vote for: Why is it in my self-interest to vote for you?
- Assess the extent to which the success or failure of your candidacy will be influenced by Democratic Party–affiliated individuals who are—literally or figuratively—in a "room" where decisions are made or, alternatively, are people who have gained recognition or respect in the literal or figurative "place where people come together." Which of these individuals can help or harm your candidacy the most, and how will you seek to work with them, or work around them, as the case may be?

Underlying all three of these questions is a broader challenge: how to inspire and engage more participation in democracy in a city where election years characterized by rising-tide movements that catalyze voter turnout are often followed by election years in which apathy and disengagement have a decisive influence on election outcomes.

PART II

Driving the New Machines

9

★★★★★★★

Women's Work

On a national level, the results of the 2018 elections have been characterized as another Year of the Woman, comparable to 1992, when an unprecedented number of women won seats in the U.S. House and Senate. In that year, as in 2018, anger over allegations of sexual misconduct on the part of public officials (Clarence Thomas, Bill Clinton) and the retirement of a large number of incumbent officeholders were significant contributing factors.[1]

In Pennsylvania, the success of women candidates for state legislative office in the 2018 elections increased the diversity of the General Assembly. Eighteen women became members of the Pennsylvania House for the first time, joining thirty-four women incumbents to increase women's representation in that body from 19 percent to about 25 percent. In the Pennsylvania Senate, five new women joined seven incumbents, increasing women's representation to about 25 percent. These outcomes, although noteworthy, show that gender parity is likely to remain only an ideal for some time. Until fairly recently, progress toward achieving this ideal has been nonexistent or slow. No women were elected to the Pennsylvania House until the 1923 session. No woman from Philadelphia was elected to the Pennsylvania Senate until 1985, when Roxanne Jones won election (Jones was also the first African American member of the Pennsylvania Senate). Before then, only two other women had been elected to that body.[2]

With respect to Philadelphia government, progress has been slow as well. Before 1980, most or all of Philadelphia's ten district council seats were occupied by men. Gender diversity increased in the years that followed, and in the 2004–2008 session of council, six of the ten district councilpeople were women. Women have been less successful with respect to council's seven at-large seats. Until the late twentieth century, most of these seats were held by men, and in four of the five Philadelphia City Council sessions that took place between 2000 and 2020, only one of the seven at-large council members was a woman.

Despite the fact that the prospects for successful candidacies by Philadelphia women were, on the whole, not favorable until fairly recently, ambitious women have found ways to gain power and make their influence felt in Philadelphia's political environment. The first two sections of this chapter are profiles of two women who gained stature in this environment during successive periods in the city's postwar history. The third section describes the initial experiences of a millennial-generation Philadelphia woman who, influenced by the outcome of the 2016 presidential election, became a successful candidate for committeeperson in the May 2018 Democratic primary.

Natalie Saxe

A group of remarkable women organized and energized the first phase of Philadelphia's postwar reform movement that began after the end of World War II and continued until the end of Richardson Dilworth's mayoral administration in 1962. They were not handmaidens or worker bees. They were go-to people: leaders, administrators, coalition-builders, recruiters, trainers, and field-operations managers, working individually and in coordination with one another. Although two men—Joseph Clark and Richardson Dilworth—were at the forefront of the reform movement, they owed much of their success to these women.[3]

One of them was Elise Bailen, who had worked for the Office of Strategic Services during the war and afterward became the first executive director of the United Council of Philadelphia, a public policy forum later renamed the World Affairs Council.[4] During Dilworth's 1947 campaign for mayor, Bailen headed the Independent Women's Committee for Dilworth, and in that year she recruited Natalie Saxe, a twenty-four-year-old Penn graduate with a degree in psychology, as a volunteer.

Although Saxe had no prior campaign experience, she quickly demonstrated her value to the Clark-Dilworth team. During the week and a half leading up to the November election, Saxe supervised a phone bank staffed by fifty volunteers that had been mobilized for the purpose of communicating directly with as many of the city's voters as possible just before election day. Although Dilworth lost the election, the reformers immediately began preparing for opportunities that would emerge in 1948 and 1949, and they used the funds remaining from the 1947 campaign to hire Saxe as their staff.[5]

Serendipitously, James Finnegan took over the leadership of the Democratic City Committee in 1948. A former army colonel who recognized that "the Democratic ward leaders were no better and no worse than their Republican opposite members,"[6] Finnegan understood the benefits to be gained from an alliance with the reformers. He provided office space for Saxe, and he approved of the School for Practical Politics, understanding its potential value as a resource for training future Democratic Party operatives. The years of Finnegan's tenure as City Committee chair (which ended in 1953) were a rare period in which Democratic party leaders and leading activists for municipal reform worked together closely to advance their mutual interests.

In her new position, Saxe was responsible for coordinating with City Committee, training volunteers, and recruiting candidates to run for committeeperson positions. When Elise Bailen left to take on an assignment from the State Department (her job was to enlist public support for the Marshall Plan in Northeastern states), Saxe and Molly Yard took over the leadership of the School for Practical Politics and worked together to advance the campaigns of reform candidates. Saxe "plunged into" the 1948 elections, and she and Yard helped deliver successful results for the Democratic Party, which picked up four congressional seats. One of them was won by William J. Green Jr., an independent Democrat whose campaign had been organized by Yard (Green was the father of William J. Green III, who became Philadelphia mayor in 1980).[7]

The national convention of Americans for Democratic Action (ADA) was held in Philadelphia in 1948, and the event generated optimism and enthusiasm among supporters of municipal reform, including Saxe. Eleanor Roosevelt delivered an address to an enthralled audience. "I quite literally adored the woman," Saxe said.[8]

Repopulating the Democratic Party infrastructure in the aftermath of a century of Republican dominance became a high priority. "In hundreds of election divisions, [Democrats] had no committeemen at all," Saxe recalled. In other divisions, "the committeemen were either sellouts or just plain lousy, and we tried to replace [them]." In addition, "We once figured out that only about 50 percent of the eligible population was registered to vote," and "that made us get into [a] full-scale registration drive."[9]

Saxe helped fuel the political ambitions of both Clark and Dilworth, and she established a good working relationship with Dilworth. She was never comfortable with his running mate. "I was made to feel very much like a paid flunky by Joe Clark," she recalled, "and rather more like a human being by Dick Dilworth."[10]

By the time Dilworth opened his 1949 campaign for city treasurer, Saxe had developed networking skills that she was able to use to good advantage. At a party, she chatted up a Republican political operative who disclosed the strategy that Sheriff Austin Meehan planned to employ in an upcoming, well-publicized debate with Dilworth: fire off a series of "nasty questions" about Dilworth's personal life (including a messy divorce in 1935) to catch his opponent off guard. Saxe traveled to Atlantic City, where Dilworth and his advisers were planning Dilworth's debate strategy, and she gave them a debriefing on what she had learned.[11] During that campaign, she also provided Dilworth and Clark (who was a candidate for city controller in the same election) with detailed information about police corruption that she had obtained from David J. Malone, a police department employee in a "middle echelon position" with whom Saxe had become well acquainted "in the early days when I wasn't permitted to know him." Saxe said that she was one of only two people in whom Malone confided about these matters.[12]

She continued to manage campaign activities at the grassroots level as well. Dilworth and Clark were running in tandem with Democratic candidates for two other offices on the 1949 ballot: coroner and registrar of wills. Saxe and the campaign team organized separate street-corner rallies for each of the four candidates—three or four rallies a night, six nights a week, for the final two months of the campaign. As a result of the outreach, recruitment, and training activities that Saxe and Yard had conducted with the encouragement of James Finnegan, "by the time 1949 came around, the City Committee was in a position to be of some help in the campaign . . . though I believe that the independent campaign [conducted in coordination with, but separately from, City Committee activities] was the single most important force in winning that election."[13]

Dilworth and Clark took office in 1950 as treasurer and city controller. However, with the encouragement of Pittsburgh mayor David Lawrence, Dilworth decided to run for governor of Pennsylvania, and he took an unpaid leave of absence during his first year in office. Lawrence helped ensure that he would secure the Democratic Party endorsement without having to face significant opposition in the spring primary election.[14]

Saxe was enlisted in the gubernatorial campaign, and she served as Dilworth's "advance man," as she put it, visiting each of Pennsylvania's counties over an eight-month period to make preparations for campaign tours and to provide the candidate with information about the political environment in each region of the state. Her appointment to this key position "became a matter of some protest on the part of the Democratic power structure who felt . . . that a young (which I was then) woman was unable to do [the job]."[15] Saxe certainly was a young woman; at the start of 1950, she was twenty-six years old.

In each county, Saxe would "meet with the county chairman, assess him as best I could . . . cross-check with other Democratic Party officials, newspaper people, business people . . . and come back and make a report to Dilworth as to what he might expect when he arrived in town."[16] She would also

> find out what rallies are planned and identify best locations for streetcorner meetings. Size up each organization and get local sentiment toward the big issues. . . .
>
> From the [county] chairmen she goes to the state committeemen and then to the newspaper offices. She was especially interested in deadlines—to make sure her boss makes a maximum of editions.[17]

Dilworth lost the election, but by the end of the year, Saxe was on a first-name basis with key political figures in municipalities and counties across the state. Mayor Lawrence urged Dilworth to place her in a position that would enable her to "be present at the legislative sessions in Harrisburg," Saxe recalled. "Since I had met all these characters around the state, I would be very useful . . . to preserve the relationships with the legislative delegation."[18]

Afterward, Dilworth sent a note to her parents: "I just want to thank you both for having let Natalie make that 67 county trip on our behalf. . . . She did a perfectly wonderful job for us, and in addition created complete good will wherever she went. . . . I don't need to tell you what a grand girl she is."[19]

Saxe's working relationship Dilworth extended until his retirement from the public sector in 1971, and she played a central role in his mayoral administration. Dilworth's first term began in 1956, only five years after the adoption of Philadelphia's Home Rule Charter, which provided new opportunities to reshape municipal government to improve the delivery of public services and position the city to take advantage of new opportunities.

> "Home rule" transfers authority over municipal matters from state laws to [what is] essentially a local constitution: it sets up the government structure and outlines its authority and its limitations.
>
> Under home rule, a county or municipality can do anything that's not specifically denied by the state constitution, the General Assembly, or the charter itself. By contrast, municipalities run by municipal codes (state laws) can only act where specifically authorized by state law. . . .
>
> Home rule . . . gives the municipal government the ability to craft ordinances and make decisions based on local needs, rather

than having to follow a one-size-fits-all state code that's decided by state legislators. . . .

For example, home rule municipalities have flexibility in setting the rate of property taxes and personal taxes for residents.[20]

Philadelphia's Home Rule Charter spelled out the roles and responsibilities of city departments and called for the creation of numerous boards and commissions, but it was not an operations manual. Important decisions about how elected, appointed, and salaried individuals in the municipal government infrastructure would interact with one another had to be made by the city administration—and Saxe was often in the best position to influence these decisions. She was a member of the mayor's cabinet (the only woman member). She was secretary of the charter-mandated Administrative Board, the purpose of which was to "determine the policy to govern administrative details of the City government."[21] She reviewed and made recommendations for appointments to boards, from the Philadelphia Housing Authority to the Police Advisory Commission, and she responded to inquiries from prospective appointees ("I have your letter containing the biographical material. You may be sure that it will be on top of the pile in the event of any Board or Commission vacancy. The mayor has asked me to thank you for sending it along."). She prepared the agendas for the regular luncheon meetings between city department heads and Democratic members of City Council. And she continued to be actively involved in lobbying for and overseeing the progress of state or federal legislation associated with city priorities. At an operational level, she may have had the biggest role in determining how the machinery of Philadelphia's new Home Rule government would be driven by Dilworth administration officeholders.

"My principal value to Dilworth was in the political arena," she recalled. "I guess I was the final authority on what he did and didn't do and who he met with and who he didn't." Lobbyists would "call me and tell me they wanted the Mayor to testify or make the rounds or whatever, and I would decide whether or not to recommend that to the Mayor."[22] The two of them had a unique synergy. He counted on her intelligence, perceptiveness, and reliability. She counted on his consistent political support. Their confidence in each other proved to be well founded.

Dilworth won reelection as mayor in 1959 but resigned to run for governor (again unsuccessfully) in 1962. In 1963, for the first time in sixteen years, Saxe was no longer professionally associated with Dilworth, and she was no longer on the city government payroll. She wrote to her former coworker and friend Elise Bailen, who had apparently inquired several months earlier about whether it would be useful for the two of them to "get together after the election to talk out my problems."[23] The letter had a somewhat plaintive tone.

> I've invested the past 2 and one half months in a combination of exploring and just plain thinking things through. It was clear to me . . . that I hadn't begun to settle down and figure out the kind of direction I wanted to take. . . .
>
> They want me back in City Hall and I've been given a "whatever you want" kind of offer. That's a NO and the "why" is simple—I've often referred to the validity of Mr. [Thomas] Wolfe's "You Can't Go Home [Again]."
>
> Next, although I've had some flattering conversations in the broad arena of Philadelphia civic stuff, I do realize that I'm spoiled rotten. There may be those who can, but I cannot do a (what seems to me to be) one dimensional thing after spending six years in the overall seat of power.[24]

Saxe eventually found her way. After a brief stint with a business consulting firm, she did local political work on Lyndon Johnson's 1964 presidential campaign and then regrouped with Dilworth after he was appointed president of the Philadelphia School District in 1965. As his executive assistant, one of Saxe's major responsibilities was lobbying with state government officials to obtain funding and other support for public education. The relationships she developed during this period (which ended with Dilworth's retirement in 1971) positioned her well for the final phase of her professional career as a self-employed consultant and lobbyist working for education and cultural-institution clients.

Marian Tasco

In 1947, the year in which Natalie Saxe was beginning to get acquainted with Philadelphia's political environment, Marian Benton was a young girl living in her great-grandmother's home in Warnersville, an African American neighborhood in Greensboro, North Carolina.

> Warnersville was probably the first area of Greensboro where African-Americans lived. They had factories and mills there. A lot of men worked in the factories; the women raised children and did housework for white families. None of us could get jobs downtown in the department stores. My grandmother was probably born at

> about the time slavery ended. She was a domestic—she worked for a white family. I went to [James Benson] Dudley High School; it was the only high school in Greensboro that [blacks] could attend.[25]

Although segregated, Greensboro possessed cultural and institutional resources that many African American communities lacked. The city is the home of Bennett College, a historically black liberal arts college for women, as well as North Carolina Agricultural and Technical State University (A&T), a land-grant institution founded in 1891.

Her great-grandmother was a member of a Pentecostal congregation led by Bishop Wyoming Wells, whose thirty-four-year ministry included tent revivals and a popular radio broadcast. Well's son, Ozro Thaddeus (O.T.) Wyoming Wells, became a prominent civil rights and defense attorney and served as president of the National Bar Association from 1972 to 1973.

Older people did not encourage her to settle for a homemaker future. To the contrary, "All I heard was 'Get an education, get an education! Go to school! Get an education.'"

> It was a well-rounded life. People were good to us. In the summer, when there was an event, they would have tables outside with white tablecloths. It was just a nice camaraderie, a nice coming together of black people, because we knew we were going to be oppressed downtown. . . . My grandmother was a domestic, but she was always "Miss Benton," and she dressed nice. She always dressed me nicely. She had beautiful furniture that I dusted many times, as far back as I could remember. In those days, the older women used to have formal teas. They used to have wonderful parties. They would have crystal. I learned a lot from them. The kids spent a lot of time on A&T's campus, riding bikes up and down the campus. The university brought the North Carolina Symphony Orchestra in to give concerts, and black kids came from all of the local schools to see them.

After graduating from high school, Marian enrolled at Bennett College and completed three years of coursework while living at home. However, fulfilling a Bennett requirement that each nonresident student live on campus for one year would have made the final year of Bennett unaffordable for her; so she moved to Philadelphia to complete her education at Temple University while living with relatives.

While at Bennett, Marian became acquainted with the four young men who initiated the 1960 sit-in at a Woolworth's lunch counter in downtown Greensboro, a landmark event in the civil rights movement. They were A&T students, and had Marian still been at Bennett at the time, she would have joined them. By then, however, she was living in Philadelphia and enrolled at Temple.

In Philadelphia some years later, an experience with her friend Emma Smith, president of the regional chapter of the Bennett Belles, the school's alumnae association, provided valuable insights that she kept in mind as her political career progressed. In a conversation with Marian—then Marian Tasco—Smith made an observation about Hess's, an Allentown, Pennsylvania-based department store chain that, in its mid-twentieth-century heyday, operated in eighty locations. As one element of its marketing strategy, the company hosted fashion shows on behalf of charitable groups at venues in the areas where stores were located.

> Emma said, "Marian, Hess's has all these fashion shows, but I've never seen one for the black community." So she put together a book about [the Bennett Belles' charitable activities]—a narrative and photographs. And we went to Allentown; my husband drove us. Emma made the presentation to the lady who was in charge of the fashion shows, and she said, "Let me keep this, and I'll get back to you." And Emma said, "If you don't select us, you're going to have to have a very good reason why not." So we got back to Philadelphia, and a day or two later we got a call: we could have the fashion show. So I went down to the Ben Franklin Hotel. We had been having [political campaign] events down there, and I had gotten really tight with the manager, and so we had the first fashion show for the Bennett group down at the Franklin. We had over a thousand people in that ballroom.

As a result of the fashion show, the Delaware Valley chapter of the Bennett Belles raised five times as much money for the college than they had in the previous year. Their success was a catalyst that sparked a series of fundraising competitions among Bennett Belles chapters in subsequent years and generated many more Hess-sponsored fashion shows.

The Hess's experience reinforced and strengthened Tasco's convictions about the need to be ambitious and persistent in pursuing one's goals and advancing one's self-interest. She already had more than a little experience in doing so. After passing the City of Philadelphia civil-service exam, she had turned down opportunities for secretarial positions in the police department, holding out for something more challenging, and was eventually placed on the registrar's staff at the Philadelphia Museum of Art. Over a period of five or six years, she learned how the unit managed its curatorial responsibilities—documenting each item that was part of the museum's collection and tracking any changes in its status or location. In the evenings, she finished up her studies at Temple while her husband cared for their child and attempted—with limited culinary skills—to cook dinner for the family. Tasco's short-term ambition had been to take over the registrar's job when the opportunity arose; but when that person retired and someone else was appointed, she moved on, looking for the next opportunity.

Not too long afterward, Tasco had a conversation with the head of an employment agency, an African American man. "He told me he was going to send me downtown to work for the biggest black guy in Philadelphia."

They both knew who he was talking about: Charles Bowser.

She got an interview with Bowser and then became his secretary at the Philadelphia Urban Coalition, an organization that Bowser headed until he resigned to run for mayor in 1975. Founded in 1969 by business and community leaders at the end of a decade characterized by racial conflict, the coalition (which later became the Greater Philadelphia Urban Affairs Coalition) was "created to fight inner city and other social inequities by bringing together the various public and private sectors in our city . . . as a new structure through which existing organizations and existing leadership can coordinate and expand their efforts."[26] The coalition received government, foundation, and private funding to provide direct services, to deliver funds and technical assistance to smaller nonprofit organizations, and to advocate for progressive changes in government and corporate policies, such as antiredlining initiatives and the creation of business development financing programs for small minority-owned firms.[27]

Through her experience at the Urban Coalition, Tasco "got to meet all the movers and shakers" for the first time: "[Bowser] mentored me. . . . He got me involved in the political world. He made me pay attention to what was going on around me. He would say, 'You have to know what is going on if you expect to change things.'"[28] After working as Bowser's secretary for two years, Tasco became a task force coordinator. The coalition's task forces, comparable to advisory committees, consisted of individuals who had interest or expertise associated with one of the coalition's priorities, such as education, employment, and housing.

> I really enjoyed it. I did a lot of organizing. We had conferences; we started the summer youth employment program. Anytime he wanted to create some new action, I would have to set up a town hall meeting: "Have a town hall meeting, Tasco!" So I stayed there, and then he ran for mayor.

She moved from an older West Philadelphia neighborhood to a section of Northwest Philadelphia that had been built up during the years leading up to and after World War II.

> We moved up onto Temple Road. One day my neighbor asked my husband, "Do you want to be the committeeman?" and my husband said no, he wasn't involved in politics, and I said, "I'll do it." So I went to the meeting. Rose Toll was the ward leader—nice lady. So I was out ringing doorbells till it was dark, passing out literature. I worked the polls for the endorsed candidates in the [1977] district attorney primary election—Emmett Fitzpatrick and Andrew Freeman.

The 50th Ward, where Tasco became a committeeperson (and where she eventually became ward leader), was one of the many wards in which Ed Rendell received more votes than Fitzpatrick, notwithstanding Tasco's door-to-door campaigning on behalf of the Democratic Party–endorsed DA candidate.

Through her work with Bowser and the Urban Coalition downtown, Tasco got acquainted with government and business leaders. Through her activities as a committeeperson in Northwest Philadelphia, she learned how to be effective at retail, neighborhood-level politics. Through her early experiences in Greensboro's African American community, she had already learned how to communicate and how to benefit from social relationships formed and sustained within an environment that, on a larger scale, was hostile and oppressive. And through her years of friendship with Emma Smith, she "absorbed her values, her patience—understanding people—and her outlook on how life works. That was all part of my caring about the community."

She met John F. White Jr. through the ward committee, and White asked her to support his campaign for state representative in the 1974 Democratic primary. The incumbent candidate was the ward leader, Rose Toll, "the lady who had been very nice" to Tasco when she had started out as a committeeperson. But Tasco "could see the neighborhood trending." From her point of view, the political future of her immediate community looked more like John White than Rose Toll, just as a few years later, West Philadelphia residents living in the 192nd state legislative district would view the political future as looking more like Chaka Fattah than Nicholas Pucciarelli.[29]

> I didn't even know John White, but I started working with him, worked his first campaign, rang every doorbell up here, passed out literature, sold chicken dinners to raise money. "Marian, we need money, go fry chicken!" That poor little house out on Temple Road—there was grease all over my dining room carpet. Charlie [Bowser] got mad at me because Rose Toll had supported Charlie when he ran

> for mayor. He had some allegiance to her, and he tried to do everything to get me not to work for John. But I worked with John, and the second time we won [in 1976]. And I just did it because I enjoyed it. I wasn't looking for anything.

After John White was elected, he persuaded Tasco to take a position in Harrisburg with the office of Commonwealth Secretary C. DeLores Tucker, the nation's highest-ranking African American woman in state government. Moving to Harrisburg was not as great a challenge as it might have been at another time. Her marriage was coming to an end, and she had relatives in Steelton Borough, four miles away.

Tucker "was a wonderful person to work with," but Tasco resigned after about a year to accept an invitation from William H. Gray III to work on his campaign for Congress in the 1978 elections. Tucker was very understanding. "You have to follow what you believe in," she told Tasco.

> I moved back to Philadelphia and got an apartment. Bill Gray had hired a gentleman to be his campaign manager—a really high-powered guy—and he told the gentleman to go look for an office for the campaign. And the guy said, "Go find an office? I'm not going to do that." The gentleman resigned. Bill Gray looked at me, and he said, "I guess you're it."
>
> So I became his campaign manager. I already had experience working with John White, running his campaign, getting the workers, doing the paperwork. Sharmain [Matlock-Turner, who later became head of the Greater Philadelphia Urban Affairs Coalition,] and I ran the office on Vernon Road; we covered the polls. On Easter, I had a houseful of company downstairs, but I was on the phone, making sure that the people I had recruited as volunteers were going to show up on election day. So I really liked politics; I really did.

During Gray's early years in Congress beginning in 1979, Tasco ran his Northwest District office and worked closely with his district office staff in North and West Philadelphia. This experience, through which she got acquainted with ward leaders, committeepeople, and political operatives in a large area of the city, placed her in a good position to mount a successful campaign for Philadelphia City Commission in 1983; after winning that citywide office, she was well positioned to be competitive as a City Council candidate in 1987.

Tasco liked the opportunity to engage people through political activity, and people liked her because she was smart, attractive, and able to speak her mind in a convincing, down-to-earth manner. Being a woman was not an obstacle to success in the political arena.

> I didn't run into any sexism—not in my community. And the white [liberal] wards were very good to me. I went to Center City—I was involved with ADA and all that. The progressive wards supported me, so I always had that cushion. No one said you shouldn't be running. Black women have always run the church, and I was very close with ministers. Bill [Gray] formed the Black Clergy group, he and Reverend [William] Moore and the ministers. On Sunday mornings, I was in two or three churches speaking with the congregation—and those people voted.

But there was more to what Tasco termed the "political dynamic" than being intelligent and engaging. The political dynamic was hard and sharp-edged. She explained that when she decided to support John White's candidacy for state representative against Rose Toll, "I had to leave the lady who had been very nice to me; I abandoned her." When DeLores Tucker was being pressured to resign from office on the basis of questionable accusations of impropriety, she said, "what was very painful for me was that some of the staff who had sucked her up [before the accusations] just turned on her. I couldn't believe it." The 1983 city commissioner race was hard fought, and "it was very painful to see the racism." When she ran for City Council in 1987, the Democratic City Committee endorsed one of her opponents, ward leader Shirley Gregory, and the *Philadelphia Inquirer* endorsed her other opponent, E. Randy Urquhart, a retired police officer.

> My friend [Northwest Philadelphia state representative] Dwight Evans told me he was going to support me—but he joined forces with [Tom] Foglietta and all the white ward leaders on the east side of Broad Street and endorsed Shirley Gregory. That was very painful, because I had worked with him all these years. We'd done a lot of work together. I began to understand the dynamics of politics then.

Tasco felt that the news media was portraying the council race as, in effect, a competition between two powerful men who owned and manipulated the two women candidates and were using them to advance their own political goals. Urquhart tried to promote this narrative to benefit his own candidacy. As one news writer reported, "Urquhart went on to accuse both Tasco and Gregory of being tools of 'machine politics.' He said they were supported by 'power brokers' like Gray and U.S. Rep. Thomas M. Foglietta."[30]

Renée Hughes, who was managing finances for Tasco's campaign, urged her not to be drawn into exchanges of charges and countercharges. "She said, 'Just stay real calm. Don't say anything.'"

Not long afterward, Tasco had a good opportunity to say something. On primary election day 1987, she received about twice as many votes as Shirley Gregory, with Urquhart finishing a distant third. The victory party, held at Lakey's Restaurant on Stenton Avenue, was jam-packed. "So a reporter said, 'What happened to Randy?' and I said, 'I told you he wasn't going to win.' And I kept on dancing."

Maya Gutierrez

Not long after Maya Gutierrez started working as a public health researcher at the Philadelphia-based Public Health Management Corporation (PHMC), she became aware of a disturbing pattern:

> It seemed like every year or so, something related to state legislation or the state budget was threatening one or more of the projects that I was working on. It became really evident that there were a lot of state policies that were related to my work and were directly impacting it. So I started to pay more attention to state politics.[31]

She already knew about the master settlement agreement that had been executed between forty-six states and the tobacco industry, with an allotment of $11 billion to Pennsylvania, and she was aware that Pennsylvania's state government had been borrowing from this funding to address budget shortfalls.[32] PHMC received government funding for research, program development, and health promotion projects, as well as for direct-service activities, and uncertainty about future funding prospects was an ongoing concern, as it was for most nonprofit institutions and service agencies. Some of her coworkers had been laid off in 2009 as the result of a funding cutback, and as a relatively new employee, she felt fortunate to have been retained.

Gutierrez's interest in politics and public policy issues had begun long before then. In 1999, during her middle school years, the father of a classmate had declared his candidacy for Philadelphia mayor in the Democratic primary, and she remembered reading newspaper articles about the campaign. The classmate was Kellan White, whose key role in the 2017 city controller primary election is described in Chapter 1. His father was John F. White Jr., who, in 1974, had enlisted Marian Tasco's support for his first campaign for state representative (the winner in the 1999 mayoral primary was John F. Street, who subsequently became a two-term mayor). In college, Gutierrez had majored in political science, but she found international relations, sociology, and geography courses most appealing. She liked the subject matter, and she found the students and faculty more engaging than those who specialized in U.S. politics.

Gutierrez did have had some experience as a campaign volunteer. She had done canvassing and voter registration on presidential campaigns for John Kerry in 2004, then for Barack Obama in 2008 and 2012, and she had helped with a congressional campaign in which a friend was involved. However, although she was not uninterested in politics or disengaged from campaigns and elections, she remained unaware of how the political system was structured at the neighborhood level. She had heard about wards, but she did not know what they were. The ward-and-division system had not been a necessary frame of reference for her volunteer activities.

She and her husband bought a house in Northwest Philadelphia, and she had a child. During the summer of 2016, Gutierrez had been thinking about volunteering for Hillary Clinton's campaign, but it was not a very opportune time to do so; the baby was still nursing and was not napping well. Besides, there seemed to be every indication that Clinton would be successful. Former Obama campaign manager David Plouffe had assured a podcast audience that Clinton was going to win. In Gutierrez's present circumstances, volunteering would be complicated and possibly a waste of time that could be better spent catching up on other responsibilities. She explained:

> I felt guilty about it afterwards. I felt kind of like I had sold out my daughter's future. So the night of or the day after the election, I was trying to come up with concrete ways that I could contribute in a way that I hadn't before. It seemed like a logical thing to run for something. I hadn't considered that before, but I was feeling really angry, and I felt I could do a better job than a lot of these people—so why shouldn't I?

Gutierrez was not particularly pleased with the performance of some of the officeholders who were currently representing her, particularly conservative Republican U.S. Senator Pat Toomey; but she was not going to run against Toomey, and he had just been elected to a six-year term. That was when she remembered that the office of committeeperson existed. During the four years in which she and her husband had lived at their current address, they had not been aware of who their committeeperson was, and no committeeperson had ever knocked on their door, dropped off a pre-election newsletter, or approached them at the polling place.

Gutierrez went online and learned that one of the two committeeperson slots in her division—the 23rd Division within the 22nd Ward—was vacant.

A short time afterward, she discovered that the person who occupied the other committeeperson position had recently moved to another division—so both positions were open. Running for committeeperson was something she could do without needing to be politically connected and without needing name recognition outside her immediate neighborhood.

At about that time, Philadelphia Neighborhood Networks (PNN) was leafletting her neighborhood to promote a committeeperson recruitment-and-training program. PNN is an advocacy organization that was founded by local activists after the 2004 presidential campaign and had received some initial assistance from the national MoveOn organization. Since then, PNN had worked to support progressive candidates and policies with a particular focus on issues such as education, health care, and criminal justice.

In anticipation of committeeperson elections that would be held in May 2018, PNN, in collaboration with Reclaim Philadelphia (which had been particularly active in South Philadelphia) was sponsoring training sessions for prospective candidates. Gutierrez attended one of the sessions, got acquainted with the organizers, and participated in small-group meetings with voters in her division. Overall, the experience was positive. The training was useful, and she liked the people who were involved.

During that time, she met Numa St. Louis, who lived in the same division as she did. He had served as a committeeperson in another area of the city before moving to Northwest Philadelphia, and they decided to work together in campaigning for the two committeeperson positions for their division that would appear on the May ballot. They circulated a joint letter letting people know they were going to run, and they held a petition-signing party. They each knew a handful of neighbors, and they contacted these residents first to collect some signatures on their petitions before knocking on the doors of people who did not know them. Gutierrez's husband was ill with the flu during the week when she had been planning to ring doorbells and ask for signatures; so she took her two-year-old daughter with her, eliciting a welcoming response from many residents.

Participants in the PNN/Reclaim training session had been encouraged to try to engage voters in a discussion of current policy issues while seeking their signatures on the nominating petitions. However, Gutierrez decided not to do so:

> I didn't because it seemed like, for that particular activity, all I needed was their signature, and if they're happy to sign the petition, that's enough. Not that I think it's a bad idea to talk with people about what issues matter to them; it's just that, as a committeeperson, I'm not going to be making any decisions about big policy issues. I may endorse one candidate or another, but I see it more as just

> being committed to helping people vote and promoting a democratic ward to the extent that I can. Some people asked me what a committeeperson does, but I don't think I had a policy conversation with anyone.

Gutierrez and St. Louis did not learn of anyone else who was interested in running for committeeperson in their division, and no one else filed a nominating petition; they would be running unopposed. Even though their election was all but guaranteed (unless another candidate were to emerge and launch an effective write-in campaign—an unlikely prospect), they both wanted to work together to promote their candidacies and generate a good voter turnout.

When the votes were tallied at the close of election day, Gutierrez was the seventh-highest vote-getter among the fifty-eight winning committeeperson candidates in the 22nd Ward, with 160 votes. Numa St. Louis received 144 votes. About half of the successful committeeperson candidates in the 22nd Ward received fewer than 100 votes, and three of these candidates were elected with fewer than 10 votes.

Before election day, Gutierrez had become acquainted with individuals who were running for committeeperson positions in other divisions, and she had participated in some informal discussions about how the ward might be organized after the election. Some of these individuals had participated in PNN/Reclaim training sessions, and others had not; several of them had been incumbent committeepeople who were reelected. The members of this ad hoc group represented a wide range of campaign and election skills and experience, from scant to sophisticated.

The two most pressing post-election issues were the questions of who would be elected ward leader and how the ward committee would operate. As described in Chapter 1, elected committeepeople meet shortly after the date of their election to vote on the selection of a ward leader. Gutierrez knew that the incumbent ward leader, Ron Cousar, would not be running for reelection. Through communication with PNN organizers and others, she learned that two 22nd Ward committeepeople who were also elected officials—district councilperson Cindy Bass and at-large councilperson Derek Green—were interested in the position. Another committeeperson, Carla Cain, who had been an unsuccessful candidate for city commissioner in the May primary election, had also expressed interest. A fourth prospective candidate eventually emerged: Alexander Talmadge, a committeeperson who, years earlier, had served three terms as a city commissioner.

Some people who are active in local politics in Philadelphia feel that it is a conflict of interest for an elected official to also be a ward leader. In their view, a ward leader who is also a candidate or officeholder is less likely to be impartial, particularly with respect to issues such as the ward's endorsements of candidates for office (including, obviously, the office that the ward leader holds). Holding both positions is not prohibited, however, and numerous local, state, and federal officeholders are or have been ward leaders. With respect to the 22nd Ward, the fact that two of the four prospective ward leader candidates were elected officials, one had served as an elected official, and one, Carla Cain, had been a candidate for office in the May primary election and might be a candidate again made it difficult to reach a decision about which of the four prospective ward leader candidates to support.

Because most of the individuals who participated in these informal conversations had not previously been acquainted with one another and were new to ward-and-division politics, each of them appeared to be reluctant to take a strong position with respect to the vote for a ward leader. Gutierrez recalled that in a meeting that was organized a short time before the date of the ward election,

> we went around the room introducing ourselves, saying who we were and who we wanted to be ward leader, and it felt very much like we were all supposed to say that we didn't know who we were supporting yet. I didn't know, and maybe a lot of other people didn't—but I think we were trying to reassure each other that we weren't coming into this with an agenda, trying to elect somebody in particular. Almost everyone said, "I don't know who I'm voting for, but I don't want to vote for an elected official." . . . But Alex had been elected before, and Carla Cain has run for office, so it's not like anyone is totally uninvolved or has no conflicts of interest. So it was a slightly confusing time. And right before the ward meeting—the day before—there were people who were saying, "Okay, I'm voting for this person." But I think that the [group's] reluctance to settle on a candidate made it harder to elect a candidate who would actually support what we wanted.

The individuals who participated in this informal discussion were not a majority of the ward's committeepeople, and it would have been premature for them to try to organize themselves as a caucus of some kind. However, because they had not been able to reach a clear decision about their choice of a candidate for ward leader, they entered the ward meeting without a spokesperson and without a plan for using their numbers to best advantage.

The ward leader election was held, and Cindy Bass won the most votes. However, in ward meetings that took place during the months that followed, disagreements arose about operational issues: How should the ward organization make decisions about candidate endorsements? In what manner would the ward organization report on financial transactions, especially those involving candidates for office? These disagreements were not resolved by the time of the next primary election in May 2019. In preparation for that election, a group of dissident 22nd Ward committeepeople, including Gutierrez, created a 22nd Ward Open Caucus, and the caucus conducted an independent review of candidates, made its own candidate endorsements, and circulated its own sample ballot to voters in the divisions they represented.

In early 2020, it appeared that the 22nd Ward, like some others in the city, would remain divided indefinitely; neither the ward leader nor the Open Caucus members seemed ready to compromise. Because the 22nd was a high-turnout ward, the dissidents had an opportunity to deliver many votes for the candidates they endorsed. Needless to say, however, the alternative—a united ward in which most committeepeople actively and energetically support ward-endorsed candidates as the result of a generally agreed-on candidate-vetting process—would be advantageous to all concerned.

Although Saxe, Tasco, and Gutierrez had very different experiences in Philadelphia politics, they had several characteristics in common that likely influenced their success. They were college educated, and they did not appear to have experienced difficulty in getting private-sector jobs before their involvement in political activity. They worked with men in pursuing their respective political interests, but they were not dependent on men for their success. Both Saxe and Tasco gravitated toward powerful men, but not any more or less than powerful men gravitated toward them. They were not owned by or beholden to any of them.

Most important, all three of them knew how to think critically about opportunities available to them within the city's complicated political infrastructure and were pragmatic in considering how best to pursue these opportunities. Those candidates for office and those individuals engaged in activism at the grassroots level who do the same will have better prospects for succeeding in a city such as Philadelphia, where political instability and uncertainty about the future are likely to be the norm in many neighborhoods.

10

★★★★★★★

Pop-Up Elections and Permanent Campaigns

The public election process has an impermanent aspect: it is seasonal and cyclical. On an annual basis, two periods of intense activity—the spring primary election and the fall general election—are followed by periods of lackluster routine.

David Thornburgh of the Committee of Seventy, a Philadelphia nonprofit organization that works to promote citizen engagement and public policy advocacy in support of "representative, ethical and effective government,"[1] characterized Philadelphia's election-administration process as "a pop-up enterprise," the deeply flawed nature of which is best understood when something goes wrong. "When you have lines of people waiting for three hours to vote at Temple University in the 2016 election, then it's clear that somebody wasn't doing the job of anticipating, planning, training staff, and allocating resources. It's a losing proposition."[2]

Not coincidentally, many campaigns for reforming the political party system or improving the election process are also impermanent, although this impermanence is more often expressed in terms of a linear, rather than cyclical timeline. Reform projects of all kinds seem to rise and fall, come and go, over a period of months, years, or decades.

A reform initiative often emerges as a reaction to a crisis or threat that makes people feel compelled to get involved in some way. Many reform projects—the passage of various forms of equal-rights legislation, for example—are focused on a single issue and are not designed to last beyond the time when the issue is resolved in one way or another or becomes less of a priority.

Are there ways in which voter engagement, in terms of both the administration of elections as well as the advancement of reform initiatives, could be made more ongoing and reliable and less sporadic and unpredictable? The experiences of three Philadelphia organizations illustrate different ways in which this challenge has been addressed, with varying degrees of effectiveness and permanence.

Liberal Evolution

Two unusual strategic partnerships were formed during the years leading up to and after Richardson Dilworth's first unsuccessful run for mayor. One was associated with the desire of Dilworth supporters to continue advancing a Democratic reform agenda after the 1947 election. As previously described, reformers who had supported Dilworth and leaders of the Democratic City Committee agreed to work with each other to pursue, among other goals, their mutual interest in recruiting and training a new generation of committeepeople and volunteers to reinvigorate the party's ward-and-division infrastructure.

The second, more unusual strategic partnership involved two groups that had no prior experience in working together: wealthy owners and managers of Philadelphia businesses and institutions and their spouses, and the heads of about a dozen Philadelphia trade unions. These individuals became the core leadership group of the Southeastern Pennsylvania chapter of Americans for Democratic Action (ADA), an organization that strongly influenced Philadelphia politics for several decades.

Americans for Democratic Action was organized on a national level as an "organization of liberals" in January 1947, and a Philadelphia chapter was founded two months later.[3] The creation of the Philadelphia affiliate provided a new advocacy vehicle for reformers who had resigned from a group called the Philadelphia Citizens Political Action Committee (PAC) in the wake of a conflict over the extent to which "PAC policies were being decided by people who were Communists, or Communist sympathizers."[4] Some of the first generation of ADA members were "social register types," including Dilworth himself.[5] Many of them already knew each other and socialized together. According to one of the labor leaders who subsequently came on board, "The original founders had developed a highly personal relationship. . . . Sometimes small intimate groups met at somebody's house to discuss a problem. There were lots of those meetings taking place."[6]

The labor group that joined forces with these upper-class Philadelphians consisted of leaders of trade unions (steelworkers, sheet metal workers, garment workers, and others) who had wanted to support Richardson Dilworth as a reform candidate in the 1947 mayoral election, instead of remaining neutral or supporting the existing Republican machine, as other unions had done.

The bluebloods and the labor leaders recognized their common interests and became comfortable interacting with one another. According to one of the union representatives:

> When we first started getting together to plan ADA, we really didn't know much about each other. They (the upper class group) did everything they could to woo us and we loved it. They wanted our support and they went out of their way to get it. I don't know what kinds of people they expected us to be, but I think they very quickly learned that we were responsible people who took our obligations seriously.[7]

In the postwar environment, the ADA provided opportunities for idealistic middle- and upper-class people with no prior political experience to educate themselves and participate in constructive ways. As Emily Sunstein described it, "Women and young people . . . entering into the reform movement were able to climb very quickly. . . . Women did very well in the reform. As I remember, nobody ever said to me, 'I don't think you'd be very good at that; we need a man to do that.'"[8] With no prior experience, Sunstein signed up to become head of ADA field operations. At the time, many ADA members lived in the suburbs and worked to advance Democratic candidacies in suburban jurisdictions while contributing to Philadelphia candidates and volunteering for Philadelphia causes.

> There was a good deal of money raised in the counties . . . [from] '46 through 1960. Even '63 [for Walter Phillips's unsuccessful mayoral campaign] . . . you would be surprised at how many of those people were suburban people. But they were so used to giving money to the Philadelphia movement that you would never think of it.[9]

To support volunteer recruitment and election day activities in each county where the ADA had a presence, Sunstein and her coworkers organized a member-list system that was especially beneficial for Philadelphia.

> [The lists] were kept in a central office. And the minute we expanded into a political campaign of any kind, those lists were there. And they were divided both alphabetically and by counties, so that if you wanted to go into a county organization, you had a cadre of people whom you knew, and who had some experience. . . . They could hand out literature, they could canvas, they could make telephone calls

> and so forth. And they did. I don't think that I would question whether there were enough bodies, particularly in the early days, to do as good a job as we were able to do on election day without *masses* of people coming in from the counties to do that.[10]

Sunstein later became chair of ADA and headed the organization during the 1960s. During the latter part of this decade, the liberal political movement in downtown Philadelphia grew much stronger. Between 1967 and 1971, nearly four thousand Democratic voters were added to the voter rolls in Center City's two major wards—the 5th and the 8th Wards, located east and west of Broad Street, respectively—while the number of registered Republicans shrank by more than two thousand, as shown in Table 10.1.

It is noteworthy that, during this period, the total number of registered voters increased by only 2,005, while the increase in registered Democrats was close to double that amount—meaning that this increase could not be attributed solely to the recruitment and registration of new voters. Two other voter groups are likely to have been major contributors to this change: former Republican, independent, or minor-party voters who changed their registrations to become Democratic Party members, and registered Democrats who moved into the area from other places during those years, at the same time as registered Republican voters were moving out.

This change was attributable in large part to the leadership of Norman Berson and other cofounders of the Central Philadelphia Reform Democrats,

TABLE 10.1 CHANGES IN VOTER CHARACTERISTICS IN TWO CENTER CITY WARDS, 1967 AND 1971

Year	Ward (area)	Total registered voters	Democrats	Republicans
1967	5 (east of Broad)	12,388	5,995	5,917
	8 (west of Broad)	16,042	7,801	7,192
Total		28,430	13,796	13,109
1971	5 (east of Broad)	12,759	7,375	4,623
	8 (west of Broad)	17,676	10,135	6,149
Total		30,435	17,510	10,772
Increase or decrease, 1967–1971	5 (east of Broad)	371	1,380	–1,294
	8 (west of Broad)	1,634	2,334	–1,043
Total increase or decrease		2,005	3,714	–2,337

Source: Philadelphia Registration Commission, *Sixty-Second Annual Report of the Registration Commission for the City of Philadelphia* (Philadelphia: City of Philadelphia, 1967); Philadelphia Registration Commission, *Sixty-Sixth Annual Report of the Registration Commission for the City of Philadelphia* (Philadelphia: City of Philadelphia, 1971).

Note: Total registered voters includes Democrats, Republicans, and all other voters.

a downtown-area group of liberal activists who had grown frustrated with the existing political structure.

> We could see that we were getting regularly beaten because of the ward organization that had been created in the city, and what we thought we would do is start at the bottom level and . . . take some of these committeemen's jobs and take over some of these wards and get some voice in the politics of Philadelphia. . . .
>
> You had a certain social cohesiveness because what you have living in Center City at the time were people who were basically from the same social class. They were middle class professional people or middle class businessmen who were in a section of the city that had not had the benefit of a great deal of city money to redevelop it.[11]

Berson ran for state representative in 1966, 1968, and 1970 and won, despite the opposition of ward leader Benjamin Donolow, who endorsed opposing candidates each time.

> By the third time that they had run candidates against me in the primary election, I decided . . . that it would be so much better if we just took over the regular ward structure in the 8th ward and what we did in 1970 was to run a slate of committeemen in every division. . . . There are 29 divisions and we ran 58 candidates. We started a year before—one solid year before—to recruit people to run.[12]

Berson's strategy was successful. Most of the committeeperson candidates he recruited won their elections, and they subsequently elected him ward leader. The Central Philadelphia Reform Democrats included many ADA members, and the two organizations worked closely together.

The ADA continued to remain strong during the years after Sunstein's retirement as chair. As in the early years, many of the most active members of this newer ADA generation were already acquainted with one another socially. As Shelly Yanoff, who got involved with ADA during the 1960s and later became executive director, explained, "It goes back to that Hal Libros thing of being social friends.[13] It was the same with us—we had dinner together and did stuff together. It was a group of young professionals."[14] The organization initiated and managed the citywide campaign to recall Frank Rizzo from office in 1976 and, a year later, loaned Rich Chapman to Ed Rendell's campaign to serve as field operations director in Rendell's successful race for district attorney. The ADA played the central role in mobilizing opposition to the charter amendment that would have allowed Rizzo to run for a third term. And every year the organization raised money and mobilized election day turnout strategies to support the campaigns of liberal candidates. ADA's membership continued to remain largely white and middle and upper class.

Through these and other activities, the ADA of the 1970s retained its influence in Philadelphia politics. But the organization had changed. Some changes were characteristic of the personalities and temperament of a new generation of leaders, including Shelly Yanoff and Mary Goldman.

Shelly Yanoff had been "raising [her] babies"[15] and attending League of Women Voters meetings until the late 1960s. Then she dropped in on an ADA meeting and saw Mary Goldman (who followed Mark Bernstein as head of the 27th Ward Democrats) stand up and speak knowledgably about a current issue—"urban renewal or something."[16]

"I was so impressed that a woman who was not an elected official stood up and raised an important issue and people paid attention," Yanoff recalled. "And I thought, 'Oh, my gosh, look at that!'"[17]

During the following years, Yanoff found lots of ways to get people to pay attention. About a decade after seeing Mary Goldman at the ADA meeting, Yanoff helped Goldman in her (unsuccessful) campaign for one of five City Council at-large seats in the 1979 primary. On election day, she spot-checked polling place operations in the 17th Ward where David Cohen, also a candidate for council at large, was ward leader.

> We thought we had made a deal [that Cohen and Goldman would promote each other's candidacies]. But then I found a Cohen [sample] ballot that did not have Mary's name on it. So I strong-armed Florence Cohen [David Cohen's wife]. I knocked on her door, and she came out. I showed her the sample ballot and said, "This is what some of your committeemen are giving out. If it's not off the street in an hour, David's going to be cut in seven wards!" It was so much fun to be on the right side of a confrontation.[18]

Yanoff had served as ADA's executive director during the early years of the Rizzo administration, and she ran for City Council at large in 1975 as one of five at-large candidates endorsed by Democratic City Committee chair Pete Camiel (all five were defeated by a slate of at-large candidates endorsed by Rizzo, who subsequently replaced Camiel with Marty Weinberg, as described in Chapter 5).

Lenora Berson, Norman Berson's wife (and his coequal as a political strategist), joined the ADA board in 1970. Berson was less genteel than some of the ADA women of the previous generation. She once referred to Congressman Bill Barrett as an "evil spider."[19] "Emily wouldn't have liked Lenora because Lenora was a street fighter," Yanoff recalled. "I can't imagine them in the same room together."[20]

As ADA chairperson during Rizzo's second term, Berson organized the publication of *The Sayings of Chairman Frank, or I Never Saw My Mother Naked*, a collection of Rizzo quotations that were intended to be humorous (e.g., "I like art. It was us Italians who started most of it"). The one-hundred-plus-page booklet was an effective attention-getter and fundraising vehicle.

Emily Sunstein's comments on the publication, made years after she had left the ADA to become a successful writer, reflect the differences between two generations of leadership.

> I thought that we tended to look down on Rizzo's class . . . in a way that we never would have tolerated if it had been black or anything but Italian Catholic. . . . I thought it was bad business. . . . We were feeding the very insecurities and resentments that made his group so loyal to him. . . . I thought the publication of that ridiculous pamphlet about him . . . was insulting! A dreadful thing to have done! It doomed us to a kind of defeat.[21]

ADA weathered some internal conflicts and some changes in the political environment as well. Union members were displeased about the ADA's support for Republican candidate Arlen Specter over James Tate in the 1967 mayoral election, which Tate won. By that time, the union presence in the ADA had weakened greatly. As the manufacturing economy became globalized during the mid- to late twentieth century, causing many industrial firms to move or go out of business, the influence of the labor movement, in Philadelphia, as elsewhere, declined as well.

Some liberals were unhappy that Hardy Williams chose to run for mayor in 1971, splitting the primary election vote between himself and Bill Green and enabling Frank Rizzo to win decisively (David Cohen had also been a candidate in that election, but Cohen withdrew his candidacy shortly before election day and threw his support to Green). Mary Goldman, who had cofounded a group called Independent Democrats of West Philadelphia—a group in which John White Sr., Hardy Williams, and Wilson Goode participated before the founding of the Black Political Forum—was not taken aback by this turn of events. "It's not surprising that Hardy ran, because this [African Americans competing for citywide political office with increasing success] was happening all over the country. The black community had to begin to make their presence known."[22]

The biggest internal division within the ADA that occurred during this period was the result of David Cohen's entry into the 1971 mayoral primary.

Cohen's ADA supporters viewed him as a candidate with genuine left-wing credentials and regarded Bill Green as an elitist politician who lacked strong ties to the traditional urban Democratic base. Green's ADA supporters viewed Cohen as an ideological purist whose candidacy would fail to gain traction with a majority of the electorate, in the same way as left-of-center presidential candidate Eugene McCarthy had failed to do on a national level a few years previously in 1968, after an unexpectedly strong showing in the New Hampshire primary. Even though Cohen had exited the mayor's race shortly before the primary election date and pledged his support to Green, bad feelings persisted. "Strong friendships were formed by the work you did for one candidate versus another," Shelly Yanoff said. "And people who had been close friends split over Cohen versus Green. It was very difficult."[23] Notwithstanding the confrontation between Shelly Yanoff and Florence Cohen on the day of the 1979 Democratic primary, Cohen's candidacy for council at large that year was successful, and Cohen served on City Council until his death in 2005.

During the 1970s, a hotel ballroom would be needed to accommodate a big ADA event. In 2019, most ADA events could be contained within a Center City coffee shop. The ADA of the twenty-first century was no longer supported by a network consisting of many people who were well acquainted with one another, who frequently got together socially, and who regularly contributed to the organization without thinking twice about it. The organization, funding, and implementation of political campaigns had changed fundamentally.

Not every characteristic of the ADA was positive. The ADA's membership had always been more white and more elite than many of its members wanted, and attempts to make the organization more diverse had not been very successful. Ironically, for all its faults, the membership of the much-reviled Democratic City Committee was far more representative of the diversity of Philadelphia's population.

In 1968, the year in which the Black Political Forum was founded, African American leaders who had participated in Independent Democrats of West Philadelphia, the group that Mary Goldman had helped organize a few years earlier, moved on. Their departure from the group was consistent with Goldman's comment about Hardy Williams's campaign for mayor: it was time for the black community to make its presence known, and the Black Political Forum had been organized for this purpose.

In *Black Voters Mattered*, his history of African American political empowerment in Philadelphia, Wilson Goode wrote:

> By the end of 1978, the Black Political Forum had achieved many of the purposes for which it had been organized. The training,

> coaching, and guidance that the BPF had provided had generated sufficient momentum to propel the Black independent political movement forward. . . . The Black Political Forum declared that its work was done.[24]

The Philadelphia ADA could be viewed as having a comparable purpose: serving as a voter-education, leadership-recruitment, and civic-engagement machine designed to help a generation of liberal voters become politically active during the postwar decades. The ADA was not well positioned for permanency. Like the Black Political Forum in some respects, the ADA was highly successful during one phase of the city's political evolution, after which it was superseded by other forms of organization that were more appropriate for a new time.

Arming the Challengers

Lenora and Norman Berson lived in Center City during a period characterized by community opposition to some controversial public-sector development projects that, if implemented, would have worsened conditions in the residential communities surrounding the central business district. During the 1940s and 1950s, residents had successfully fought a proposal to turn Rittenhouse Square into a parking lot.[25] During the 1960s and 1970s, they had campaigned in opposition to a plan to replace South Street with an expressway that would have extended across the width of Center City. At the time, suburban real estate markets were growing stronger, while Philadelphia's downtown and neighborhoods were becoming increasingly distressed. Supporters of these government-sponsored projects had viewed them as an appropriate response to these circumstances—as asset-creation initiatives that would improve the city's competitive position in a new economy.

Fifty years later, during the first quarter of the twenty-first century, Center City's market potential had changed in ways that few would have imagined. High-rent apartments and high-priced condominiums overlooked Rittenhouse Square. Newly constructed and rehabilitated housing on South Street was selling for up to and over $1 million. Vacant land and buildings that had little value during the late twentieth century had become pricey in the twenty-first.

Although city government agencies owned some of the vacant properties that were attracting developer interest in this reinvigorated real estate market, the city had not successfully realigned property-disposition policies to respond to new opportunities. Most sales of publicly owned properties were subject to a cumbersome process that required the district councilperson in whose district the property was located to sign off on the transaction. If the signature was not forthcoming, for whatever reason, the transaction came to a halt.

Not surprisingly, this process provided an opportunity for council members to support favored developers in ways that are not consistent with the public interest. For one developer, a property could be conveyed without being subject to a competitive bid process required by the city.[26] For another developer, the price of a property could be reduced to an amount substantially below its appraised fair market value.[27]

Because council members are elected to four-year terms, there is, in theory, an opportunity for a challenger who supports an honest and equitable property-disposition policy to receive enough votes to replace an incumbent who plays favorites. However, because most incumbent candidates are routinely endorsed by the Democratic City Committee, most ward leaders and committeepeople in a particular council district work to support the incumbent's campaign. And, recognizing this advantage, many individuals and businesses who want to maintain good working relationships with the incumbent do not want to support that person's political opponents. For these reasons and because council members are not subject to term limits, some district council members may remain in office for decades.

Council's complicity in maintaining the status quo with respect to an inefficient and inequitable property-disposition process was not the only reason why Philadelphia 3.0 was founded, but this frustrating problem provides one example of why the founders of Philadelphia 3.0 felt strongly about the need for a new kind of political engagement.

Philadelphia 3.0 executive director Alison Perelman commented:

> The challenge in Philadelphia is the fear that those who push back against the party establishment will face some kind of retaliatory response. And so you have to build this political structure . . . that needs to be able to challenge incumbents and beat them in an atmosphere where people are scared of doing that publicly.[28]

Since its founding in 2014, Philadelphia 3.0 has endorsed a small number of candidates in each election, in contrast to the Philadelphia ADA which, in its heyday, served as a kind of big tent for a variety of political candidates who held liberal views. Endorsed candidates are supported through a political action committee, the original funders of which included several older-generation business leaders.[29]

Between elections, Philadelphia 3.0 has devoted much of its attention to voter education and advocacy for public policy reform, as the ADA had done. The vehicle for these activities is a 501(c)(4) entity, an organization that the Internal Revenue Service allows to engage in lobbying activities associated with a "social welfare" core mission. In 2019, the 501(c)(4) had two employees: Perelman and Jon Geeting, who managed the organization's online presence and much of its advocacy work. Both were Democratic committeepeople who live in gentrifying areas: Perelman in South Philadelphia's 2nd Ward, where Joseph Vignola had been ward leader several decades previously, and Geeting in Fishtown's 18th Ward, where Congressman Raymond Lederer was ward leader at the time of his indictment in the Abscam scandal.

Although the connection between a new generation of political advocacy and "dark money" funding from business establishment sources is unusual and, to some, may appear to be suspect, Philadelphia 3.0 has gained credibility with some of the individuals and organizations that have been most active in advancing a government reform agenda. Perelman commented on the dark money concern.

> Would you feel comfortable writing a check to support a challenger in a district race where you have a relationship with the [incumbent] representative of that district? Very few people would say, "Sign me up for that." And, in the absence of people being able to do that without the fear of some kind of retaliatory action, it isn't clear to me how you would build a political apparatus that would be able to challenge . . . the institution of incumbency. . . . There isn't a totally A-1 version of building a political organization in Philadelphia that can account for this retaliatory stew that I think a lot of people find themselves marinating in.[30]

In the 2015 municipal election, Philadelphia 3.0 endorsed six candidates for City Council: incumbent district Councilperson Maria Quiñones-Sánchez and five candidates for council at large. The money that Philadelphia 3.0 spent on print advertisements and campaign fliers supporting the organization's endorsed candidates may have made a critical difference for Quiñones-Sánchez, given her narrow margin of victory in that primary.

One of the Philadelphia 3.0-endorsed candidates, Derek Green, was the top vote-getter in the at-large race. However, because he had served in Marian Tasco's office as her legal counsel and already had a broad base of support within the ward system, it would be difficult to determine the extent to which 3.0's endorsement contributed to his success. Another candidate, Isaiah Thomas, came within 1,300 votes of winning an at-large seat.

Philadelphia 3.0 hired Neil Oxman (one of the "young Turks" who, decades earlier, had worked with Joseph Vignola and others to get Tom Foglietta elected to Congress) to produce television commercials in support of the endorsed candidates. After the election, Oxman expressed the view that Philadelphia 3.0 regarded its activities in 2015 as part of a "long-term venture." "They view this as being involved for some number of elections over a reasonably long period of time," he observed.[31]

In 2016, the organization joined with the Committee of Seventy to create the Better Philadelphia Elections Coalition as a way of advocating for changes in the management and oversight of Philadelphia elections. The group called for the replacement of the City Commissioners (three elected officials assigned those responsibilities, as required by the Philadelphia Home Rule Charter) with an election director appointed by the mayor and an unpaid bipartisan board of elections.[32]

A year later, the coalition filed a lawsuit against the president judge of Common Pleas Court, charging her with failure to uphold what the coalition viewed as a charter requirement calling for a panel of judges to take the place of the City Commissioners in managing any elections in which a proposed city charter amendment appears on the ballot as a referendum question. After examining thirty-one past municipal elections in which a charter-amendment referendum question was on the ballot, the coalition had concluded that the City Commissioners should have recused themselves (and allowed election-management responsibilities to be taken over by a judicial panel) in two-thirds of these elections. "This further raises the absurdity of the [City Commission] office," David Thornburgh commented.[33] The Pennsylvania Supreme Court dismissed the case in April 2017 without issuing an opinion on the reasons for its action.

After the 2016 election, Philadelphia 3.0 spent more time pursuing opportunities to refresh the ward-and-division system with a new generation of committeepeople who might be more inclined to make voter education and outreach a higher priority and to make their own judgments about candidate endorsements instead of simply following ward leaders' directives. Perelman said:

> The 2016 election was a punch in the face. If Clinton had won, we'd probably still try to work on the ward elections [such as the 2018 primary, in which all of the committeepeople seats would be on the ballot], but it wouldn't have had the same resonance and it would have been a lot harder to get people interested. . . .
>
> We knew we were onto something when we put the first event up on Facebook in late November [the "get mad, then get elected" invitation to an informational meeting about running for committeeperson, referenced in Chapter 1]. The second Jon put it up, it sold out. We were only intending to do one version of that type of thing—and then we're like, "Oh!" And we did a second one and a

> third one, and they just kept filling up. So I think that helped steer the process.[34]

Philadelphia 3.0 was well positioned to take advantage of this new opportunity, and the organization devoted months to educating prospective committeeperson candidates. The work paid off; 170 of the 3.0-supported candidates won election.

In the 2019 Democratic primary, Philadelphia 3.0 endorsed Jamie Gauthier, a challenger running against longtime incumbent district Councilperson Jannie Blackwell in West Philadelphia's 3rd District. Gauthier had been employed as head of the Fairmount Park Conservancy, as executive director of the Sustainable Business Network, and as a program officer at the Local Initiatives Support Corporation's Philadelphia office.

The 3rd District includes the University of Pennsylvania and other institutions, rapidly gentrifying residential communities, and, farther west, distressed neighborhoods with high levels of poverty and social need. Younger, college-educated voters who live in the district's Penn-area neighborhoods might feel that they have more in common with Gauthier than Blackwell (a ward leader who grew up in public housing). However, it would not necessarily follow that all voters of this type would automatically support Gauthier and would respond positively to 3.0's advocacy on her behalf. Facebook user Gregory Laynor expressed his view:

> It's disgusting when rich people try to use progressive rhetoric to grab power.
>
> Billionaire Super PAC Philadelphia 3.0 is trying to buy West Philly's City Council seat, dumping tons of money into ads that co-opt the language of reform. . . .
>
> We need to organize to replace Blackwell—not with a candidate beholden to the anti-Philly Philadelphia 3.0 billionaires—but with a candidate accountable to our pro-labor, pro-affordable housing movement.[35]

Speaking, in general terms, about negative comments posted on Philadelphia 3.0's website, Perelman said:

> If you're trying to do something that's designed to totally change the system, and no one's upset with you, then I don't think you're doing it right. I don't say that because I like being in contentious relationships—I don't think that's productive. I'm more inclined to try to find that really narrow place where we can work together and build a bridge—that's our sensibility; that's the way we like to do things.[36]

New Partnerships, Broader Strategies

On first glance, it might appear to be an unlikely collaboration: the still-new Philadelphia 3.0 and the century-old Committee of Seventy. However, in the post-2016 environment, the two organizations found common ground in terms of their mutual interest in opening up the ward-and-division system.

David Thornburgh said:

> We've got this millennial generation, and we're sort of on the bubble about whether these folks will dive into local politics or get involved in something else. So we're trying to figure out ways to work with them and the generation after them. But it's obvious that you can't encourage people to get active and at the same time have this local ward organization that doesn't want any part of them.[37]

In a separate conversation, Alison Perelman had a related observation.

> It's not incidental—it's by design that [the ward-and-division structure] is a closed loop. We and the Committee of Seventy are both really passionate about democratizing the ward system, so it was a very obvious place to work together. You need a clearinghouse and a laboratory for that kind of work; it has to live somewhere. There needs to be a center of gravity for people who are interested in that stuff.[38]

In in the wake of the 2016 elections, the Committee of Seventy had an experience similar to that of Philadelphia 3.0.

> We had been working with the Young Involved Philadelphia group to plan a "How to Run for Office" event that would take place two weeks after the November election. A week before, we had like thirty people sign up for it. By the time the event was held—270 people. The place was packed.[39]

Following the election of many new Democratic committeepeople in the May 2018 primary, staff members of the two organizations convened a series of informal meetings to work with them and others to consider ways to improve the operation of the ward organizations that represented them or—for the successful committeeperson candidates—that they were now part of. Most participants had similar priorities: making ward endorsements of candidates for office through a majority vote of committeepeople rather than by a unilateral decision on the part of the ward leader; scheduling regular ward meetings and conducting them according to rules of order approved by the ward organization; and filing finance reports that identified funds received and spent by the organization, among other concerns. By primary election day 2019, several ward organizations that had already been conducting their activities according to open-ward principles were continuing to do so; other ward organizations were considering adoption of some or all of the principles; and several wards were experiencing disagreements about the principles. Regardless of how individual wards resolved open issues—to the extent that they were able to do so—this sequence of activity was the first time in decades that the "opening" of the ward-and-division system had gained such high visibility and elicited support from a somewhat organized group of people, many of whom were participating in the system as elected committeepeople.

The Committee of Seventy was created as part of a reform movement that began at the end of the nineteenth century. The organization's leadership has viewed its role as a watchdog, providing independent oversight of elections and municipal governance, as a priority. At the time of its founding, at the height of the Republican machine's dominance in Philadelphia politics, the need for such a role was clear. In monitoring the election of 1909, for example, the committee found evidence that "not less than 38,000 ballots had been marked by some person other than the voter[, an] evil [that] had not been thoroughly understood by the public at large."[40]

During the late twentieth century, the Committee of Seventy recruited and trained individuals—frequently volunteers from businesses and law firms—to be available outside polling places on election days to provide information, answer any questions that voters approaching the polling place might have, and report any problems that they observed. Ellen Mattleman Kaplan, Seventy's policy director from 2005 until 2014, characterized this activity as a "hallmark" of the organization, but said that she and Zack Stalberg, who was president and CEO of the organization during that time, decided it would make sense to start deemphasizing it in order to devote more attention to city governance issues.[41]

David Thornburgh, who became head of Seventy after Stalberg's retirement, continued the organization's transition away from poll monitoring to focus on other voter education and engagement activities. He found that preparing to mobilize volunteers for poll oversight consumed a lot of staff time and that it was difficult to determine the extent to which voters' rights were protected and illegal behavior was deterred. Seventy's volunteers could not gain the same status as partisan poll watchers, who can enter the polling place and review election records, because the poll-watcher certificates they must carry can be issued only by campaign organizations or political parties. For this reason, it was hard to determine how much added value the volunteer program provided. As an alternative, Thornburgh repositioned this program for a much younger group—high school students—who were recruited and trained to distribute election information to voters and respond to basic questions. "It gives them the impression that they have a stake in this," Thornburgh said. "It makes them feel important, and it's good resume fodder." He would hear back from candidates: "I saw your kids at the polls." "It was a take on the new Committee of Seventy," Thornburgh added. "Enabling young people to interact with voters rather than having them play a less active, and possibly less effective, oversight role."[42]

In another context, the watchdog image illustrates a particularly difficult challenge that an organization such as Seventy has to address. A group with a political agenda, such as Philadelphia 3.0, has the ability to take positions on candidates, campaigns, and parties to the extent that doing so might serve the interests of the candidates it supports. However, a group with charitable organization status, such as the Committee of Seventy, has two particular challenges: in addition to refraining from participating in political activity, the organization has to make careful decisions about how its advocacy initiatives will be regarded by people in the public and private sector who have been supportive in various ways in the past. If an organization of this kind starts to be viewed as an unrelenting critic, then at some point supporters in both government and the private sector will stop paying attention. Some people will respect a watchdog; fewer people will respect a gadfly.

Ellen Mattleman Kaplan identified another challenge that such an organization has to address. "With a capital fundraising campaign, you can show a bricks-and-mortar result," she observed. "With a municipal reform campaign, it may be difficult to quantify the impact, regardless of the amount of time and paperwork involved."[43] Kaplan's tenure coincided with the final years of the administration of Mayor John F. Street, during which city officials were investigated in connection with a pay-to-play scandal that led to a prison sentence for the city treasurer. In preparation for the next city administration, Seventy published an "ethics agenda" and asked candidates for mayor and City Council to sign on. Influenced in part by this initiative, then-mayoral candidate Michael Nutter supported several of the proposed reforms and, after his inauguration as mayor, created a Task Force on Ethics and Campaign Finance Reform that published recommendations on policies related to lobbying, conflicts of interest, and other issues. Seventy had a major influence throughout; but, in keeping with Kaplan's comment, the impact of Seventy's leading role in this activity was probably not widely known.

Encouraged in part by the Nutter administration's emphasis on municipal reform, the Committee of Seventy published a research report,

"Needless Jobs: Why Six Elected City Positions Should Die," in 2009. In an introductory page, Seventy characterized itself as "aggressively non-partisan" while stating that "the current financial crisis has prompted us to move government effectiveness higher on our agenda."[44]

In this instance, Seventy could focus on a specific target—obsolete government offices—and could describe a quantifiable outcome in terms of savings to taxpayers. The report called for the "elimination of the Clerk of Quarter Sessions, the City Commissioners, the Sheriff, and the Register of Wills as independently elected offices and the transfer of all necessary tasks from those offices to governmental entities that can handle them efficiently and professionally."[45] These elected positions, which had been created more than a century earlier, were held by officials who did not report directly to the mayor, and the offices were staffed to a considerable extent by patronage employees. Based in part on Allegheny County's experience in eliminating unnecessary elective offices several years previously, the report specified ways in which the responsibilities of these offices could be reallocated.

> The functions of the Clerk of Quarter Sessions and most functions of the Register of Wills can be transferred to the local court system. The Sheriff's duties can be split between the courts and the Police Department, with sheriff's sales shifting to the City's Finance department as in New York City. The responsibility for running elections can be moved from partisan City Commissioners to a professional administrator with experience in managing and supervising local government elections.[46]

In 2010, Mayor Nutter abolished the office of clerk of quarter sessions, and its functions were reassigned to the county court system, as Seventy's report had recommended. Several years later, the *Needless Jobs* report served as a frame of reference for the Seventy-3.0 campaign to restrict or end altogether the Philadelphia City Commissioners' role in administering elections.

In recent years, the Committee of Seventy has "tried to build the brand as less of a watchdog and more of a reform organization—not what are we against but what are we for. We say, 'Here are the things that we'd like to make happen,' and we operate as sort of a quasi-permanent campaign organization, trying to figure out opportunities—and to move on some of those things."[47]

In 2018, Seventy found an opportunity to move on the issue of gerrymandering, which became an especially contentious issue after the Pennsylvania Supreme Court instituted new state and congressional legislative district boundaries, as the result of a finding that 85 percent of the existing district boundaries had been drawn in ways that favored Republicans.

The court action was a short-term fix, not the equivalent of a new state policy on redistricting. In the interest of creating a future policy that would not be driven primarily by politics, the Committee of Seventy became one of the cofounders (with the League of Women Voters of Pennsylvania, Common Cause Pennsylvania, the Pennsylvania Council of Churches, and others) of Fair Districts PA in 2016. This statewide coalition's primary mission is to "reform . . . redistricting rules to promote competitive elections and partisan fairness," with particular concern about the need to institute reforms in time for the redrawing of district boundaries after the 2020 census.[48]

As a related project, Seventy created Draw the Lines PA. Thornburgh described the project as "a massive open source public mapping competition that had people from around Pennsylvania taking the software that we've given them to draw their own congressional maps, as a way of making it clear that citizens want to and can participate in this conversation."[49] The initial competition, undertaken in coordination with three regional steering committees, drew the interest of more than 2,500 people from around the state, with 318 map entries. As Chris Satullo of Seventy described it, "Essentially, we asked people to try to do a map [showing appropriate boundaries for Pennsylvania's eighteen congressional districts] that was better than . . . the one the State Supreme Court imposed last year."[50] After the end of the 2018 competition, Seventy announced that it would continue to sponsor similar mapping challenges, timed to coincide with academic semester calendars, through 2021.[51]

The Committee of Seventy also scaled up its role in promoting voter education and awareness, largely through an online presence known as WeVote. According to Thornburgh, WeVote is "a suite of voter tools—find your elected officials, find your polling place, review candidates on the ballot, develop your own personal sample ballot, and then send it to your family and friends and post it on Facebook." He described WeVote, which reached 65,000 people in 2018, as "the best online voter guide in the country."[52]

> The tagline on WeVote is that it's part of an effort to support the culture of voting in Philadelphia. I think that's an interesting lens for looking at voting—it's a cultural phenomenon. So when it's part of your identity, it's not a question of it's raining, it's early, it's late, it's whatever—it's just what you do. It's, "I owe this to my family, to the people in my community, my church, my company," whatever it is. A hundred years ago, voting was a young people's game, with youth gangs swarming around the city beating people up to get them to the polls, like in the *Gangs of New York* movie. And then

> there was a pushback, this feeling that voting should not only be private but kind of somber—so now it's like we suck all the fun out of it. We sucked the community spirit out of it. So I'm intrigued about ways to try to put that back.[53]

Part of the "fun" associated with ADA was the organization's roots in social networks involving friends and business associates within the twentieth-century middle and upper class. When these networks weakened or dissipated, the fun began to disappear, and the organization became anemic.

For both Philadelphia 3.0 and the Committee of Seventy, the Internet provided energy for new social-network machines. However, each organization's approach to voter education and civic engagement has its own limitations. A person who understands why Philadelphia 3.0 chooses not to disclose the identities of its funders might, at the same time, justifiably question whether the organization has an agenda that involves more than supporting qualified candidates for office. In response to this question, Alison Perelman would probably suggest reviewing the credentials and viewpoints of the candidates that 3.0 endorsed in 2019.

> We're looking for people who have demonstrated professional success in careers prior to running for office and people who are willing to take the kind of risks that we think are going to be required for us to have a City Council that's capable of digging into really challenging issues. . . . If you were to look at the six candidates that we're supporting this time around, you'd be really hard pressed to put them in a box where they all fit comfortably. . . . What does feel right is to say that these are all people who are deeply invested in solving the problems of city government as an institution.[54]

One significant limitation associated with the Committee of Seventy's approach is the organization's nonprofit status, which requires a separation from political candidates and campaigns. Like Philadelphia 3.0, the Committee of Seventy has found creative ways to draw on the energy that followed the 2016 election without overstepping the boundaries associated with tax-exempt status. However, because simply promoting the principles of good government and participation in voting will not, by itself, generate much enthusiasm, the Committee of Seventy in particular has to find new ways to refresh the agenda and attract new interest by, for example, instituting Draw the Lines PA as an annual competition linked to the academic calendar. As ADA's lifecycle demonstrated and as David Thornburgh suggested, to be really successful, municipal reform and civic engagement have to be fun.

11

★★★★★★★

The Perfect Ward

You and a group of your neighbors wanted to improve the ward organization that was supposed to serve as the Democratic Party's presence in your community but had not fulfilled this responsibility for years. Most registered Democrats in the neighborhood did not even know a ward organization existed. So you and several other residents who shared your concerns filed nominating petitions to run for committeeperson positions in the upcoming primary election—and you all won. So now what?

This chapter provides profiles of three ward organizations that experienced a change in leadership after the May 2018 primary election in which committeeperson positions were on the ballot. The narrative that follows describes different ways in which these organizations addressed transition-period challenges and how each of them did or did not respond to the opportunity to reconstitute the ward organization based on open-ward principles promoted by the Committee of Seventy and Philadelphia 3.0.

2nd Ward

The 2nd Ward is located in South Philadelphia, just south of the Center City downtown district. A portion of the street frontage on one of the area's many mixed-use retail-residential blocks is shown in Figure 11.1.

After the 2017 Democratic primary election in which Lawrence Krasner and Rebecca Rhynhart won by large margins, Nikil Saval came to the same

Figure 11.1 South 3rd Street, 2nd Ward

conclusion as the one that Norman Berson had reached with respect to his own neighborhood two dozen blocks away on the other side of Broad Street, half a century previously (as described in Chapter 10). Promoting democracy at the neighborhood level is a worthwhile goal. So to achieve this goal, why keep trying to work around an established ward organization that has a history of unresponsiveness to the interests of community members? Why not just take over the ward organization and make it work to the benefit of the neighborhood?

> Krasner won the 2nd Ward without ward organization endorsement, and he won quite handily [Krasner won 55 percent of the votes, beating his second-place opponent, Joe Khan, 2,684 votes to 1,183]. . . . I and others felt that we were kind of trying to run around the party [organization] in certain directions; that worked in the Krasner election, but it wouldn't always work. We thought we wanted to root ourselves in the neighborhood; we had already done so through our canvassing. We thought it would make sense to bring those values into the party itself, through the ward-and-division structure. That was the initial impulse, the related idea being that we wanted to make these ward-and-division-level decisions open to voting. A lot of the endorsements that would come down, that we would see handed out—it was clear that they were not reflective of the ward [residents].[1]

In every division in Philadelphia, committeepeople are elected every four years in the same primary election as the one in which candidates for governor of Pennsylvania are selected. Shortly after the date of the primary elections, the City Commissioners certify election results and send certificates of election to the winning candidates. Then the elected committeepeople in each ward meet to elect a ward leader and officers of the ward organization.

This initial organizational meeting is not presided over by an unaffiliated individual who is intended to serve as a neutral party; it is convened and opened by the incumbent ward leader or the ward leader's designee. So when a group of committeepeople comes to the ward meeting with the goal of replacing that ward leader and reorganizing the ward committee, there is good reason to be concerned that trouble will start immediately.

> There had been history in the ward of the rules being used to take people out or of people having their certificates of election taken at the door. We were all terrified of that, actually—that after all of this effort, we would somehow not actually be able to organize the ward. But none of that ended up happening. It was actually a fairly smooth reorganization. There was a rumor that there had been some kind of directive from the party leadership not to make [the ward organization process] an issue. It was very clear what the election results were, and it was reported in the newspaper. Even so, the ward chair suggested that the results were not what we suggested they were. But that turned out not to amount to anything.[2]

Reclaim Philadelphia, the primary driving force behind the reorganization of the 2nd Ward, was created in 2016 by former staffers and volunteers from the Bernie Sanders presidential campaign. Within a few years, Reclaim had grown to an organization of "300 dues-paying members and hundreds of volunteers."[3] Nikil Saval was a founding member of Reclaim and vice chair of the organization's Democratic Party Transformation Taskforce.

Reclaim functioned in part as an advocacy organization that participated in issue-oriented campaigns; for example, Reclaim was a member of a coalition that lobbied Philadelphia City Council to divest $2 billion from Wells Fargo, based on the bank's "racist lending practices, investment in dirty energy and funding of privatized prisons."[4] However, Reclaim had been most successful in building support for political candidates at the neighborhood level. The founders of the organization helped produce a large turnout for Sanders in South Philadelphia in 2016, and one Reclaim founder, Amanda McIllmurray, managed Elizabeth Fiedler's successful campaign for state representative in 2018.

Nikil Saval, who was to become leader of the 2nd Ward in 2018, had moved to Philadelphia in 2011. In addition to pursuing his career as a writer (he is a coeditor of the literary magazine *n + 1* and a frequent contributor to the *New Yorker*), he had participated in labor organizing and had been a volunteer for the hospitality workers union UNITE HERE. In Philadelphia, Saval ran voter-canvassing operations out of his house for Sanders in 2016 and then for Krasner in 2017. He characterized Reclaim Philadelphia as

> an organization of the left that seeks to bring critical issues that affect people's lives—like housing, education, and criminal justice—into people's homes by focusing on key electoral issues; to bring together social movements around particular candidates. So Krasner was an ideal version of this, where you get a candidate who's really connected to a movement [i.e., criminal justice reform] linked to a political campaign. Reclaim endorsed Krasner early and connected with a number of criminal justice groups.[5]

In the months leading up to the May 2018 Democratic primary, three groups were taking an active interest in 2nd Ward committeeperson candidacies. Many of the incumbent committeepeople were seeking reelection, and Reclaim and Philadelphia 3.0 were each separately recruiting or encouraging prospective challengers. Reclaim and Philadelphia 3.0 both wanted to see the 2nd Ward reconstituted as an open ward, but the two groups were distinctly different from each other. Philadelphia 3.0 could not be characterized as "an organization of the left," did not have a social-issues agenda comparable to that of Reclaim, and, in some instances, endorsed candidates who were competing against Reclaim-endorsed candidates.

By the deadline for submitting nominating petitions, each of the three groups could claim between twenty and forty candidates running for the fifty-four committeeperson positions in the ward's twenty-seven divisions (with two positions elected for each division). In some divisions, six candidates were running for the two available positions: two candidates from each of the three groups.

Reclaim and Philadelphia 3.0 were committed to an approach involving direct contact with voters—doorbell ringing and doorstep conversations—activities that had not occurred in the ward for years. The 2nd Ward was a different place from the ward that Joseph Vignola had led in the early 1980s, where everyone knew everyone else on their block and households were linked by family, social, and political ties that spanned generations. The twenty-first-century ward population was much more transient, with fewer ties to local churches and schools. Fewer residents were homeowner-occupants. Much of the new development in the area consisted of rental housing, and the conversion of older row houses to apartments had become commonplace.

The incumbent ward organization had not undertaken door-to-door canvassing for years. Many residents were unable to identify the committeeperson who represented their division. So it was not surprising that about two-thirds of the candidates who were supported by Reclaim and Philadelphia 3.0 were elected, producing a strong majority in favor of the open-ward approach.

Nikil Saval was elected ward leader with no opposition and one abstention. The open-ward organizing process began right away. On the basis of Democratic City Committee rules that provided for the formation of subcommittees at the discretion of the ward leadership, several subcommittees were formed: a Get Out the Vote Subcommittee, an Election Day Subcommittee to recruit people to manage polling-place activities on election day, a Bylaws Subcommittee, a Communications Subcommittee, and a Fund-Raising Subcommittee.

Notwithstanding the broad support for an open ward shared by most of the new committeepeople, the related organizational development process was far from tranquil. "The first two meetings were ugly affairs," said George Donnelly, one of the participants. "There were real differences."[6] But in the end, according to Donnelly, there was agreement on 95 percent of the provisions of the new bylaws.

During the previous four years, the ward organization had met only twice. Now the ward organization was holding monthly meetings, sometimes meeting more frequently. In preparation for the May 2019 primary election, candidate forums were held for most of the major offices. Candidates were asked to respond to a questionnaire before the date of the forum in which they would appear.

Two lawyers headed a subcommittee that was assigned to evaluate judicial candidates. After examining each candidate's application to the bar and getting answers to questions about the candidate's values and reasons for wanting to become a judge, the subcommittee produced a list of recommended candidates. The recommendations were subsequently supported by the ward organization by a nearly unanimous vote.

A leadership team consisting of the ward's nine elected officers set the agenda for each ward meeting. However, ward decision-making was consistent with principles of transparency and democratic process. Any committeeperson could participate on any subcommittee. Every candidate endorsement was made on the basis of a simple majority vote by the committeepeople. With respect to the May 2019 primary, most of the candidates who were recommended by the candidate review subcommittees received a substantial majority of votes from the committeepeople—in many instances, more than 60 percent. A committeeperson who disagreed with one or more of the ward endorsements was free to promote alternative candidates, as long as it was made clear that the latter were not ward endorsed.

The ward organization produced a sample ballot containing the names of the endorsed candidates and posted the ballot on a newly designed website. The Democratic City Committee leadership made it known that wards that had adopted a ballot with candidate endorsements that differed from those of City Committee would not receive "street money" to support election day expenses. So the ward organization had to raise funds from other sources to pay for printing its own sample ballots and funding other election expenses. However, candidates were not asked to make contributions to the ward as a condition of receiving ward endorsements.

On primary election day, four out of five City Council at-large candidates endorsed by the 2nd Ward organization won the ward (a total of twenty-eight candidates were running for five positions in this election). All of the ward-endorsed candidates for the judiciary carried the ward. Tiffany Palmer, a common pleas court candidate who had been endorsed by the ward organization and had received a "highly recommended" designation from the Philadelphia Bar Association but had a poor ballot position (bottom row, fifth column to the right, in a field of twenty-five candidates), received the most votes.

The ward organization's approach proved successful in terms of promoting broad civic engagement as well. In the 2018 general election, the 2nd Ward placed within the city's top ten wards in terms of total turnout as well as percentage increase in turnout—the only ward in Philadelphia to place in the top tier of both categories. "The results speak for themselves," George Donnelly said. "If the goal is to turn out the vote and educate people, it couldn't have been done better."[7]

51st Ward

The 51st Ward is located in West Philadelphia south of Market Street, with its eastern edge overlapping the western edge of the University of Pennsylvania–influenced real estate market. Figure 11.2 shows a representative row house block.

Gregory Benjamin first became acquainted with neighborhood politics during the years in which Hardy Williams and other young African American activists were running for office and defeating older white politicians who had enjoyed incumbency for years. During that time, Benjamin's ward got its first African American ward leader—Harold Lloyd Barksdale—but Barksdale proved to be a disappointment. In 1982, he was indicted for defrauding the federal government after it was discovered that he had been collecting rent subsidies for rat-infested apartments that lacked gas and electricity.[8]

Vivian Miller followed Barksdale as ward leader, and she held this position for the next quarter-century, fending off a series of challengers, one of

Figure 11.2 Springfield Avenue, 51st Ward

whom was Benjamin. During much of this time, she also served as the city's clerk of quarter sessions, one of the offices featured in the Committee of Seventy's "Needless Jobs" report (the office's duties included processing bail and defendants' fees and fines). Miller resigned from this position in 2010 after nineteen years, following a report that financial records were not being managed appropriately and that her office had an uncollected debt of $1 billion in forfeited bail.[9]

"One thing I learned from Vivian Miller," Benjamin recalled, remarking on his previous attempts to be elected ward leader, "is that you'd better know what the numbers look like." He continued:

> I started organizing people—block captains and others—to become committeepeople. I already had a base of fifteen of the current committeepeople who supported me. I knew I needed another fifteen to get across the threshold. So I went out, and I made sure that all of my people went on petition drives and got their petitions. I'll never forget that morning when I went to submit my petition [as a candidate for committeeperson in his division] at City Hall. I was the first in line. Later, I found out that two or three petitions were submitted [for the two committeeperson positions] in some divisions, but in other divisions, none at all. So then I realized that I had a good chance of winning. When we took the vote, I received thirty-three votes. So I saw that as a referendum for change.[10]

Before becoming a committeeperson and then ward leader, Benjamin had focused on community services and neighborhood improvement rather than political activism. When he and his wife moved into the area, they found themselves on a block that had three drug houses and was frequented by prostitutes. "People at that time were of the impression that that block could not change," he said. "People thought that was the way it would always be."

Benjamin was determined to change that perspective, and he did so by drawing on the experience he had gained in his past career as a youth counselor and clinician. He started sweeping the block regularly. He opened up his garage for bible study sessions. He struck up conversations with the prostitutes. He recalled:

> I used to clean the block by myself sometimes. That was just to demonstrate to people that I was sincere—but I wanted people to get on board. It was really about engagement and what leadership looked like. If people see leadership, if they see consistency, then they begin in their own time to change some of their thinking. We don't want to incarcerate ourselves out of the problem.

Conditions on the block began to improve. Neighbors joined in on the cleanups. The drug houses and the prostitution disappeared. Benjamin began recruiting residents of nearby blocks to serve as block captains, and he started organizing a block-captain network.

The city announced a plan to shut down the Kingsessing Library, an important neighborhood resource, and Benjamin and others organized a movement to stop the plan. The movement succeeded; the library stayed open. "After that experience," he said, "I decided that I would run for ward leader. I did that because I felt that I could tie the pieces together between community and politics."

Benjamin's plan as incoming ward leader in 2018 was not to remake or rebuild the ward organization. His plan was twofold: to broaden the ward organization's scope of activity to include a neighborhood improvement agenda and to instill in committeepeople a sense of responsibility for implementing that agenda. As a result of that perspective, he did not feel the need to appoint a committee to draft new bylaws for the ward, as the incoming 2nd Ward leadership had done. From Benjamin's perspective, the decades' old "Rules of the Democratic Party of the City and County of Philadelphia" were satisfactory. "It's just like the Constitution of the United States," he said. "There are some things that need to be worked on; it's not perfect. But everything we need is there. They're clear."

In preparation for the May 2019 primary, Benjamin organized a candidate's night for council at-large candidates. He communicated directly with candidates for some of the lesser-known offices. He spoke with other party leaders about candidate endorsement options. At that time, he had been ward leader for less than a year. He did not want to be regarded as a politician who could be bought, but he wanted to be pragmatic. He decided that it would make sense to support City Committee candidate endorsements in those instances in which the party's endorsements seemed to align with the views of 51st Ward voters.

Another important consideration was the need to support his committeepeople with street money. Good committeepeople were "overworked and overlooked," he felt, and he wanted to recruit and keep good committeepeople. The ward population was, by and large, not wealthy. Benjamin was a human services professional who had retired early after an injury. There were no funding sources within the ward that could be tapped to pay for the printing of sample ballots, and thousands of sample ballots would be needed to supply all of the polling places in the ward. So—in the 2019 election at least—Benjamin felt that it would be best to support all the candidates on the party-endorsed ticket. In future years, he would be in a better position to make informed decisions about the circumstances under which his endorsements might diverge from those of the party.

"I believe in the people having a voice. I believe in running an open ward," Benjamin said. But, with regard to candidate endorsement decisions, the final decision would be his.

> My definition of an open ward may be different from that in some affluent areas. When people say open wards, sometimes it seems like it means that everybody should be able to say whatever they want to. We want cohesiveness. We don't want to be unproductive because we're spending most of our time complaining and arguing. Yes, I do believe my committeepeople should have involvement in the process. I want to make room for people to speak. I also believe that the committeeperson should respect that I would make decisions that would have some influence. I believe in being a very active ward leader, and I believe that people will trust my suggestions.

Benjamin also made it known that he had certain expectations of 51st Ward committeepeople. He expected them to show up for monthly ward meetings and to participate in ward-sponsored initiatives, some of which would be demanding of their time and energy. He enlisted them to help him organize movie nights at Kingsessing Playground and to distribute information about community programs and services to the families who came to see the movies. In 2019, Benjamin planned to travel through the ward with the committeepeople, division by division, block by block, to determine the extent to which the "street list" of registered voters published by the city was consistent with reality and to help any unregistered residents register to vote, just as the Black Political Forum had done decades earlier.

As it turned out, several of the candidates that the Democratic City Committee had endorsed in the May 2019 Democratic primary—and that Benjamin had endorsed as well, following the party's lead—were defeated by substantial margins, in two cases by women who successfully challenged incumbent male candidates. The experience made Benjamin aware that longer-term success as a ward leader would depend in large part on his ability to gauge community sentiment on issues of broad interest and to anticipate how these bigger issues might influence voting decisions. Simply endorsing the party ticket every time would not be adequate and would not be in his self-interest as a ward leader.

The community was challenged by serious problems. One of them was gentrification: real estate values were steadily increasing on the residential blocks at the ward's eastern edge. Another was community mental health. Benjamin had been employed in human services jobs at the time when, as a result of late-twentieth-century "deinstitutionalization" policies, individuals with chronic mental illness were released into residential neighborhoods without the benefit of community-based supportive services. "And now those people who were overlooked have families," Benjamin observed. These problems were beyond the capacity of any ward organization to resolve. But in this environment, Benjamin's approach—linking political activism with community services and neighborhood improvement initiatives—seemed to be the most promising one.

50th Ward

In the 50th Ward, located along a portion of the city's northwestern border, most residential development took place in the post–World War II years. A representative block is shown in Figure 11.3.

Cherelle L. Parker was born in Philadelphia and raised by her grandparents, who had moved there from South Carolina and Virginia, respectively. They lived in North Philadelphia for a time and then bought a home in an area of Northwest Philadelphia that had been developed in postwar suburban style: block after block of brick houses with front yards and driveways.

Figure 11.3 Rugby Street, 50th Ward

"It was like *The Jeffersons* [TV show]," Parker said. "It was a big deal to move into that community. I remember as a kid still having white neighbors on our block. But as more African American people moved into the community, you saw white flight."[11]

Parker was seventeen years old and a student at Parkway Center City High School when her grandmother died. With the encouragement of her English teacher, Jeanette Jimenez, Parker wrote an autobiographical speech as a way of working through her grief. Then she delivered the speech as a participant in the citywide Black History Month Oratorical Competition. Parker had entered the competition in the previous year but had not been successful; this time she won.[12]

As the competition winner in the high school category, Parker delivered her speech to a session of Philadelphia City Council. Marian Tasco, then district councilperson for Northwest Philadelphia's 9th District, took note. So did councilperson at-large Augusta Clark, who chaired the council's Education Committee. "I met Gussie and Tasco, and they sort of took me under their wings," Parker recalled. She began working with Tasco while still a high school student.

Through this experience, Parker began learning about neighborhood politics at a time when the population of the 9th District was turning majority black. Tasco had become councilperson for the district in 1988, succeeding John F. White Jr. after White resigned to accept an appointment as secretary of the Pennsylvania Department of Welfare. She and White were part of a new generation of independent African American political leaders who, in Parker's words, created "a high level of expectation" about participation in neighborhood politics:

> I learned very early on that no matter how well intentioned someone [outside the community] may be, the community must speak for itself. No one can speak better for you or your community. And if you're concerned about preserving the quality of life in your neighborhood, you will roll up your sleeves and do something. . . . Black people have a right to lead their own politics and be unapologetic about it. But you have to earn it—no one is given anything.

The 50th Ward avoided some of the adverse effects associated with neighborhood change that had challenged the 2nd and 51st Wards. Although the racial makeup of the neighborhood underwent a transformation, African American homeowners replaced white homeowners with relatively little loss of population or decline in owner occupancy. In contrast, the 2nd and the 51st Wards had been affected, over several decades, by depopulation, housing abandonment, the deterioration of century-old existing housing, and the conversion of many single-family houses to multifamily apartments. Housing in the 50th Ward had been developed much more recently, and owners were not plagued by the kinds of major systems repair and replacement needs that were emerging in houses that had been built decades earlier. In the late-twentieth-century demographic churn that occurred in this section of Northwest Philadelphia, the neighborhood lost some homeowner occupants, but the dominant pattern remained single-family homeownership, and because the neighborhood was stable and attractive, many of the renters who lived there stayed on long term.

Parker was aware of how this characteristic of the 50th Ward affected neighborhood political dynamics:

> Ownership means equity and value. Whenever you see a high rate of homeownership, you will also undoubtedly see a high rate of civic engagement. When people own, they are going to do everything they can to protect the value of their greatest asset; and in this instance it was their home. So in our community, being engaged civically was extremely important.

Parker graduated from Lincoln University in 1994. She later completed postgraduate studies at the University of Pennsylvania's Fels Institute of Government, receiving her master's in public administration degree in 2016. By that time, she had been a committeeperson for two decades.

Committeepeople, block captains, and neighborhood organization members in her Northwest Philadelphia neighborhood were linked more closely than they were in other wards such as the 51st, where Gregory Benjamin had to devote time to organizing his own block and then recruiting people to serve as block captains on other blocks.

Parker said:

> At that very early age, civic engagement was ingrained in me. I don't know what it's like in other areas, but in the 50th and the 10th, right next to it, being a committeeperson was a big deal. That meant you had to have a block captain on every block in your division; and if there was not a block captain or a block contact, you better go find one. . . . You can't simply be a committeeperson if you're not engaged. And so we come to meetings—and that's not just ward meetings. We have a Mount Airy Community Council. Practically everybody in the ward is a part of the Mount Airy Community Council.

What Parker characterized as the "sense of pride, ownership, and responsibility" that came with being a committeeperson was accompanied by unarticulated but palpable social pressure:

> You couldn't become a block captain or a committeeperson in the 50th Ward without doing the work. . . . .If we're in a meeting and Tasco would say, "Something happened on the 8600 block of Provident—who's the committeeperson over there? That's you? Who's the block captain over there?" If you didn't know who the block captain was, it was like you were falling down on the job, and all of the other committeepeople would look at you like, "Oooh, she's a lazy one. You don't even know your people?"

The 50th Ward also benefitted from several decades of continuity in political leadership that had no counterpart in the 2nd and 51st Wards. Marian Tasco had succeeded John White as both 9th District councilperson and ward leader. When Parker succeeded Tasco as district councilperson, the two of them had worked together directly or in close coordination for twenty years. But there was no succession plan and no guarantee that the committeepeople would automatically vote for Parker as ward leader in 2018. She explained:

> When I asked for support, I had already been a vice chair of the ward [organization]. Before then and before becoming state representative [from 2005 to 2015], I had been a committeeperson, sitting in the same chair they were sitting in. I was one of them. I came from them; I'm a product of them. They've seen me grow, they've seen my sweat equity, they've seen my advocacy. . . .
>
> Don't talk about Marian Tasco giving it to me—it wasn't hers to give! I had to earn it through service. Now you see politicians on social media—"I did a block cleanup today." Don't get me wrong—I'm elected, and I've got to do that too; it's another vehicle of communicating. But the hard work that we do in the community, it's not on social media. It's when Ms. Johnson calls. It's when Mr. Brown calls. "Something happened on my block." "Something happened with my husband." "Something happened with my daughter." "My grandchild needs this." It's the service—and it's the service that's not in the newspaper. It's not on social media. That's the sauce! And you can't fake that.

The 50th Ward has a candidate endorsement process that, in general terms, is similar to that adopted in other wards. But the 50th Ward can deliver more value to candidates than many other wards for two reasons: the ward has more "supervoters" who vote in every election, not just the presidential elections, and these voters are particularly attentive to recommendations from committeepeople because they know their committeepeople as neighbors who can solve problems or help them get access to services. Parker explained:

> You don't have to tell people in the 50th Ward that all politics is local; they know that. So if you're doing your work [as an effective committeeperson], it's highly likely that people will want your recommendation about who to vote for. And I'm not just talking about Cherelle. They want the recommendations of their commiteepeople because the committeepeople have analyzed which candidate's platform is best for our community. Anybody who gets the support of the people of the 50th Ward, rest assured, it's going to be earned.
>
> I get a little frustrated when I hear people talk about the ugliness of the process. It is almost as if they want you to feel guilty about being transparent, about requiring a candidate to explain the return on investment for the people of the community that you want to support you. "You're going to run for City Council at large? If we support you, what are you going to advocate for that will benefit the quality of life in our neighborhood?" To me, that is fundamentally the question that every ward, every community in the city, has a right to ask. Every neighborhood is uniquely situated, and there is no one-size-fits-all remedy to public policy. One policy may work very well over there, but the needs of the people who live over here are a little bit different. Every neighborhood should be requiring everyone who's elected to public office to say, "What is going to be your prescription for us, and how will you apply it?" I want to hear more people saying—more people who claim to be interested in democracy—saying, "What's going to be the return on investment for the people in each neighborhood?" I want someone affirming that—and that's what we do through our work.

Although candidates for office can get through to the 50th Ward organization to promote their candidacies, Parker is not enthusiastic about requiring candidates to fill out questionnaires or to appear at candidates-night meetings:

> We won't waste people's time parading people through—that's just pageantry. Personality and charisma and a good speech won't get us. A three-minute speech or answers on a questionnaire are not a

> sufficient process for vetting candidates. We must dig deeper to achieve as much of an authentic view as possible—of who folks are when they are not in front of a camera.
>
> We benefit—the ward benefits—from an engaged constituency. Somebody has a great commercial on television during an election; but our committeepeople and our block captains are communicating with the residents on the block, and they're like, "That person put some heavy commercials on television, but we have to comb through the record. What will be their position on the commercial corridors? What's their record on infrastructure? What's their record on predatory lending? What's their record on public safety? What's their record as far as being accountable on city services and what they expect from law enforcement? What's their philosophy about restorative justice and criminal justice reform?" Our people ask tough questions, and they want data. They're a gritty group.

Ward endorsements are made on the basis of a show-of-hands vote by committeepeople at a ward meeting. The group's preference is frequently known before the meeting has even begun, but not always. In 2018, many committeepeople were enthusiastic about the candidacy of Nina Ahmad for lieutenant governor. Ahmad was a Philadelphian with strong credentials in government, the private sector, and academia. However, it was very unlikely that Ahmad would win. Her campaign had begun late. She was a candidate with liberal credentials running for a statewide office in a conservative state. She was a woman of color competing in a state in which voters across the state, in general, did not favor either women or people of color as candidates. The leading candidate for lieutenant governor, John Fetterman, had been the mayor of a western Pennsylvania municipality, and he had a much higher statewide profile than Ahmad, as well as a strong campaign narrative. He was the likely winner of the election. So why would the ward consider supporting a loser?

"Normally we know who we're going to end up supporting, but we had to go to a paper ballot on this one," Parker said. Ahmad won the ward endorsement, and she won 62 percent of the ward's votes in the primary. However, voters statewide gave Fetterman more than 40 percent of the vote, compared with about 23 percent for Ahmad. Parker said:

> Someone from outside of the 50th Ward might have said that wasn't a smart decision to make. Why would you waste the 50th Ward's endorsement on someone who wouldn't win? Why didn't you just go with the winner? It doesn't work that way. Would they vote whatever way the ward leader tells them? It doesn't work that way! Because the

> moment I, Tasco, or John White started acting as if we knew what was best for them without talking with them, without going through a process of figuring out who's best to represent the interests of our community, they would kick us out. . . . We want to keep it that way, and the way we do it is by delivering results when there's no election. It's the service, the service, the service. People want it to be magic—it's not magic. We're not dictators. You try being a dictator in the 50th Ward—you'll get your head cut off!

In the 2019 primary election, voter turnout in the 50th Ward was 36 percent, compared with about 23 percent citywide. Parker recalled:

> People were saying, "The mighty 50th—they're so good!" But if these people had been in our ward meeting [afterward], they would have said, "Why are these people so frustrated?" Because 36 percent's not good enough—our goal is 50. And after we get to 50, it's going to be 60. It's never good enough—and that's what keeps you motivated. Everybody's always pushing. And when they see it's 36 percent, they're all looking at each other. "Well, what are we going to do? How are we going to do it different next time? We've got to find a way." They don't give you a chance to rest—no! Because the presidential is coming. You're talking about fired up! What is going to be the strategy to get our people out? We wanted 50 percent for this election, so they were disappointed. They've been talking about 80 percent for the presidential. Those are not numbers that are coming from me—these are numbers that are coming from the committeepeople, many of whom are block captains or are connected to block captains. What are we going to do to get our people out? So they're always keeping my wheels spinning because they're always trying to figure out how we're going to do it.

The Perfection Dilemma

The 2nd Ward and the 50th Ward organizations have two characteristics that make it possible for them to produce higher turnouts and better educated voters: a strategy for effective communication with voters and agreement on a plan for operating the ward organization.

However, both wards possess inherent advantages that most others do not. The populations of both are more likely to include more people with higher incomes, higher levels of educational attainment, and more work experience than people elsewhere in the city. The 2nd Ward is home to many residents with new-economy jobs and associated skill sets, and the 50th has an unusually high level of homeownership. Both wards are more homogenous than the rest of the city: the 2nd as a result of gentrification, the 50th because the transition from majority white to majority black was completed years ago. Notwithstanding these advantages, the ward-organizing success in each ward was achieved only through energetic and sustained work on the part of those individuals who made it a priority.

More areas of Philadelphia have characteristics resembling those of the 51st Ward, along with the kinds of challenges that Gregory Benjamin has been addressing through a combination of ward organizing and neighborhood improvement activity. The eastern edge of the ward—49th Street—is adjacent to one of the city's higher-priced neighborhood real estate markets; farther west, the interior of the ward contains areas where 40 percent or more of the residents live in poverty.[13] Health care and community mental health needs are pervasive. The community does not have the financial wherewithal to support expenses associated with some key open-ward activities—for example, the cost of printing and distributing an independent sample ballot not authorized by the Democratic City Committee. And because wards similar to the 51st do not at present have the capability to deliver large numbers of votes for endorsed candidates, soliciting contributions from candidates might be harder than in the 2nd or 50th Ward.

On the basis of these circumstances, the approach that Benjamin adopted—initially supporting every candidate endorsed by the Democratic City Committee—was likely to have been the best option for this ward. If open-ward initiatives begin to take hold in other parts of the city, Benjamin may gain an indirect benefit: as the number of wards under City Committee control decreases, party leaders may look for opportunities to be more helpful to wards such as the 51st that are becoming better organized but, for the moment, remain in the fold. And if wards of this kind build their voter education and voter turnout capacity during the coming years, they will be well positioned to find new opportunities for elevating their profile and strengthening their influence.

12

****

The Word

Touch

I held a stranger's hand—not for a moment but for about ten minutes, standing quietly in a big room with a vaulted ceiling, along with hundreds of other people. I was an outsider attending the Sunday morning worship service at Canaan Baptist Church in Germantown, a Northwest Philadelphia neighborhood. I was a white person in the midst of an African American congregation. As everyone stood for the beginning of a series of prayers, the woman next to me extended her hand without speaking, conveying the understanding that we were to join hands, as everyone else was doing, while the pastor descended a few steps toward the congregation and began to speak.

For me, this experience was an unusual one. It was different from another part of the Canaan Baptist worship service, known in some congregations as the Peace, when the order of service is momentarily suspended so that, as described in the Episcopal Church's *Book of Common Prayer*, "the Ministers and People may greet one another in the name of the Lord."[1] Members of the congregation rise from their seats and exchange greetings, handshakes, or embraces, often engaging in a few moments of friendly conversation. Encounters with others during the Peace are informal and fleeting and are not intended to be consequential or freighted with significance. You can decide what you want to do or not do during the Peace—and that, in a way, is the point.

By contrast, the joining of hands at Canaan Baptist Church was, as I understood it, intended to be one of the most meaningful parts of the worship service. Everyone was literally joined and, in effect, constrained by the hand holding. During the prayers, you might be deeply immersed in prayer or meditation, or alternatively, you might be thinking random thoughts or not thinking at all. But for that time, you and everyone else shared an intimacy—another person's touch—for an extended time. I doubt that the hand holding was intended to produce revelations or generate euphoria, but it was unusual. At what other time and place in the outside world would you touch a stranger's hand and feel that person's touch, that intimacy, for one moment after another in an environment of stillness and calm?

The American church and the American government are both institutions that were created in the service of ideals that can never be achieved—the former in making humanity godly, the latter in making society equitable. In broad terms, both institutions have some similar interests: in encouraging good behavior and celebrating good works; in preventing and resolving conflicts; and in supporting the pursuit of happiness—ways in which individuals (figuratively, for the most part) touch one another in a social environment. In Philadelphia and everywhere else, much can be learned about the prospects for advancing social change and political reform by studying how these institutions interact with each other in seeking to deliver value to their constituencies.

Federal regulations that confer tax-exempt status on congregations of faith prohibit them from directly engaging in politics. However, these institutions are allowed to provide information about elections and the electoral process and, from the pulpit and in church-sponsored events, to comment on and promote dialogue about politically charged issues such as immigration and voting rights. Although the scope of their activism has to be narrower than that of other organizations in the political environment, faith-based congregations can play an important role in fueling political activism and policy reform.[2]

Leaking Vessels

Many members of the generations that grew up after World War II began to regard institutions of government, as well as institutions of faith, as archaic at best and criminal at worst.

The government lied about the Tonkin Gulf incident, triggering the Vietnam War, and then lied repeatedly about the war's progress. The government tried to keep the Pentagon Papers secret and tried to cover up the Watergate break-in. The government sponsored assassinations and coups that disrupted or displaced the leadership of emerging nations. The government deprived African Americans and other citizens of their property and their access to education, employment, and justice.

Although the scope and frequency of government misconduct might have been just as great before World War II as it was afterward, postwar media brought the worst news of this kind into wider circulation. Then the media industry became expert in weaponizing news as well, with government wrongdoing and incompetence as popular themes. In the past, politicians of the left and right were accustomed to blaming government for causing problems; now they began insisting that government itself was the problem. In his 1981 inaugural address, Ronald Reagan famously said, "In this present crisis, government is not the solution to our problem; government is the problem" and then contrasted "self-rule" favorably with "government by an elite group."[3]

On the left, Saul Alinsky, whose writings still inspire activist movements, has little good to say about government, and his *Rules for Radicals* includes a somewhat Manichean categorization of humanity into Haves, Have-Nots, and Have-a-Little, Want Mores.[4] To be fair, Alinsky was candid about the nature of his topic: the practice of an in-your-face brand of activism. He did not claim expertise in policy development, and it seems unlikely that he would have considered authoring a book titled *Rules for Moderates*. However, although Alinsky describes compromise as "a key and beautiful word,"[5] he does not devote much attention to explaining how compromise may be achieved after the kinds of disruptions that he describes have served their purpose in terms of drawing attention to a critical issue. And if those who are doing the disrupting believe that, in general, people in authority are inherently bad, why would they want to consider compromising?

Also characteristic of this period was a questioning of the traditional authority of church leaders and a steady decline in church attendance. Harvey Cox's *The Secular City*, published in 1965, stimulated national dialogue and debate about the role and relevance of the church in modern society.[6] Churches and church facilities that had once been closely linked to the identities of the neighborhoods where they were located were vacated as depopulation and white flight took hold. Some were repurposed for other uses, and many were demolished. When Catholic priests were exposed as sexual predators and church authorities were revealed to have enabled this behavior, the decline in church membership was accompanied by costly financial settlements to resolve related legal action. *God Is Not Great*, a foundational work of what was known as the "new atheism," was published in 2007.[7] Serious internal divisions emerged in Protestant and Catholic churches with respect to LGBTQ issues, particularly after the 2015 Supreme Court decision supporting gay marriage.

With an awareness of the transformations that American government and the American church underwent during the past half-century, traditional congregations of faith that remain in Philadelphia, like their counterparts elsewhere, have explored opportunities to reposition themselves to provide value in a changed environment.

Clubhouse or Lighthouse

Reverend Dr. W. Wilson Goode Sr., who served as mayor of Philadelphia from 1984 to 1992, categorized two different ways in which congregations of faith may present themselves to their members and the public. "Congregations have an opportunity to remain a clubhouse for members that pay their offerings and tithes," he said, "Or to become a lighthouse for the community. They need to be a lighthouse in the community and the city."[8]

The lighthouse role is fully documented in *The Other Philadelphia Story: How Local Congregations Support Quality of Life in Urban America*. In this work, University of Pennsylvania scholar Ram A. Cnaan describes the results of research that he and his team conducted on more than two thousand Philadelphia-based congregations, describing "the heroic role [they] play in improving the quality of life of people in Philadelphia. . . . [T]aken together, they comprise a massive force, almost a social movement, of doing good locally and beyond."[9]

The Other Philadelphia Story focuses on the role of churches in complementing or adding value to existing government-supported health and human service resources—or, in some instances, creating new resources where none previously existed. One example cited is Amachi, a program through which individuals belonging to a particular congregation, after being screened and trained, work as a team to provide mentoring services to children of incarcerated parents. The program, which began in Philadelphia and expanded nationally, is headed by Goode.[10]

Through church-affiliated development corporations or joint ventures with private real estate developers, congregations of faith have also produced new community-serving assets in urban neighborhoods in Philadelphia and elsewhere for well over a half-century. Friends Neighborhood Guild, a pioneer in affordable housing development, was founded by the Religious Society of Friends (Quakers). Advocate Community Development Corporation, a project of the North Philadelphia-based Church of the Advocate, produced the first of a series of affordable housing ventures in 1970.[11] Presby's Inspired Life, affiliated with the Presbytery of Philadelphia, is one of many affordable housing developers that have secured federal and state funding to support housing ventures across the city.

For the most part, these contributions of faith-based institutions have little or no political frame of reference and, for the most part, were not designed to produce outcomes in the political environment. Opportunities to increase voter engagement and the election of qualified candidates for office must be pursued in other ways.

Icons to Coalitions

"In the twentieth century, the black preacher was the best access to the political process," Reverend Dr. Alyn E. Waller of Enon Tabernacle Baptist Church told me during a conversation in his office.[12] He gestured to a nearby photograph of Reverend Martin Luther King Jr. (pictured with a three-year-old Alyn Waller), which hung next to a framed photograph of Waller's father, Reverend Alfred M. Waller. Alfred Waller had been pastor of Shiloh Baptist Church in Cleveland, and in 1973, he had run (unsuccessfully) for mayor of Cleveland to succeed Carl Stokes.

Waller's statement seems to be applicable to Philadelphia: there are no twenty-first-century counterparts to Reverend Leon Sullivan of Zion Baptist Church (whose congregation had responded so enthusiastically to Sullivan's introduction of Casey Five judicial candidate Darnell Jones), or to Reverend Paul Washington, pastor of the Church of the Advocate. During Washington's ministry, Advocate hosted the third national conference on black power and a convention of the Black Panther Party, and the church served as the venue for the 1974 ordination of eleven women into the Episcopal priesthood (an action taken in defiance of the Episcopal church's prohibition against women priests, a policy that was ended three years later).

Since the late twentieth century, faith-based activism has been driven less by individual leaders like King and Sullivan, who had dominated the political landscape at the height of the civil rights movement, and more often by church and interfaith coalitions. In 1981, a group of Philadelphia African American pastors felt compelled to take action to bring a two-month-long teachers' strike to an end. Organizing themselves on an ad hoc basis as the Concerned Clergy to Open Our Schools, members of the group were arrested for blocking traffic as part of a downtown protest, after which the group entered into meetings with then–managing director Wilson Goode and Mayor William J. Green III to lobby for a proposal that included "provisions for teacher accountability, involvement of citizens in a search for a new schools superintendent and specific concessions from all parties in the strike."[13]

After the strike was resolved, the group formally organized as Black Clergy of Philadelphia and Vicinity and began pursuing a social-action agenda. In 1982, after a six-month advocacy campaign undertaken in coordination with Operation PUSH/Philadelphia, the group secured a commitment by the Coca-Cola Bottling Company of Philadelphia to provide employment opportunities, business support, and philanthropic support to the black community.[14] In 1983, members of the Black Clergy worked individually and together to support Wilson Goode's campaign for mayor in the Democratic primary election and in the November general election. Goode's appearances at church venues drew crowds of enthusiastic voters. These events and related activism by individual members of the Black Clergy made a big impact. Referring to the Black Clergy's influence on the election outcome, Goode's campaign manager said, "They registered voters, raised money, and they sent a pretty strong message on Sunday."[15]

Not all black pastors were enthusiastic about this approach, however. In a letter published in the November 21, 1983, edition of the *Philadelphia Inquirer*, Reverend William L. Banks of Faith Fellowship Baptist Church charged pastors who had supported Goode's campaign in this manner with "violating one of the major tenets of their faith—separation of church and state. . . . Someone should inform these pastors that it is not their prerogative to tell parishioners how to vote."[16] Oher pastors were reluctant to join the group because of its practice of endorsing candidates for office. Some of them may have felt justified in their concerns when Black Clergy members found themselves unable to agree on whether to endorse Lucien E. Blackwell or George R. Burrell Jr. in the 1991 election to succeed Goode, in a sequence of events that included a "surreptitious" meeting and charges of backroom deal making that one pastor characterized as "a comedy of errors."[17]

Although the Black Clergy continued to endorse candidates for office (the group endorsed Anthony Hardy Williams for mayor in the 2019 primary), most of its actions were closely tied to issues of broad concern such as public education, services for children and youth, and criminal justice. In 1989, the group created a separate entity to fund and implement programs and services for young people, to provide conflict mediation training, and to educate congregation members about financial management and health issues. Some of the education and training activities that had been initiated by this affiliated organization are now part of the Black Church programs offered by the Philadelphia Lutheran Theological Seminary's Urban Theological Institute.

People of Influence

As iconic leaders of the civil rights era faded into history, faith-based coalitions increasingly became viewed as effective vehicles for political activism. During the late twentieth century, the term "institution-based community organizing" (IBCO) became popular among philanthropic supporters of faith-based activism. This approach is designed to increase the effectiveness of community organizing by "bridging social capital" to "overcome the strategic limitations that previously undermined the field" by bringing together constituencies that had often been separated from one another based on differences of race, ethnicity, socioeconomic status, geography, and "immigrant-narrative background."[18] National organizations, such as the Industrial Areas Foundation (IAF) founded by Saul Alinsky, have assisted in planning, recruiting, training, and supporting startup activities associated with these coalitions. During the Rendell administration, an IAF-facilitated faith-based coalition, Philadelphia Interfaith Action (PIA), proposed to develop one thousand new homes at a cost substantially lower than the per-unit cost that the city had been subsidizing. Although the implementation of the plan fell short of expectations, the PIA experience helped stimulate thinking about the best ways to make faith-based coalitions effective and sustainable.

A 2011 census of IBCOs nationally found that the median number of member institutions per IBCO was twenty-one and that the number of non-congregational, secular members of IBCOs had doubled during the decade leading up to this census, from about five hundred to one thousand. These noncongregational members include schools, nonprofit organizations, unions, and neighborhood organizations.[19] POWER, an IBCO created in Philadelphia in 2011, represented more than fifty congregations in the city and region in 2019.[20]

Planning for POWER began when representatives of an organization now known as Faith in Action (formerly PICO National Network) contacted several religious leaders in Philadelphia to inquire about the possibility of creating an IBCO in the city through which faith organizations would join together to address social justice issues. Reverend Robin Hynicka of Arch Street United Methodist Church (ASUMC) was one of several leaders who, after this initial contact, participated in a series of planning meetings to pursue their interest in this proposal.

Arch Street United Methodist Church, located a block north of City Hall in downtown Philadelphia, was established in 1862. Like many older churches in Philadelphia, it is housed in a large, historically noteworthy building that had been designed more than a century ago for a much larger congregation (the sanctuary seats more than nine hundred people). Hynicka was very familiar with the health and human service needs of Philadelphia's population. He had previously been pastor at Methodist churches in North Philadelphia and Frankford, two neighborhoods challenged by poverty, crime, and social need. During Hynicka's ministry, Arch Street United Methodist Church became known as a resource for services and emergency shelter for homeless people and as a participant in the Sanctuary City movement. ASUMC hosted the initial assemblies of the Occupy Philadelphia Movement, which set up an encampment at City Hall in 2011.

As a result of this experience and Reverend Hynicka's presentation of the coalition's overall plan and vision, the ASUMC Church Council was ready to authorize ASUMC to join POWER without a lot of questioning or debate. The church was one of about two dozen congregations that were represented at an organizational meeting for POWER held in 2011.

A rabbi representing a congregation in another area of the city had a more drawn-out experience in forming an association with POWER. When contacted by a PICO organizer, he was excited to learn about the plans to create a faith-based coalition in Philadelphia—an interfaith voice on public issues in the city. The idea appealed to him. He viewed active cooperation among different congregations in support of a shared goal as superior to "interfaith dialogue" that might not lead to any constructive outcomes. And there were more than a few issues that different congregations could consider working on together. For example, everyone is likely to agree that hungry people should be fed, and many congregations are engaged in addressing this need to the extent of their capability to do so; but neither Republicans nor Democrats are making this issue enough of a political priority—hunger remains a critical problem in the United States.

After his conversation with the PICO organizer, the rabbi spoke with members of his congregation about joining the POWER coalition. They were not excited about the idea. Many of them were concerned about making a commitment to the coalition without knowing what kinds of activities it would be engaged in. So no action was taken.

Two years later a representative of POWER contacted the rabbi. By that time, POWER had grown to about two dozen congregations. Coincidentally, the synagogue's social action programs had undergone some changes during that time, and now the idea of becoming a member of POWER was attracting more interest. Even so, getting the congregation comfortable with entering into a formal commitment took about eighteen months. There was real concern about signing on to an organization that was going to take positions on political issues. How would POWER use the funding that the synagogue paid as dues? And where would that funding come from—how would it be raised? When these questions were resolved and the congregation joined POWER, five members became very active, and another fifty or so became less active but were still involved.

The rabbi had several observations about this experience.

- He liked the straightforward criteria that POWER used in choosing a particular issue to focus on: the issue should be local; the issue should be one that the coalition members agreed POWER should address; and the activism taken by POWER should have the potential to achieve a specific result. POWER's advocacy for substantially increasing the minimum wage for airport workers (associated with a larger campaign to enable Philadelphia airport workers to join the Service Employees International Union) met these criteria and produced an early win for POWER.

- Some critical issues cannot be addressed by local activism alone. The need for more funding for public education, based on a fair funding formula, was an example. The members of the Pennsylvania General Assembly who represented legislative districts in Philadelphia all agreed with POWER's position, but the Philadelphia delegation was not strong enough to produce a majority vote in the legislature as a whole. With this consideration in mind, POWER leaders began exploring opportunities to expand its geographic reach and extend the group's organizing activities to enlist the participation of residents of areas outside the city that shared this concern.
- The strength of POWER is based on its status as a moral voice—speaking on the basis of morality and religion, not politics—and politicians recognize that religious people are frequent voters.

POWER's advocacy for a fair distribution of state funding for public education provides a good example of the way in which members of local congregations can support a broad advocacy initiative. David Mosenkis, a data analyst whose synagogue, Germantown Jewish Centre, is a member of POWER, correlated data on state public school funding levels with data on the racial makeup of school districts and documented the results of his analysis in a report that was released in November 2014.

> Mosenkis' study of Pennsylvania's funding of school districts for the 2014–2015 school year shows there is an evident racial bias in the distribution of funds based on the number of students of color versus white students. According to the study, "An analysis of enrollment, demographics, and basic education funding of Pennsylvania's 501 public school districts reveals dramatically higher per-student funding in districts with predominantly white populations compared to economically similar districts with more racial diversity."[21]

Mosenkis's findings were published by the *Philadelphia Public School Notebook* and picked up by the mainstream media. A state-appointed commission had been meeting since August 2014 to study how state education funds should be distributed, and the commission had scheduled meetings on November 18 and 19, less than two weeks after the report's release. POWER requested an opportunity to make a presentation at the hearing and received no response. A second request produced a message that "there is no space on our agenda" for such a presentation.[22] With assistance from Faith in Action staff, POWER made it known publicly that it wanted the report to receive the attention it deserved. Plans were made for demonstrators to appear at the hearing site. Some POWER activists were preparing to be arrested, and the news media was informed of POWER's plans. As time grew short, the head of the commission contacted POWER representatives and invited POWER to send representatives to the hearing, which would be held in public. Other public testimony would be invited, and the same format would be adopted for other hearings to be held around the state.

In 2016, legislation authorizing school funding in a manner consistent with POWER's position was passed by the General Assembly. However, the authorization applies only to "new money"—future funding over and above 2016 budget levels. As a result, most public education funds continue to be allocated unfairly. Legislation has been introduced in the Pennsylvania House and Senate to produce the fair funding formula for which POWER had advocated;[23] but this experience illustrates how difficult it can be for even a well-organized advocacy initiative to contend against defenders of the status quo who are skilled in using the levers of government to their advantage.

The Church in the Middle

"The black church has never been fully aligned with either Democrats or Republicans," Alyn Waller told me in a 2019 conversation. And in many instances, African American churches cannot be precisely categorized as conservative or liberal. Members of some black churches might be comfortable with a characterization of their congregations as "theologically conservative and socially liberal," while others might not be.[24]

On a personal basis, Reverend Waller had experienced a sense of not belonging to either of two men's movements that were popular during the late twentieth century. "Every time I left a Promise Keepers meeting," he said in a 2018 lecture at the Urban Theological Institute, "I felt like they were forcing me to define my manhood by where I am on sex and sexuality and abortion—and will I vote Republican." And although he had a positive view of the Million Man March, his experience at the event made him feel "like Mary when she was at the tomb: 'They took my Lord, and I don't know where they laid him.'"[25]

What was constant, however, was an understanding of the word of God in a political context. "In the black church, we understand that the Bible is a book written to people under oppression. . . . [F]rom Genesis to Revelation, that book was written to somebody who's dealing with political realities."[26]

Waller's church, Enon Tabernacle Baptist Church, a Philadelphia-area megachurch with more than 15,000 members, is located on the Philadelphia side of Cheltenham Avenue, the border between the city and the neighboring Cheltenham Township. The church has a strong presence in and beyond the community. According to its website:

> The church provides every student [in the Germantown neighborhood, where the church was originally founded] with a backpack full of school supplies annually. Once Enon's students are ready to pursue a postsecondary education, they have the opportunity to earn college scholarships, including a number of full four-year scholarships. . . . The church's competitive athletics program provides a haven for roughly 600 young people.[27]

"My job is to preach to the issues," Waller told me. "In any good sermon, the Bible is in one hand and the newspaper is in the other. . . . If ten people get shot over the weekend, that has to be in my sermon." His role is to "overlay the word of God with today's themes."[28]

"I don't have to tell people who to vote for," he said. Like other pastors, he can place current issues in a biblical context without being overtly political. In a sermon that I heard Reverend Dr. Derick Brennan deliver at Canaan Baptist Church a month earlier, Brennan referred to the hardships experienced by migrants seeking asylum on America's southern border, comparing the situation to the oppression of the Israelites by Pharaoh. Everyone in the congregation seemed to have no doubt about what and who he was talking about.

Like other preachers, Waller can be supportive of elected officials without delivering political endorsements. He can speak favorably about Cherelle Parker's presence at a meeting, demonstration, or rally concerning an issue that he feels is important. By the same token, there is an expectation of reciprocity. The day after our conversation, Waller, along with African American leaders of religious congregations and advocacy organizations, was scheduled to meet with Mayor Kenney to demand that the mayor take action in response to the revelation that more than three hundred Philadelphia police officers had made racist and violent posts on Facebook. Not long afterward, he could expect Cherelle Parker to introduce a resolution calling for City Council hearings on the issue, and she did.

Waller will make a point of being present at a public event when doing so will encourage participation by members of his congregation. "I might attend a town hall meeting on violence—so people say, 'If he was there, I should get involved.'" More often, Waller's priority is to use his stature as a leader to "get a seat at the table" where problems are to be solved. In this sense, his view of his role parallels that of Chaka Fattah, who did not want to be just another legislator raising his hand in support of a policy; he wanted to write the policy.

In his UTI lecture, Waller described how, in response to especially heated arguments between him and his siblings during his childhood, his mother would call for a temporary, nonnegotiable truce. "Wait till your father gets home," she would say. "Then we're going to settle the whole thing." In a similar vein, speaking about the internal tensions challenging the African American church in today's world, Waller told his audience, "We're going to get along in the house until God gets here."[29]

Making it Right

About two months before the May 2019 Democratic primary election, I attended the People's Forum, a candidate forum for council at-large candidates sponsored by POWER and the MLK D.A.R.E. Coalition and held at the Congregation Rodeph Shalom, a synagogue located a few blocks north of Arch Street United Methodist Church on Broad Street. The venue was filled to capacity with an audience of about a thousand people. The crowd was representative of Philadelphia's citywide demographic in terms of race, ethnicity, and age.

More than two dozen candidates had filed nominating petitions to have their names placed on the May primary ballot for council at-large seats (for various reasons, a number of them withdrew or were removed from the ballot before the election). Because no political party was allowed more than five of the seven at-large seats, Democratic voters would select five candidates as their party's nominees. Most of the at-large candidates were in attendance, arrayed in rows bleacher-style at the front of the crowded room.

The program was introduced by Mark Kelly Tyler, pastor of Mother Bethel A.M.E. Church and cohost of *Mark and Denise in the Mornings*, a talk show broadcast on WWDB-AM radio and sponsored in part by POWER, of which Tyler was a member. As a related activity, the show had begun a series of daily interviews with each of the council at-large candidates. During each broadcast day leading up to the primary election, Tyler and his cohost, Denise Clay, would interview a different at-large candidate—forty-one candidates in all—on forty-one separate mornings.

In preparation for the People's Forum, POWER had contacted advocacy organizations across the city, asking that their members identify issues that should be brought to the candidates participating in the event. The candidates, in turn, were sent a questionnaire containing questions similar to those that they could expect to be asked at the event. Tyler called out the names of groups whose members were in attendance: 215 People's Alliance, ACT UP Philadelphia, Asian Americans United, Philadelphia Neighborhood Networks, Reclaim Philadelphia, Women's Community Revitalization Project, and others. "None of our organizations are powerful enough by themselves," Tyler said in his introduction. "But when people in this city speak with one voice, things begin to happen, things begin to change. All the power we need is in this room."[30]

During the second part of the program, the candidates, one by one, would be given an opportunity to introduce themselves and speak briefly about their candidacies. First, however, the candidates would be asked to respond to a series of questions. Each of them had received a yes placard and a no placard to hold up to respond after each question was asked.

Each of the questions was introduced by an individual who had a personal connection and a direct experience of some kind with the issue raised. For example, a question about the Philadelphia Police Department's stop-and-frisk policy was asked by an African American man who, while driving home from a Hillary Clinton fundraiser in 2016, had been pulled over, handcuffed, and detained for fifteen or twenty minutes by a police officer who had mistakenly identified his vehicle as a stolen car. "I'm forty-five at the time," he said. "I'm working; I have a professional career. You're thinking, 'I'm okay'—no! See the color of my skin? If it affects one, it affects all."[31]

The question he asked the candidates was "Do you believe City Council should enact legislation to end stop-and-frisk, which unjustly affects people of color?" Most of the candidates held up yes placards; a few did not.

Another question, raised by another participant, was "Do you believe that gun violence is a public health emergency in Philadelphia and support increasing funding for victim services and funding to address root causes of violence, such as poverty and our underfunded educational system?"

The questions were associated with the People's Platform for a Just Philadelphia, described as "a progressive policy agenda that we believe every leader in our city government should live up to." Platform items included "invest in healthy schools, jobs and re-entry, and affordable accessible housing," "make Philadelphia safe and healthy," and "ensure a democracy where we can all participate."[32]

The People's Forum approach was one that Cherelle Parker would not have supported for the 50th Ward. She had said, "Just parade thirty or forty people in a room and give them two or three minutes, or even a questionnaire—that doesn't tell me who you are! Because you're going to respond in a way that you think will impress me and impress the committeepeople—so that's a low bar."[33] What was also clear was that the right answer to every question, in terms of making a favorable impression on the audience, was yes: yes to healthy schools, affordable housing, and funding for victim services. There were other limitations associated with the forum as well. That afternoon you could hold up your yes placard in response to the question about ending stop-and-frisk and then ardently support a continuation of current policy at a Fraternal Order of Police session that evening—and who would know? More to the point, the appropriate answer to many of the questions that were being asked was the response that Barack Obama, as president, had made in framing responses to some questions: "It's complicated." Some issues cannot be resolved by choosing between two absolutes. The candidates were not given the option to hold up "We need to discuss" placards.

But in another sense, any criticisms of the People's Forum that might be made on the above basis would be off the mark. The 50th Ward candidate vetting process was highly sophisticated and had been designed and refined over more than a generation of ward leadership. In terms of their knowledge of the political dynamic, the 50th Ward committeepeople were a highly educated group, better educated politically than most of their counterparts anywhere in the city. In contrast, members of the People's Forum audience represented wide variations in educational attainment, as well as wide variations in political sophistication. For that audience, the yes-or-no questions and the three-minute candidate pitches provided information and insights that many of them—not only those from high-poverty communities—might not otherwise have received.

As important, the People's Forum approach was consistent with the approach that Waller had adopted: bringing a faith-informed view to the political process and overlaying the word of God with today's themes, allowing people to make the connections and put the pieces together with some degree of independent judgment. The People's Forum was a way of communicating with people who had been oppressed, and the reality of this oppression was reflected in the questions that were asked of the candidates. It was as much about sharing common experiences of oppression with the other participants, particularly the candidates sitting up front. "God is the God of the underdog," Waller had told the audience at the Urban Theological Institute. "He's always on the side of the one who has a foot on his or her neck. So he becomes the God who makes it right for those for whom life is wrong."[34]

As I understood it, the forum was designed to address two questions related to Waller's preaching: How could life be made more right for those Philadelphians who lived in the worst of circumstances? And what, if anything, could any of these candidates do to make it so?

PART III

Common Threads

13

★★★★★★★

The May 2019 Election

What to Expect

Philadelphia's May 2019 Democratic primary election was going to be noteworthy, if only because of circumstance. In 2017, the most recent year in which citywide offices had appeared on the ballot, the outcomes had been dramatic. Powered by the energy of criminal justice advocates and supported by PAC-funded promotions, winning district attorney candidate Lawrence Krasner had beaten his second-place opponent by more than 25,000 votes in a seven-person race; and, as described in Chapter 1, city controller candidate Rebecca Rhynhart spectacularly defeated incumbent Alan Butkovitz, winning by substantial margins in almost every area of the city. The 2019 primary would be the first post-Clinton/Trump election in which nearly all citywide offices, as well as City Council district offices, would be on the ballot.

But how likely was it that the 2019 outcomes would be as noteworthy as the outcomes had been two years previously? Although many new candidates had won committeeperson seats in the previous year, the leadership structure of most wards had remained unchanged. Although Philadelphia 3.0's PAC was making large expenditures to promote certain candidates, large PAC expenditures were no guarantee of success, as evidenced by state Senator Anthony Hardy Williams's dismal results in the 2015 mayoral campaign. Notwithstanding $7 million in campaign promotions funded by a

PAC associated with three hedge-fund financiers, the winning candidate in 2015, James Kenney, defeated Williams by a two-to-one margin.

In addition, the 2019 primary might not be as much of a draw for younger and newer voters as the 2017 primary had been. The top of the ticket—the mayor's election—was boring: three older men with deep roots in the Democratic Party establishment were competing for the nomination. Incumbent James Kenney came from an old-school South Philadelphia political background. He had been employed for more than a decade as an aide to South Philadelphia state Senator Vincent Fumo. He was at work in Fumo's office during the years in which Tom Foglietta had won and held onto his congressional seat, aided by Joseph Vignola and his political allies.

Kenney had two challengers, Alan Butkovitz (again) and Anthony Hardy Williams. Both challengers had several common points of disagreement with Kenney over certain policy issues. But they also had another characteristic in common: they had both been badly beaten in recent citywide elections.

During the months leading up to the 2019 primary, Kenney had adopted an extreme form of the traditional incumbent-candidate strategy, maximizing opportunities to be viewed by the public in his capacity as mayor rather than as one of three candidates competing for office. Kenney's opponents criticized his refusal to engage in any substantive form of debate; Kenney was unfazed. "When I ran in 2015, I didn't have a job," he said. "I was like Butkovitz. Now I have a job; a job and a half. I have to be a candidate, too. I'm sorry if my opponents are disappointed."[1]

In a poll of registered voters conducted a month before the May primary election, the *Philadelphia Inquirer* found that 48 percent of the respondents approved of Kenney's performance, notwithstanding opposition to the soft-drink tax instituted during his first term (62 percent of respondents termed it a failure) and concerns about the rising homicide rate (cited by 37 percent of respondents as their top-priority issue).[2]

The results of this race had seemed predetermined weeks earlier. In Philadelphia, incumbent mayors who had sought election to a second term had always been successful, and it appeared that Kenney would be as well. Reality turned out to be consistent with appearance; on May 21, Kenney beat Williams, 67 percent to 24 percent, with Butkovitz collecting the remaining 9 percent of the vote.[3]

Some mayors develop relationships with protégés or political allies who, as time goes on, come to be viewed as possible candidates to succeed them after they leave office. As of 2019, there did not appear to be a likely successor to Kenney. Kenney's two most powerful allies, City Council president Darrell Clarke and Congressperson Dwight Evans, might not be interested in the job. Instead, the more likely candidates in the 2023 mayoral election might be younger people from the local, state, or federal legislatures—or someone from outside the public sector altogether.

City Commissioners

Traditional political party organizations are particularly effective in delivering vote majorities for little-known candidates campaigning for lesser-known offices in low-turnout elections. Philadelphia's Democratic City Committee performed this function reasonably well in 2019.

One such low-profile office is the Office of the Philadelphia City Commissioners, which is responsible for conducting voter registration, administering elections, and maintaining voting machines and voting records. The Home Rule Charter requires that no more than two of the three commissioners be individuals who belong to the same political party; as a result (given the Democratic Party's overwhelming majority of registered voters), the two individuals who are elected in the Democratic primary every four years are assured of winning these seats in the general election.

In 2019, this race was somewhat noteworthy because one of the incumbent commissioners, Anthony Clark, had chosen not to run for reelection and also because Clark had gained notoriety in light of his chronic absences from work (a full-time position that, in 2019, paid $130,668) and because he had not voted in several elections. Notwithstanding this baggage, Clark had won reelection in 2015 and, in fact, was the top vote-getter, beating his closest challenger by 11 percentage points; so his decision not to run again in 2019 was apparently based on something other than fear of being defeated at the polls.

The Democratic City Committee–endorsed candidates in the 2019 primary were incumbent Lisa Deeley and Omar Sabir. Deeley had longstanding family and professional ties to the party. Sabir was a committeeperson in Bob Brady's ward who had worked for state legislators and had been a candidate in the 2015 City Commissioners election (in which he came in next-to-last, with 13 percent of the vote).

Based on generally available information about Deeley and Sabir—of which there was not a great deal—there seemed to be nothing wrong with either of them, particularly in comparison with the soon-to-depart Anthony Clark. However, most voters were probably not aware that Deeley had lost her notary license in 2018 for notarizing a signature without verifying the signer's identity, an action that resulted in the approval of documents that fraudulently deprived a woman of her right to her husband's death benefits. Then Deeley tried to mislead the media by denying that she had been sanctioned by the state because of this incident.[4]

As an alternative to Deeley or Sabir, one of the unendorsed candidates in the 2019 election, attorney Kahlil Williams, seemed to be extraordinarily well qualified for a City Commissioner seat. While a graduate student at Penn, Williams had worked for the NAACP Legal Defense Fund on reauthorizing the Voting Rights Act and for the Brennan Center for Justice on redistricting reform. Referring to this experience, Williams told *Philadelphia Magazine*:

> I'm the only candidate in the race who has worked on voting rights or election reform issues as part of their profession. Having overseen hundreds of election protection volunteers in my pro bono work, I know how to recruit, train, and advise folks on how to fix problems on Election Day.[5]

Although not endorsed by the Democratic City Committee, Williams succeeded in obtaining endorsements from some individual Democratic ward organizations, several of them representing high-turnout areas in Center City and South Philadelphia.

This City Commissioner election also attracted a high level of interest from other prospective candidates, in part because of the heightened awareness of voter-participation issues that followed the 2016 presidential election. The fact that only one of the candidates—Lisa Deeley—was an incumbent provided an additional incentive to run. Thirteen candidates' names appeared on the May ballot.

City Committee accomplished the goal of getting both of its two endorsed candidates elected. Omar Sabir won the most votes, and Kahlil Williams trailed Deeley, the second-place winner, by about 12,400 votes. Ten other candidates, none of whom individually received more than 25,000 votes, split the remaining votes, as shown in Table 13.1.

As shown in Figure 13.1, Sabir was particularly successful in South, West, North, and Northwest wards with high levels of African American population, and Deeley was particularly successful in South, Northwest, and Northeast wards with high levels of white population. Williams won Center City's two wards, along with liberal wards in West, South, and Northwest Philadelphia.

Two Council Districts

Who could be trusted to promote equitable development in South Philadelphia's 2nd Council District? Was it incumbent Councilperson Kenyatta Johnson, who had helped a childhood friend obtain city-owned lots at bargain prices, after which the friend flipped them and made a substantial profit?[6] Or was it challenger Lauren Vidas, who had led a community organization in another part of the district that, in Johnson's words, had "totally gentrified the entire neighborhood?"[7]

TABLE 13.1 VOTES RECEIVED BY MAJOR CANDIDATES IN DEMOCRATIC PRIMARY FOR CITY COMMISSIONER, 2019

Candidate	Votes	Percentage of total
Omar Sabir	71,303	24
Lisa Deeley	61,278	21
Kahlil Williams	48,884	17
Subtotal	181,465	62
Ten other candidates, plus write-ins	111,583	38
Total votes cast	293,048	

Source: Data from Philadelphia City Commissioners *View Election Results* database, https://www.philadelphiavotes.com/en/resources-a-data/ballot-box-app.

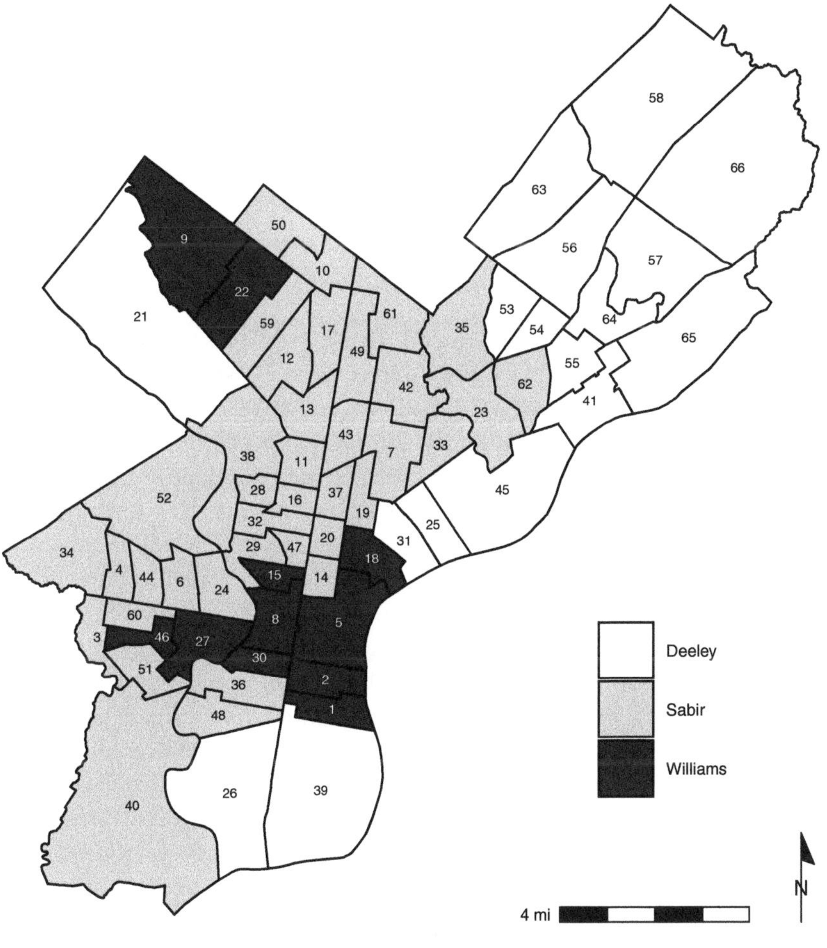

Figure 13.1 Highest number of votes received in 2019 Democratic primary for city commissioner by ward

Source: Data from Philadelphia City Commissioners *View Election Results* database, https://www.philadelphiavotes.com/en/resources-a-data/ballot-box-app; map by Michael Fichman.

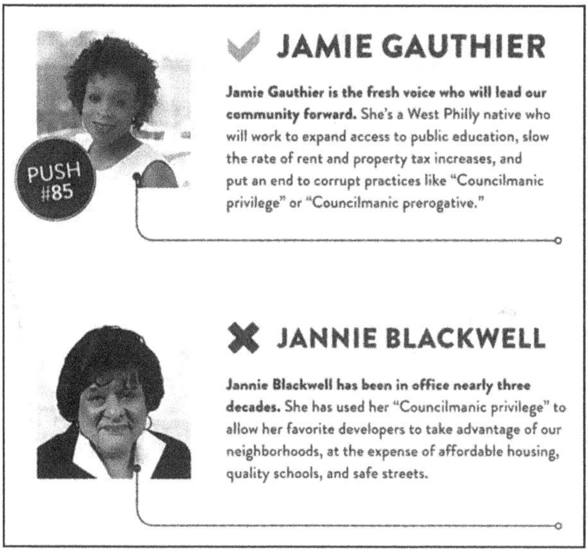

Figure 13.2 Campaign flier published by Philadelphia 3.0 in support of Jamie Gauthier

Source: In the author's possession.

In West Philadelphia's 3rd Council District, who was the candidate who would be most likely to place the interests of real estate developers over those of community members? Was it incumbent Councilperson Jannie Blackwell, who, in late 2018 and early 2019, held up a community-endorsed sale of public land to leverage support for a favored developer?[8] Or was it her opponent, Jamie Gauthier, whose campaign was benefitting from promotions funded by Philadelphia 3.0's PAC (an example of which is shown in Figure 13.2), as part of what an anonymous flier circulated in West Philadelphia had labeled "a hidden Republican/Donald Trump Plan"?[9]

Back in 2015, Johnson had faced a well-financed challenge from developer Ori Feibush; he defeated Feibush by a large margin after a fiercely fought campaign. Blackwell, who had represented West Philadelphia's 3rd District since 1992, had not encountered significant opposition for years.

Gentrification and displacement were hot topics in both districts. South Philadelphia's Point Breeze neighborhood, located west of Broad Street and a dozen blocks south of City Hall, had been a center of poverty, depopulation, and abandonment for decades; then, after the turn of the century, the real estate market began to change. The revitalization of Philadelphia's downtown business district, facilitated by the city's ten-year tax abatement, a generous development incentive that provided the greatest benefit to the highest-cost projects, had brought new value to neighborhood blocks

TABLE 13.2 VOTES RECEIVED BY MAJOR CANDIDATES IN 2019 DEMOCRATIC PRIMARY IN 2ND AND 3RD COUNCIL DISTRICTS

2nd Council District		3rd Council District	
Candidate	Votes	Candidate	Votes
Kenyatta Johnson	13,358	Jamie Gauthier	13,460
Lauren Vidas	8,995	Jannie Blackwell	10,588

Source: Data from Philadelphia City Commissioners *View Election Results* database, https://www.philadelphiavotes.com/en/resources-a-data/ballot-box-app.

extending far north and south of Center City. By 2019, high-priced new townhouse construction was commonplace in Point Breeze.

During the same period, reinvestment activity that had begun on the residential blocks just west of the University of Pennsylvania campus during the 1990s expanded into neighborhoods to the north and farther west. Population grew from about 46,400 in 1990 to about 54,300 in 2018. Median home sales prices increased from $100,000 in 2000 to $400,000 in 2017. The area's office occupancy rate had become the highest in the city, second-highest in the region. Real estate development completed in 2017 totaled 1.3 million square feet.[10]

During the months leading up to the May primary, both incumbent candidates and challengers had made gentrification a defining theme of their candidacies. However, one of the incumbents, Kenyatta Johnson, held his seat, while the other incumbent, Jannie Blackwell, lost hers, as shown in Table 13.2.

Blackwell had served on council far longer than Johnson—she had taken office in 1992, twenty years before Johnson—and she was better known by voters throughout her district than Johnson was. So if one of the two incumbents was going to be beaten in 2019, why would it have been Blackwell rather than Johnson?

Gauthier had established a candidate profile and campaign narrative that set her apart from Blackwell in ways that proved to be effective. Gauthier could describe how poverty and addiction had affected members of her extended family.[11] Blackwell had a hardship narrative as well, but she rarely mentioned her personal background, possibly because (like other women of her generation) she may not have felt comfortable doing so, even in passing.

Gauthier was a young leader—she had been director of two public-serving nonprofit organizations. Blackwell could be characterized as an old politician, and that characterization might have been all that some voters needed. However, many people who were familiar with Blackwell's overall career would have found it grossly inaccurate and unfair. Blackwell was devoted to acting on behalf of individuals and households that were struggling with deep poverty, threatened with homelessness, or maintaining an existence on the streets. A row of chairs could be seen outside her office in City Hall, and those chairs would be occupied by people who were in desperate need of services and were seeking her help. She was in the best position to assist them because she was familiar with the public-sector resources that were available to address housing, health, and human service needs and because she knew how to communicate with the people who managed these resources. It was not unusual for one of them to receive an early-evening phone call from her: "I have a family here that needs a place to stay tonight—is there something we can do for them?" She was skilled in finding solutions for people who had fallen through the cracks of the public-sector infrastructure, and that skill represented a major contribution to the well-being of the city and its communities. Blackwell's performance as a councilperson left much to be desired in some respects; but her successor would be challenged by the need to deliver value that Blackwell represented to these constituencies in another way.

Gauthier addressed the issue of institutional responsibility for gentrification in an evenhanded manner ("I think there are ways to work with those institutions to create more local jobs and more procurement opportunities"[12]) but strongly emphasized the need to do more to protect renters threatened by displacement and to preserve a supply of affordable rental housing, possibly by adopting some form of rent control.[13]

Independent expenditures by Philadelphia 3.0 involving "robust field, mail and digital programs" made an impact. An early March poll had shown Blackwell ahead by 42 points. During the weeks that followed, voters received one direct-mail flier after another (reading, for example, "Jamie Gauthier: A Forward-Looking Leader Who Will Put the People Before the Powerful" and "OUR BASIC NEEDS ARE BEING IGNORED. TOGETHER WE CAN CHANGE THE SYSTEM."). Two months later, Blackwell's lead over Gauthier shrank to 2 points.[14]

Gauthier conducted an energetic door-to-door campaign and made use of opportunities to introduce herself to voters in person. "We have talked to voters all over the district," she told a reporter. "No matter what neighborhood I've been in, I've heard the same thing: People are ready for a change."[15]

Although Gauthier's margins of victory were highest in wards that had been most affected by gentrification, she won or came close to winning in seven of the nine wards that make up the district, as shown in Table 13.3.

Blackwell did not mount an ambitious fundraising drive or engage in doorbell ringing on a large scale. Instead, her approach was similar to Kenney's, focusing on her commitment to doing her job as an elected official rather than engaging in debate with a competitor. Asked after the election whether she felt that she had campaigned hard enough, Blackwell said, "I work seven days a week, all my legislation comes from the people. . . . I go

TABLE 13.3 3RD COUNCIL DISTRICT VOTE TOTALS BY WARD IN 2019 DEMOCRATIC PRIMARY

Ward	Jannie Blackwell	Jamie Gauthier
3	1,796	1,432
6	1,072	1,090
24	787	1,293
27	526	1,615
40	237	117
44	1,105	910
46	1,687	3,576
51	1,769	1,804
60	1,609	1,623

Source: Data from Philadelphia City Commissioners *View Election Results* database, https://www.philadelphiavotes.com/en/resources-a-data/ballot-box-app.

to meetings all the time."[16] However, a Kenney-like approach was not going to be effective against a candidate who possessed advantages that Kenney's two challengers lacked.

In terms of the level of energy devoted to the campaign, the difference between Jamie Gauthier and Jannie Blackwell was similar to the difference between Tom Foglietta and Joseph Smith in the 1st Congressional District election in 1982. Gauthier, like Foglietta, knew that direct contact with voters, requiring a massive commitment of time spent in the streets and on doorsteps, was essential. Blackwell, like Smith, was a much older person who had been accustomed to winning reelection routinely and who was not willing or able to try to match the time that her challenger was spending in the public arena.

Kenyatta Johnson, the 2nd District incumbent, was not like Blackwell and Smith. In his first campaign for public office, running for state representative in the 186th District, he had achieved a surprising upset victory over incumbent state representative Harold James, defeating the ten-term officeholder by a nearly two-to-one margin. And in 2015, he had organized a successful defense of his council seat against Ori Feibush, a developer with deep pockets.

A commitment to face time on the street was not the only reason Gauthier and Johnson were successful, but without it, neither of them might have succeeded in 2019.

City Council at Large

The council at-large ballot included the names of twenty-eight candidates. The top five vote-getters would become the Democratic nominees for this position, assuring them of victory in the November general election. Three incumbents were running: Allan Domb, Derek Green, and Helen Gym. The other two individuals serving at-large terms in 2019, Blondell Reynolds Brown and William Greenlee, had chosen not to run for reelection. The Democratic City Committee would endorse two individuals as candidates for the two positions that Greenlee and Brown would be vacating, but City Committee endorsement was no guarantee of success, particularly in the post-2016 political environment.

In the midterm congressional elections that had taken place in 2018, numerous seats in the U.S. House of Representatives were won by first-time candidates, many of whom were termed "progressive" because of their support for policies such as universal health care that had been opposed by the conservative Republican majority then in power. In Philadelphia, several of the new candidates for council at large had credentials that some would associate with progressive political views. They included a gay Latino member of the Democratic Socialists of America (Adrián Rivera-Reyes), an openly transgender LGBTQ activist (Deja Lynn Alvarez), an organizer of Philadelphia's version of the 2017 Women's March (Beth Finn), and a prominent immigration rights activist (Erika Almirón), among others. However, the difference between the advocates for change and the defenders of the status quo was far less well defined in Philadelphia than it was on a national level.

A comparison of how Philadelphia voters responded to the candidacies of two of the most prominent at-large candidates illustrates this ambiguity. The candidate most likely to be characterized as progressive by the greatest number of people was Helen Gym. Before her initial election to council in 2015, she had organized protests against the development of a stadium north of the Chinatown community and, years later, against the construction of a casino half a block south of the neighborhood (the protestors defeated both proposals). As a council member, she introduced a "Fair Workweek" bill that called for, among other things, an increase in the minimum wage to $15.[17] After the violent aftermath of a white-power demonstration in Charlottesville, Virginia, Gym called for the statue of former mayor Frank L. Rizzo to be removed from its place across from City Hall.[18] During her first term in office, Gym also introduced several bills that were designed to limit the ten-year tax abatement to channel more tax revenues to Philadelphia schools.

The at-large candidate most likely to be characterized as conservative was Allan Domb, owner of a Center City real estate firm that had been highly successful in marketing condominiums in Center City. Like Gym, Domb first won election to council in 2015.

The fact that Domb was the only at-large candidate with a recognizable private-sector resume is noteworthy. Although it would not be accurate to label most of the other at-large candidates anti-business, most of them were known for careers in the nonprofit sector or (to a lesser extent) in government, not in business. Although City Council members are allowed to take on other employment (subject to conflict-of-interest standards), businesspeople who wish to be active in politics are more likely to pursue this interest by fundraising for preferred candidates or—particularly in the liberal wards—running for committeeperson. Domb's decision to become a candidate for public office was very unusual.

As many conservative politicians might do, Domb had identified taxes and jobs as the two issues that needed to be addressed to improve Philadelphia's economic condition. However, his campaign focused on the need to reduce poverty by investing in public education, with particular consideration to creating and improving resources for financial literacy, information technology training, entrepreneurship training, and workplace-based mentorships.[19] Although Domb expressed general support for the ten-year tax abatement, he introduced legislation calling for the reduction of the abatement term to eight-and-a-half years. And Domb donated his council salary to the Philadelphia schools. Clearly, these characteristics are not comparable to those associated with many of the legislators with business backgrounds who held seats in the state and federal legislatures at that time.

The election results show that many voters regarded both Gym and Domb as worthy of their support. As shown in Figure 13.3, both candidates received majority votes in many of the same wards.

For the two at-large seats that would be vacated by Blondell Reynolds Brown and William Greenlee, the Democratic City Committee endorsed Isaiah Thomas and Katherine Gilmore Richardson. Although both candidates were successful, Thomas outpolled Richardson by nearly twenty thousand votes, as shown in Table 13.4.

Thomas had broad support both within and outside the party establishment. As an unendorsed candidate in the 2015 council at-large race, he had come within 1,300 votes of displacing Helen Gym from fifth place (Thomas had also been a candidate in 2011). Thomas was an engaging speaker, and he had a powerful background narrative in support of his proposed Youth Agenda.

> I grew up in the Northwest neighborhoods of Philadelphia. My parents both had full time jobs . . . and I learned a strong work ethic and family values from their example. Although I did not realize it at the time, like many young people in our city today, I attended under-resourced schools. . . . My elementary school . . . had almost no playground equipment for us to explore at recess, and my middle and high schools . . . lacked technology and a curriculum designed to

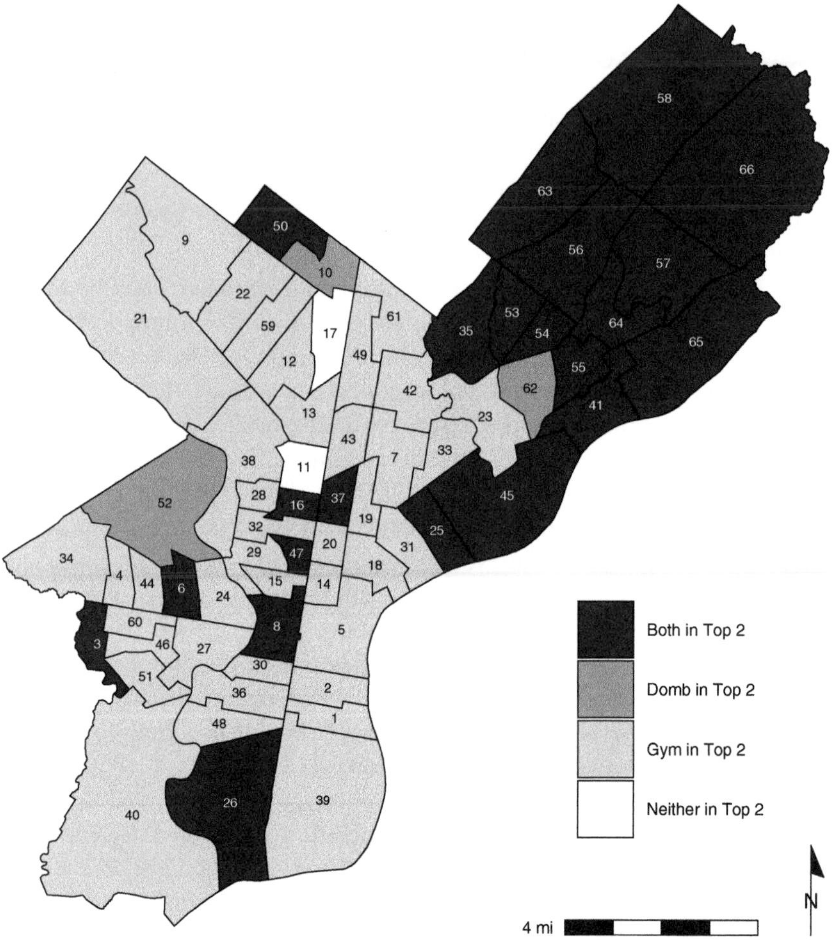

Figure 13.3 Wards that generated the most votes for Helen Gym and Allan Domb in the 2019 Democratic primary for city council at large

Source: Data from Philadelphia City Commissioners, "Archived Data Sets: 2019 Primary," https://www.philadelphiavotes.com/en/resources-a-data/ballot-box-app/additional-election-results-data; map by Michael Fichman.

prepare us for the 21st century. Gun violence and fighting was commonplace, and I was forced to walk past drug dealers and prostitutes on my way to and from school each day. Further, like many young men of color, negative interactions with police were the norm for me as early as middle school. . . .

Looking back, I credit my parents with realizing that if I did not have an opportunity to develop a positive identity and leadership

TABLE 13.4 DEMOCRATIC PRIMARY COUNCIL-AT-LARGE VOTE TOTALS FOR SELECTED CANDIDATES, 2019 AND 2015

Candidate	Votes (rank) in 2019	Votes (rank) in 2015
Helen Gym	108,604 (1)	49,270 (5)
Allan Domb	67,193 (2)	57,691 (3)
Isaiah Thomas	64,045 (3)	48,000
Derek Green	61,070 (4)	68,505 (1)
Katherine Gilmore Richardson	45,470 (5)	
Blondell Reynolds Brown		62,922 (2)
William K. Greenlee		50,849 (4)
Justin DiBerardinis	42,643	
Adrian Rivera-Reyes	35,565	
Eryn Santamoor	35,026	
Erika Almirón	34,329	
W. Wilson Goode Jr.		46,555
Sherrie Cohen		45,847
Ed Neilson		40,786

Source: Data from Philadelphia City Commissioners *View Election Results* database, https://www.philadelphiavotes.com/en/resources-a-data/ballot-box-app.
Note: Votes for winning candidates are shown with rankings in parentheses.

> skills, I could have fallen victim to many of the same negative forces that enveloped my community. They enrolled me in basketball and volleyball programs, the Freedom Schools project, and other extracurricular programs that gave me a chance to grow into my own person and become resistant to peer pressure. I became a coalition-builder, bringing together students, teachers, coaches and community leaders to advocate for better resources and fairer justice.[20]

Regardless of their views about Thomas, Democratic Party leaders may have felt that he would win an at-large seat with or without a party endorsement—and, to all appearances, party leaders did seem to be enthusiastic about Thomas's candidacy, as his election results suggest.

The performance of Gym, Domb, and Thomas is illustrative of former House speaker Robert O'Donnell's observations about the nature of the Democratic Party, as quoted at greater length in Chapter 8.

> To think about the party as an entity is not the most useful thing. And to think of candidates who oppose incumbents as independents—which may suggest that they're the reformers—doesn't really represent what actually occurs. . . . The party is just like a place where people come together.[21]

In 2015, Gym, Domb, and Derek Green (who had been employed as an aide to Councilwoman Marian Tasco) were able to defeat three party-endorsed candidates—incumbents W. Wilson Goode Jr. and Ed Neilson, and newcomer Sherrie Cohen—but they did not campaign as reformers. And although all three were subsequently endorsed by the Democratic City Committee in 2019, none of them appeared to be obligated to the party in ways that would affect their popular support. Because they were popular, Gym and Domb would probably have won reelection even without the party's endorsement. So, after being elected in 2015, was it likely that Gym, Domb, and Green became more supportive of the party establishment in ways that were not apparent to most of their supporters? Or is it also accurate that they were embraced by party leaders in part because they had been successful at the polls?

Gym's strong showing generated some speculation about an alternative scenario: what if Gym had decided to run for mayor rather than City Council in 2019? She had received more than 108,000 votes in the council at-large election, while Kenney had received about 134,000 votes in the mayoral election; but as a mayoral candidate in 2019, Gym would have had the potential to attract voters who regarded Kenney, Williams, and Butkovitz as three lackluster choices. Kenney had intentionally made the mayoral campaign boring; Gym would have made it exciting. She would have brought out many young voters. She would have assembled an army of inspired volunteers whom she could have mobilized citywide. She was an organizer; she knew how to do it. Unions liked her; she would have cut into the union support that had enabled Kenney to win past elections.

Had she chosen to run for mayor in 2019, Gym would have been a formidable candidate. As a practical matter, however, considering this possibility as a potential opportunity for 2023 or later would make more sense (assuming that she wanted to consider it at all). In 2019, it is unlikely that many people, including many of Gym's supporters, had any idea of how she would govern the city. Gym might not have known either. She might not have been interested in considering this possibility in 2019, even if she had an awareness of her strong potential as a mayoral candidate; and she might not be interested in considering this possibility at a later time either.

District Council: Kensington

There was no ambiguity with respect to the party's position regarding Maria Quiñones-Sánchez's candidacy. Because the ward leaders in her district opposed her, the Democratic City Committee did not endorse her. As in past 7th District elections, old-school principles prevailed: past victories at the polls did not guarantee party endorsement; the vote of the ward-leader

TABLE 13.5 DEMOCRATIC PRIMARY RESULTS FOR 7TH COUNCIL DISTRICT, 2019

Ward	Total votes	Sánchez votes	Cruz votes	Sánchez %
7	1,678	711	967	42
18	853	455	398	53
19	1,629	681	948	42
23	1,957	1,380	577	71
25	140	89	51	64
31	176	105	71	60
33	1,450	692	758	48
42	995	534	461	54
43	1,004	575	429	57
49	113	59	54	52
54	284	169	115	60
62	1,513	689	824	46
Totals	11,792	6,139	5,653	

Source: Data from Philadelphia City Commissioners *View Election Results* database, https://www.philadelphiavotes.com/en/resources-a-data/ballot-box-app.

caucus is what mattered. In 2019, the ward leaders endorsed state representative Angel Cruz for the 7th Council District seat. Quiñones-Sánchez and Cruz were the only names on the ballot.

As shown in Table 13.5, Quiñones-Sánchez won by a narrow margin, as she had in 2015. She lost four of the six wards in which more than one thousand voters participated, with a significant loss in the 33rd Ward, which she had won by nearly two hundred votes in 2015. However, she made up for these losses—barely—with a big majority in the 23rd Ward and narrow wins in most of the other wards.

"In every election, we have to get our target number," Quiñones-Sánchez told me. "In this case, the number we got from the professionals was 6,300. So our goal was to touch 7,500 people before election day and get them to commit to vote for us; then we try to be strategic about pulling out those 7,500 [on election day]. So that's been our winning strategy."[22] As it turned out, the experts were right. As shown above, the number of votes needed to win was 5,654 (Cruz's total plus one); Quiñones-Sánchez's actual total was 6,139.

After the years of infighting between Quiñones-Sánchez and the other ward leaders, did City Committee chair Bob Brady try to bring everyone together to resolve their differences? Not exactly, Sánchez told me:

> For the first time in my four elections, Brady made the ward leaders sit in front of me and at least listen to my case. But you have to put that into context. There were three highly qualified Latinas who ran

> at large. There were two open at-large slots. He didn't support them. Instead, he facilitated a process in which the only Latina incumbent was challenged by another Latino elected official. So that encompasses how Brady really feels about our community. It's the divide-and-conquer. He had his chosen Latino—Angel Cruz, who's assistant secretary of the party. So Angel Cruz can throw whatever tantrums he wants, and the Brady style is "We take care of incumbents," except when it comes to me.[23]

Luck of the Draw

Ballot position in Philadelphia primary elections is determined by lottery, and in a race with many candidates, ballot position can sometimes decisively influence the outcome. In the 2019 council at-large election, Derek Green's name was posted in the bottom row of the fifth column. Although he had finished in first place in 2015, he finished in fourth place in 2019.

In the May primary, the competition for the fifth at-large seat (based on the assumption that the three incumbents and Isaiah Thomas would win four of the seats) was, in effect, between Katherine Gilmore Richardson and Justin DiBerardinis. Both had served on City Council staff, working for influential council members (Cherelle Parker and Maria Quiñones-Sánchez, respectively), and both had strong ties to neighborhood constituencies. The fact that Richardson was an African American woman and DiBerardinis was a white man may have made a difference. However, it is very likely that ballot position made as much as, if not more, of a difference. Richardson's name appeared on the ballot in the third column to the right, and DiBerardinis's was in the sixth column. DiBerardinis came in fewer than three thousand votes behind Richardson.

As described in Chapter 7, ballot position always matters with respect to common pleas court candidacies for two reasons: a larger number of candidates are competing, and most voters know little or nothing about them. A citizen who comes to the polls to vote for the next mayor or district council member and who is confronted by the multiple columns of unfamiliar names that appear on the judicial ballot may decide not to vote for any candidates or to simply vote for candidates in the left-hand columns and then move on.

In a blog post the week before the May primary, urban demographer Jonathan Tannen introduced his analysis of the upcoming common pleas court election with this background narrative.

> The court is responsible for the city's major civil and criminal trials. Its judges are elected to ten-year terms. And we elect them by drawing [ballot numbers] out of a coffee can.

> The result is that Philadelphia often elects judges who are unfit for the office. In 2015, Scott DiClaudio won; months later he would be censured for misconduct and negligence and then get caught having given illegal donations. . . . He was in the first position on the ballot. Lyris Younge was at the bottom of the first column that year and won. She has since been removed from Family Court for violating family rights and made headlines by evicting a full building of residents with less than a week's notice.[24]

Tannen examined the extent to which several factors appeared to influence the outcome of past common pleas court elections, including candidate endorsements promoted by the Democratic City Committee; candidate recommendations by the Philadelphia Bar Association ("highly recommended," "recommended," or "not recommended"); and candidates' ballot positions. His findings included the following:

- Democratic Party endorsement is especially important in the traditionally strong African American wards but not as influential in Hispanic wards or in Northeast Philadelphia.
- Candidates who are designated as recommended by the bar association "receive about 1.8 times as many votes [as other candidates] on average, drawing almost all of that advantage from Center City and Chestnut Hill & Mount Airy [i.e., wealthier neighborhoods with a more highly educated population]."[25] In 2019, the bar association also designated four candidates as highly recommended.
- "Unfortunately, all of these effects are swamped by ballot position. Candidates in the first column receive twice as many votes in every single type of ward, but especially many in lower-income wards."[26]

Noting that seven of the eight candidates listed in the first two columns of the ballot had received a "recommended" designation from the bar association, Tannen anticipated that "probably at worst" only one "not recommended" candidate would win.

As it turned out, all of the winners were Recommended or Highly Recommended candidates. Only three of the winning candidates had ballot positions in the first two columns; the other three occupied ballot positions in the fourth, fifth, and sixth columns. The bar association's promotion of its recommendations, tested in 2017 and expanded in 2019, seemed likely to have contributed to this outcome. Winning candidates and the bar association's 2019 handout are shown in Table 13.6 and Figure 13.4.

TABLE 13.6 VOTE TOTALS FOR WINNING CANDIDATES IN 2019 DEMOCRATIC PRIMARY FOR COMMON PLEAS COURT JUDGE

Candidate	Votes
Jennifer Schultz*	59,547
Anthony Kyriakakis†	58,128
Joshua Roberts*	55,702
Tiffany Palmer†	55,586
James C. Crumlish†	39,217
Carmella Jacquinto*	38,920

Source: Data from Philadelphia City Commissioners *View Election Results* database, https://www.philadelphiavotes.com/en/resources-a-data/ballot-box-app; Philadelphia Bar Association, "2019 General Election Ratings—Candidates: Philadelphia Court of Common Pleas," https://judges.philadelphiabar.org.

* Recommended by Philadelphia Bar Association

† Highly recommended by Philadelphia Bar Association

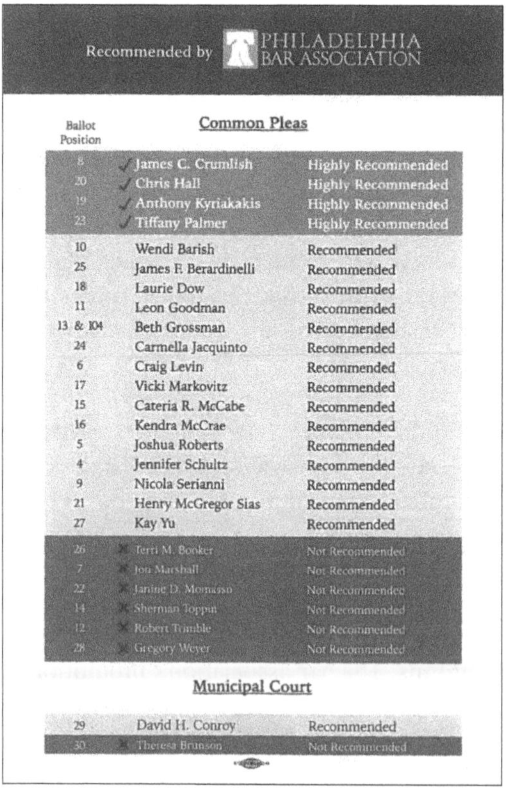
Recommended by PHILADELPHIA BAR ASSOCIATION

Common Pleas

Ballot Position		
8	✓ James C. Crumlish	Highly Recommended
20	✓ Chris Hall	Highly Recommended
19	✓ Anthony Kyriakakis	Highly Recommended
23	✓ Tiffany Palmer	Highly Recommended
10	Wendi Barish	Recommended
25	James F. Berardinelli	Recommended
18	Laurie Dow	Recommended
11	Leon Goodman	Recommended
13 & 104	Beth Grossman	Recommended
24	Carmella Jacquinto	Recommended
6	Craig Levin	Recommended
17	Vicki Markovitz	Recommended
15	Cateria R. McCabe	Recommended
16	Kendra McCrae	Recommended
5	Joshua Roberts	Recommended
4	Jennifer Schultz	Recommended
9	Nicola Serianni	Recommended
21	Henry McGregor Sias	Recommended
27	Kay Yu	Recommended
26	✗ Terri M. Booker	Not Recommended
7	✗ Jon Marshall	Not Recommended
22	✗ Janine D. Momasso	Not Recommended
14	✗ Sherman Toppin	Not Recommended
12	✗ Robert Trimble	Not Recommended
28	✗ Gregory Weyer	Not Recommended

Municipal Court

29	David H. Conroy	Recommended
30	✗ Theresa Brunson	Not Recommended

Figure 13.4 Philadelphia Bar Association 2019 primary election common pleas court candidate recommendations

Source: Handout from Philadelphia Bar Association.

Curiosities

Changes occurred with respect to two of the elective offices featured in the 2009 Committee of Seventy report, "Needless Jobs: Why Six Elected City Positions Should Die": the Philadelphia sheriff and the register of wills.

Two sheriff's office employees had charged the incumbent sheriff, Jewell Williams, with sexual harassment, and the city had agreed to pay $127,500 to settle one of them (Williams denied harassing the employees).[27] The Democratic City Committee endorsed Williams for reelection anyway, generating a public outcry. Soon after, the party withdrew its endorsement without endorsing one of the other two major contenders, Rochelle Bilal or Malika Rahman. The winner of the election was Bilal, a former police officer and former head of the Guardian Civic League who captured 41 percent of the vote, compared with 27 percent for Williams and 25 percent for Rahman.

The ten-term incumbent register of wills, Ronald Donatucci, lost his bid for reelection to Tracey Gordon, who received 44 percent of the vote compared with 40 percent for Donatucci.

Both offices were among the city's relatively few twenty-first-century patronage-job resources. So why did the Democratic Party not devote more attention to these two races? In the #MeToo era, when, in 2018, a woman candidate for Congress (Mary Gay Scanlon) had easily defeated the party-endorsed candidate (Richard Lazer, a candidate who had not been the subject of sexual harassment charges), the Democratic City Committee's support for Jewell Williams and subsequent ham-handed withdrawal of the endorsement set the stage for an upset. And why had the party not anticipated that a much younger African American woman, a challenger with past experience as a municipal government official (deputy city commissioner) and political campaigner in previous years (unsuccessfully, for state representative and City Council), might pose a problem for Donatucci in 2019? Thinking in terms of former House speaker O'Donnell's perspective, there was not a sufficient critical mass of "people coming together" to make sure that party-favored candidates were going to win these two offices. Some critical number of people associated with the Democratic City Committee who might have helped make the difference with respect to these two elections apparently felt that their involvement was not needed or was put to better use on higher-profile elections. Not enough of them, apparently, had considered the potential outcomes of these two elections or had cared enough about their consequences.

What Just Happened?

The May election lacked the drama of Ed Rendell's victory over Emmett Fitzpatrick. The May election lacked the closure of the overwhelming no vote with respect to the referendum-question election that ended the prospects for a three-consecutive-term Rizzo administration. What happened was less clear-cut and less susceptible to the kind of analysis that could be conveyed in the form of sound bites or takeaways.

The Democratic City Committee could claim credit for having done its job (City Commissioners), but the Democratic City Committee had also blundered (sheriff, register of wills). Advocacy organizations such as Philadelphia 3.0, Reclaim, and Philadelphia Neighborhood Networks could declare victory with respect to some of the campaigns they had supported, but none of them could claim exclusive ownership of any of these victories (Jamie Gauthier, Maria Quiñones-Sánchez) or be held solely responsible for any of the losses that candidates they favored had experienced (Kahlil Williams, Justin DiBerardinis).

There was no clear division between liberal Philadelphia and conservative Philadelphia, comparable to the division between blue-state and red-state America that existed in 2019. However, Philadelphia's political condition was nothing like a state of harmony. Philadelphia was in a political transition that was strongly influenced by the city's history of racial discrimination, racial and ethnic conflict, and discriminatory criminal justice; by the long-term effects of 9/11; and by national and regional immigration patterns and real estate market trends.

The Philadelphia results of the 2016 primary and general elections had illustrated this absence of clear lines of political division. In the presidential primary, Bernie Sanders had finished strongly, with 129,353 votes compared to Hillary Clinton's 218,959 votes. Sanders won majorities in seven wards: three in South Philadelphia, one each in West and Northwest Philadelphia, and two on the Delaware River. Then, in the general election, Donald Trump won one ward in far Northeast Philadelphia and one ward in deep South Philadelphia. One of these wards, the 26th, had delivered a primary-election majority for Sanders six months previously. In 2019, the 26th Ward results for council at-large candidates were consistent with the citywide results: Helen Gym and Allan Domb placed first and second.

Citywide voter turnout in the May 2019 primary was characteristically low—less than 23 percent of the city's registered voters showed up to vote. However, turnout in that election was higher than in 2017, the year of the hotly contested district attorney primary in which all candidates were nonincumbent; and turnout was higher than in 2018, the year of the congressional midterm elections.

The barely visible backdrop for the 2019 primary was Mayor Kenney's poverty-reduction policy agenda. Although no one is in favor of poverty, reducing poverty is not the ideal platform for a political campaign, particularly in a city in which most voters are not poor people. With full awareness of this political disadvantage, Mayor Kenney had made the reduction of poverty his administration's top priority and had made the Philadelphia Beverage Tax, the controversial soft-drink tax, the primary vehicle for addressing this issue constructively. The tax would generate funding for prekindergarten and community-schools programs and would pay debt service on bond financing for the upgrading of parks, recreation centers, and libraries.

In year one, revenue from the tax funded 2,000 pre-K seats and nine community schools. In mid-2018, litigation against the tax was resolved in the city's favor. In year two, the tax funded 2,250 pre-K seats and twelve community schools.[28] Playground improvement projects were started in February of the election year, and funding awards for recreation center and library upgrades were announced during the months leading up to the election.

Mayor Kenney was a pragmatic politician, and it is likely that his first-term goals with respect to this issue had been to get the tax approved, to resolve the litigation that would inevitably be brought against the tax, and then to start using initial tax revenues to begin delivering some of the promised benefits. Engaging in debate with his two competitors in the mayoral primary, Alan Butkovitz and Anthony Hardy Williams, would make it harder for Kenney to accomplish these things; and (as indicated previously) giving opposing candidates an opportunity to air their views in public debates was not a good strategy for an incumbent in Kenney's position.

So, in many respects, the 2019 primary was boring, and Kenney had played a large role in making it boring. He had done so, in part, with political considerations in mind. But doing so also enabled him to continue to advance an unpopular but necessary policy that he had designed to address the city's biggest and most intractable problem.

14

★★★★★★★

Unfinished Business

On May 15, 2019, Alabama governor Kay Ivey signed into law a bill that would prohibit abortions at nearly every stage of pregnancy, making no exceptions for cases of rape or incest.[1] In a statement issued by her office, Governor Ivey said, "This legislation stands as a powerful testament to Alabamians' deeply held belief that every life is precious and that every life is a sacred gift from God."[2]

The governor's declaration about the preciousness of life is at odds with her state's poor performance in promoting health and welfare practices that have proven successful in other states and that, if adopted in Alabama, would affirm the value of life on a much larger scale. Alabama is one of the nation's worst-performing states with respect to addressing infant mortality and low birthweight rates.[3] Because of its rejection of Medicaid expansion, made possible through the Affordable Care Act, the state missed out on an opportunity to reduce the cost of services to pregnant women by a projected $43 million over a four-year period.[4]

Why would public officials who claim to care so deeply about life consistently fail to support measures that would improve the lives of their constituents? When questions of this kind are raised about situations such as this one, a familiar response is "It's just politics." On the face of it, that response may be accurate, but the underlying reality is this: they do not care.

Uncaring lawmakers and the substitution of symbolic gestures for constructive action are nothing new in American politics. What is new is the fact that this combination of political pageantry and empty policies is being made routine at a time when, for millions of households, wealth is steadily eroding and quality of life is steadily worsening. As economic hardships increase for many Americans, the population of this country is coming to more closely resemble that of nations governed by nationalistic and authoritarian leaders. The quality of U.S. education and health care systems has fallen below that of two dozen other nations.[5] In 2016, nearly half of the nation's renter households were "cost-burdened"—spending more than 30 percent of income for housing.[6] In that year, food insecurity—a household's inability to obtain adequate food because of lack of money or other resources—remained elevated above pre-recession levels, affecting about 13 million children in 2016.[7]

Many of these problems will not be resolved in the short term. The replacement of bad politicians on election days will not necessarily be followed by an era of positive, transformative change. Seating a whole new generation of much more responsible leaders may take decades.

Much of the constructive political change that needs to happen will not originate in the White House or the Capitol. At the federal level, bipartisanship has been a rare phenomenon, and gridlock may continue to be Washington's default position for the foreseeable future. Instead, the best new public policies are likely to emerge as initiatives that are introduced and tested at the state and local level, then authorized by the federal government and expanded on a national basis. The best-known example of this policy development sequence is the Affordable Care Act, modeled after the 2006 health care reform law approved in Massachusetts during the administration of then-governor Mitt Romney.

Other policies that are formulated by state governments and do not conflict with federal mandates will be replicated in other states without the need for any federal involvement. Legislation authorized in Michigan enabled Genesee County treasurer Dan Kildee (who was later elected to Congress) to organize a county land bank as a vehicle for facilitating the acquisition and development of vacant and abandoned properties in Flint, Michigan. After witnessing the positive results that land banks produced in Flint and other Michigan communities, many other states adopted land bank legislation, giving themselves a more systematic approach for addressing blighted property challenges in rural as well as urban areas.

Most of the political leaders of the future, like the political leaders of the past and present, will get their start in politics at the local level. In terms of their career path, they will look more like Dan Kildee (who won his first election as a candidate for the Flint Board of Education) and Maria Quiñones-Sánchez than like Mitt Romney and Donald Trump.

This book is primarily about how ambitious individuals succeeded in long-odds elections by employing creative campaign strategies, by finding the most effective ways to communicate with voters, and by understanding the political opportunities available in the social and economic environment in which their campaigns were taking place. In this way, the book is intended to convey a positive message: under certain circumstances, a reform candidacy can succeed; under certain circumstances, reform candidacies can succeed again and again. Citizens who are concerned about the future of American democracy need to be aware that elections held every year at the municipal and county level will, in the aggregate and over the long term, determine the extent to which government at the national level could fundamentally improve, or not.

The campaigns described in Part I are analyzed in terms of the ward-and-division system populated by ward leaders and committeepeople. This system functioned most effectively during the late nineteenth and early twentieth centuries, when government jobs and contracts could be offered in exchange for political support or campaign contributions. Because this system could not (and should not) be reconstituted on that basis, it could be worthwhile to consider the possibility of dismantling it in favor of an alternative that might be more appropriate for the present time. However, before accepting this conclusion as inevitable, consideration should be given to the fact that, in terms of its design, Philadelphia's ward-and-division system is an excellent model for representative government. As described in Chapter 1, the city of Philadelphia is conceived, in this model, as consisting of about 1,500 "villages"—the small geographic units known as divisions. Political party members in each division elect two representatives—the committeepeople—and this pair meets with counterpart pairs in nearby divisions to elect a ward leader. That person joins with other ward leaders in organizing the resources of the political party they represent and in (it is assumed) promoting voter registration and education.

Although this model may appear to be ideal from an academic perspective, it has become, in many respects, a failure in practice. But is it a failure because of some inherent, uncorrectable flaw—or is it a failure because the leaders of the system have been, more often than not, the wrong people?

The "right people" are not some group of elites that should be appointed to take charge of the ward-and-division infrastructure. Many of the right people already occupy committeeperson positions and would be prepared to take on greater leadership responsibilities if they could be joined by others who share their views; and some of the right people who are not committeepeople would consider running for that office if they had a better understanding of how the system works and of its potential value to their communities.

Although the current system is deeply flawed, the fact that the composition of each ward organization's leadership—consisting, collectively, of the ward leader and committeepeople—is, in most instances, highly reflective of the composition of the community it represents (in terms of diversity of age, race, income, employment status, and other factors) should not be taken lightly. In many instances, the leadership of the typical ward organization is more representative of its community than the leadership of the vast majority of neighborhood-based organizations, service agencies, and community-serving institutions within Philadelphia, as it is any many other municipalities.

Is the ward-and-division system like a horse-drawn buggy that has no utility in today's environment? Or is it instead like an older factory building that can be rehabilitated and repurposed to become successful in today's economy as housing, work space, or an eating-and-drinking place—successful, in part, because the underlying structure is sound and capable of adaptation? To the extent that more people learn more about how the system works and why it is not working effectively, the more likely it is that any changes that are subsequently instituted will be the best ones.

Next Steps: Giant or Incremental?

The events of the first quarter of the twenty-first century have demonstrated that some fundamental changes in public policy and political leadership that many would never have dreamed of can happen in the short term—with great or terrible consequences. Recent political history demonstrates the obvious: if more citizens are committed to political activism at the grassroots level and are educated about the best ways to join in—whether the vehicle be the Tea Party or Black Lives Matter—it becomes more likely that big results will be achieved.

So, if we had our way, what big opportunities would we pursue? With respect to voting and election day activity, innovations such as lowering the voting age, making voter registration automatic, instituting ranked voting, and expanding the use of mail-in ballots have found support in a variety of states, the populations of which represent a diversity of political views.[8]

Making Election Day a federal holiday is a proposal that apparently has strong bipartisan support but has not been advanced in Congress.[9] Making that new holiday, in part, a day of celebratory events as well—actually making Election Day fun rather than simply a time when one observes an obligation to interact with a voting machine—would broaden its appeal.[10] If this proposal were to be adopted, then, in Philadelphia, the Committee of Seventy could expand the program described in Chapter 10 on a citywide basis, recruiting and training high school students to provide voter information and answer questions at every polling place in the city. Then more people would gain an understanding of, for example, how to evaluate candidates for the judiciary or how to respond to referendum questions that are often included on the ballot.

Because the Democratic Party's dominant role in Philadelphia's political system makes the city, in effect, a one-party municipality, the election day that is nearly always decisive is the spring primary; with relatively few exceptions, the Democrats who are successful in the primary will win by wide margins in the fall general election. In Philadelphia and similar cities, this system could be made more consistent with principles of democracy if an "open primary" approach were to be adopted, in which any voter, regardless of party affiliation, would be permitted to vote for any candidate, regardless of party affiliation, in the primary election. In the primary election at present, registered Democrats and other voters who are members of a particular party may vote only for candidates belonging to that party; independent and unaffiliated voters may not vote for any candidates and can vote only on referendum questions. This change would restore value to the fall general election and give the election-day holiday authenticity.

Consideration should also be given to activities that are undertaken in a political context but are designed to benefit the public at large, not just party insiders. As the open-wards initiative supported by Philadelphia 3.0 and the Committee of Seventy illustrates, democratizing ward-meeting management and the candidate endorsement process is likely to produce better-qualified endorsed candidates and, in this way, reduce the number of underachieving officeholders and elected officials who are subsequently convicted of criminal activity.

Although this book is primarily about political activism and civic engagement at the municipal level, it is not unreasonable to also consider ways in which statewide civic engagement and coalition building could lead to major policy changes that yield broad benefits. Through dialogues at annual conferences and in consultations with local and county leaders in urban and rural areas, Elizabeth Hersh, then–executive director of the nonprofit Housing Alliance of Pennsylvania, found that communities that may have political differences share similar views about the urgency of addressing the widespread problem of blighted and neglected real estate. Regardless of political orientation, no one liked vacant, abandoned houses and industrial properties. No one liked absentee owners of neglected properties. Most people were concerned about the risks associated with speculator participation in tax-sale auctions. Some people were unequivocally opposed to the use of eminent domain power as a means of acquiring property, but many of them were not opposed to the use of conservatorship, a court-ordered assignment of a neglected vacant property to a responsible developer. As a result of coalition-building activity undertaken by the Housing Alliance in close coordination with legislators and their staff, Pennsylvania created a portfolio of state-authorized interventions that municipalities or counties can use to support blight prevention measures and reinvestment strategies. As it happened, some of the leaders who were most responsible for securing legislative authorization for these actions were Republican legislators who represented largely rural districts.

Persistent Habits and Small Changes

Small plastic bottles of water can be found in the executive offices of national charitable foundations that fund smart growth advocacy initiatives sponsored by nonprofit organizations. They can be found in the workplaces of many of the grantee organizations that these foundations support. They are delivered by the caseload to conferences hosted by academic institutions, research institutes, and industry groups that promote sustainability and green building policies and practices. They are present in the chambers of general assemblies where officeholders deliberate over environmental protection laws and regulations, as well as in the legislative offices and district offices of the representatives and senators who have made the enactment of these measures a top priority.

Bottled water is a necessity in communities where the water supply is contaminated or threatened by hazards. But when did consumers in the broader marketplace decide to start buying small plastic bottles of water, and why did they continue to do so until the presence of these items became regarded, in a way, as a necessity? Many people living today remember a time when water was never purchased and consumed in this manner and when the term "hydrate" was not commonly heard in the public realm. Is it possible that there are other, less environmentally harmful ways to "hydrate"?

Ideally, small plastic water bottles would disappear from the marketplace altogether at some time in the future. However, although eliminating these items immediately would provide enormous benefits, doing so at once would also have serious economic consequences, the burden of which would be borne largely by working people. Would it be possible to plan for a gradual phase-out of this product over some period of time? Working to create such a plan would be desirable even though, at present, it would be difficult to imagine what it would look like. With the plastic water bottle as an example, people who seek to reform government and improve society should be mindful of the need to distinguish between changes that require immediate action and changes that cannot be implemented in the short term and will need to be worked on.

They also have to be self-aware. Those who strive for political reform and positive social change do not need to adopt a monastic lifestyle or subject themselves and their allies to Cultural Revolution–style self-criticism and reeducation, but they do have to be self-critical. With respect to plastic water bottles and other issues, they have to think about and act on lifestyle changes that they will choose to require themselves to make—in some cases, while refraining from insisting that others do so as well.

Benediction

In a 2019 conversation with me, former Philadelphia mayor W. Wilson Goode criticized elected officials past and present, who had campaigned as reformers but who, once elected, had failed to follow up in advancing a reform agenda.

> They ran as reformers, but they became the people they sought to replace. . . . They really don't clearly understand that they're policy people. They're there to make changes in policy. They're not there to have community meetings or summer festivals in the park—to do what community leaders and nonelected people can do. They're there to develop ways to perfect a broken system and to help people. We need people in elective office who understand what their job description is. It's not to do what others can do—it's to do what only they can do, and that's to pass laws to bring about change.[11]

In this time of deep uneasiness and uncertainty, it would not be inappropriate to consider how these comments relate to ourselves individually, not just to elected officials. Political reform is not going to be achieved without bold and constructive action by individuals like those who, in the aftermath of the 2016 election, decided they had to do something. We should feel compelled to ask ourselves questions similar to those that they, as well as the challengers whose stories are described in Part I, must have asked themselves: What should I do? What can I do that others cannot do? What is that thing that only I can do?

Notes

★★★★★

ACKNOWLEDGMENTS

1. John Kromer, *Neighborhood Recovery: Reinvestment Policy for the New Hometown* (New Brunswick, NJ: Rutgers University Press, 2000), 210–213.

2. Karen Bojar, *Green Shoots of Democracy in the Philadelphia Democratic Party* (Berkeley, CA: She Writes Press, 2016).

3. Russell F. Weigley, ed., *Philadelphia: A 300-Year History* (New York: W. W. Norton, 1982); Sal Paolantonio, *Rizzo: The Last Big Man in Big City America* (Philadelphia: Camino Books, 1993); W. Wilson Goode Sr., *Black Voters Mattered: A Philadelphia Story* (n.p.: BookBaby, 2018).

INTRODUCTION

1. The troubled history and unexpectedly positive outcome of this community development venture is described in John Kromer, *Fixing Broken Cities: The Implementation of Urban Reinvestment Policies* (New York: Routledge, 2010).

CHAPTER 1

1. Kellan White, interview by the author, Philadelphia, March 30, 2018.

2. See the organization's home page, at http://www.phila3-0.org.

3. Jon Geeting, "Get Mad, Then Get Elected," *Philadelphia 3.0* (blog), November 11, 2016, http://www.phila3-0.org/get_mad_then_get_elected.

4. Kelly Dittmar, "Women Candidates in Election 2018," Rutgers University Center for American Women and Politics, November 20, 2017, http://www.cawp.rutgers.edu/sites/default/files/resources/a_closer_look_2018_outlook_final.pdf (emphasis in original).

5. Max Marin, "Ward Lords: The Endorsements That Matter in the Philly DA's Race," *Philadelphia Weekly*, May 9, 2017, p. 1.

6. White, interview by the author.

7. Ibid.

8. Rebecca Rhynhart, personal communication with the author, July 18, 2019.

9. White, interview by the author.

10. The coattails issue is analyzed in more depth in Jon Geeting, "Larry Krasner's Coattails Don't Explain Rebecca Rhynhart's Sweep," *Philadelphia 3.0* (blog), May 18, 2017, http://www.phila3-0.org/krasner_doesnt_explain_rhynhart.

11. White, interview by the author.

12. Ibid.

13. Ibid.

14. Sarah Stuart, interview by the author, Philadelphia, April 30, 2018.

15. Brandy Bones, interview by the author, Philadelphia, April 7, 2018.

16. Attorney, interview by the author, Philadelphia, April 30, 2018.

17. 22nd Ward resident, interview by the author, Philadelphia, April 23, 2018.

18. White, interview by the author.

19. Committee of Seventy, *How to Run for Committeeperson: A Campaign Guide for Philadelphia Candidates* (Philadelphia: Committee of Seventy, 2016), 6.

20. Tom Ferrick, Jr., "Election Day? A Big Payday for Philly Political Bosses," *Philadelphia Inquirer*, October 28, 2015, https://www.inquirer.com/philly/news/politics/mayor/Ferrick_Election_Day_A_big_payday_for_Philly_political_bosses.html.

21. Holly Otterbein, "Why Is Bob Brady Still in Charge?" *Philadelphia Magazine*, April 15, 2017, https://www.phillymag.com/news/2017/04/15/bob-brady-democratic-party/.

CHAPTER 2

1. For example, see Joseph S. Clark Jr., and Dennis J. Clark, "Rally and Relapse, 1946–1968," in *Philadelphia: A 300-Year History*, ed. Russell F. Weigley (New York: W. W. Norton, 1982), 649–703.

2. Peter Binzen with Jonathan Binzen, *Richardson Dilworth: Last of the Bare-Knuckled Aristocrats* (Philadelphia: Camino Books, 2014), 97.

3. Philadelphia Registration Commission, *Forty-Third Annual Report of the Registration Commission for the City of Philadelphia* (Philadelphia: City of Philadelphia, 1948), 24, 25.

4. Peter McCaffery, *When Bosses Ruled Philadelphia: The Emergence of the Republican Machine, 1867–1933* (University Park: Pennsylvania State University Press, 1993), 98.

5. Ibid., 89.

6. Arthur P. Dudden, "The City Embraces 'Normalcy,' 1919–1929," in Weigley, *Philadelphia*, 583.

7. Ibid., 580, 581.

8. Philadelphia Registration Commission, *Forty-Third Annual Report*, 1, 2.

9. Philadelphia Registration Commission, *Forty-Seventh Annual Report of the Registration Commission for the City of Philadelphia* (Philadelphia: City of Philadelphia, 1952), 6.

10. Ibid., 12. Twentieth-century immigration trends are described in Dudden, "The City Embraces 'Normalcy,'" 587–591.

11. G. Terry Madonna and John Morrison McLarnon III, "Reform in Philadelphia: Richardson Dilworth, Joseph S. Clark and the Women Who Made Reform Possible, 1947–1949," *Pennsylvania Magazine of History and Biography*. 127, no. 1 (2003): 65.

12. Ibid., 67.

13. Hal Libros, *Hard Core Liberals: A Sociological Analysis of the Philadelphia Americans for Democratic Action* (Cambridge, MA: Schenkman, 1975).

14. Madonna and McLarnon, "Reform in Philadelphia," 68, 69.

15. Clark and Clark, "Rally and Relapse," 656.

16. Ibid., 657.

17. His projects are described in detail in Gregory L. Heller, *Ed Bacon: Planning, Politics, and the Building of Modern Philadelphia* (Philadelphia: University of Pennsylvania Press, 2013).

18. Clark and Clark, "Rally and Relapse," 657, 658.

19. Ibid., 659, 660; Binzen, *Richardson Dilworth*, 129, 130.

20. Clark and Clark, "Rally and Relapse," 660.

21. Madonna and McLarnon, "Reform in Philadelphia," 86–88.

22. Matthew Smalarz, "Northeast Philadelphia," in *The Encyclopedia of Greater Philadelphia* (London: Rutgers University, 2014), https://philadelphiaencyclopedia.org/archive/northeast-philadelphia-essay/.

23. Amy Hillier, "Redlining in Philadelphia," in *Past Time, Past Place: GIS for History*, ed. Anne Kelly Knowles (Redlands, CA: ESRI Press, 2002), 86.

24. Ibid., 87–88, 90. See also Alex F. Schwartz, *Housing Policy in the United States*, 2nd ed., (New York: Routledge, 2010), chap. 3.

25. Commonwealth of Pennsylvania Department of the Auditor General, *Performance Audit Report: Philadelphia Parking Authority, Employment Policies and Procedures* (Harrisburg, PA: Commonwealth of Pennsylvania, 2017), i.

26. Commonwealth of Pennsylvania Department of the Auditor General, *Performance Audit Report: Philadelphia Parking Authority, Financial Objectives* (Harrisburg, PA: Commonwealth of Pennsylvania, 2017), 2.

27. John Baer, "Goodbye Mr. Cohen . . . or Not?" *Philadelphia Inquirer*, November 28, 2016, https://www.inquirer.com/philly/columnists/john_baer/20161128_Goodbye__Mr__Cohen_____or_not_.html.

28. Holly Otterbein, "Progressives Hoping to Shake Up Philly's Democratic Party Get Good, and Bad, News," *Philadelphia Inquirer*, March 15, 2018, https://www.inquirer.com/philly/columnists/clout/progressives-bob-brady-democratic-party-ward-leaders-20180315.html.

CHAPTER 3

1. Vanessa Williams, "Rookie of the Year: Chaka Fattah Rode to Congress on a Landslide; Problem Is, So Did the Other Party," *Philadelphia Inquirer Magazine*, January 15, 1995, p. 22.

2. Curtis Jones Jr., interview by the author, Philadelphia, August 9, 2018.

3. Ibid.

4. Ibid.

5. Paul Taylor, "Forum Endorses Bowser: Black Delegates Favor Him, 54–9," *Philadelphia Inquirer*, March 12, 1979, p. B-1.

6. Pamela Smith, "Jones, Fattah, Run for Comm. of Elections," *Philadelphia Tribune*, March 23, 1979, p. 2.

7. "City Commission Needs New Faces, New Policies," *Philadelphia Inquirer*, May 10, 1979, p. 18-A.

8. Arthur P. Dudden, "The City Embraces 'Normalcy,' 1919–1929" in *Philadelphia: A 300-Year History*, ed. Russell F. Weigley (New York: W. W. Norton, 1982), 583.

9. Stephanie G. Wolf, "The Bicentennial City, 1968–1982," in Weigley, *Philadelphia*, 707.

10. U.S. Department of Commerce, Bureau of the Census, *County and City Data Book, 1967* (Washington, DC: Bureau of the Census, 1967); Philadelphia City Planning Commission, *Highlights of the 1980 Census for Philadelphia: Technical Information Paper* (Philadelphia: City of Philadelphia, 1982); Philadelphia City Planning Commission, *Preliminary Population Data for Census Tracts: Technical Information Paper* (Philadelphia: City of Philadelphia, 1991).

11. Douglas S. Massey and Nancy A. Denton, *American Apartheid: Segregation and the Making of the Underclass* (Cambridge, MA: Harvard University Press, 1993), 72.

12. Tom Infield, "Racial Tension Is Not Limited to S.W. Phila.," *Philadelphia Inquirer*, December 8, 1985, p. D01.

13. Ibid.

14. Sarah Mack, "Memory from Sarah A. Mack," in *Cedar Park Centennial Commemorative Booklet* (Philadelphia: Cedar Park Neighbors, 2011), 36.

15. W. Wilson Goode Sr., *Black Voters Mattered: A Philadelphia Story* (n.p.: BookBaby, 2018), loc. 263.

16. Jones, interview by the author.

17. Pamala Haynes, "Hardy Williams: 'How We Beat an Incumbent Legislator,'" *Philadelphia Tribune*, June 6, 1970, p. 32.

18. Wilson Goode's *Black Voters Mattered* provides a detailed overview of late-twentieth-century African American political activism in Philadelphia with profiles of individuals who played key leadership roles. Matthew J. Countryman's *Up South: Civil Rights and Black Power in Philadelphia* (Philadelphia: University of Pennsylvania Press, 2006) is a well-documented history of the evolution of black political power, from the New Deal era to Wilson Goode's mayoral administration.

19. Goode, *Black Voters Mattered*, loc. 551.

20. "Blacks Should Control Democrat Party, Says Angry Hardy Williams," *Philadelphia Tribune*, February 22, 1972, p. 1.

21. Christopher K. Hepp, Tom Infield, and Vernon Clark, "Charles W. Bowser, Towering Political Figure in Philadelphia, Dies," *Philadelphia Inquirer*, August 12, 2010, https://www.inquirer.com/philly/obituaries/20100812_Charles_W__Bowswer__towering_political_figure_in_Philadelphia__dies.html.

22. Jim Davis, "Wilson Has Goode Chance of Winning," *Philadelphia Tribune*, April 20, 1982, p. 6.

23. Chaka Fattah, interview by the author, Lewis Run, PA, October 14, 2018.

24. As it turned out, Hardy Williams chose to run for state Senate in 1982, instead of seeking reelection to the House. Williams was successful, and Peter Truman was elected to fill the 191st District House seat that Williams was to vacate.

25. Terry E. Johnson, "192D: Not Black and White Election—State House District Has Changed its Character," *Philadelphia Inquirer*, May 11, 1982, p. B08.

26. Fair Districts PA, "How Redistricting Works," https://www.fairdistrictspa.com/the-problem/how-redistricting-works (accessed February 14, 2020).

27. Fattah, interview by the author.

28. Ibid.

29. Ibid.

30. Ibid.

31. Ibid.

32. Chaka Fattah, quoted in Richard F. Fenno, *Going Home: Black Representatives and Their Constituents* (Chicago: University of Chicago Press, 2003), 118.

33. Lynette Hazelton, "Fattah: Not Just Another Candidate," *Philadelphia Tribune*, February 23, 1982, p. 3.

34. Ibid.

35. Johnson, "192D," B08.

36. Fattah, interview by the author.

37. Mike Leary, "Mullen, 2 Other Incumbents in City Trail for PA House," *Philadelphia Inquirer*, May 19, 1982, p. A07.

38. Beth Gillin and Maida Odom, "Fattah's Vision Raises Eyebrows: Critics Say the Legislator's Plan to Transform Public Housing Is Impractical," *Philadelphia Inquirer*, March 8, 1990, p. B01.

39. Ibid.

40. Ibid.

41. William Yardley, "William H. Gray III, Pastor and Lawmaker, Dies at 71," *New York Times*, July 2, 2013, https://www.nytimes.com/2013/07/03/us/william-h-gray-iii-pastor-and-lawmaker-dies-at-71.html.

42. Since this contest was the equivalent of a general election rather than a primary, Blackwell, as the endorsed Democratic Party candidate, was the only one to have his party affiliation displayed on the ballot. As a result, "pulling the Democratic lever" in this election meant delivering a vote for Blackwell, creating a significant disadvantage for the two other candidates, who happened to be members of the Democratic Party. In that election, Fattah ran as the Consumer Party candidate, White as an Independent.

43. Vanessa Williams, "Fattah Will Seek Re-election Forgoes 2nd Bid for Congress," *Philadelphia Inquirer*, February 24, 1992, p. B01.

44. Fattah, interview by the author.

45. Vanessa Williams, "Fattah Is Giving Blackwell a Battle in the Primary, Pitting Two Generations of Democrats," *Philadelphia Inquirer*, April 24, 1994, p. B01.

46. Ibid.

47. Fattah, interview by the author.

48. Patrick Kerkstra, "Philadelphia Power Broker Carol Ann Campbell Has Died," *Philadelphia Inquirer*, November 19, 2008, https://www.inquirer.com/philly/blogs/heardinthehall/Carol_Ann_Campbell.html.

49. Fattah, interview by the author.

50. Eugene Scott, "The Democratic Party Owes Black Female Voters a Big 'Thank You,'" *Washington Post*, November 9, 2017, https://www.washingtonpost.com/news/the-fix/wp/2017/11/09/the-democratic-party-owes-black-women-voters-a-big-thank-you/.

51. Fattah, interview by the author.

52. Ibid.

53. Williams, "Rookie of the Year," 26.

54. Laurie Asseo, "U.S. Supreme Court Upholds PA Redistricting Plan," *Philadelphia Inquirer*, October 6, 1992, p. B02.

55. Fattah, interview by the author.

56. Vanessa Williams, "Hot Races Just Didn't Materialize: Despite New Boundaries and Voter Anger, the City's Congressmen Appear Safe," *Philadelphia Inquirer*, March 16, 1992, p. B01.

57. Fattah, interview by the author.

58. Keegan Gibson, "PA Republicans Win Redistricting Game," *PoliticsPA*, November 9, 2012, http://www.politicspa.com/pa-republicans-win-redistricting-game/44201/.

59. Karen Bojar, *Green Shoots of Democracy in the Philadelphia Democratic Party* (Berkeley, CA: She Writes Press, 2016).

60. Christopher Ingraham, "Pennsylvania Supreme Court Draws 'Much More Competitive' District Map to Overturn Republican Gerrymander," *Washington Post*, February 20, 2018, https://www.washingtonpost.com/news/wonk/wp/2018/02/19/pennsylvania-supreme-court-draws-a-much-more-competitive-district-map-to-overturn-republican-gerrymander.

61. Bojar, *Green Shoots*, loc. 3748.

62. Fair Districts PA, "Measuring Fairness," https://www.fairdistrictspa.com/solution/measuring-fairness (accessed February 14, 2020).

63. Carrie Arnold, "The Mathematicians Who Want to Save Democracy," *Scientific American*, June 7, 2017, https://www.scientificamerican.com/article/the-mathematicians-who-want-to-save-democracy/.

CHAPTER 4

1. Joseph Vignola, interview by the author, Philadelphia, January 10, 2019. All quotations by Vignola in this chapter come from this source.

2. Curtis Jones, interview by the author, Philadelphia, August 9, 2018.

3. Henry B. Cianfrani was a state representative from 1952 to 1962, as well as a Democratic ward leader. His son, Henry J. "Buddy" Cianfrani, succeeded him both as state representative and ward leader. He was elected to the state Senate in 1966, where he became head of the Appropriations Committee, a position that gave him great influence over the allocation of state funding to Philadelphia. Both Cianfranis were powerful political leaders in South Philadelphia east of Broad Street; Barrett was more influential west of Broad, where his home ward was located.

4. Holly Otterbein, "Why Is Bob Brady Still in Charge?" *Philadelphia Magazine*, April 15, 2017, https://www.phillymag.com/news/2017/04/15/bob-brady-democratic-party/.

5. John R. Maneval, *An Ethnic History of South Philadelphia, 1870–1980: A Research Tool for Demographic Studies* (Philadelphia: Balch Institute for Ethnic Studies, 1992), II-104.

6. Frank DiCicco, interview by the author, Philadelphia, December 27, 2018.

7. Ibid.

8. Peter McCaffrey, *When Bosses Ruled Philadelphia: The Emergence of the Republican Machine, 1867–1933* (University Park: Pennsylvania State University Press, 1993), 135.

9. Murray Dubin, *South Philadelphia: Mummers, Memoirs, and the Melrose Diner* (Philadelphia: Temple University Press, 1996), 96, 97.

10. Ibid., 96, 97.

11. "Emanuel Weinberg," *Wikipedia*, October 3, 2019, https://en.wikipedia.org/wiki/Emanuel_Weinberg.

12. McCaffrey, *Bosses*, 135.

13. S. A. Paolantonio, *Frank Rizzo: The Last Big Man in Big City America* (Philadelphia: Camino Books, 1993), 68.

14. Ibid., 87.

15. City of Philadelphia Registration Commission, *Sixty-First Annual Report of the Registration Commission* (Philadelphia: City of Philadelphia, 1967); City of Philadelphia Registration Commission, *Sixty-Ninth Annual Report of the Registration Commission* (Philadelphia: City of Philadelphia, 1975).

16. Paolantonio, *Rizzo*, 108.

17. Paul Taylor, "Green Gets His First Taste of Defeat," *Philadelphia Inquirer*, February 14, 1980, p. 1-A.

18. Paolantonio, *Rizzo*, 188.

19. Russell Cooke, "Foglietta, Tayoun Have Lively Debate," *Philadelphia Inquirer*, March 13, 1984, p. B01; Larry Eichel, "Campaign '82—Who's on First? Committeemen Hold the Key," *Philadelphia Inquirer*, April 21, 1982, p. B01.

20. Dianna Marder, "One Pol Relies on Principle, the Other, Power Connections," *Philadelphia Inquirer*, June 25, 1995, p. B1.

21. Geoffrey T. Gibbs, "Dead but Still Running," *Harvard Crimson*, November 3, 1980, https://www.thecrimson.com/article/1980/11/3/dead-but-still-running-pperhaps-ozzie/.

22. Steve Twomey, Murray Dubin, and Daniel R. Biddle, "Myers Beaten; Lederer Wins Easily," *Philadelphia Inquirer*, November 5, 1980, p. 1.

23. Ibid.

24. Paul Taylor, "In Phila.'s 3rd District, Hand-to-Hand Political Combat," *Philadelphia Inquirer*, July 20, 1981, p. 8-B.

25. Paul Taylor, "In Upset, Smith Trounces Glancey for Seat in House," *Philadelphia Inquirer*, July 22, 1981, p. A01.

26. Larry Eichel, "In Pa. Redistricting, They Played the Republicans' Song," *Philadelphia Inquirer*, March 7, 1982, p. F01.

27. Frederick Cusick, "Pa. Legislature Passes GOP Redistricting Plan," *Philadelphia Inquirer*, March 3, 1982, p. A01.

28. Eichel, "In Pa. Redistricting," F01.

29. Connie Langland, "City Commission: Have 3 Mixups in Votes Doomed It?" *Philadelphia Inquirer*, September 23, 1979, p. 1-M.

30. Ibid.

31. Ibid.

32. In this instance, "college" is a euphemism for "prison." Cianfrani served twenty-seven months in federal prison after being convicted of racketeering, mail fraud, and other charges associated with the payments from the Senate budget to two "ghost" employees.

33. Eichel, "Campaign '82—Who's on First?"

34. Larry Eichel, "The Primary: By Nov., Maybe Just a Footnote," *Philadelphia Inquirer*, May 23, 1982, p. F01.

35. Mike Mallowe, "They Call It a Council," *Philadelphia Magazine*, March 1976, pp. 196, 197.

36. Tony West, "The Multifaceted Life of Jimmy Tayoun," *Philadelphia Public Record*, November 9, 2017, http://www.phillyrecord.com/2017/11/the-multifaceted-life-of-jimmy-tayoun/.

37. Linda Loyd and Susan FitzGerald, "Foglietta Announces for 3rd Term—Tayoun Expected to Enter Primary," *Philadelphia Inquirer*, January 8, 1984, p. B01.

38. Thomas Ferrick Jr., "Tayoun Wins Ward Support over Foglietta," *Philadelphia Inquirer*, January 10, 1984, p. B01.

39. Thomas Ferrick Jr., "Challengers Gearing up for the Primary," *Philadelphia Inquirer*, December 20, 1983, p. B04.

40. Ferrick, "Tayoun Wins Ward Support."

41. L. Stuart Ditzen, "For a Primary Contest with Spice, Foglietta and Tayoun Are Hard to Beat," *Philadelphia Inquirer*, April 2, 1984, p. 5.

42. Paul Nussbaum, "Foglietta, Rovner and Borski Win," *Philadelphia Inquirer*, May 21, 1986, p. A01.

CHAPTER 5

1. Jonathan Neumann, "Rendell: 'The People Had Minds of Their Own,'" *Philadelphia Inquirer*, May 19, 1977, p. B01.

2. Edward G. Rendell, interview by the author, Philadelphia, February 26, 2019.

3. Rendell, interview by the author.

4. Paul Critchlow, "Rendell, Klenk Score Upset over Ticket Backed by Rizzo," *Philadelphia Inquirer*, May 18, 1977, p. 1-A.

5. Ibid., 4-A.

6. Ed Rendell, *A Nation of Wusses: How America's Leaders Lost the Guts to Make Us Great* (Hoboken, NJ: John Wiley, 2012), 12.

7. Rendell, interview by the author.

8. Joseph H. Miller, "Specter Wins by 38,000, Hemphill Victor; Hughes Re-elected; Lindsay Beats Beame," *Philadelphia Inquirer*, November 3, 1965, p. 1.

9. S. A. Paolantonio, *Frank Rizzo: The Last Big Man in Big City America* (Philadelphia: Camino Books, 1993), 86.

10. Miller, "Specter Wins," 4.

11. Philadelphia District Attorney's Office, "What We Do," October 17, 2018, https://www.phila.gov/departments/philadelphia-district-attorneys-office/.

12. Tina Rosenberg, "The Deadliest D.A.," *New York Times Magazine*, July 16, 1995, sec. 6, p. 22.

13. Chris Palmer, "Philly DA Larry Krasner Won't Seek Cash Bail in Certain Crimes," *Philadelphia Inquirer*, February 21, 2018, https://www.inquirer.com/philly/news/crime/philadelphia-larry-krasner-cash-bail-reform-20180221.html.

14. "Legal Aid May Cost $1 Million, Tate Says," *Philadelphia Inquirer*, January 6, 1966, p. 4.

15. Joseph H. Miller, "Cutting Court Backlog Is No. 1 Job, DA Says," *Philadelphia Inquirer*, February 3, 1966, p. 5.

16. "Specter Warns Magistrates of Record Checks," *Philadelphia Inquirer*, February 18, 1966, p. 13.

17. Joseph H. Miller, "Tate and Hemphill Swamped by Specter in GOP Mayor Poll," *Philadelphia Inquirer*, February 26, 1967, p. 1.

18. "GOP Is 'Sure' Specter Will Heed Mayoral Call," *Philadelphia Daily News*, March 4, 1967, p. 4.

19. "Philadelphia G.O.P. Bids Specter Oppose Tate for the Mayoralty," *New York Times*, March 4, 1967, p. 11.

20. Homer Bigart, "Tate Beats Specter in Philadelphia Mayor's Race," *New York Times*, November 8, 1967, p. 39.

21. Ibid.

22. Paolantonio, *Rizzo*, 87.

23. Jon Katz, "Key to City's Off-Year Election: Getting Voters Out," *Philadelphia Inquirer*, October 23, 1973, p. 2-D.

24. Jon Katz, "D.A. Race Dull, but Pivotal for the Politicians," *Philadelphia Inquirer*, November 4, 1973, p. 1-A.

25. Rendell, *Nation of Wusses*, 13.

26. Mike Leary, "Fitzpatrick Didn't Believe it—until Specter Conceded," *Philadelphia Inquirer*, November 7, 1973, p. 1-A.

27. Paolantonio, *Rizzo*, 218.

28. Jon Katz and Mike Leary, "Rizzo Opposes Fitzpatrick, Klenk: Mayor Accuses Camiel of 'Bossism,'" *Philadelphia Inquirer*, March 6, 1973, p. 2-D.

29. Ibid.; Jon Katz, "Rizzo Seeks Ouster of Camiel, Shakeup in City Committee," *Philadelphia Inquirer*, March 7, 1973, p. 1-D.

30. Aaron Epstein, "Rizzo Will Name 'Soft' Judges Too Late for Response," *Philadelphia Inquirer*, October 3, 1973, p. B-1.

31. Jon Katz, "Fitzpatrick Upsets D.A. Specter," *Philadelphia Inquirer*, November 7, 1973, p. 1-A.

32. Jon Katz, "Specter and Fitzpatrick Are Cautious in TV Debate," *Philadelphia Inquirer*, November 3, 1973, p. 1-B.

33. Jon Katz, "D.A. Campaign—Study in Contrasts," *Philadelphia Inquirer*, October 28, 1973, p. 1-A.

34. Ibid.

35. Dan Lynch, "Fitzpatrick to Drop Practice," *Philadelphia Inquirer*, May 21, 1973, p. 1-B.

36. Jon Katz, "Interview with Democratic D.A. Candidate: 'Justice System Is a Shambles,'" *Philadelphia Inquirer*, September 9, 1973, p. 1-H.

37. Jon Katz, "Fitzpatrick Calls for Rizzo Inquiry," *Philadelphia Inquirer*, October 12, 1973, p. 8-B.

38. Rendell, interview by the author.

39. Paul Critchlow, "Democrats Square Off in D.A. Race," *Philadelphia Inquirer*, April 4, 1977, p. 3-B.

40. Paul Critchlow, "Fitzpatrick Is Criticized at Forum," *Philadelphia Inquirer*, March 23, 1977, p. 1-B.

41. Rendell, *Nation of Wusses*, 14, 15.

42. Ibid., 15.

43. Rendell, interview by the author.

44. Ibid.

45. Ibid.

46. Paul Critchlow, "Democrats Deny Klenk Support," *Philadelphia Inquirer*, March 5, 1977, p. 1-A.

47. Rich Chapman and Shelly Yanoff, interview, December 6, 1976, pp. 4, 5, Collection ID SCRC 128, Walter Massey Phillips Oral Histories, Special Collections Research Center, Temple University Libraries, Philadelphia.

48. Paolantonio, *Rizzo*, 190, 196, 198–201; Chapman and Yanoff, interview, 4, 5.

49. Richard Chapman, interview by the author, Ocean City, NJ, May 16, 2019.

50. Rendell, interview by the author.

51. A. W. Geiselman Jr., "Rizzo Helps Parking Authority Staff Grow," *Sunday Bulletin*, p. 5.

52. Rendell, interview by the author.

53. Paul Critchlow, "Phila. Party Backs Rendell, Klenk," *Philadelphia Inquirer*, April 1, 1977, p. 2-B.

54. Paul Critchlow, "Can Klenk and Rendell Beat the Machine?" *Philadelphia Inquirer*, March 13, 1977, p. 1-D.

55. Paul Critchlow, "Fitzpatrick Makes Newspapers His Target," *Philadelphia Inquirer*, May 9, 1977, p. 1-B. S. A. Paolantonio expresses a contrary view: "Rizzo saw no advantage in expending too much energy trying to keep Fitzpatrick in office." Paolantonio, *Rizzo*, 218.

56. Rendell, interview by the author.

57. Michael Petrowsky, *Race, Poverty, and Unemployment Task Force: Interim Report* (Philadelphia: Center for Philadelphia Studies, University of Pennsylvania, 1981), 14.

58. Ibid., 31, 33, 34, 37.

59. Joseph S. Clark Jr. and Dennis J. Clark, "Rally and Relapse, 1946–1968," in *Philadelphia: A 300-Year History*, ed. Russell F. Weigley (New York: W. W. Norton, 1982), 661.

60. Joseph H. Miller, "Green Vows to Fight Mayor's 'Iron Grip' on Democratic Party," *Philadelphia Inquirer*, November 15, 1969, p. 1.

61. Howard S. Shapiro, "Poll: Voters Saw Goode as Honest," *Philadelphia Inquirer*, March 18, 1983, p. 1.

62. Kellan White, interview by the author, Philadelphia, March 30, 2018.

CHAPTER 6

1. Max Marin, "Pro-Morales Latino Coalition Drops Díaz to Support Kenney," *Al Día*, April 20, 2015, https://aldianews.com/articles/elections-2015/pro-morales-latino-coalition-drops-diaz-endorse-kenney/38703.

2. Holly Otterbein, "How Johnny Doc Almost Took Out Maria Quiñones-Sánchez," *Philadelphia Magazine*, June 25, 2015, https://www.phillymag.com/citified/2015/06/25/johnny-doc-council-election/.

3. Nelson Díaz, *Not From Here, Not From There/No Soy de Aquí Ni de Allá: The Autobiography of Nelson A. Díaz* (Philadelphia: Temple University Press, 2018), 225.

4. Philadelphia City Council, "District 7," http://phlcouncil.com/MariaQSanchez/ (accessed February 14, 2020).

5. Pew Charitable Trusts, "The State of Philadelphians Living in Poverty, 2019," April 2019, p. 3, https://www.pewtrusts.org/-/media/assets/2019/05/state_of_poverty.pdf.

6. Philadelphia Land Bank, "2017 Strategic Plan and Performance Report," February 2017, p. 5, https://static1.squarespace.com/static/5342bfabe4b076ea499631f5/t/58e260982994caf20b4d8473/1491230946416/philadelphia-land-bank-strategic-plan-february-2017.pdf.

7. Alfred Lubrano, "How Kensington Got to Be the Center of Philly's Opioid Crisis," *Philadelphia Inquirer*, January 23, 2018, https://www.inquirer.com/philly/news/kensington-opioid-crisis-history-philly-heroin-20180123.html.

8. Stephen Metraux, Meagan Cusack, Fritz Graham, David Metzger, and Dennis Culhane, "An Evaluation of the City of Philadelphia's Kensington Encampment Resolution Pilot," University of Pennsylvania, March 5, 2019, p. 6, https://www.phila.gov/media/20190312102914/Encampment-Resolution-Pilot-Report.pdf.

9. Holly Otterbein, "The Sánchez Insurgency," *Philadelphia Magazine*, January 24, 2016, https://www.phillymag.com/citified/2016/01/24/maria-quinones-sanchez-profile/.

10. Bobby Allyn, "Renee Tartaglione Sentenced to Nearly 7 Years in Prison for Defrauding Nonprofit," *WHYY*, July 12, 2018, https://whyy.org/segments/renee-tartaglione-sentenced-to-nearly-7-years-in-prison-for-defrauding-nonprofit.

11. Chris Brennan and Dylan Purcell, "How Philly's Electricians Union and Johnny Doc Converted Payroll Deduction into Political Influence," *Philadelphia Inquirer*, February 25, 2019, https://www.inquirer.com/news/local-john-dougherty-campaign-money-elections-mayor-council-20190225.html.

12. Ibid.

13. Lee Nentwig, "Angel Cruz Speaks on Primary Election Clash with Maria Quiñones-Sánchez," *Al Día*, April 24, 2019, https://aldianews.com/articles/politics/angel-cruz-speaks-democratic-primary-election-clash-maria-quinones-sanchez/55463.

14. Max Marin, "Quiñones-Sánchez Endorsed by 7th District Leaders," *Al Día*, April 30, 2015, https://aldianews.com/articles/elections-2015/qui%C3%B1ones-s%C3%A1nchez-endorsed-7th-district-leaders/38818.

15. María Quiñones-Sánchez, interview by the author, Philadelphia, June 25, 2019.

16. Otterbein, "Sánchez Insurgency."

17. Nentwig, "Angel Cruz Speaks."

18. Greta Anderson, "María Quiñones-Sánchez: 'I Picked My Enemies'; The City Council Veteran Reveals Her Strategy to Defeat Her Nemesis State Rep. Angel Cruz," *Al Día*, March 21, 2019, https://aldianews.com/articles/politics/elections/maria-quinones-sanchez-i-picked-my-enemies/55254.

19. Nelson Díaz, interview by the author, Philadelphia, April 16, 2019.

20. Díaz, *Not From Here*, 235.

21. Díaz, interview by the author.

22. Committee of Seventy, "A Troubled History: The Office of the City Commissioners," https://seventy.org/issues/elections-and-voting/better-philly-elections-coalition/city-commissioners-history (accessed February 14, 2020).

23. Michael Decourcy Hinds, "Vote-Fraud Ruling Shifts Pennsylvania Senate," *New York Times*, February 19, 1994, https://www.nytimes.com/1994/02/19/us/vote-fraud-ruling-shifts-pennsylvania-senate.html.

24. "'Massive . . . .Ballot Fraud, Deception, Intimidation, Harassment, Forgery,'" *Philadelphia Inquirer*, February 20, 1994, p. E4.

25. Ibid., E4.

26. Philadelphia City Commission, "Guide for Election Board Officials in Philadelphia County," February 2018, p. 27, https://www.philadelphiavotes.com/files/election-workers/Election_Board_Training_Guide.pdf.

27. Maria Quiñones-Sánchez, Facebook post, April 27, 2019 (now removed).

28. Maria Quiñones-Sánchez, Facebook post, April 30, 2019 (now removed).

29. Maria Quiñones-Sánchez, Facebook post, May 3, 2019 (now removed).

30. Angel Cruz, "City Council District 7 Candidate, Angel Cruz—2019 Philly-CAM Video Voter Guide," *YouTube*, May 1, 2019, https://www.youtube.com/watch?v=1X0VvKM04zs&t=79s.

31. Nentwig, "Angel Cruz Speaks."

32. Bobby Allyn, "Supporters Sue to Open Safe Injection Site in Philadelphia, Citing Religious Freedom," *NPR*, April 13, 2019, https://www.npr.org/sections/health-shots/2019/04/13/710253334/supporters-sue-to-open-safe-injection-site-in-philadelphia-citing-religious-free.

33. Nentwig, "Angel Cruz Speaks."

34. Otterbein, "Sánchez Insurgency."

CHAPTER 7

1. Common pleas court candidate, interview by the author, Philadelphia, May 24, 2018.

2. Mark Bernstein, interview by the author, Philadelphia, March 26, 2018.

3. Fredric N. Tulsky, "In the Lurch: 3 Rejected Judicial Nominees Caught Unawares by Politics," *Philadelphia Inquirer*, April 9, 1987, 1-A.

4. John L. Puckett and Mark Frazier Lloyd, *Becoming Penn: The Pragmatic American University, 1950–2000* (Philadelphia: University of Pennsylvania Press, 2015), chap. 4.

5. C. Darnell Jones II, interview by the author, Philadelphia, June 7, 2018.

6. Tulsky, "In the Lurch."

7. Fredric N. Tulsky, "Bench Wars: Patronage Stakes High in Judicial Races," *Philadelphia Inquirer*, May 18, 1987, p. 5-B.

8. Legrome D. Davis, interview by the author, Philadelphia, June 29, 2018. All quotations by Davis in this section come from this source.

9. Flora Barth Wolf, interview by the author, Philadelphia, April 18, 2018.

10. Mark Bernstein, interview by the author, Philadelphia, March 26, 2018.

11. C. Darnell Jones II, interview by the author, Philadelphia, June 7, 2018.

12. Flora Barth Wolf, interview by Senior Judge Oral History Project, *YouTube*, December 9, 2014, https://www.youtube.com/watch?v=SyqEExpfJH0.

13. Wolf, interview by the author.

14. Annette Rizzo, interview by the author, Philadelphia, April 6, 2018.

15. Ibid.

16. Ibid.

17. Ibid.

18. Ibid.

19. Emilie Lounsberry and Thomas Fitzgerald, "The Rocky Road to Pa. Supreme Court," *Philadelphia Inquirer*, March 22, 2007, https://www.inquirer.com/philly/news/local/20070322_The_rocky_road_to_Pa__Supreme_Court.html.

20. Jones, interview by the author.

21. Jennifer Schultz, interview by the author, Philadelphia, May 24, 2018. All quotations by Schultz in this section come from this source.

22. Jonathan Tannen, "Newly Engaged in Politics, Anxious for 2018?" Econsult Solutions, December 16, 2016, https://econsultsolutions.com/judicial-elections-2017-philadelphia/.

23. Ibid. (emphasis in original).

24. Ibid.

25. See Philadelphia Bar Association, "Guidelines for Evaluation of Attorney and Judge Candidates," July 2016, https://www.philadelphiabar.org/WebObjects/PBAReadOnly.woa/Contents/WebServerResources/CMSResources/Guidelines2019.pdf.

26. Ibid., 1.

27. Ibid., 4, 7.

28. Ibid., 5.

29. Jonathan Tannen, Alison Shott, and Matthew Olesh, "The Effect of Handing Out Candidate Recommendations outside of Polling Places," Econsult Solutions working paper, July 7, 2017, https://econsultsolutions.com/wp-content/uploads/ESI_Bar_Working-Paper.pdf.

30. Schultz, interview by the author.

31. Pennsylvania merit selection issues are discussed in depth in Shira J. Goodman and Lynn A. Marks, "A View from the Ground: A Reform Group's Perspective on the Ongoing Effort to Achieve Merit Selection of Judges," *Fordham Urban Law Journal* 34, no. 1 (2006), 424–452.

32. Schultz, interview by the author.

33. Bernstein, interview by the author.

CHAPTER 8

1. Larry Platt, "What Change Feels Like," *Philadelphia Citizen*, March 1, 2019, https://thephiladelphiacitizen.org/what-change-feels-like/.

2. Roxanne Patel Shepelavy, "The Pro-Choice Election," *Philadelphia Citizen*, May 11, 2017, https://www.rebeccaforphiladelphia.com/news-1/2017/5/11/the-pro-choice-election.

3. Dave Davies, "Outside Spending for Congressional Candidate Tops $600K," *WHYY*, April 30, 2018, https://whyy.org/articles/outside-spending-for-philly-congressional-candidate-tops-600000/.

4. Center for American Women and Politics, "Results: Women Candidates in the 2018 Elections," November 29, 2018, https://cawp.rutgers.edu/sites/default/files/resources/results_release_5bletterhead5d_1.pdf.

5. Center for American Women and Politics, "Results: Record Number of Women Elected to State Legislatures Nationwide," January 8, 2019, https://cawp.rutgers.edu/sites/default/files/resources/press-release-state-legislatures-results-2018.pdf.

6. Matthew J. Countryman, *Up South: Civil Rights and Black Power in Philadelphia* (Philadelphia: University of Pennsylvania Press, 2006), 220.

7. W. Wilson Goode Sr., *Black Voters Mattered: A Philadelphia Story* (n.p.: BookBaby, 2018), loc. 666.

8. Madonna and McLarnon, "Reform in Philadelphia," 73.

9. Emily Sunstein, interview by Walter Phillips, Philadelphia, May 8, 1980, p. 2, Walter Massey Phillips Oral Histories, Special Collections Research Center, Temple University, Philadelphia, https://libdigital.temple.edu/oralhistories/catalog/transcript:AOHWMPJZ2015010048xp16002coll22x46.

10. Goode, *Black Voters Mattered*, loc. 493.

11. Ibid.

12. Countryman, *Up South*, 310.

13. Karen Bojar, *Feminism in Philadelphia, the Glory Years: Philadelphia NOW, 1968–1982* (North Charleston, SC: Createspace, 2013), 98.

14. Ibid., 99.

15. Colt Shaw, "How Elizabeth Fiedler Beat the Odds and the Establishment in the 184th," *City and State Pennsylvania*, June 26, 2018, https://www.cityandstatepa.com/content/how-elizabeth-fiedler-beat-odds-and-establishment-184th.

16. Anna Orso, "City Council Side Jobs: All the Totally Legal Ways Philly's Electeds Supplement Income," *Billy Penn*, May 31, 2016, https://billypenn.com/2016/05/31/city-council-side-jobs-all-the-totally-legal-ways-phillys-electeds-supplement-income/.

17. Jeremy Roebuck, "Can a Paycheck Be a Bribe? Johnny Doc's Lawyers Say No, Push to Dismiss Case involving Council Member Henon," *Philadelphia Inquirer*, July 8, 2019, https://www.inquirer.com/news/johnny-doc-bobby-henon-philadelphia-local-98-ibew-judge-schmehl-20190708.html.

18. Jeremy Roebuck and David Gambacorta, "Local 98 Leader Johnny Doc, Councilman Bobby Henon Charged in Sweeping Conspiracy Case," *Philadelphia Inquirer*, January 30, 2019, https://www.inquirer.com/news/johnny-doc-john-dougherty-bobby-henon-ibew-local-union-philadelphia-investigation-city-council-20190130.html.

19. Ed Rendell, interview by the author, Philadelphia, February 26, 2019.

20. Joseph Vignola, interview by the author, Philadelphia, January 10, 2019.

21. Rendell, interview by the author.

22. This information was conveyed to me as part of the city's response to a Right to Know request.

23. "Specter Wins by 38,000, Hemphill Victor; Hughes Re-elected; Lindsay Beats Beame," *Philadelphia Inquirer*, November 3, 1965, p. 1.

24. Saul Kohler, "Tate Ready to Oust Smith; Shafer Hails Charter Victory," *Philadelphia Inquirer*, May 16, 1967, p. 1.

25. Paul Critchlow, "Rendell, Klenk Score Upset over Ticket Backed by Rizzo," *Philadelphia Inquirer*, May 18, 1977, p. 1.

26. Robert W. O'Donnell, interview by the author, Philadelphia, November 27, 2019.

27. This and the following paragraphs are my own commentary, which may or may not be consistent with O'Donnell's and Bernstein's views.

28. Justin Miller, "How Big Money Lost in Philly's Mayoral Race," *American Prospect*, May 20, 2015, https://prospect.org/article/how-big-money-lost-philly%E2%80%99s-mayoral-race.

29. Vignola, interview by the author.

30. Darrell Clarke described this incident to me years ago, during my tenure as Philadelphia housing director (1992–2001), at a time when Clarke was employed as an aide to John F. Street, City Council president at the time.

CHAPTER 9

1. Li Zhou, "The Striking Parallels between 1992's 'Year of the Woman' and 2018, Explained by a Historian," *Vox*, November 2, 2018, https://www.vox.com/2018/11/2/17983746/year-of-the-woman-1992.

2. Samantha Melamed and Anna Orso, "After Another 'Year of the Woman,' How Close Is Pa. to Gender Parity in Politics? (Not Very)," *Philadelphia Inquirer*, December 27, 2018, p. 1.

3. Their participation in the early years of the reform period is described in detail in G. Terry Madonna and John Morrison McLarnon III, "Reform in Philadelphia: Richard-

son Dilworth, Joseph S. Clark and the Women Who Made Reform Possible, 1947–1949," *Pennsylvania Magazine of History and Biography* 127, no. 1 (January 2003): 57–88.

4. "Elise Bailen, 62, Former Member of Boards of Community Centers," *New York Times*, June 21, 1979, sec. D, p. 19.

5. Natalie Saxe, interview by Walter Phillips, July 23, 1974, p. 5, Walter Massey Phillips Oral Histories, Special Collections Research Center, Temple University, Philadelphia, https://libdigital.temple.edu/oralhistories/catalog/transcript:AOHWMPJZ2015040012xp16002coll22x148.

6. Ibid., 7. See also Joseph S. Clark Jr. and Dennis J. Clark, "Rally and Relapse, 1946–1968," in *Philadelphia: A 300-Year History*, ed. Russell F. Weigley (New York, W. W. Norton, 1982), 653.

7. Madonna and McLarnon, "Reform in Philadelphia," 77, 88.

8. Saxe, interview by Walter Phillips, 5.

9. Ibid., 9.

10. Ibid., 11.

11. Ibid., 14.

12. Ibid., 1.

13. Ibid., 4.

14. Peter Binzen with Jonathan Binzen, *Richardson Dilworth: Last of the Bare-Knuckled Aristocrats* (Philadelphia: Camino Books, 2014), 104.

15. Saxe, interview by Walter Phillips, 1.

16. Ibid., 2.

17. Earl Selby, "In Our Town: The Lady and the Politicians," *Philadelphia Bulletin*, July 26, 1950, p. 14.

18. Saxe, interview by Walter Phillips, 4, 5.

19. Richardson Dilworth, letter to Mr. and Mrs. Nathaniel Saxe, May 20, 1951, Natalie Saxe Randall Papers, Historical Society of Pennsylvania, Philadelphia.

20. Kate Lao Shaffner, WPSU, "What Is Home Rule?" WHYY, July 24, 2014, https://whyy.org/articles/what-is-home-rule/.

21. See Philadelphia Home Rule Charter, §3-103, available at https://www.coj.net/city-council/docs/consolidation-task-force/2014-01-09-philadelphiacharter.aspx.

22. Saxe, interview by Walter Phillips, 4, 5.

23. Natalie Saxe, letter to Elise Bailen, March 8, 1963, p. 1, Natalie Saxe Randall Papers, Historical Society of Pennsylvania, Philadelphia.

24. Ibid.

25. Marian Tasco, interview by the author, Philadelphia, April 18, 2019. All other quotations in this chapter are from this source unless otherwise indicated.

26. Urban Affairs Coalition, "History," http://www.uac.org/history (accessed April 19, 2020).

27. Bowser's role in providing assistance to business enterprises in the Hispanic community is described in detail in Nelson A. Díaz, *Not From Here, Not From There/No Soy de Aquí ni de Allá* (Philadelphia: Temple University Press, 2018), 97–101.

28. Christopher K. Hepp, Tom Infield, and Vernon Clark, "Charles W. Bowser, Towering Political Figure in Philadelphia, Dies," *Philadelphia Inquirer*, August 12, 2010, https://www.inquirer.com/philly/obituaries/20100812_Charles_W__Bowswer__towering_political_figure_in_Philadelphia__dies.html.

29. John F. White Sr., John White's father, was a cofounder of the Black Political Forum and a leader in the phase of Philadelphia's African American political

empowerment that began with Hardy Williams's candidacies in West Philadelphia, as described in Chapter 3.

30. William W. Sutton Jr., "Candidate: Gray Upset Bid for White's Support," *Philadelphia Inquirer*, April 15, 1987, p. 11-B.

31. Maya Gutierrez, interview by the author, Philadelphia, April 17, 2019. All other quotations from Gutierrez in the chapter come from this source.

32. "Pa. to Fill Budget Holes by Borrowing against Tobacco Fund," *WHYY*, November 14, 2017, https://whyy.org/articles/pa-fill-budget-holes-borrowing-tobacco-fund/.

CHAPTER 10

1. Committee of Seventy, "About Us," https://seventy.org/about/about-us (accessed February 23, 2020).

2. David Thornburgh, interview by the author, Philadelphia, April 23, 2019.

3. Hal Libros, *Hard Core Liberals: A Sociological Analysis of the Philadelphia Americans for Democratic Action* (Cambridge, MA: Schenkman, 1975), 14.

4. Ibid., 22.

5. Ibid., 24.

6. Ibid., 27, 28.

7. Ibid., 28.

8. Emily Sunstein, interview by Walter Phillips, Philadelphia, May 8, 1980, p. 8, Walter Massey Phillips Oral Histories, Special Collections Research Center, Temple University, Philadelphia, https://libdigital.temple.edu/oralhistories/catalog/transcript:AOHWMPJZ2015010048xp16002coll22x46.

9. Ibid., 5.

10. Ibid.

11. Norman Berson, interview by Walter Phillips, Philadelphia, February 8, 1979, pp. 1, 2, 6, Walter Massey Phillips Oral Histories, Special Collections Research Center, Temple University, Philadelphia, https://libdigital.temple.edu/oralhistories/catalog/transcript:AOHWMPJZ2014110018xp16002coll22x19.

12. Ibid., 3.

13. For Libros's description of early ADA social relationships, see Libros, *Hard Core Liberals*, 14.

14. Shelly Yanoff, interview by the author, Philadelphia, May 7, 2019.

15. Ibid.

16. Ibid.

17. Ibid.

18. Ibid.

19. Lenora Berson, interview by Walter Phillips, Philadelphia, November 16, 1978, p. 4, Walter Massey Phillips Oral Histories, Special Collections Research Center, Temple University, Philadelphia, https://libdigital.temple.edu/oralhistories/catalog/transcript:AOHWMPJZ2014110017xp16002coll22x17.

20. Yanoff, interview by the author.

21. Sunstein, interview by Walter Phillips, 21.

22. Mary Goldman, interview by the author, Philadelphia, May 7, 2019.

23. Yanoff, interview by the author.

24. W. Wilson Goode Sr., *Black Voters Mattered: A Philadelphia Story* (n.p.: BookBaby, 2018), loc. 1021.

25. Norman Berson, interview by Walter Phillips, 6.

26. Mark Fazlollah and William Bender, "Philadelphia Councilman Kenyatta Johnson Helped Friend Make $165,000 Flipping City-Owned Lots," *Philadelphia Inquirer*, November 20, 2018, https://www.inquirer.com/philly/news/kenyatta-johnson-councilman-felton-hayman-house-flip-profit-philadelphia-20181120.html.

27. William Bender, "How Philly Developer 'Mr. Bigg,' Backed by Darrell Clarke, Got a Bargain on City Land near Temple," *Philadelphia Inquirer*, February 22, 2019, https://www.inquirer.com/news/philadelphia-real-estate-sales-shawn-bullard-darrell-clarke-temple-20190222.html.

28. Alison Perelman, interview by the author, Philadelphia, April 17, 2019.

29. Holly Otterbein, "Ali Perelman: New Philly's Old Money," *Philadelphia Magazine*, October 21, 2017, https://www.phillymag.com/news/2017/10/21/ali-perelman-philadelphia-3-0/.

30. Perelman, interview by the author.

31. Dave Davies, "Updated: Dark Money Group Pulls the Shades," *WHYY*, July 9, 2015, https://whyy.org/articles/philadelphia-dark-money-secret-contributions/.

32. Claudia Vargas, "Pressure Grows to Eliminate City Commissioners," *Philadelphia Inquirer*, May 4, 2016, https://www.inquirer.com/philly/news/politics/20160505_Pressure_grows_to_eliminate_ciy_commissioners.html.

33. Claudia Vargas, "Committee of Seventy, Others Sue Head Common Pleas Judge over City Commissioners," *Philadelphia Inquirer*, March 27, 2017, https://www.inquirer.com/philly/news/politics/Committee-of-Seventy-others-sue-Common-Pleas-Court-President-Judge-over-City-Commissioners.html.

34. Perelman, interview by the author.

35. Gregory Laynor, Facebook post, May 18, 2019 (now removed).

36. Perelman, interview by the author.

37. Thornburgh, interview by the author.

38. Perelman, interview by the author.

39. Thornburgh, interview by the author.

40. Committee of Seventy, *Revision of Election Laws: Explanatory Statements concerning Proposed Bills in Reference to "Assistance to Voters," Abolishing the Party Square, Making the Vote at the Primary the Test of Party Existence and Providing for the Enrollment of Voters Participating in Primaries, Editorial Comment and Drafts of Bills* (Philadelphia: Committee of Seventy, 1912).

41. Ellen Mattleman Kaplan, interview by the author, Philadelphia, May 6, 2019.

42. Thornburgh, interview by the author.

43. Kaplan, interview by the author.

44. Committee of Seventy, "Needless Jobs: Why Six Elected City Positions Should Die," March 16, 2009, p. iii, https://seventy.org/uploads/files/624204592740589766-954823571103424434-needless-jobs-why-six-elected-city-positions-should-die-3-16-2009.pdf.

45. Ibid., 2.

46. Ibid., 4.

47. Thornburgh, interview by the author.

48. Fair Districts PA, "About," https://www.fairdistrictspa.com/about (accessed February 23, 2020).

49. Thornburgh, interview by the author.

50. Chris Satullo, "Yes, It's Mapping Time Again, Pennsylvania," Draw the Lines, February 4, 2019, https://drawthelinespa.org/news/yes-it-s-mapping-time-again-2.

51. Ibid.
52. Thornburgh, interview by the author.
53. Ibid.
54. Perelman, interview by the author.

CHAPTER 11

1. Nikil Saval, interview by the author, Philadelphia, May 31, 2019.
2. Ibid.
3. Reclaim Philadelphia, "About," https://www.reclaimphiladelphia.org/our-history (accessed February 28, 2020).
4. Reclaim Philadelphia, "Success Stories," https://www.reclaimphiladelphia.org/success-stories (accessed February 28, 2020).
5. Saval, interview by the author.
6. George Donnelly, interview by the author, Philadelphia, June 7, 2019.
7. Ibid.
8. "Philadelphia Ward Chief Held on Fraud Charges," *New York Times*, March 21, 1982, sec. 1, p. 26.
9. Craig R. McCoy, "Controversial Vivian Miller Will Step Down," *Philadelphia Inquirer*, March 9, 2010, https://www.inquirer.com/philly/news/homepage/20100309_Controversial_Vivian_Miller_will_step_down.html.
10. Gregory Benjamin, interview by the author, Philadelphia, June 6, 2019. All quotations by Benjamin in this section come from this source.
11. Cherelle Parker, interview by the author, Philadelphia, June 18, 2019. All quotations by Parker in this section come from this source.
12. Another winner that year was Leslie Odom Jr., who later gained renown for his performance as Aaron Burr in the Broadway musical *Hamilton*.
13. Pew Charitable Trusts, "Philadelphia's Poor: Experiences from Below the Poverty Line," September 2018, p. 3, https://www.pewtrusts.org/-/media/assets/2018/09/phillypovertyreport2018.pdf.

CHAPTER 12

1. Church Hymnal Corporation and Seabury Press, *The Book of Common Prayer* (Kingsport, TN: Kingsport Press, 1977), 360.
2. My frame of reference is narrow as well, as a result of my lack of appropriate academic credentials and the fact that my familiarity with the subject of this chapter is primarily with African American and white churches of the Protestant denomination. I hope this topic will be addressed in a more comprehensive fashion by others who are better qualified to do so and who may find this chapter to be a useful starting point for further investigation.
3. Ronald Reagan, inaugural address, January 20, 1981, https://avalon.law.yale.edu/20th_century/reagan1.asp.
4. Saul D. Alinsky, *Rules for Radicals: A Practical Primer for Realistic Radicals* (New York: Random House, 1971), 18.
5. Ibid., 59.
6. Harvey Cox, *The Secular City: Secularization and Urbanization in Theological Perspective* (Princeton, NJ: Princeton University Press, 2013).

7. Christopher Hitchens, *God Is Not Great: How Religion Poisons Everything* (New York: Hatchette, 2007).

8. W. Wilson Goode, interview by the author, Philadelphia, April 17, 2019.

9. Ram A. Cnaan, *The Other Philadelphia Story: How Local Congregations Support Quality of Life in Urban America* (Philadelphia: University of Pennsylvania Press, 2006), xvi, xvii.

10. Ibid., 236–238. See also Amachi, "Reverend Dr. W. Wilson Goode, Sr.," http://www.amachimentoring.org/bio.html (accessed February 29, 2020).

11. Sally A. Downey, "Christine J. Washington, Community Advocate," *Philadelphia Inquirer*, March 28, 2012, https://www.inquirer.com/philly/obituaries/20120328_Christine_J__Washington__community_advocate.html.

12. Alyn E. Waller, interview by the author, Philadelphia, June 18, 2019.

13. Lucinda Fleeson, Mary Bishop, and Linda Loyd, "Two Issues Block Progress in Teacher Contract Talks," *Philadelphia Inquirer*, November 7, 1981, p. 3-B.

14. "PUSH, Clergy to Monitor Coke Pact," *Philadelphia Tribune*, November 9, 1982, p. 3.

15. S. A. Paolantonio, "United to Elect Goode, Now Split on Nominee," *Philadelphia Inquirer*, April 7, 1991, p. 1-C.

16. Reverend William L. Banks, letter to the editor, *Philadelphia Inquirer*, November 21, 1983, p. 14-A.

17. Paolantonio, "United to Elect Goode," 2-C.

18. Richard L. Wood, Brad Fulton, and Kathryn Partridge, *Building Bridges, Building Power: Developments in Institution-Based Community Organizing* (Denver: Interfaith Funders, 2012), i.

19. Brad Fulton and Richard L. Wood, "Interfaith Community Organizing: Emerging Theological and Organizational Challenges." *International Journal of Public Theology* 6, no. 4 (2012): 406, 407.

20. POWER, "About POWER," https://powerinterfaith.org/about/ (accessed February 29, 2020).

21. POWER, "POWER Study Shows Racial Bias in PA Public School Funding," November 6, 2014, https://powerinterfaith.org/power-study-shows-racial-bias-in-pa-public-school-funding/.

22. David Mosenkis, interview by the author, Philadelphia, June 14, 2019.

23. For more information, see POWER, "POWER Interfaith 100% Fair Funding Campaign," https://sites.google.com/view/power100fairfundingcampaign/home (accessed February 29, 2020).

24. Waller, interview by the author.

25. Alyn E. Waller, 2018 Annual Urban Theological Institute Lecture, Philadelphia September 18, 2018.

26. Ibid.

27. Enon Tabernacle Baptist Church, "Our History," https://enontab.org/our-history/ (accessed February 29, 2020).

28. Waller, interview by the author.

29. Waller, 2018 Annual Urban Theological Institute Lecture.

30. Mark Kelly Tyler, opening remarks at People's Forum, Philadelphia, March 24, 2019.

31. David Lipscomb, presentation at People's Forum, Philadelphia, March 24, 2019.

32. Action Network, "Sign on to the People's Platform," https://actionnetwork.org/forms/i-support-the-peoples-platform-for-a-just-philadelphia (accessed February 29, 2020).

33. Cherelle Parker, interview by the author, Philadelphia, June 18, 2019.

34. Waller, interview by the author.

CHAPTER 13

1. Chris Brennan, Julia Terruso, and Claudia Vargas, "It's Crunch Time for Candidates in the Philadelphia Races," *Philadelphia Inquirer*, May 20, 2019, p. B5.

2. Jonathan Lai, Claudia Vargas, and Julia Terruso, "Voters' No. 1 Issue: Crime," *Philadelphia Inquirer*, April 29, 2019, p. A1.

3. Data in this chapter consist of machine votes only (i.e., absentee ballots are not included).

4. Mark Fazlollah, "In Charge of Philly Elections, Commissioner Lost Notary License for Violating the Law," *Philadelphia Inquirer*, May 1, 2019, https://www.inquirer.com/news/lisa-deeley-city-commissioner-fraud-sanctioned-department-of-state-20190501.html.

5. Ernest Owens, "City Commissioner Candidate: We Must Fight 2020 Voter Suppression Efforts," *Philadelphia Magazine*, March 19, 2019, https://www.phillymag.com/news/2019/03/19/kahlil-williams-city-commissioner/.

6. Mark Fazlollah and William Bender, "Philadelphia Councilman Kenyatta Johnson Helped Friend Make $165,000 Flipping City-Owned Lots," *Philadelphia Inquirer*, November 20, 2018, https://www.inquirer.com/philly/news/kenyatta-johnson-councilman-felton-hayman-house-flip-profit-philadelphia-20181120.html.

7. Julia Terruso, "Kenyatta Johnson Faces Lauren Vidas in Race to Represent Point Breeze, Philly's Second District," *Philadelphia Inquirer*, April 8, 2019, https://www.inquirer.com/news/lauren-vidas-20190408.html.

8. Jake Blumgart, "Philadelphia Councilwoman Delayed Major City Land Deal to Help a Developer," *PlanPhilly*, February 8, 2019, http://planphilly.com/articles/2019/02/08/philadelphia-councilwoman-delayed-major-city-land-deal-to-help-a-developer.

9. Julia Terruso and Chris Brennan, "Dark Money under Spotlight as Campaign Finance Law Changes Right before Philly Primary," *Philadelphia Inquirer*, May 2, 2019, https://www.inquirer.com/news/primary-politics-campaign-finance-gauthier-blackwell-third-district-west-philly-philly-30-dark-money-20190502.html.

10. University City District, "The State of University City, Philadelphia, 2019," December 2018, pp. 8, 29, 49, 54, https://issuu.com/universitycity/docs/the_state_of_university_city_2019?e=4547788/65469041.

11. Julia Terruso, "Jannie Blackwell Has Represented West Philly for 27 Years: Jamie Gauthier Thinks Her Time's Up," *Philadelphia Inquirer*, March 28, 2019, https://www.inquirer.com/news/jannie-blackwell-election-jamie-gauther-philadelphia-city-council-20190324.html.

12. Ryan Briggs, "Fairmount Park Conservancy Leader to Challenge Blackwell for Philly Council Seat," *PlanPhilly*, January 30, 2019, https://whyy.org/articles/fairmount-park-conservancy-leader-to-challenge-blackwell-for-philly-council-seat/.

13. Jake Blumgart, "How Philly's City Council Candidates Say They'd Deal with the Housing Crisis," *PlanPhilly*, May 19, 2019, https://whyy.org/articles/how-phillys-city-council-candidates-would-deal-with-the-housing-crisis/.

14. "Philadelphia 3.0 Highlights Successes in 2019 City Council Primary," *Philadelphia 3.0*, May 28, 2019, http://www.phila3-0.org/philadelphia_30_highlights_successes_in_2019_primary.

15. Julia Terruso, Michaelle Bond, and Juliana Feliciano Reyes, "Jamie Gauthier Ousts Councilwoman Jannie Blackwell in Council 3rd District," *Philadelphia Inquirer*, May 22, 2019, https://www.inquirer.com/politics/election/jamie-gauthier-wins-primary-election-third-district-jannie-blackwell-20190522.html.

16. Julia Terruso, "Blackwell Points to PAC for Losing Seat: Councilwoman Said Developers, Others Came after Her District," *Philadelphia Inquirer*, May 24, 2019, p. B1.

17. David Maas, "Philly Passes Fair Workweek Law, Raises Minimum Wage," *Al Día*, December 7, 2018, https://aldianews.com/articles/politics/state-and-local/philly-passes-fair-workweek-law-raises-minimum-wage/54618.

18. Jay Scott Smith, "Philly Councilwoman Helen Gym Unflinching in Calls to Remove Rizzo Statue," *WHYY*, August 18, 2017, https://whyy.org/articles/helen-gym-shows-no-fear-in-calls-for-removal-of-rizzo-statue/.

19. Pete Mazzaccaro, "Councilman Domb Talks School Reform, Taxes at CH College," *Chestnut Hill Local*, February 13, 2019, https://www.chestnuthilllocal.com/2019/02/13/councilman-domb-talks-school-reform-taxes-at-ch-college/.

20. Isaiah Thomas, "Youth Agenda," http://www.isaiahthomas4philly.com/youth-agenda (accessed March 1, 2020).

21. Robert W. O'Donnell, interview by the author, Philadelphia, November 27, 2018.

22. Maria Quiñones-Sánchez, interview by the author, Philadelphia, June 25, 2019.

23. Ibid.

24. Jonathan Tannen, "Who Will Win the Court of Common Pleas?" *Sixty-Six Wards* (blog), May 13, 2019, https://sixtysixwards.com/home/2019/05/page/2/.

25. Ibid.

26. Ibid.

27. Mensah M. Dean, "City Settles Lawsuit Accusing Philadelphia Sheriff Jewel Williams of Sexual Harassment," *Philadelphia Inquirer*, January 23, 2019, https://www.inquirer.com/news/philadelphia-sheriff-jewell-williams-sexual-harassment-lawsuit-settled-20190124.html.

28. Office of the Controller, "Data Release: Beverage Tax Revenue and Expenditures," December 12, 2019, https://controller.phila.gov/philadelphia-audits/data-release-beverage-tax/.

CHAPTER 14

1. Alan Blinder, "Alabama Governor Signs Abortion Bill: Here's What Comes Next," *New York Times*, May 15, 2019, https://www.nytimes.com/2019/05/15/us/alabama-abortion-facts-law-bill.html.

2. Quoted in Kim Chandler and Blake Peterson. "Alabama GOP Governor Signs Nation's Toughest Abortion Law," *Philadelphia Inquirer*, May 16, 2019, p. A3.

3. National Center for Health Statistics, "Stats of the States—Alabama," 2017, https://www.cdc.gov/nchs/pressroom/states/alabama/alabama.htm.

4. Alabama Hospital Association, "Alabama Medicaid Expansion: Summary of Estimated Costs and Savings, SFYs 2020–2023," February 2019, p. 8, https://www.alaha.org/wp-content/uploads/2019/02/MedicaidExpansionReportCostsSavings.pdf.

5. Aria Bendix, "The US Was Once a Leader for Healthcare and Education—Now It Ranks 27th in the World," *Business Insider*, September 27, 2018, https://www.businessinsider.com/us-ranks-27th-for-healthcare-and-education-2018-9.

6. Joint Center for Housing Studies of Harvard University, "The State of the Nation's Housing, 2018," 2018, p. 5, https://www.jchs.harvard.edu/sites/default/files/Harvard_JCHS_State_of_the_Nations_Housing_2018.pdf.

7. Lauren Bauer and Diane Whitmore Schanzenbach, "Children's Exposure to Food Insecurity Is Still Worse than It Was before the Great Recession," Brookings Institution, June 29, 2018, https://www.brookings.edu/blog/up-front/2018/06/29/childrens-exposure-to-food-insecurity-is-still-worse-than-it-was-before-the-great-recession/.

8. "Ideas for Change: Making More Votes Count," *Philadelphia Inquirer*, May 5, 2019, p. C1.

9. Drew DeSilver, "Weekday Elections Set the U.S. Apart from Many Other Advanced Democracies," Pew Research Center, November 6, 2018, https://www.pewresearch.org/fact-tank/2018/11/06/weekday-elections-set-the-u-s-apart-from-many-other-advanced-democracies/.

10. Ashley Hahn, quoted in Joshua A. Douglas, "Radicalizing the Vote: 10 Ideas That Just Might Save Democracy," *Philadelphia Inquirer*, May 5, 2019, https://www.inquirer.com/opinion/commentary/voting-election-solutions-ideas-change-20190502.html#loaded.

11. W. Wilson Goode, interview by the author, Philadelphia, April 17, 2019.

Index

★★★★★

John Kromer is a planning and development consultant, an instructor in urban development policy at the University of Pennsylvania, former Director of Housing for the city of Philadelphia under Mayor Edward G. Rendell, and a participant in local political campaigns and elections. He is the author of *Fixing Broken Cities: The Implementation of Urban Development Strategies* and has written extensively on downtown and neighborhood development issues.